American Guides

American Guides

The Federal Writers' Project and the Casting of American Culture

WENDY GRISWOLD

The University of Chicago Press Chicago and London

Wendy Griswold is professor of sociology and the Bergen Evans Professor in the Humanities at Northwestern University.

The University of Chicago Press, Chicago 60637
The University of Chicago Press, Ltd., London

Printed in the United States of America

25 24 23 22 21 20 19 18 17 16   1 2 3 4 5

ISBN-13: 978-0-226-35766-9 (cloth)
ISBN-13: 978-0-226-35783-6 (paper)
ISBN-13: 978-0-226-35797-3 (e-book)
DOI: 10.7208/chicago/9780226357973.001.0001

Library of Congress Cataloging-in-Publication Data

Names: Griswold, Wendy, author. | Griswold, Wendy. Regionalism and the reading class. Sequel to (work):
Title: American guides: the Federal Writers' Project and the casting of American culture / Wendy Griswold.
Description: Chicago; London: The University of Chicago Press, 2016. | Includes bibliographical references and index.
Identifiers: LCCN 2015038316 | ISBN 9780226357669 (cloth: alk. paper) | ISBN 9780226357836 (pbk.: alk. paper) | ISBN 9780226357973 (e-book)
Subjects: LCSH: Federal Writers' Project. | Federal Writers' Project—Influence. | American guide series. | Books and reading—United States—History—20th century. | United States—Intellectual life—20th century. | United States—Civilization—1918–1945. | United States—History—1933–1945. | Regionalism—Social aspects—United States. | Social change—United States.
Classification: LCC E175.4.W9 G75 2016 | DDC 028.0973—dc23 LC record available at http://lccn.loc.gov/2015038316

⊗ This paper meets the requirements of ANSI/NISO Z39.48-1992 (Permanence of Paper).

To Theda Skocpol—distinguished scholar, dear friend, and companion on the road.

Contents

Tables and Illustrations

Tables

Figures

Maps

Preface

During the Great Depression, the Federal Writers' Project gave jobs to white-collar workers. At the same time, inadvertently, it defined the contours of American culture in general and diversified American literature in particular. The cultural transformation effected by the Project's American Guides is the subject of this book. It has as its central thesis that the Federal Writers' Project, the agency of the Works Progress Administration (WPA) designed simply to employ destitute writers, ended up casting American literature into state molds and bringing women and minorities into the nation's literary pantheon.

This is the second book of a three-book project. The first was *Regionalism and the Reading Class* (University of Chicago Press, 2008), which looked at literary regionalism in a variety of settings, including Italy, Norway, and America. Using comparative and empirical analysis, it demonstrated the persistence of literary regionalism in spite of globalization and the cultural homogenization that some feared would produce a total eclipse of place. The present book, *American Guides*, is a case study of how regionalism operates through "casting." I use "cast" in two senses: to select the characters that populate the regionalist imagination (as in casting a play), and to pour a substance into a mold so it solidifies and takes a specific shape (as in cast iron). The third volume will cover cultural regionalism in the United States from the nineteenth to the twenty-first centuries, comparing the social origins and aesthetic-intellectual consequences of the artistic and literary movements that have represented and fostered different interpretations of American place cultures.

Support for the research that has gone into *American Guides* came from the John Simon Guggenheim Memorial Foundation and from the Institute for Advanced Study, Princeton. Eugene Morris, reference specialist at the National Archives and Records Administration of the United States, knows where all the WPA records are hiding, and he was immensely patient in guiding me to the materials on the Federal Writers' Project at the National Archives. Many booksellers helped me track down guidebooks, in particular Arnold Greenberg of the Complete Traveller in New York City; Penelope Daly of Wellread Books in Northport, New York; and Lucinda Boyle at Bernard J. Shapero Rare Books in London, England. Finally, I join the long stream of sociologists who offer praise and thanks to University of Chicago Press Senior Editor Doug Mitchell, and an extra thanks to Editorial Associate Kyle Wagner.

INTRODUCTION

Casting Culture

The Federal Writers' Project was that rarest of American birds: a massive federal government intervention into the arts. There has never been anything like it before or since. Lasting less than seven years, the Project's most extraordinary products were the state guidebooks of the American Guide Series. These books shaped and continue to shape American culture.[1]

"Shape" is critical here: Culture's initial, sine qua non impact comes through form, not content. Shapes, boundaries, classifications, and categories make up the vessels through which people receive their stories and symbols and objects and values—their culture. This is not a new insight. Back in the eighteenth century Edmund Burke was specifying the geometric qualities that distinguished the sublime from the beautiful, and more recently sociologists and anthropologists have studied symbolic boundaries, particularly those that demarcate an "us" from a "them." Neither aestheticians nor social scientists, however, have paid much attention to how shapes and boundaries get established in the first place.

The Federal Writers' Project gave rise to a historically specific and singularly influential instance of cultural shape-shifting. During the late 1930s, the Project's American Guide Series cast American culture into state-shaped molds, where it has remained ever since, and into those molds it poured a cast of characters that was more diverse than ever before.

1. The American Guide Series included one volume for each of the forty-eight states, two territorial volumes for Alaska and Puerto Rico, two for New York City, and one for the District of Columbia. A number of city and local guides also carried the American Guide Series designation.

How this happened is intrinsically important for understanding American culture, then and now. Moreover, the story of the American Guides shows how people pursuing strictly political and economic agendas can accidently create radical cultural change simply by playing with shapes.

Regionalism and Federalism in American Culture

Americans have always felt a tension between centralization and decentralization, the national and the local, federal, and state. The Civil War resolved this tension politically but not culturally. While intellectuals of the 1930s argued over conservative versus progressive regionalism, the federal government, for reasons that had nothing whatsoever to do with culture, was about to reshape regional cultures by casting them into forty-eight new molds. State boundaries set the form; the content resulted from East Coast elitism versus heartland experience, Washington high-handedness versus local stubbornness, and the political, economic, and literary context at both the national and the state levels in which the federal-state struggles took place.

Regional cultures are the product of geography, climate, migration flows, and people's interpretation of their lives and histories. Prior to the middle decades of the nineteenth century, cities, states, and territories of the not-very-United States had their own folkways, communications media, and central nodes of trade and knowledge, with relatively little intercourse among them on a cultural level. To be sure, Americans were never living in isolated islands of humanity; there was too much commerce, too much mobility, and too much immigration for that. But in 1850 even those of European background—the schoolteacher in Iowa, the planter in Georgia, the Hispano farmer in New Mexico, and the merchant in Massachusetts—did not share a great deal in terms of culture, while people of African, Asian, or indigenous descent were even more sequestered in their own worlds. The Civil War per se did not change this.

Federalism—the balance of power between a single center and multiple units on the periphery—has two dimensions: political and cultural. Political federalism was an eighteenth-century achievement in the colonial, then the confederated, and finally the *united* states, an achievement that had to be finally ratified by civil war. Cultural federalism did not follow automatically; indeed just when war was settling the question of American political unification once and for all, American cultural unification was just beginning.[2]

2. It is still a work in progress; pressures for cultural centralization continue to meet with local and regional pushback, and at times the very forces promoting homogeneity have themselves encouraged and shaped distinctive place cultures (Griswold 2008).

"Shape" refers to the forms within which we view cultural objects and practices. Shapes may conform to jurisdictional boundaries (New England folkways, California cuisine) or cross them (Appalachian music, Great Plains writing). Such forms are dynamic: Shapes can fade away (aside from the names of my home university and of a Milwaukee insurance company, the old conception of the "Northwest," based on the Northwest Territory, has disappeared) while others rise (the "Sunbelt" became meaningful in the 1970s). Although it is misleading to think of American culture as having congealed into specific shapes once and for all, certain shapes take hold. Before the 1930s, the containers for regional culture were not state-shaped. After the Federal Writers' Project, they were. This book tells how this happened and what in particular the literary consequences were.

American cultural unification came about, to the extent that it did, as a technological by-product. In the middle of the nineteenth century the telegraph, the railroad, and the postal service tied the country together.[3] Infrastructure set the tracks for unification, and reading was the engine. The Industrial Revolution had put the printed word in the hands of anyone who wanted it. Weekly magazines had appeared in the early nineteenth century, daily newspapers even earlier, and they published fiction, poetry, and essays in addition to news, travel reports, and commentary on current events.[4] Periodicals were expensive, however, so the audience was limited until the 1840s, when inventors in Germany and in Canada (unaware of each other) discovered how to make paper from wood pulp instead of rags. At almost the same time the steam-powered rotary press made it possible to print much more quickly and cheaply than with the flatbed presses of the past. These inventions, together with the Postal Act of 1863, which allowed publishers cheaper distribution, ushered in the golden age of the American magazine, with magazines more national in coverage, more varied in terms of quality and audience, and far more numerous than before.[5]

Everyone was reading. Magazines, novels, and newspapers littered both parlors and tenements. Libraries sprang up everywhere. Literacy (not nec-

3. The telegraph connected the two coasts in 1861. The First Transcontinental Railroad connected them in 1869. Railway mail service also began in the 1860s.

4. The *Saturday Evening Post* was founded in 1821, the *Saturday Press* in 1838, the *New York Ledger* in 1847. Later and even more important in terms of the literature they published were the monthlies: *Harper's New Monthly Magazine* (1850), the *Atlantic Monthly* (1857), the *Galaxy* (1866), the *Overland Monthly* (1868), *Scribner's* (1870), and *Century Illustrated Monthly Magazine* (1881).

5. "The Act of March 3, 1863 (12 Stat. 704), based postage for a letter on its weight and eliminated all differences based on distance, thus providing universal service to customers no matter where they lived in the country. The act also created three classes of mail: First-Class Mail, which embraced letters; second-class mail, which covered publications issued at regular periods; and third-class mail, which included all other mailable matter." "The Postal Role in US Development," http://about.usps.com/publications/pub100/pub100_010.htm.

essarily in English) was becoming all but universal, lighting was improved, and most people, especially if they had moved off the farm, had some leisure time. Moreover, there was little competition for this leisure time; the seductions of electronic media were yet to come. Men had their clubs and saloons, of course, and women their own clubs and social worlds, but in the evenings Americans read.[6]

Paradoxically, although all Americans were reading the same magazines and books, these magazines and books impressed on them just how different they all were. The late nineteenth and early twentieth centuries were the heyday of local color stories, dime novel Westerns, and postbellum fantasies about southern belles and/or southern decay. Although centralized media and better communications did not create regional cultures, they packaged them for entertainment and they made everyone aware of them. Fascinated by their own cultural variation, American readers embraced regional writing.

This symbiotic relationship between centralization and localism mutually reinforcing one another was not exceptional. American culture has always been pulled between unification and differentiation, core and periphery. While we sometimes associate a uniform, media-disseminated American culture with modernity, envisioning an inexorable and largely one-directional movement toward homogeneity, with regional differences an attractive but fading remnant, such a view is incorrect. Activities at the center—technological innovations, the growth of media and commercial culture, national museums and libraries, and the activities of the federal government—have always contributed to the invigoration and stabilization of regional cultures, just as regional cultures have been marketed and celebrated by institutions at the nation's core.

This book looks at one such period, a time when the federal government, for reasons of its own that had nothing whatsoever to do with culture, undertook a series of steps that ended up promoting regional cultures, determining their shapes, filling them with individuals, and locking them into place. New Deal centralism encouraged regionalism of a particular kind: For the first time, states, not broader territories like the Midwest or New England, were the cultural units of regionalism. It was as if the federal government poured preexisting cultural differences into state-shaped molds, where they then hardened. And as a by-product, again totally unintended, the process introduced gender and ethnic diversity—a cast of heterogeneous characters in the nation's definition of its own culture—

6. See Pawley (2001) for the impressive range of reading materials and practices in small-town Iowa during the late nineteenth century.

the likes of which had never been seen before. In terms of the shapes and in terms of the personnel, the process was one of casting American culture.

Regionalism before the 1930s

Regionalism was an old story in the new nation. Had history taken a slightly different turn, the area that is now the United States of America could have looked more like contemporary Africa, a postcolonial landmass with different nations speaking different languages and developing different cultures. In the eighteenth century, French (then Spanish, then French again) Louisiana, Spanish New Mexico, and British New England had little in common culturally although they happened to share a continent. True, the inexorable and rapacious push westward from the initial English settlements, along with fortunate developments in France and Spain that enabled the new nation to gain control of their colonies, prevented an African model from developing, but as noted above, this unification was political and not cultural.

Indeed, it could be said that regionalism defined American culture. Antebellum literature featured local humor and dialect. Washington Irving, among America's first bestselling authors, wrote about the Dutch in New York, ever after known as the Knickerbockers. Publishers operating out of Charleston and Baltimore maintained a largely separate literary world devoted to southern writers. Publishers in Boston, Philadelphia, and later Chicago fostered writing from and about their regions. Smaller but even more separate were the literary worlds of French-speaking New Orleans or Spanish-speaking Santa Fe.

The mid-nineteenth-century golden age of magazines entertained Americans by depicting one another's strange regional folkways. Many of the most influential periodicals had appeared just before the war—*Harper's* in 1850, *Leslie's Weekly* in 1855, the *Atlantic* in 1957—and after Appomattox, magazine circulation exploded. Americans could choose from 700 different magazines in 1865, 1,200 in 1870, 2,400 in 1880, 3,300 in 1885; overall 8,000 to 9,000 different magazines appeared, with an average life of four years.[7] At the same time railroads were both facilitating print distribution and making travel available for average Americans, including readers curious about places they might actually visit.

Magazines needed material; writers and readers were traveling; supply and demand were in place. The result was the Local Color Movement, the

7. Tebbel and Zuckerman (1991): 57–58.

fiction and sketches about singular American locales that had its heyday between the 1870s and the early years of the twentieth century. Local Color writers were of two minds: On the one hand they promulgated homespun, dialect-speaking, regional characters (New England eccentrics, western braggarts, midwestern stoics) of the sort that had been popular since the early nineteenth century, while on the other hand they presented these as endangered species, disappearing in the same wave of industrialization and urbanization that had made the movement possible and popular in the first place. Nostalgia was woven into Local Color writing.

The focus on a vanishing past gave rise to a vogue for Americana, the desire to collect and preserve those traditional cultural patterns and objects that were disappearing. Wealthy collectors had been interested in Americana since the late nineteenth century—in *The House of Mirth* Lily Bart unsuccessfully attempts to land a dull-but-wealthy collector who bores her by going on about the stuff—and the popular vogue for Americana grew through the 1920s.[8] Celebrations of disappearing folkways, together with scholarly and philanthropic preservationist movements institutionalized in museums, libraries, collections, and historical societies, enabled what the historian Michael Kammen called the Party of Memory to resist the centralization advocated by the Party of Modernity. While the decades before and immediately after the First World War saw the rise of cultural modernism, they also saw the maintenance of a contrary value embracing the traditional and regional. This tension between Memory and Modernity, the regionally distinctive and the nationally (or internationally) standardized, would come to a head in the 1930s.

Regionalism during the 1930s

Well before the federal government's cultural intervention, before the New Dealers decided to—as FDR put it—"try something," intellectuals and artists debated the role of American regionalism. The question was, does

8. Kammen (1991) described Americana as part of a dialogue between traditionalists and modernists. Prior to about 1870, Americans rejected the past in favor of Progress and Nature. Orators rarely invoked a common tradition, writers took a very selective approach to history (e.g., Longfellow's *Hiawatha*), and overall the nation was present-and-future oriented. In the late nineteenth and early twentieth centuries, however, there emerged a "hunger for history." Out of the desire for sectional reconciliation, the centennial celebration, new technologies like the camera, and ubiquitous print emerged collective memory as a national project. Tourists made "pilgrimages" to historical sites like Civil War battlefields. There was renewed interest in colonial architecture. Annual celebrations such as rural festivals, "pioneer days," and "old home weeks" proliferated. Philanthropists turned their resources to preserving historical sites, notably the Colonial Williamsburg restoration funded by John D. Rockefeller in the 1920s.

the celebration of the local contribute to the celebration of the national, a national narrative, or does it assert itself in opposition, offering an alternative narrative? The New Dealers who would design the Federal Writers' Project argued that the regional and the national were complementary, indeed symbiotic. Regionalists in art and literature argued to the contrary, that the regionally specific was opposed to and a refuge from the centralizing and homogenizing tendencies of the modern state. These two extremes obscure the fact that during the thirties, "regionalism" had four distinct strands—inventorial, American gothic, romantic conservative, and romantic progressive—and all four had an impact on the regionalism that the Federal Writers' Project codified.

First, the desire to document, preserve, and catalog the nation's historical and cultural experience grew out of the earlier interest in Americana. Nowadays we associate documentaries with images of the Great Depression, but the goal was broader. The urban, educated photographers, filmmakers, musicologists, and folklorists who did the fieldwork of documenting American lives sought to capture fading local cultures, which were especially manifest in the lives of the rural, the poorly educated, the less sophisticated Americans. New Dealers, who believed in gathering social data of all sorts, heartily supported this impulse, the most lasting products of which would be the Historical Records Survey, *The Index of American Design*, and the fieldwork of John and Alan Lomax for the Archive of American Folk Song of the Library of Congress.[9]

Second, today we associate thirties regionalism with Regionalists, the painters like Grant Wood and writers like William Faulkner, who represented a strand I'm calling "American gothic" that emphasizes the regional past as brooding, distorting, inescapable. Although Faulkner's famous line "The past is not dead. It's not even past" came later, it captures the outlook.[10] American gothic presented local history as unsettling, regional natives as strange and, to urban sophisticates, unfathomable. Critics in the twenties had called the work of Sinclair Lewis (*Main Street*), Sherwood Anderson (*Winesburg, Ohio*), and Edgar Lee Masters (*Spoon River Anthology*) as the "revolt against the village," but where these earlier writers depicted the necessity of escape, the American gothics asserted its impossibility.

It was the two other strands of regionalist thinking that would ani-

9. The Historical Records Survey was part of the Federal Writers' Project from the fall of 1935 until November 1936, when it separated as a fifth unit under Federal One. Its goal was organizing, inventorying, and documenting public archives. Precedence was given to the county level, except in New England where the town was the principal political subdivision.

10. "The past is not dead. It's not even past." From William Faulkner, *Requiem for a Nun* (New York: Random House, 1951).

mate the Federal Writers' Project most directly. Romantic conservatives celebrated the past, contrasting it with the present, while romantic progressives saw the past as contributing to modernity itself. Both positions emanated from the South and both began with the question of the South's relation to the rest of the nation, especially the Northeast. As we have seen, industrialization and urbanization seemed to be rendering regional variations—in cuisine, dialect, outlook, style, manners, humor, values—increasingly obsolete. Between 1910 and 1920 the majority of the American population became urban, and the ratio of urban to rural increased steadily throughout the century.[11] Regions like the West and New England, which during the Local Color era had seemed exotic to the cultural centers of the Northeast, were losing much of their distinctiveness. The South, on the other hand, remained obdurately different: poor, rural, unindustrialized, racially divided, and brooding on the past. This prompted two types of response: The conservative one celebrated and cherished regional differences, while the progressive one viewed regional differences as an intrinsic part of a unified whole.

The sunnier works of Regionalists expressed the distinctiveness and Grant Wood set out its claims in his essay aptly titled "Revolt against the City." This conservative impulse also influenced the folklore and documentary movements. Most notably the Agrarians, a brilliant cadre of poets and literary scholars born in a poetry club at Vanderbilt University, asserted that regionalism was a value. Dismayed by northern scorn, which had come to a head in the 1925 Scopes trial, they defended a rural way of life in opposition to the industrialization, materialism, and inhumanity of the North and "New South." Agrarians rejected the label of backwardness because they rejected the dominant image of what it meant to be advanced in the first place; defining progress in terms of industrial modernity was a misconception by which a metropolitan cultural elite class flattered itself. Satanic mills, urban anomie, a despoiled environment, social Darwinism: The Agrarians wanted none of it—but they also wanted none of the sentimental nostalgia for the Lost Cause perpetuated by history's losers and commodified for tourists. Their 1930 manifesto *I'll Take My Stand* urged that the South shape its future along the lines of their (highly selective) reading of the Old South: an agrarian, organic community combining the virtues of the yeoman farmer's work ethic and the planter's benevolence. This premodern vision found little favor in academia (even Vanderbilt's chancellor disassociated himself from the Agrar-

11. US Census Bureau, October 1995, table 1, "Urban and Rural Population: 1900 to 1990," sources: table 16, 1990 CPH-2-1; table 25, 1990 CPH-2-1; and table 13, 1980 PC80-1-1.

ians' anti-industrialism) and alarmed other southern scholars, especially the social scientists.

The heartland of romantic progressivism was southern as well. At the University of North Carolina, the sociologist Howard W. Odum and colleagues responded to conservative regionalism by redefining the terms, arguing that isolationist, anti-industrial tendencies amounted to "sectionalism," which was divisive and doomed. Odum contrasted sectionalism with regionalism: *Regional* differences were real, and scholars working on such issues as poverty needed to recognize them, but such differences contributed to an organic whole. Applying a federal political model to culture, Odum maintained that distinct regions came together in a unified national culture. In a series of studies Odum's research center amassed statistics on different American regions to show (1) that regionalism was not confined to the South but was characteristic of the American nation as a whole, and (2) that regionalism, far from being a misty nostalgia for some imagined past, offered social scientists and planners data and tools with which to craft social policy.

Such romantic progressive regionalism was the stance of the Federal Writers' Project, the subject of this book. Project New Dealers in Washington and in the state offices believed that local place-based characteristics could be analyzed, depicted, and turned to progressive ends, those of employing writers, encouraging tourism, and educating people about their own history. In the American Guide Series, the Project set out to produce travel guides that not only would direct people on which routes to take and what to see but also would reveal and celebrate the distinctive characteristics of individual states—their histories, their cultures, their cities and roads—and in so doing would contribute to the American project.[12]

Although this was the New Dealers underlying cultural belief, it was not their purpose. The mission of the Project, and of the WPA as a whole, had nothing whatsoever to do with culture, regional or otherwise. The mission was much simpler: jobs.

From Jobs to Culture

American Guides will trace how a jobs program concocted in Washington cast American culture into new shapes and with new contents. It is the result of research that posed questions at three levels. The substantive

12. In his fine intellectual history of the Project (published, of course, by University of North Carolina Press), Jerrold Hirsch (2003) calls this "romantic nationalism."

ones were: How did the State Guides of the Federal Writers' Project come about and why were they the way they were? How did their cultural essays define and present American literature? How did people actually use the Guides? What impact did they have on American culture? To answer these substantive questions meant first tackling methodological questions: How can we tell what people do with books? What counts as evidence? Can materiality play a role? And finally there were theoretical questions: How does culture change? How does the interplay of cultural agents—the producers' intentions and constraints, the receivers' applications and innovations, the unexpected twists of history, the lock-in of institutionalization, the shifts in the market—shape the meaning and impact of cultural objects? The book before you offers answers I have come up with to these substantive, methodological, and theoretical questions.

It begins with part 1, "Jobs for Writers." The first chapter, "Putting People to Work," emphasizes that the Federal Writers' Project was first and foremost a jobs program. Its roots were in the Depression, the New Deal, the Works Progress Administration, and Federal One, the four WPA Arts Projects that put the white-collar unemployed to work. The threatening political context, especially the incessant accusations of boondoggling, government interference, and subversion, would profoundly influence the Project's organization, activities, and cultural impact. The second chapter, "Keeping Writers out of Trouble," sets out how Federal Writers' Project officials, like New Dealers overall, saw their mission through the lens of progressive politics, elite East Coast backgrounds, and cosmopolitanism. They encountered resistance from radicals, from conservatives, from parochial interests, from a skeptical press, and from an uninterested public. The Project's problem was to come up with something for destitute writers to do that would pacify the opposition and convert the ambivalent. The solution was to have them turn out travel guides.

Part 2, "Guides for Travelers," explores the history of travel guides as a genre and travel as a practice. Chapter 3, "Guiding Travelers," shows how travel guides solved the Federal Writers' Project's problem of giving unemployed writers something socially useful to do. Although guidebooks were an ancient genre, before the Industrial Revolution they mainly directed the journeys of religious pilgrims, scholars, merchants, and elite youth on the Grand Tour. This changed in the nineteenth century when steamships and railroads brought travel within the reach of the growing middle class. Guidebooks for this new market exploded, with Baedekers setting the standard. This was the Federal Writers' Project's model when it set itself the task of writing "American Baedekers." The fourth chapter, "Seeing America," covers travel in twentieth-century America, where the automobile offered new possibilities, particularly to growing numbers of vacationers. The Federal Writers' Project's American Guide Series was part of a wide-ranging response to the new model of leisure travel. Tourism was booming in the 1930s, and travel guides for American motorists abounded. The American Guides would have to carve out their niche within a crowded field.

Part 3, "Cultural Federalism," takes up how the Federal Writers' Project set about its task. The fifth chapter, "Negotiating Federalism," shows how, for better or for worse, the Federal Writers' Project was committed to writing travel guides for every state. Project administrators in Washington wanted standardized Guides, and they stressed efficiency, style, and attention to what they considered significant. The states, on the other hand, had their own priorities, their own ideas about what was significant, and sometimes their own styles as well. Wrestling between Washington and the states took place in the fraught political context of the New Deal, the recession of 1937–38, and the rising alarm about subversion. These struggles gave the Guides their form and their peculiar blend of conventional and idiosyncratic. Chapter 6, "Describing America," focuses on the Guides themselves. Over its up-and-down existence, the Project (which devolved to the states as the Writers' Program in 1939) always saw the State Guides as its top priority. Impressive as physical objects, the books told a comprehensive story of every state's natural, social, and cultural heritage, its cities, and how motorists should experience it. Each Guide was an odd mix of travel guide, reference work, and armchair reading, and each bore traces of the struggle between Washington standardization and state individualism.

Part 4, "Readers and Authors," focuses more directly on American readers and American literature. The seventh chapter, "Guiding Readers," looks at the assumptions about reading built into the American Guide Series. Although it was politically expedient to write travel guidebooks for tourists, the Project directors aimed for readers as well as travelers. Leisure reading was booming in the 1930s; the nation was almost entirely literate and books were widely available even for those who couldn't afford to buy them. The more avid readers tended to be urban and educated, as were the Project directors, and their tastes had a powerful influence on the Guides in general and on the Literature essays in particular.

Chapter 8, "Choosing Authors," turns to the authors covered in the State Guides' Literature essays. While some states embraced the federal mandate to come up with an essay on their local literature and other resisted the task, in the end the Guides' Literature essays discussed over 3,000 authors. The organization of the Project by state had a geographically leveling effect: States in the South and in the Plains had to come up with their authors just like states in the Northeast. It also had a diversifying effect: In their scramble to uncover authors, states—especially those outside the Northeast—found women and minority authors that had previously been ignored.

Part 5, "Casting Culture," demonstrates the American Guide Series' lasting impact on American literature. Chapter 9, "Defining Literature," shows that before the Guides, the American literary canon was white, male, Northeastern, and traditional in terms of genre; after the Guides, it was less of all these. The Guides marked a shift in literary definition that took place three decades before civil rights, second-wave feminism, and identity politics blew the canon wide open. Unlike these movements, the Federal Writers' Project pursued no cultural agenda and had no goal of inclusion or diversity. Nevertheless, the Guides' presentation was more diverse than had been any of the previous attempts to define what American literature encompassed.

Chapter 10, "Using Books," tackles the question of correlation versus causality by assessing the evidence that the Guides actually made a difference in how Americans conceptualize literature in terms of form (those state-shaped molds) and content (increased diversity). The Guides' definition of the American literary canon was more diverse than any before, pointing toward a change that, by the end of the century, would revolutionize American culture. To suggest that it had independent cultural influence, however, requires evidence. Such evidence—from the Guides' design, from their materiality, from their initial reception, from the timing of their rollout, and from their endurance and use in subsequent decades—supports the thesis that the Guides unobtrusively normalized conceptions of diverse literary voices and distinctive state cultures.

The concluding chapter, "Casting American Culture," summarizes the book's claims, starting from the premise that cultural change does not always come about through the gradual congealing of ideas. In the case of the State Guides, institutionalization came before ideas, and for reasons that had nothing to do with culture. The resulting diversification was not intentional, not the result of a high-minded view about inclusivity but of politically strategic decisions, bureaucratic logics, and struggle between snobbish, metropolitan intellectuals and stubborn, you-can't-push-me-around locals. The fruits of cultural federalism were twofold: an American regionalism cast into state-shaped molds and a far more heterogeneous set of players cast into lead roles. The American Guides Series demonstrates the cultural power that comes from transposing a form from one field (politics) to another (culture) and from filling that form with the contents readily at hand. It is the Federal Writers' Project's inadvertent casting of American literature that we have brought into the twenty-first century.

PART ONE

Jobs for Writers

ONE

Putting People to Work

> The unemployed
> without a stake in the country
> without jobs or nest eggs
> marching they don't know where
> marching north south west—
> and the deserts
> marching east with dust . . .
> these lead to no easy pleasant conversation
> they fall into a dusty disordered poetry
>
> CARL SANDBURG, *THE PEOPLE, YES*

The unemployed—the faces of the Great Depression, victims and symbols of America's economic collapse—were the problem. And just as Carl Sandburg was finishing his American epic, the Works Progress Administration was putting together the solution. The WPA's goal was simple: take men and women off the relief roles and put them to work.

The Great Depression gave rise to the New Deal; the New Deal generated the WPA; the WPA produced Federal One; and Federal One launched the Federal Writers' Project, the subject of this book. This sequence unfolded from the spring of 1933 to the summer of 1935. As a response to unemployment, the charge of the Federal Writers' Project was jobs, nothing else. Nevertheless, both the work that the Project would undertake and the cultural impact that it would have were a direct result of the rocky, scorpion-infested political landscape in which it struggled to survive.

"Try Something": The Early Years of the New Deal

When Franklin Delano Roosevelt was inaugurated president of the United States on March 4, 1933, a quarter of the American workforce was out of a job. Unemployment had been growing every year since the stock market crash, going from an average of 3.3 percent during the 1920s to 8.9 percent in 1930, 15.9 percent in 1931, 23.6 percent in 1932, and 24.9 percent in 1933. The situation—"no easy pleasant conversation" indeed—was dire.[1]

Herbert Hoover, FDR's predecessor, believed that the free market would eventually correct itself so the crisis did not require much government interference, but late in his administration he made one move that, though modest in its ambitions, established key precedents for New Deal programs including the Writers' Project. In July 1932 Hoover authorized the Reconstruction Finance Corporation, under the Emergency Relief and Construction Act, Title I, to give aid to state and local governments and to make loans to banks, railroads, and other businesses. (See appendix A for the acronyms and organizations of the New Deal era and appendix B for the key dates.) Not a jobs program per se, the RFC channeled funds to state relief programs. Its rules required that recipients be not just unemployed but destitute; it further stipulated that projects undertaken should be on public, not private, property (so they could not be turned to private gain), that they be "worthwhile," and that they not replace work already being done by employed workers.[2] Continuing throughout the New Deal and the Second World War, the RFC rules set the pattern for federal action—that projects undertaken by the government not compete with or duplicate what the private sector was doing and that they be intrinsically worth doing—although the RFC itself was more a banking than a relief program and gave no hint of what was to come.

In the 1932 presidential election, Roosevelt, then governor of New York, campaigned against Republican Al Smith by advocating aggressive government intervention in the economy: "The country needs and, unless I mistake its temper, the country demands bold, persistent experimentation. It is common sense to take a method and try it: If it fails, admit it frankly and

1. Figures are from VanGiezen and Schwenk (2003). Nineteen thirty-three had the highest unemployment, but the recovery was slow: 21.7 percent in 1934, 20.1 percent in 1935, 17.0 percent in 1936, 14.3 percent in 1937, and then jumping again in 1938 to 19 percent. The rate stayed high (17.2 percent in 1939 and 14.6 percent in 1940) until the military buildup and then America's entrance into the Second World War bought full employment. The unemployment rate in 1941 had dropped to 9.9 percent and by 1942 it was 4.7 percent.

2. McDonald (1969): 15–16.

try another. But above all, try something."[3] Many intellectuals at the time favored such government experimentation; as Stuart Chase, the economist who coined the term "New Deal," put it, "Why should Russians have all the fun remaking a world?" This "try something" message resonated with the voters as well, who had grown impatient with government passivity. Carrying all but six states, Roosevelt won in a landslide.

Roosevelt would indeed try many things. He began his presidency with an explosion of legislation known as the Hundred Days: banking reform, farm relief, the Civilian Conservation Corps, the Tennessee Valley Authority, the Federal Emergency Relief Administration.[4] On Sunday evening at the end of his first week in office Roosevelt delivered his initial fireside chat, in which he reassured Americans that their savings were safe and that "together we cannot fail." His eloquence and energy buoyed the nation's spirits. "America hasn't been so happy in three years as they are today," Will Rogers concluded. "The whole country is with him, just so he does something. If he burned down the Capitol we would cheer and say 'well, we at least got a fire started anyhow.'"[5]

The Hundred Days' crowning achievement was the National Industry Recovery Act / National Recovery Administration, passed on June 16, 1933. The act contained two parts: Title I, the NRA, entailed economic planning and regulation, while Title II authorized borrowing over $3 billion for building projects. Although the NRA only lasted two years—the Supreme Court ruled it to be unconstitutional in 1935 (in any case, its economic impact had been disappointing)—Title II established the Public Works Administration, under Interior Secretary Harold Ickes. Working on the logic of priming the pump, the PWA contracted with private firms for its projects, which then hired their workers on the private market, so PWA employees were never on the government payroll. The PWA poured money into massive construction projects like New York City's Triborough Bridge and Lincoln Tunnel, the Grand Coulee Dam in Washington State and Fort Peck Dam in Montana, the Overseas Highway that connected Key West to the rest of Florida, as well as thousands of road, sewage, school, and airport construction projects.

The Hundred Days also brought Harry Hopkins to Washington, DC, as coordinator of federal relief efforts. "A welfare worker from the Cornbelt, who tended to regard money (his own as well as other people's) as something to be spent as quickly as possible, [Hopkins was] a studiously

3. Address at Oglethorpe University, May 22, 1932, http://newdeal.feri.org/speeches/1932d.htm, retrieved July 14, 2009; see also N. Taylor (2008): 62.

4. For a detailed account of the Hundred Days, see Cohen (2009).

5. Quoted in Schlesinger (1958): 13.

unsuave and often intolerant and tactless reformer."[6] Born in 1890, raised in Iowa, and educated in the progressive tradition of Grinnell College, Hopkins built a career in social work administration in New York City that culminated in his directorship of the state's Temporary Emergency Relief Administration. Under Hopkins's leadership, TERA put 80,000 New Yorkers to work. While most of their jobs involved road construction, sanitation, or parks and schools, a few were clerical or white-collar positions, including one program specifically for artists.

Hopkins's TERA experience convinced him that government had the ability and the responsibility to provide both relief and jobs for the unemployed. When Roosevelt took office in March 1933, Hopkins met with fellow New Yorker Frances Perkins, the new secretary of labor, to pitch his ideas: Federal money should go directly to the states (an arrangement the RFC had already established) and a single agency, working through state branches, should manage grants, provide relief, and create jobs. Perkins took the plan to FDR, a week later it went to Congress, and the Federal Emergency Relief Act, allocating $500 million in outright grants to states for relief, became law on May 12. The president put Hopkins at the head of the new agency.[7] (Table 1.1 compares TERA and the various federal relief and/or arts programs.)

Harry Hopkins spent FERA money fast, making grants to seven states his first day on the job. The *Washington Post* fretted that "the half-billion dollars for direct relief of States won't last a month if Harry L. Hopkins, new relief administrator, maintains the pace he set yesterday in disbursing more than $5,000,000 during his first two hours in office" and Hopkins cheerfully responded, "I'm not going to last six months here, so I'll do as I please." Determined to avoid political patronage, Hopkins hired staff as dedicated as he was and as expansive in their view of government's responsibilities. A piece of this expansive view that came directly from his TERA experience was Hopkins's conviction that white-collar and professional workers ought to be included in employment programs. At a conference of social workers in June, he promised that under FERA "at least two million men are going to be put to work," and not just the unskilled but professionals as well.[8]

At the same conference, Hopkins vented his growing frustration. The states were slow to act. PWA moved at a snail's pace (Hopkins and Ickes

6. "A welfare worker" is from Sherwood (1948): 1.

7. See N. Taylor (2008): 100 for an account of the meeting.

8. The *Washington Post* quotation and "I'm not going to last six months . . ." are from Sherwood (1948): 44–45. Sherwood notes that Hopkins's staff "agreed with his own unrestricted conception" of what the federal government should take on (49). The June 17 conference is from N. Taylor (2008): 111.

Table 1.1 Relief and arts programs during the Great Depression

Program	Purpose	Jobs program	Structure	Cultural impact
Temporary Emergency Relief Administration (TERA) 1931–33	New York State relief program	Yes. Direct and work relief. Means test.	State program, became model for FERA	Employed some artists and white-collar workers
Reconstruction Finance Corporation (RFC) 1931–57	Loans to banks, railroads, businesses, and to state and local governments	No. Not itself a relief program, supported state programs.	Made loans to states for relief programs	No direct impact
Federal Emergency Relief Administration (FERA) 1933–35	Manage grants to states for relief programs	Yes. Direct and work relief.	Made outright grants to states for relief	No direct impact; few white-collar positions
Civil Works Administration (CWA) 1933–34	Temporary, short-term program for jobless	Yes. No means test.	Federal government hired directly without channeling money through states	No direct impact
Treasury Department's Section on Painting and Sculpture 1934–43	Art to beautify federal buildings	No. Not a relief program.	Competitions among blind submissions	Murals in post offices and other federal buildings
Resettlement Administration / Farm Security Administration Information Division 1935–46	Promoting FSA to media, documenting poverty and New Deal programs	No. Not a relief program.	Photographers hired by Information Division's Historical Section (Roy Stryker)	Documentary photography and films
Works Progress Administration / Work Projects Administration (WPA) 1935–42	Large-scale federal effort to provide jobs for the unemployed	Yes. Work relief only. Means test.	State WPA directors; unlike other projects, Federal One reported to DC, not to state WPA directors	Four Federal One projects: Art, Theater, Music, Writers

had very different styles of management, and the rivalry between them was intense). FERA's goal of two million jobs was nowhere near enough to meet the demand. Hopkins had come to believe that the federal government should not just channel funds through states and localities but should provide jobs directly.

In the fall of 1933 unemployment remained high, winter was coming, and Hopkins worried about how the jobless would manage. So he persuaded FDR to create a temporary jobs program, the Civil Works Administration. The CWA focused on small projects like road repair that could be launched quickly. Half of its workers came from FERA's work relief rolls and half were hired directly into the program. CWA did not require workers to pass a means test, and as a result it had many more applicants than it did jobs. On its first payday in November, CWA issued checks to over 800,000 workers, a figure that rose to 2.6 million by mid-December. Field investigators sent out by Hopkins reported on the energizing impact of CWA. At its peak in January 1934 the CWA employed 4,264,000 workers.[9]

Having been stung by criticism that FERA jobs were pointless leaf raking, Hopkins tried to ensure that CWA jobs were, as Frances Perkins put it, "socially useful."[10] (This much-repeated phrase was the progressive spin on Hoover's "worthwhile.") Although most CWA workers were manual laborers, some 190,000 were "non-manual and professional"; most of these were teachers, but the category included 3,000 artists, writers, and musicians, recalling TERA's employment of artists.[11] Republicans and conservative Democrats criticized the CWA in general and its employment of artists and writers in particular, to which Hopkins famously responded, "Hell! They've got to eat just like other people."[12]

For all the expectations it raised, CWA was never intended to be other than a short-term emergency program and it was demobilized in February and March 1934. Once again FERA became the chief work-relief agency, though it never had more than 2.5 million workers. The PWA funded massive projects in virtually every county in the nation, but it worked through private contracting, and the hiring was based on skills, not on

9. Payroll figures from N. Taylor (2008): 122; see also Cohen (2009): 312.

10. See Cohen (2009): 312. Perkins and Hopkins repeatedly referred to jobs that were "socially useful." For example, in a radio address in February 1935 Perkins described the employment package, then before Congress, that would become the WPA as "the largest employment program ever considered in any country. As outlined by the President, it will furnish employment for able-bodied men now on relief, and enable them to earn their support in a decent and socially useful way." Hon. Frances Perkins, "Social Insurance for U.S.," national radio address delivered February 25, 1935, http://www.ssa.gov/history/perkinsradio.html, retrieved June 3, 2010.

11. N. Taylor (2008) gives the overall figure for nonmanual and professionals employed by CWA as 190,000, of which Sherwood claimed there were 3,000 writers and artists.

12. Figures and "Hell, they've got to eat" from Sherwood (1948): 57.

who needed the paycheck.[13] Hopkins continued to push for a more ambitious federal jobs program, but FDR held back for months, hoping the economy would rebound. Instead, as 1934 ground on, things got worse. Unemployment barely budged. A persistent drought in the Midwest brought dust storms and rural dislocation. Calls for action came from the left, for example, the American Communist Party, through popular movements and populists like the Townsend movement, Father Coughlin, and Huey Long, and from the right, for example, the anti–New Deal American Liberty League.[14]

When a Democratic surge in the midterm elections strengthened Roosevelt's hand, Hopkins made his move. Over the Thanksgiving holiday he pursued the president to his Warm Springs retreat to pitch a more aggressive approach for an expanded jobs program. Reports of the gigantic plan leaked out—the *New York Times* called it Hopkins's "End Poverty in America" plan, coming with an $8–9 billion price tag—but Roosevelt was persuaded.[15]

On January 4, 1935, FDR addressed Congress on the State of the Union. Article II of the US Constitution requires that the president "from time to time give to Congress information of the State of the Union and recommend to their Consideration such measures as he shall judge necessary and expedient." Presidents traditionally deliver this address in January, and in outlying their legislative agendas, they speak as much to the American people as to Congress. In his address Roosevelt argued that long-term relief, also known as government handouts or the dole, fostered dependence and passivity. Relief was "a narcotic, a subtle destroyer of the human spirit. . . . Work must be found for able-bodied but destitute workers."[16] Employment was not primarily an economic issue but a moral one. Five million people were currently on the relief rolls. Of these, a quarter were unable to work and needed direct relief from state and local government and private charities, but all the rest were able and eager for jobs. Roosevelt asked Congress

> to make it possible for the United States to give employment to all of these three and one-half million employable people now on relief, pending their absorption in a rising tide of private employment.

13. Smith (2006) notes that the PWA spent money in 3,068 out of the nation's 3,071 counties (p. 2).

14. See Brinkley (1982) for the background and careers of two of the most influential voices, Father Coughlin and Huey Long.

15. N. Taylor (2008): 157–58.

16. Franklin D. Roosevelt, "Annual Message to Congress," January 4, 1935, online by Gerhard Peters and John T. Woolley, *The American Presidency Project*, http://www.presidency.ucsb.edu/ws/?pid=14890.

It is my thought that with the exception of certain of the normal public building operations of the Government, all emergency public works shall be united in a single new and greatly enlarged plan.

He set out his vision, actually Hopkins's vision, of a program that would give the unemployed work, and work that was "useful—not just for a day, or a year, but useful in the sense that it affords permanent improvement in living conditions or that it creates future new wealth for the nation." Wages would be higher than the dole but less than what industry paid. Projects should not compete with private enterprise or with works already undertaken; instead, "*if it were not for the necessity of giving useful work to the unemployed now on relief, these projects in most instances would not now be undertaken* [emphasis added]." The president reeled off the types of projects he had in mind—slum clearance, rural housing, rural electrification, reforestation, soul erosion prevention, highway construction—and assured the nation that "beyond the material recovery, I sense a spiritual recovery as well." Useful work would contribute to both.

While the plan's legislative prospects were rosy, a persistent thorn emerged. The House quickly passed legislation authorizing $4 billion for the jobs program, but as the more deliberate Senate debated for weeks, in the course of its committee hearings a new word entered the nation's vocabulary. A craft teacher named Robert Marshall explained to the senators that he taught "boon doggles," which he defined as "a term applied back in the pioneer days . . . things men and boys do that are useful in their everyday operations or recreations or about their home. They might be making belts in leather, or maybe belts by weaving ropes . . . maybe a tent or a sleeping bag." Critics pounced. The *New York Times* ran headline "$3,187,000 Relief Is Spent Teaching Jobless to Play. 'Boon Doggles' Made." "Boondoggles" came to mean the government shelling out for pointless work, and the term stuck. The *New York Sun* even ran a column featuring "Today's Boondoggle." Throughout the history of the WPA, critics and humorists prospected for boondoggles, especially in construction and in artistic or intellectual projects.[17]

Boondoggles notwithstanding, the Senate finally voted through its ver-

17. Quotations from N. Taylor (2008): 167, 168. The Senate hearings brought up objections to the earlier white-collar FERA jobs such as New York City projects that compiled a Jewish encyclopedia, a history of safety pin manufacturing, and a sociological investigation of teachers' interests. The Senate committee counsel called this type of thing "high-spun theoretical bunk," but when Hopkins was asked if he was going to investigate, he responded characteristically: "Why should I? There is nothing the matter with that. They are damn good projects—excellent projects. . . . You know some people make fun of people who speak a foreign language, and dumb people criticize something they do not understand, and that is what is going on up there—God damn it!" (N. Taylor [2008]: 167)."

sion of the jobs bill, and on April 8, 1935, both houses passed the Emergency Relief Appropriations Act authorizing $4.8 billion for work relief. Roosevelt signed it the same day. Although both Ickes and Hopkins had been candidates, the president chose Hopkins to run the new program because he had demonstrated that he could spend money fast putting people to work. The act established a three-part structure: (1) Applications and Information to vet proposals from states and cities; (2) Allotments, which Ickes headed, to pass vetted proposals on to the appropriate agency; and (3) the Works Progress Division, with Hopkins in charge, to track projects and keep things moving. When announcing the new program in a fireside chat on April 28, Roosevelt promised it would be free from politics:

> I well realize that the country is expecting before this year is out to see the "dirt fly." . . . This is a great national crusade to destroy enforced idleness, which is an enemy of the human spirit generated by this depression. Our attack upon these enemies must be without sting and without discrimination. No sectional, no political distinctions can be permitted.

Inviting the public to criticize freely and to expose corruption or chiselers, Roosevelt promised "two hundred and fifty or three hundred" different kinds of work. When he signed the executive order on May 6, Hopkins began to put his organization together.

What the act had called the Works Progress Division immediately became the "Works Progress Administration." This name seemed an awkward jumble of words even at the time—Florence Kerr, who worked in the Women's and Professional Projects Division and became its head in 1939, recalled that, "nobody knew what that meant. It was a very, very odd name. I don't know where they ever picked it up"—but they knew what the WPA was to do: encompass projects that would lighten relief rolls as well as all projects under $25,000.[18] While the PWA required a 55 percent

18. Phillips (1963b): 1. In October 1963 a historian named Harlan Phillips, who had published a book of interviews with Felix Frankfurter three years earlier, interviewed Florence Kerr over a period of two weeks. Kerr was a Grinnell classmate and lifelong friend of Harry Hopkins, and he brought her into the WPA to head the Midwestern regional office of the WPA's Division of Women's and Professional Projects, which she did from 1935 until the end of 1938. A natural administrator, both diplomatic and frank, she was considered by Hopkins as the best of the five regional directors, and when Ellen Woodward resign as Hopkins's assistant in Washington, Hopkins promoted Kerr to her position. Once in Washington her duties included acting as liaison with both Congress and the White House. Kerr enjoyed a close relationship with Eleanor Roosevelt as well as with FDR himself, being a social as well as professional friend and a frequent guest at their Hyde Park weekends. Following the WPA reorganization in the spring of 1939, Kerr's division became the Division of Professional and Service Projects. Kerr maintained her relief programs oriented toward women even as the WPA shifted to war work, and when it closed down in 1943, she became the director of war public services under the Federal Works Agency. The Phillips interview is valuable for Kerr's candid and extensive insider's recollections of the

contribution from state or local sponsors, the WPA did not; not surprisingly, most proposals went to the WPA. Hopkins brought in his FERA assistants Jacob Baker, to head the Professional and Service Projects Division, and Ellen S. Woodward, to head the Women's Projects. In May when a unanimous Supreme Court struck down the NRA as unconstitutional, the focus of the New Deal turned to Social Security and to the WPA.

Over its eight-year life, the WPA would provide eight million jobs. In some respects the WPA was a compromise between FERA and CWA. Like FERA and unlike CWA or the PWA, the WPA was strictly a relief program; except for some supervisory personal, its employees had to come from the relief rolls. Like CWA, it paid a predictable monthly wage. Another key difference was that FERA had been a grant-in-aid program in which federal money was channeled through states and localities. In contrast, the WPA employees, like those of the former CWA, worked directly for the federal government. The administrative responsibilities and political headaches lay in Washington.[19] Despite its eventual size, the WPA was always considered temporary, an emergency stopgap rather than a permanent program.

Jobs, Not Art

The Works Progress Administration's purpose was to create jobs. It was not to produce buildings or infrastructure, let alone culture. Recognition of the WPA's essential mission has faded over time because the jobs and most of those who held them are gone while the structures and cultural objects remain. So Americans' collective memory tends to forget the program's raison d'être.

Nick Taylor's fine history of the WPA, for example, opens with a typically lyrical account of its legacy:

> [WPA workers] shouldered the tasks that began to transform the physical face of America. They built roads and schools and bridges and dams. The Cow Palace in San Francisco, LaGuardia Airport in New York City and National (now Reagan) Airport in Washington, D.C., the Timberline Lodge in Oregon, the Outer Drive Bridge on Chicago's Lake Shore Drive, the River Walk in San Antonio—all these accomplishments

WPA during its entire eight-year existence. Kerr returned to the name later in the interview: "Wasn't that an odd name that we got? I always thought that was a gasser. 'Work Progress.' Nobody ever knew what it meant. Now Public Works Administration was easy to understand but Works Progress wasn't" (43). See also https://libweb.grinnell.edu/archives/?p=collections/findingaid&id=59&q.

See table 5.1 for the Federal Writers' Project's Washington staff and field operatives. State project directors appear in table 5.2.

19. McDonald (1969): 103–6.

> and countless others are WPA creations. Its workers sewed clothes and stuffed mattresses and repaired toys; served hot lunches to schoolchildren; ministered to the sick; delivered library books to remote hamlets by horseback; rescued flood victims; painted giant murals on the walls of hospitals, high schools, courthouses, and city halls; performed plays and played music before eager audiences; and wrote guides to the forty-eight states that even today remain models for what such books should be.[20]

LaGuardia Airport and Lake Shore Drive, many of the murals, and all of the guidebooks are still with us. Nevertheless the WPA was a jobs program, and the political survival of both the WPA and its Federal Writers' Project depended not on what it produced but on its success in employing the destitute.[21]

During the thirties, "WPA" connoted muscular men riveting girders and hauling bricks, or muscular men leaning on their shovels. This imagery is no accident. The WPA concentrated on relatively small jobs, urban construction being the supreme case; more massive projects like dams and tunnels remained under the PWA. Thus WPA workers were highly visible to city newspapermen and sidewalk superintendents. Moreover, like other New Deal agencies, the WPA was superb at public relations and its photos and press releases documented WPA projects in heroic terms (figure 1.1). Given such imagery, it comes as something of a surprise that the very first WPA project was one that sought to employ not those hard-bodied he-men but their gentle brothers and sisters who worked in—of all things—the arts.

It happened by chance, not design. Even as late as during a mid-June 1935 conference of state WPA administrators, Washington had no plans for a federal arts program. The idea had been in the air for some time, and Arthur Goldschmidt had sketched out a national arts project back in February, but no one was committed to moving ahead. For the WPA overall, the months between April and August were ones of "doubt and confusion. . . . The passage of the bill did not remove the veil that hid the

20. N. Taylor (2008): 2. This entire section draws heavily on Taylor's detailed history of the WPA. Taylor is unapologetic in his over-the-top enthusiasm: "Franklin Roosevelt and Harry Hopkins believed that people given a job to do would do it well, and the fact that their paychecks were issued by the government would not make a whit of difference. They were right. The workers of the WPA shone. They excelled. . . . They were golden threads woven into the national fabric" (530). For a more skeptical view, see Shlaes (2007).

21. A stylistic note: In this book I will follow the common practice of referring to guidebooks, guides, and travel guides interchangeably. Of course each term has meanings—guidebooks for identifying birds, guides to take hunters through the north woods, travel guides as locals who assist tourists with bookings and transport—but I am using them in their overlapping sense of written books about a specific place that are intended to introduce visitors (actual or armchair) to what there is about that place that is distinctive and interesting. When I refer to books in the American Guide Series, I will capitalize them as Guides.

1.1 WPA poster

President's plan."[22] Initial supporters of the arts programs idea, like Bruce McClure, who directed the WPA's white-collar programs under Jacob Baker's supervision, insisted that any such programs would have to have local sponsorship and control. Late June and July, however, brought an abrupt change of fortune. Baker, Hopkins's assistant director, had close ties with New York artists and writers, and like Hopkins, he regarded them as appropriate recipients of government patronage. Goldschmidt had been associate director of the FERA Section for Professional and Service Projects, which carried over into the WPA, and he brought his ideas with him. Most critically, although the details remain murky, the Washington WPA office believed that they needed to spend the $300 million earmarked for white-collar and professional jobs immediately or risk losing the appropriation.[23]

22. McDonald (1969): 122.

23. McDonald (1969): 126–30. McDonald notes the irony: before July there had been "no intent on the part of the Washington staff to operate the arts program as a WPA-sponsored project," so "a program as fiscally unorthodox and as administratively unprecedented as was Federal One . . . [had been] prompted by an innocent legal interpretation from the General Accounting Office" (128).

So in July the Washington WPA officials threw together a flurry of white-collar projects, thirteen in all though only six proposals made it to submission. The very first was "WPA-Sponsored Federal Project Number One," which contained subprojects covering the four arts fields: writing, art, music, and theatre. Baker engaged four directors and made the official announcement on August 2:

> It is the intention of this Administration to sponsor nation-wide projects intending to employ persons now on relief who are qualified in the fields of Art, Music, Drama, and Writing. The following persons have been appointed by Mr. Hopkins to direct each of the nation-wide projects: Art, Holger Cahill; Music, Nikolai Sokoloff; Drama, Hallie Flanagan; and Writers, Henry G. Alsberg.
>
> Each of these directors will have a staff in Washington and the field to insure the unified planning and execution of the programs.[24]

The proposal, known forever after as Federal One, got final executive approval on September 12 along with a six-month allocation of a little over $6 million.[25] The Federal Writers' Project was born.

Federal One was almost, but not quite, the first time the federal government had paid for creative work. Unlike their European counterparts, American artists and writers have always had to depend on the market for their livings, with private individuals or foundations offering what little arts patronage there was to be had. Government support was rare, and most previous funding had been for commissioned projects. Arts patronage runs on a continuum from less to more artistic freedom, and commissioned work is on the less-free end: A government body or institution hires an artist to produce a particular object or representation. The government had done this on occasion, most famously in the decoration of the Capitol; in 1865, for example, it paid Constantino Brumidi $40,000 to create *The Apotheosis of Washington* fresco on the ceiling of the rotunda. The other end of the patronage continuum is when an artist receives support but has no particular responsibilities, he or she being free to create anything (or nothing). Such government-funded support is virtually unknown in the United States, though it was common at European courts and is found today in some social welfare states like Norway, where artists and writers receive generous, nonspecified stipends.[26]

24. McDonald (1969): 129.

25. Penkower (1977), ch. 1. A fifth project, the Historical Records Survey, was initially part of the Writers' Project; it became an independent division in October 1936.

26. The poet laureate of the United States comes close to this, for unlike elsewhere, he or she is not

While nothing on the scale of Federal One, there had been some New Deal precedents for the Arts Projects. In December 1933 the Civil Works Administration established the Public Works of Art Project, operating under the Treasury Department, to decorate public buildings. After CWA ended, PWAP evolved into the Treasury Department's Section on Painting and Sculpture, later Section on Fine Arts (1934–43), which commissioned murals for federal buildings and over 1,100 post offices. The Treasury Department's program, which became known as "Section Art," employed artists based on competence, not on need: The department would announce competitions, and juries would chose the winning designs from blind submissions, with the section having the final say. So Section Art was not a relief program, and the left was highly critical (untalented artists needed to eat too). The post office murals were especially popular and town boosters celebrated their dedications, although sometimes the artist's obvious unfamiliarity with the local culture pained the residents.[27]

Critiques notwithstanding, the Treasury Department's post office murals were not just beloved (as are those remaining today) but radical. As two historians put it:

> It was daring for the federal government to step in and patronize art on such a scale. It was unheard of for the government to place works of art outside the capital, much less in isolated towns without galleries or museums. It was radical for the government to take the position that art was a necessity rather than a luxury—that people needed paintings as well as highways.

Daring perhaps, yet the argument that art was some sort of necessity never would have the political traction that jobs programs had.[28]

New Deal documentary photography made an even more powerful impact on the American consciousness. The images produced by the Resettlement Administration, renamed the Farm Security Administration in

---

required to compose poems for ceremonial occasions, although the laureate does have to preside over readings and lectures at the Library of Congress.

27. Park and Markowitz (1984); see also Mangione (1972), ch. 2; Penkower (1977), ch. 1. The program was also criticized from the right, as in the attacks on the leftwing symbols on San Francisco's Coit Tower (Mangione). For analyses of post office murals, see Marling (1982) and Beckham (1989). In addition to Mangione and Penkower, D. Taylor (2009) offers a useful popular history of the Federal Writers' Project; his book was published in conjunction with a television program of the same name produced by the Smithsonian Channel. Christine Bold's (1988, 1999, 2006) scholarly work on the Project is also extremely useful. See also Schindler-Carter's (1999) discussion of the Project and summaries of the individual Guides.

28. "It was daring . . ." is from Park and Markowitz (1984): 28.

1937, are "now recognized as probably the most felicitous esthetic fallout of New Deal patronage."[29] Under Roy Stryker, the Information Division of the RA/FSA undertook to document the beneficial social interventions of the New Deal programs (Stryker would later handle public relations for Standard Oil.) The division went beyond its self-serving mandate. Stryker aimed to make the Depression visible and, moreover, to "introduce America to Americans"—a theme later picked up by the Federal Writers' Project.[30] The portraits of rural poverty that Walker Evans, Dorothea Lange, Arthur Rothstein, and their peers produced have been the faces of the Great Depression ever since. The FSA had the goal of documenting social conditions, however, not of generating employment. Like Section Art, it was not a jobs program and it did not draw its personnel from the relief rolls.

In contrast to all of these earlier programs, Federal One explicitly targeted artists and intellectuals who were destitute, regardless of whether or not they were skilled. Like the WPA in general, it was a work relief program in the lineage of FERA and CWA, and the whole point was to come up with jobs. For the next seven years Federal One put unemployed men and women to work producing plays and concerts and arts classes and guidebooks. The Theatre Project was the most notorious of the four; it mounted highly acclaimed, and often very political, productions; it trained a generation of theatrical talent; it infuriated many people; and it was the first of the four to be shut down. The Art and Music Projects did their work with comparatively little controversy, giving community art lessons and concerts, but since much of their work was ephemeral, today they are largely forgotten. It was the Federal Writers' Project that left an enduring legacy comparable to that of the construction projects. The books of the American Guide Series were its "product," the print parallel to LaGuardia Airport, and ultimately they will last longer. The books, like airports and roads, were not ends in themselves, however, but a means to people to work.

29. Sporn (1995): 41.

30. The classic work on New Deal documentary is William Stott's *Documentary Expression and the Thirties* ([1973] 1986). Stott describes how invisible the Depression was; e.g., men who lost their jobs often just dropped out of sight. Stores had fewer people. It's hard, he points out, to see things *not* happening. He sees the documentary impulse as lying in the desire to render visible, available to the senses, the hidden social pain. "By the time the Great Depression entered its third (and worst) winter, most Americans had grown skeptical of abstract promises. More than ever they became worshippers in the cult of experience and believed just what they saw, touched, handled, and—the crucial word—felt" (73). Communication then and now has to be documentary, "the presentation of actual facts in a way that makes them credible and telling to people at the time" (73).

The Critics

Somewhat obscured by the mists of time, the fact is that WPA was never popular with everybody.[31] Polls and letters to the president show the public to be strongly opposed to cash relief and ambivalent about work relief programs such as the WPA and its predecessors. "Public sentiment was often harsh toward the poor, and the public's sympathies were limited to those who could be put to work. Those who found work courtesy of the government were not to be accorded equal respect or rights" (the public believed they should not have the right to join unions or strike, and should be paid less than those in private employment).[32] The left attacked the WPA as inadequate and demeaning; the right attacked it as interfering with the labor market. Moreover, despite Hopkins's vow to keep politics out of the WPA, it was never far away and occasionally entailed outright corruption.[33] Opposition to the WPA expressed itself politically through Congress and popularly through the press. Drawing on interviews conducted in the early 1940s, William McDonald summed up the climate in Washington: "At no time can it be said that Congress, as a whole, truly and genuinely supported the principle of work relief. Congress merely permitted its use, because in 1935 it was afraid to do otherwise and, having started the WPA, was, after 1935, afraid to stop it."[34]

In spite of Hopkins's expectations, public ambivalence toward the WPA did not melt away in time (this is something that later generations have

31. Neither was the New Deal itself. As Newman and Jacobs (2010) have pointed out, political leaders like FDR are often out in front of public opinion on the question of government help for poor people. The most popular comic strip of 1937 was *Little Orphan Annie*, which was so anti-Roosevelt and anti-government intervention in the economy that one left-wing commentator, Richard Neuberger of the *New Republic*, called it "Hooverism in the funnies." Ben Schwartz, "Little Ideological Annie: How a Cartoon Gamine Midwifed the Graphic Novel—and the Modern Conservative Movement," *Book Forum*, September/October/November 2008, http://www.bookforum.com/inprint/015_03.

32. Newman and Jacobs (2010); quotation is from p. 52.

33. In 1939 journalist Tom Stokes won a Pulitzer for investigating corruption in Kentucky. Years later Florence Kerr remarked, "Tom Stokes won the Pulitzer Prize for exposing political activity from the Kentucky WPA. You know, it could just as well have been any one of the other fifty [*sic*] states. I mean, it was a pretty mild business, you know, but Stokes made a great thing of it" (Phillips [1963b]: 27). Kerr seems to be suggesting that "mild" low-level corruption was rampant.

34. McDonald (1969): 112; see 112–15 for a general discussion of opposition to the WPA. McDonald cites the agreed-on limits as indicators of the public's general distaste for work relief: It was not to compete with private enterprise, was to undertake projects that were not already being done by government via public works, and was not to pay workers as much as private enterprise would. "Thus bounded, work relief was 'made' work, not because it was necessarily useless, but because it was work that, if there were no depression, would not be undertaken either by a public or a private body" (14). (The Guides certainly qualify.) Repeatedly MacDonald contrasts the "advanced point of view of the social worker," which operated at the national level of the WPA, with the opposition to work relief, which was strong at the state level, exerted pressure through Congress, and was voiced by the press (110–113).

tended to forget). In June 1939, when the WPA had been up and running for four years, a nationwide Gallup survey asked Americans what they considered to be the New Deal's "greatest accomplishments" and "worst things done." "Relief and the WPA" came in as the greatest accomplishment, named by 28 percent of the respondents. It also led the field of worst things done (23 percent). Unsurprisingly, people with lower income, especially those actually on relief, were more approving than people with higher incomes. The *New York Times* summarized the poll's findings as follows: "The New Deal's experiment with Federal relief stands out as the most important and most controversial issue in the whole field of New Deal policy."[35]

And in this atmosphere of controversy, the Arts Projects were the WPA's weakest link. They helped people many Americans felt didn't deserve any help to begin with, people who were socially extraneous, producing luxuries that could and should be forgone in hard times. Throughout its seven-year history, Federal One faced bitter criticism. Some was philosophical. Conservatives argued that the federal government had no business meddling in the culture or supporting the arts. These critics opposed New Deal economic interventions in general, and they regarded Federal One as an extreme case of interfering with the market and wasting taxpayers' money. Leftists, on the other hand, argued that the government supports were both too stingy and too restrictive on artistic freedom. These critics advocated a generous and stable government stipend that allowed artists to follow their own (often radical) muses.

Sniping from the left, including strikes following cutbacks, continued throughout the life of the Arts Projects, and the anti–New Deal right could never be placated. The political middle of the road was more open to the Projects but had to be reminded, repeatedly, of their social usefulness. Federal One administrators were constantly beating back a set of specific criticisms from the press and in Congress, and although nowadays paeans to the WPA generally downplay the fact, the charges were not totally without merit. The criticism fell into three categories:

1. Boondoggling: Federal One put well-educated layabouts and drunks, who did nothing useful, on the public payroll.

35. "Relief Top Issue, Survey Indicates," *New York Times*, June 4, 1939. The WPA was not the only program that generated mixed feelings. Early in the Hundred Days, at FDR's instigation, Frances Perkins supported the popular Civilian Conservation Corps for young men. Although it was much more popular than the WPA, it was nevertheless initially criticized from both directions: An American Federation of Labor "leader told a congressional committee the plan smacked of 'Sovietism,' while a communist blasted it as 'forced labor'" (Downey [2010]: 151).

2. Big government: Federal One exerted too much federal control with too little sensitivity to state and local inputs.
3. Subversion: Federal One nurtured Communists and radicals who produced left-wing anti-American propaganda.

First, boondoggling: Though this accusation was not restricted to Federal One, the Arts Projects were especially vulnerable.[36] WPA road crews might lean on their shovels, but the roads themselves were obviously useful. Concerts, paintings, and historical research were another matter. Federal One administrators constantly had to defend their work by demonstrating that they were both turning out results and rooting out boondoggles. For example, James G. Dunton, an Ohio-born, Harvard-educated author of romantic fiction who directed the Ohio Writers' Project, had tried to keep his writers employed by producing copy that Washington would find acceptable, but on New Year's Day of 1937 he wrote to his district supervisors to advise them that cuts were coming. More pointedly he warned: "There will be no place for boondogglers, time-chiselers, soldiers-on-the-job, lazy research workers, unreliable reporters, careless clerical workers or any other inefficient producers of unsatisfactory copy." The fact that Dunton could reel off a list like this suggests how routine such accusations had become.[37]

Second, big government: Initially Baker wanted the Arts Projects to be, like every other WPA project, under the control of the state WPA administrations. All four Federal One national directors opposed this. They believed that only federal control would protect the arts in places that did not already have strong arts communities to fight for the jobs, places that included most of the country outside the big cities of the Northeast and the West Coast. The directors pressured Hopkins via Eleanor Roosevelt, a great champion of the Arts Projects (unlike her husband who was distinctly uninterested), to keep the Washington office in charge. They won the battle, and Washington kept control of the Arts Projects, but subsequent tension between Washington and the states was incessant. Disputes over the projects to be undertaken, over the specific content, over the format, over the political tone, and over the employment of workers on and off the relief rolls vexed the Project during its entire existence.

36. Criticism of intellectual and artistic programs preceded the WPA, as in note 17.

37. January 1, 1937, memorandum from James G. Dunton, state director, to his district supervisors conveying Washington's dissatisfaction with Ohio copy as being unreliable and uninteresting. National Archives and Records Administration (NARA), Record Group: 69, Stack area: 530, Row: 69, Compartment: 20, Entry 13. [Hereafter I will refer to this as NARA 69.] Box 40–41: Ohio.

These conflicts both shaped the State Guides and were symptomatic of more general local resistance to the expanded role the federal government was playing in peoples' lives, a resistance that the local press often took up with enthusiasm.

The third line of criticism, and ultimately the one that destroyed the Theatre Project and all but crippled the Writers' Project, was subversion: Politicians and the media claimed that radicals infested Federal One, eager to pump out anti-American propaganda, and this charge dogged the Arts Projects at every level. Such accusations were not completely unfounded; major writers' unions of the time were in fact Communist fronts and in large cities some writers believed they should be allowed to propagate their political views while on the government payroll. Although such radicals were a minority, they created a cloud of suspicion and encouraged skepticism and legislative meddling. In an all-too-typical case Oklahoma congressman R. P. Hill wrote to Harry Hopkins on January 8, 1937, demanding that State Director William Cunningham be fired because he is "a source of constant annoyance" and "mixed up in communistic activities."[38] Hopkins said he'd look into it, and nothing further ensued, but neither Hopkins nor the project directors ever succeeded in shaking off such criticism, which eventually found its voice in the House Committee Investigating Un-American Activities chaired by Texas congressman Martin Dies Jr.[39] In his classic study of Roosevelt and Hopkins, Robert E. Sherwood concluded that the Federal Arts Projects "were subjected to more derision and more charges of 'un-American activities' than almost any other part of the huge relief program. And, they were the first to be lopped off by Congress."[40]

The Great Depression, white-collar unemployment, suspicion of government art patronage, and a Congress increasingly fixated on rooting out subversion: This then was the context in which Federal One tried to carry out its charge of putting artists to work. Its goal was to come up with jobs for them, pure and simple. To achieve that goal, it had to survive. So the first problem, the sine qua non of the Federal Writers' Project, was to give the writers something to do that would keep them and the Project itself out of trouble.

38. Letter from Oklahoma congressman R. P. Hill to Harry Hopkins, January 8, 1937. All letters here and below from NARA 69.

39. NARA 69. Box 41: Oklahoma.

40. Sherwood (1948): 59. Robert E. Sherwood was a playwright who had been a speechwriter for FDR, and his insider study of the administration and the relationship between the president and Hopkins won both a Pulitzer Prize and a Bancroft Prize in 1949. He would later win an Academy Award for his 1946 screenplay, *The Best Years of Our Lives*.

TWO

Keeping Writers out of Trouble

The designers of Federal One intended to generate jobs, not culture. Nevertheless, although the sole purpose of the four Arts Projects was to come up with work for the creative and white-collar unemployed, the unavoidable result was to produce something: plays, concerts, murals, classes, performances, exhibits, recitals. And print: The Federal Writers' Project produced *books* (as well as pamphlets and the occasional magazine). And while the books were a by-product of the jobs-creation goal, they came to have an independent cultural life of their own.

Understanding these books and their cultural impact means, first, understanding what the people who ran the Project were thinking as they tried to get it off the ground. Who steered the Federal Writers' Project away from the rocks? Art is a collective endeavor, and the books produced by the Project had layers of authors, accomplices, and adversaries. These included the New Dealers as a whole, the WPA administration under Harry Hopkins, the Project's central administration in Washington, the writers' organizations that tried to pressure it, Congress, the press, the state directors and editors, local civic and business leaders, and individual employees in every state.

This chapter focuses on the top of the organizational pyramid—the New Dealers that set the agenda, the Washington Project officials that tried to implement it, and the writers' organizations that put pressure on everyone involved—because their intentions, the thinking and decisions made at the top, shaped the creative possibilities below. The art historian Michael Baxandall suggested that the analyst of "intentions" should break down the inquiry into a "charge" and a "brief."[1] A "charge" is the immediate call for action, the mission. The charge of the WPA was to put people to work. A "brief" is the set of constraints and influences, practical and material and intellectual, including all the factors that bear on decisions made and actions taken in order to fulfill the charge. Examining the charge and the briefs for the people who piloted the Project illuminates the extraordinary circumstances in which they operated and, ultimately, why the books they produced came out the way they did.

The New Dealers

When he began to campaign for the presidency following his 1930 reelection to New York's governorship, Franklin Delano Roosevelt sought advice from a circle of intellectuals who came to be known as the Brain Trust. Roosevelt had plenty of political advisors but lacked policy experts, so Samuel Rosenman, his legal counsel and speechwriter, suggested he put together a team of academics with whom he could consult. Raymond Moley, a law professor at Columbia University, would be in charge. Moley recruited Rex Tugwell, an agricultural economist, and Adolf Berle, a professor of corporate law, both from Columbia; others in the inner circle included banker James Warburg, agricultural economist George Peek, and former business executive and economic advisor Hugh S. Johnson. The Brain Trust focused on policy issues and remained aloof from the political strategists during the campaign. They wrote memos that Moley then turned into campaign speeches, including one that introduced the striking figure of "the forgotten man at the bottom of the economic pyramid."[2]

Roosevelt campaigned on a platform to help this forgotten man. He called for relief in the form of emergency public works, as well as for tariff reform and an end to Prohibition. At his nomination he said that the American people "want two things: work, with all the moral and spiritual values that go with it, and with work, a reasonable measure of security—

1. Baxandall (1985). See also Griswold (1987), which lays out the advantages of Baxandall's model for cultural sociological analysis.

2. Franklin D. Roosevelt: "Radio Address from Albany, New York: 'The "Forgotten Man" Speech,'" April 7, 1932, online by Gerhard Peters and John T. Woolley, *The American Presidency Project*, http://www.presidency.ucsb.edu/ws/?pid=88408.

security for themselves and for their wives and children. . . . I pledge you, I pledge myself, to a new deal for the American people."[3]

So the charge for the New Dealers as a whole was work and security. Putting Americans to work and offering them security required action on multiple fronts. Advised by his Brain Trust and his cabinet, Roosevelt launched a wide range of initiatives during his hyperactive Hundred Days. FDR's political genius was that he recognized and responded to the concerns of regular men and women, and nothing concerned them more than jobs. In his inaugural address he put it simply: "This nation asks for action, and action now. Our greatest primary task is to put people to work."[4] And as we have seen, over the next several years Roosevelt initiated a series of programs, culminating in the WPA, to do just that.

Who were the people on the president's team who would carry out the charge of putting people to work? Table 2.1, "New Dealers," gives the background of eighteen central players involved in the early New Deal, including the president, his Brain Trust, and the most prominent cabinet members and advisors during his first administration.

Two things stand out. First, the architects of the New Deal were all white and were almost all men, Frances Perkins being the sole exception. Diversity was not a priority back in the 1930s, and the leadership of the New Deal looked like the leadership of just about any firm, university, or public institution of the day.

The second striking and more unexpected characteristic: Almost all New Dealers came from, were educated in, or had careers in the Northeast. In fact, half had studied at or taught at Columbia University, and the rest came from Harvard or other elite schools. This point was not lost on contemporary observers. In 1934 the anti-Roosevelt *Chicago Tribune* published a political cartoon depicting New Dealers, including Tugwell, Ickes, and Wallace, shoveling government money onto the road and "depleting the resources of the soundest government in the world," to the

3. Two recent books have been particularly useful in understanding the early years of the New Deal. My discussion of the Hundred Days draws from Cohen (2009), and discussion of the origins of the WPA draws especially on N. Taylor (2008). The closing words of FDR's speech accepting the Democratic nomination were, "I pledge you, I pledge myself, to a new deal for the American people. Let us all here assembled constitute ourselves prophets of a new order of competence and of courage. This is more than a political campaign; it is a call to arms. Give me your help, not to win votes alone, but to win in this crusade to restore America to its own people." Franklin D. Roosevelt, "Address Accepting the Presidential Nomination at the Democratic National Convention in Chicago," July 2, 1932, online by Gerhard Peters and John T. Woolley, *The American Presidency Project*, http://www.presidency.ucsb.edu/ws/?pid=75174.

4. Franklin D. Roosevelt, "Inaugural Address," March 4, 1933, online by Gerhard Peters and John T. Woolley, *The American Presidency Project*, http://www.presidency.ucsb.edu/ws/?pid=14473. Much of the following discussion draws on Cohen (2008).

great satisfaction of Stalin and Trotsky who were observing. The money shovelers rode with cap-and-gown academics hoisting a bottle of "Power" and were labeled "Young Pinkies from Columbia and Harvard" (figure 2.1). Exaggerated fears of "Young Pinkies" notwithstanding, the fact remains that no one in the New Deal core represented the South Atlantic states from Delaware on down; no one came from the Deep South or the West Coast; and the few early New Dealers who came from outside the Northeast didn't last long.[5]

Thus the New Dealers, while often disagreeing over tactics, shared a worldview that had been shaped not just by politics but also by race, gender, education, and region. That view was that of white men with elite educations who lived in New York City or the Northeast. So their collective brief, the influences and constraints on early New Deal decision making, looked like this:

- Backgrounds in New York and the Northeast, and in elite universities
- Liberal, progressive outlook, favoring federal government action
- Urge to act quickly, do something, experiment
- Opposition from the right, i.e., from Republicans and conservative Democrats, especially from the South
- Opposition from the left, i.e., populists, radicals, unions
- Internal disagreements over wisdom of deficit spending
- FDR's preference for local government action when possible

If the charge of the New Deal as a whole was "work and security," the charge of the Works Progress Administration was simpler: jobs. As has been seen, Harry Hopkins's background included his midwestern progressivism and his social work career in New York City that culminated in his TERA directorship, and he enjoyed Roosevelt's confidence. All of these shaped his approach and were to his advantage. Nevertheless, the organization Hopkins was now set to run faced an extraordinarily challenging brief.

The president's State of the Union message had promised work that was "useful—not just for a day, or a year, but useful in the sense that it affords permanent improvement in living conditions or that it creates future

5. Arizona's Lewis Douglas disagreed with the direction the New Deal took (he championed balancing the budget and opposed deficit spending), left the administration in 1934, and became a fierce critic of FDR; Utah's George Dern opposed the president over Western issues such as water development and the proposed National Resources Board; and Illinoisan George Peek fought with various members of FDR's cabinet, resigned, and became a Republican who supported Alf Landon in the 1936 presidential election.

Table 2.1 New Dealers

Name	Position	Career	Born	Place	Gender	Ethnic	Education	Notes
Berle, Adolf	Brain Trust, informal advisor econ policy	Academics	1895	MA	1	1	Harvard	Columbia law professor
Cummings, Homer	Attorney general	Attorney, mayor Stamford, CT	1870	IL	1	1	Yale, Yale Law	
Dern, George	Secretary of war	Utah governor	1872	NE	1	1	University of Nebraska	Often at odds with FDR
Douglas, Lewis	Director of the budget	Mining, history teacher, congressman	1894	AZ	1	1	Amherst, MIT	Wanted balanced budget, opposed public works, relief spending; resigned 1934; became ND critic
Farley, James	Postmaster general	Politician, business (General Building Supply)	1888	NY	1	1	Packard Business School, New York	FDR's campaign manager 1932, 1936; chair NY State Dem. Comm. 1930–44; Dem. National Comm. 1932 on
Hopkins, Harry	Federal relief administrator (FERA, WPA)	NY social work	1890	IA	1	1	Grinnell College	Social work career in New York City
Hull, Cordell	Secretary of state	Lawyer, judge	1871	TN	1	1	Cumberland Law School	ANBO says FDR offered SS position "to reward the South" for Dem victory
Ickes, Harold	Secretary of interior	Journalist, reform politics in Chicago	1874	PA	1	1	University of Chicago	BA, law degree from UC
Johnson, Hugh S.	Brain Trust, later head of National Recovery Administration (NRA)	Military (brigadier general), business executive	1881	KS	1	1	West Point; UC Berkeley Law	

Moley, Raymond	Brain Trust; top aide to FDR; asst. sec. of state	Academics	1886	OH	1	1	PhD, Columbia	Columbia govt prof; conflict with Hull; close advisor to FDR; became ND critic by late 1930s
Peek, George	Brain Trust, head Agricultural Adjustment Adm. and Import-Export Bank	Economist and business executive	1873	IL	1	1	Northwestern	Fought with Wallace and Hull; resigned 1935; joined Republican Party; supported Landon in 1936
Perkins, Frances	Secretary of labor	NY industrial commissioner under FDR	1880	MA	2	1	Master's degree, Columbia	At odds with Douglas over spending for public works
Rosenman, Samuel Irving	Speechwriter and advisor to FDR	Lawyer, New York State assemblyman	1896	TX	1	1	Columbia Law School	Advocated FDR form a brain trust of academics and policy experts
Roosevelt, Franklin Delano	President	Law, Dept of Navy, politics, NY governor	1882	NY	1	1	Harvard, Columbia Law	
Tugwell, Rex	Brain Trust; asst. sec. of agriculture	Economist	1891	NY	1	1	Wharton	Columbia econ prof.
Wallace, Henry	Secretary of agriculture	Agricultural journalist, editor *Wallace's Farmer*	1888	IA	1	1	Iowa State College	
Warburg, James	Brain Trust, FDR's financial advisor	Banker and lawyer	1896	Germany	1	1	University of Chicago, Harvard Law	
Woodin, William	Secretary of the treasury	Corporate exec steel	1868	PA	1	1	Columbia School of Mines	

2.1 "Planned Economy or Planned Destruction: Young Pinkies from Columbia and Harvard" by Carey Orr. From *Chicago Tribune*, April 21. © 1934 Chicago Tribune. All rights reserved. Used by permission and protected by the Copyright Laws of the United States. The printing, copying, redistribution, or retransmission of this Content without express written permission is prohibited.

new wealth for the nation." The reaction was guarded but largely favorable. Business groups, wary of government activism, were relieved that WPA jobs would not compete with private industry since they paid less by design. On the other hand, some unions responded negatively to the same provision, so the very thing that relieved the business community antagonized organized labor. And soon enough came the cartoons depicting shovel leaners and the *New York Sun*'s "Today's Boon-Doggle."

Nevertheless, the WPA accomplished its charge: It gave jobs to people who were unemployed and on relief. Its organizational brief included those attributes of the New Deal in general along with some WPA-specific additions that might be summarized as:

- Continued high unemployment that previous programs like FERA and CWA had not alleviated
- Extraordinary expectations
- The need for an organization and staff in every state
- Local and state politics, patronage
- Unions wary of wages being undercut
- Business wary of labor-market interference
- Press searching for boondoggles, patronage, corruption
- Congress searching for radicalism, subversion, Communism, waste

Given such an extraordinary brief, success would require some extraordinary individuals.

Once Roosevelt had issued his (what Florence Kerr called "really sudden") executive order establishing the Works Progress Administration on May 6 and had appointed Harry Hopkins to head it, the first item on the agenda was to come up with something for WPA employees to do.[6] Hopkins and FDR seemed to have the vague idea that "jobs" meant manual labor, seeing the "dirt fly" as the president put it. A few types of jobs didn't involve flying dirt, however, and the WPA lumped these together as "women's and professional" jobs. Hopkins appointed FERA's Jacob Baker to head the Division of Women's and Professional Projects and Ellen S. Woodward to be director of women's work.[7]

Although Baker and Hopkins were sympathetic to the needs of writers and artists, coming up with jobs for such white-collar workers was a delicate business. Back in the winter of 1933–34 the CWA had employed about 1,000 writers, who promptly showed their appreciation by demanding long-term jobs and by complaining about their assigned tasks of working on public records and state research projects. New York City writers in particular had agitated for more federal aid, forming the Unemployed Writers Association in 1934, which, along with the Authors League, urged

6. Kerr later stressed how unprepared the public, as well as state and congressional officials, were for such a massive effort. "You know how sudden this program was, really sudden, and as far as educating people as to why we had a work relief program, that wasn't—well, I don't say that it wasn't done at all. It certainly never was done adequately" (Phillips 1963b: 58).

7. As an operating matter, the distinction between women's work and professional work was never clear, and there was friction between the two. Woodward controlled arts projects at state and local levels, while Baker was in charge of federal arts initiatives directed from Washington.

the CWA to come up with some work for writers that would demonstrate obvious social benefit to justify putting them on the federal payroll. Some prominent writers threw out ideas, with several, including Marianne Moore and Ridgely Torrence, suggesting some form of state histories or guidebooks. Baker set up a section for "Professional and Non-Manual Projects" under Arthur "Tex" Goldschmidt, which undertook a few writing projects but never enough to satisfy the league's demands.

The ideas of the federal government paying writers to do something, something both satisfying and useful, something big that would take months or even years, had thus been around for over a year by the spring of 1935. Hopkins, unfortunately, had no idea of what that something would be. At a cocktail party in the spring he told Florence Kerr, "The President told me last week that he wants to hurry this work program and get jobs for unemployed musicians and artists—people like that. God, if I've had trouble before, what do you think I'm going to have now. But it's the thing to do."[8] For the writers, what was needed was some all-purpose, noncontroversial project that would give them paychecks, employ them in "useful" way, and, critically important, keep them out of trouble.

Writers' Organizations

Keeping the writers out of trouble—collectively and individually—was no small order. Writers tended to be independent and antibureaucratic by nature, and making them conform to rules set in Washington was never going to be easy. The more direct challenge came from various writers' organizations that pressured the Project.[9]

The most established of such was the Authors League of America, particularly its Authors Guild. The Authors League was an organization of published authors, formed in 1912, to advance its members' professional interests. In 1921 the Authors League split into two branches: the Authors Guild for fiction and nonfiction writers, both book and magazine, and the Dramatists Guild for radio and stage writers. The league had set up an Authors League Fund in 1917 to assist writers in need, so the organization leadership had experience with the ups and downs of writers' financial lives and had developed firm views on how aid should be offered.

The Authors Guild was aggressive in protecting its established writers.

8. Phillips (1963b): 1. This account seems a bit unlikely, in that Roosevelt (unlike his wife) never expressed any particular concern about artists, so Hopkins may have been putting his own interest in helping the white-collar and creative unemployed into the president's mouth.

9. Appendix A, "Organizations and Acronyms," lists the major writers' organizations.

Most guild members lived in New York or other large cities. Accustomed to having volatile personal finances, they felt that going on relief would be humiliating and they tried strenuously to avoid it. As a consequence of this attitude, a recurring bone of contention between the Authors Guild and the WPA was the "means test," the rule that 90 percent of workers hired, including those of Federal One, had to come from the relief roles. Early in 1936 Henry Alsberg published a letter in the *Saturday Review of Literature* announcing that with the new Federal Writers' Project, the government was taking care of destitute writers for the first time. The president of the Authors League of America shot back that although "certain writers have been put to work, . . . others are starving," and the head of the Authors League Fund wrote to Hopkins directly:

> The means test, together with the stupid arrangement by which each state has been given a certain amount of money regardless of whether the state has writers or not, has defeated your purpose and our hope. As you know, writers are largely grouped in various centers. As a consequence, three quarters of the states are utterly unable to find writers to fill their quotas, while in a city like New York the quota is utterly inadequate to take care of the professional writers who are desperately in need of work.[10]

The league and its offshoots continued to press for more relaxed requirements while disdaining the Project's employment of nonprofessionals from the hinterlands whose claims of being actual "writers" were modest. The conflict was fundamental: The league's charge was to secure jobs for established professional writers, while the Project's charge was to come up with jobs in every state for people whose skills had some relationship, however tenuous, to the written word.

Other writers' organizations were more explicitly radical. During the twenties and thirties, many authors and editors, encouraged by the events in Russia that fascinated American intellectuals, promoted proletarian literature and other left-wing literary agendas.[11] Mike Gold, one of the few of these who actually held membership in the Communist Party, was especially influential when he founded the *New Masses* in 1926. After a brief period of political openness when it published nonradicals like D. H. Lawrence and Allen Tate, the *New Masses* concentrated on proletarian writing. In a July 1928 editorial Gold described the voices he was looking to publish as:

10. Quoted in Mangione (1972): 98.

11. See Denning (1997) for an overview of the cultural front; see especially chapter 5 for the rise, fall, and continued influence of the proletarian literature movement.

Confessions—diaries—documents—
Letters from hoboes, peddlers, small town atheists, unfrocked clergymen and schoolteachers—
Revelations by rebel chambermaids and nightclub waiters—
The sobs of driven stenographers—
The poetry of steelworkers—
The wrath of miners—the laughter of sailors—
Strike stories, prison stories, work stories—
Stories by Communist, I.W.W. and other revolutionary workers[12]

Gold's thrust was populist and he was especially interested in publishing promising but unprofessional writers, but the *New Masses* was always torn between the market's desire for established writers and the editorial focus on the inexperienced and unpublished.

These competing demands eventually led to a split. In November 1929 the journal's editorial board established the John Reed Club, organized first in New York City, as an offshoot that would focus on younger, would-be writers, while the *New Masses* would maintain itself by publishing the better known and more experienced. Attracting the struggling and politically disenchanted in the early years of the Depression, John Reed Clubs soon were operating in thirty cities. Writers gathered to debate Marxist and radical ideas, celebrate their solidarity, and discuss literature in general. Although the clubs were not Communist organs per se, they took their cues from the party.

This proved to be their undoing. In response to the growing fascist threat and to shifts of party line at the Kharkov conference, the American Communist Party's literary mission turned away from specifically proletarian writing toward a broader "people's front." When the second national convention of John Reed Clubs met in Chicago in September 1934, Central Committee representative Alexander Trachtenberg announced the shift. The John Reed Clubs were soon to be dissolved, and younger writers would have no special place in the reorganization. Richard Wright strenuously opposed the change of direction away from novices in favor of prominent radicals, but to no avail.[13] The *New Masses* called for an American Writers Congress to take place May 1, 1935 (it actually opened April 26), and there the League of American Writers formally replaced the John Reed Clubs. This move cast adrift many young writers with leftist sympathies who had high hopes but embryonic careers and no

12. The quotation from Gold's editorial is quoted by Homberger (1979): 229.

13. Much of what we know about the clubs' operations, and about the tensions between their political and literary agendas, comes from Richard Wright, who was active in the Chicago chapter.

jobs. Of course these were exactly the sorts of people the Federal Writers' Project wanted to help.[14]

More focused on employment and less on political theory was the Unemployed Writers Association, later to become the Writers Union, which was organized in 1934 to pressure Washington to establish "a national project that would give jobs to creative writers." New York City again was where the action was. In January 1934 about twenty-five writers got together to discuss their economic distress and formed the Unemployed Writers Association. Membership quickly swelled to 500, with over twice that many on the mailing list. The UWA petitioned Congress, demanding that it appropriate funds to pay each member a weekly stipend and establish a national plan for supporting all writers. "Demanding for each writer a minimum of $30 a week, the association asked that Congress appropriate the necessary funds a year in advance and establish a 'national plan for all writers.'" Since the on-its-way-out CWA had already hired some writers and the PWA was employing artists, this idea was not altogether novel, but the UWA was now demanding something permanent that would be specifically for writers. The federal government was unresponsive. In April the UWA members, strongly influenced by the Communist Party, voted to become the Writers Union. Its leadership included many Communists and the organization was largely a party front, though most of the rank and file were not formally affiliated. Over the next two years it organized picket lines in New York, held weekly meetings that would attract 200 or so unemployed writers, and held a Conference of Professional, Cultural, and White Collar Workers calling for federal relief programs.[15] The Writers' Union would continue to represent New York City writers in the Federal Writers' Project, holding sit-ins and strikes in 1936 and 1937, and was a constant thorn in the side of the Project there, though it also claimed credit for having influenced the Project's development.[16]

Tensions beset the various writers' organizations: between pure and

14. This summary is based on Homberger (1979). The shift from the John Reed Clubs to the league was part of a more general change of emphasis away from proletarian culture toward antifascism; for the origins of what was called the people's front, the Popular Front, and—by Denning—the cultural front, see Aaron (1961) and Denning (1997).

15. Denning (1997): 87. Denning says that the Writers' Union remained "weak" in light of its revolutionary aspirations, but Mangione (1972) describes at length the difficulties they caused for the New York City Project (see esp. chapter 5).

16. See Penkower (1977): 12–15 for the history of the Writers' Union; see footnote 19, p. 15 for the claiming of credit. See also N. Taylor (2008): 291–292. "A national project . . ." Mangione (1972): 34. Folsom (1994) says he had been on the executive board of the Unemployed Writers Association and had helped form the Writers Union. In August 1937 Folsom became executive secretary of the League of American Writers. One of the letters he received was "a plea asking the League to oppose efforts that were being made to terminate the Works Progress Administration (WPA) Writers Project" (6); he does not indicate the date of this letter, but it gives a sense of the Writers Union activities.

more inclusive political views (e.g., over whether bourgeois writers and fellow travelers could be included); between younger, unpublished writers and established professionals; between literary and political agendas; between party control and local, democratic control; between writers in the cities and writers in the sticks. The Federal Writers' Project inherited these tensions along with the unemployed writers everyone was trying to help. It also inherited the urban professional writers' reputation for radicalism and subversion, which drew constant scrutiny from Congress and the media. Henry Alsberg and his staff had to manage all this while they were getting the Writers' Project off the ground, running it, producing something useful, and keeping things from exploding.

Problem and Solution

Since the WPA had the overall charge of providing jobs, the Federal Writers' Project had to come up with work for writers. No one was terribly concerned about what that work would actually be, for at the most basic level, the Project just needed to keep the writers busy and out of trouble. As Florence Kerr recalled, "There were so few people who grasped [the Project's] potential, or who really knew what the philosophy was back of it. . . . They regarded it as an emergency. And it will soon be over. Therefore what you did didn't matter too much one way or the other."[17]

The Project needed to give unemployed writers something to do in every state in the union. Moreover, they needed to do it under a particular set of constraints, over and above the briefs for the New Deal and WPA, constraints that included:

- Continuous criticism of the Arts Projects as boondoggles[18]
- Agitation from writers' unions and organizations, often radical and sometimes Communist
- Congressional and media hunts for subversion
- The need to come up with work for writers in every state regardless of whether the state actually had professional writers

17. Phillips (1963b): 56. When she made this comment to Phillips, it is unclear if Kerr was referring to the Writers' Project or to the WPA as a whole; during the interview she repeatedly made the same point about both.

18. While skeptics charged the WPA as a whole with being a nest of boondoggles, Federal One was a favorite target. Critics continually questioned its usefulness; e.g., a *New York Times* September 1, 1936 editorial complaining that 25 percent of the state WPA budget was being spent on arts and white-collar projects—"Such boondoggling tends to bring the engineering projects into discredit with it" (N. Taylor [2008]: 248). Unlike the construction work, the Arts Projects had to be on the defensive all the time.

- The enormous urban/rural and coastal/heartland differences in numbers and skills of professional writers

Given this context, how could the Writers' Project come up with useful jobs?

The people making the decisions held a range of attitudes toward arts patronage and how free the artists should be. One possibility that the Washington administrators considered was to have Project employees work on government manuals and reports. This was quickly scotched, for everyone remembered the writers' bitter protests under the CWA, and as Mangione recalls, "even the more conservative members of the WPA administration conceded that such bureaucratic tasks would only add to the depression of the writers and the nation." Going to the opposite extreme, groups like the UWA argued that Project employees should simply work on their own novels, poetry, essays, or whatever. Baker rejected this as too risky, for given the radicalism of many urban writers, such a policy might well produce manuscripts "so subversive in content as to create undue embarrassment for the administration." Federal One needed something that would occupy the writers while keeping them—and the Project as a whole—out of hot water.[19]

The solution turned out to be an idea that had been kicking around for over a year. Back when the CWA was employing people, the Authors Guild had urged it to devise projects for writers that would clear "social usefulness," and while their definition might not have been identical with what Frances Perkins had in mind, the guild understood that it was public benefit, not literature, that might justify putting writers on the federal payroll. A few authors had suggested that a worthy project might take the form of state histories or guidebooks. Out in Michigan a FERA supervisor had proposed "a sort of public Baedeker, which would point out to the curious traveler the points to real travel value in each state and county."

19. "Even the more conservative" and "so subversive" both from Mangione (1972): 42. The fears about subversion were well grounded. In late April at the New York congress of the League of American Writers, the Popular Front replacement for the John Reed Clubs that was designed to attract all radical writers and not just party members, Earl Browder, the executive secretary of the Communist Party in the United States, told the audience that the party was seeking "a growing audience for revolutionary writing." While some experienced writers argued that there was a difference between revolutionary art and propaganda, the distinction was lost on most. As Mangione recalls, "Communist smitten writers from all strata of society became leftwing activists. Whether they were party members or fellow travelers, they worked zealously on large and small tasks—manning mimeograph machines, distributing leaflets or copies of the *Daily Worker*, participating in strikes and antifascist demonstrations, trying to organize farm workers in the south or white collar workers in the publishing firms of Manhattan. Except for the hard-boiled functionaries on the party payroll, . . . they were as idealistic and as eager for sacrifice as the early Christians" (43–44).

Most of these ideas went nowhere until Federal One came along, but Connecticut, which had recently gathered historical materials in celebration of its tercentenary, began working on a state guide.[20]

A year later in May 1935, when the WPA had been launched and Jacob Baker was casting about for white-collar projects, Katharine Kellock, a Washington insider working for the Resettlement Administration, began promoting the idea of having writers produce travel guides. For a century the Baedekers, produced by the German company of the same name, had set the standard for guidebooks. Having worked in Europe with a Quaker relief program following the First World War, Kellock knew firsthand how useful Baedekers were. She also knew that in the automobile age, the 1909 Baedeker for the United States was obsolete. At a cocktail party she cornered Baker's assistant Arthur Goldschmidt and urged, "The thing you have to do for writers is to put them to work writing Baedekers."[21]

That same month *The Connecticut Guide, What to See and Where to Find It,* initially developed through FERA and CWA funding, appeared. Though somewhat plodding and fixated on the past, *The Connecticut Guide* was surprisingly successful; it sold 10,000 copies in two months, returning all its costs, and it earned praise from the Yale English Department. The timing could not have been better for Kellock's advocacy of "Baedekers" (a "Baedeker" had become the generic term for a travel guide). Goldschmidt presented the concept to Baker, while Kellock herself pitched it to Henry Alsberg, who happened to be a Columbia classmate of her husband's as well as a member of Baker's inner circle.[22] Consensus built around the idea. "American Baedekers" would promote tourism, stimulate business, please congressmen and state officials, and employ white-collar workers in "useful" way while keeping them from being bored on the one hand or running amok with idiosyncratic or radical projects on the other. Kellock and WPA staffers Nina Collier and Clair Laning developed a proposal and budget, which became the blueprint for the Federal One proposal.[23]

In July 1935 Jacob Baker announced that he had appointed Alsberg to be the national director of the Federal Writers' Project. He also chose

20. "A sort of public Baedeker" from Henry S. Curtis, quoted in Mangione (1972): 46.

21. Quoted in Mangione (1972): 46.

22. Harold Kellock and Henry Alsberg were both Class of 1900 at Columbia. They remained friends all their lives. On February 19, 1954, Alsberg wrote to Katharine Kellock on the stationery of Hastings House, the publisher where he worked: "I was glad to get your letter telling me all about Kel, the work he was doing and his last illness. It is wonderful to die quickly; what everyone in Kel and my age bracket (he was only a few years older than I) fears most is a lingering illness." Katharine Kellock papers, Folder #1, Correspondence, Personal, 1924–67.

23. See Penkower (1977): 18–29. In respect to this policy making via casual conversations embedded in social ties, Penkower comments on "the ease with which the New Deal was done in those days" (22).

Hallie Flanagan to head the Federal Theatre Project; Holger Cahill, the Federal Arts Project; and Nikolai Sokoloff, the Federal Music Project. Baker officially launched Federal Project Number One, the WPA's first federally sponsored project, on August 2, with final executive approval and the a six-month allocation of over $6 million coming on September 12. "American Baedekers" it would be.

Now it was Alsberg's job to build the Project. Born in 1881 to a German-Jewish family, Henry Garfield Alsberg fit right in to the New Deal template in that he was white, male, East Coast, a man of the left, and had attended *both* Columbia and Harvard. He had worked as a journalist and playwright, he had traveled widely (including a period doing relief work for Russia Jews), and he was well known in New York literary circles. In mid-1934 Baker had recruited Alsberg to edit a CWA compilation called *America Fights the Depression.* Baker and Hopkins saw Alsberg as creative, though not very organized, and as left-wing but, thankfully, not too much so; Jerre Mangione later remarked that "New Deal agencies served as a convenient haven for tired radicals of the twenties like Alsberg."[24] In any event, Alsberg had stayed on with FERA, with Reed Harris as his assistant, and when Federal One came along, Baker saw him as the obvious person to direct the Writers' Project. As Baker recalled later, "He was an old acquaintance of mine here in New York. . . . He was there and he presented himself so sadly, [saying] that he wanted to run the WPA project. I knew damned well that he didn't have exactly the administrative ability, but by that time I had come to the conclusion there was one big thing to be done. . . . That was a guide book of the nation."[25]

The stars were aligned—*The Connecticut Guide* appeared in the same month as the WPA was being signed into law and as Baker's proposal for Federal One was taking shape—but the players saw different constellations. Kellock envisioned that the ultimate products would be travel guides for tourists. Alsberg had in mind that the guides would be collections of historical essays, with the tours as something of an afterthought. Hopkins and the WPA administrators just wanted jobs that would not create any political problems.

Baker had sketched out the format—the Writers' Project would compile a guidebook for the entire country, divided into five regional volumes, while also turning out things like WPA progress reports and an encyclopedia of government—and this structure was what the Federal One proposal actually contained. Once having been appointed as national direc-

24. Mangione (1972): 56.
25. Phillips (1963a): 15.

tor, however, Alsberg and his colleagues immediately began objecting to the five-region organization. George Cronyn, the Project's associate director, and Katharine Kellock both argued that the borders of many regions were unclear: Is Missouri, for example, in the South or the Midwest? More important to the viability of the Project, they pointed out that a regional structure would lack automatic political support—states, not regions, elect congressmen and senators—and it was apparent from the outset that the Project was going to need all the friends on Capitol Hill that it could get. With this in mind Cronyn proposed that the Project produce individual guides, one for every state, and by October his arguments had prevailed. So this would be the form: State-shaped boxes would contain Baedeker-type contents.

Contents, however, posed an equally critical question: Would the books be collections of essays with tours appended or collections of tours with introductory essays? The original idea had been a tourist's guidebook, an American Baedeker, and Katharine Kellock continued to champion this view. Intellectuals like Alsberg and Cronyn focused on essays, however. They wanted to "attract attention to the whole of American civilization and its development." In other words, they conceived of the books' primary audience as *readers and students*, while Kellock, with her focus on highways and routes, conceived of the audience as *motorists and tourists*. In the type of awkward compromise not uncommon in federal bureaucracies, the question of audience was never settled, and the final format of the American Guides included appeals to both reader and traveler.[26]

This quality of being slapped together to suit multiple agendas typified the Federal Writers' Project as a whole, but no one was particularly concerned. Some New Deal arts programs like Section Art aimed at producing artworks, but Federal One aimed at producing jobs. No one cared what the creative outcomes were, so long as they kept the political and media hounds at bay and kept the artists busy, "useful," and out of the spotlight. Alsberg and his staff recognized that they would need to define "writers" very loosely; as Mangione recalled, the Project was "made up largely of workers with little or no writing experience, most of whom had to qualify as paupers before they could be employed."[27] For the Writers' Project, travel guidebooks were a solution to political and practical problems, a way to give largely inexperienced writers something socially useful and not too demanding to work on, and not ends in themselves.

Federal One was no Ministry of the Arts, and to think of the Federal

26. The "attract attention" quotation is from Penkower (1977): 21.
27. Magione (1972): 8.

Writers' Project works and particularly the American Guides as somehow being the results of state planning would be entirely misleading. Lacking any overarching vision, the Guides were conceived from urgency, politics, and expediency. The books were compromises geared toward satisfying as many constituencies as possible without causing unnecessary trouble.

Nevertheless, the Federal Writers' Project introduced and sold its books, labeled the American Guide Series, first and foremost as travel guides. Guidebooks were a genre that had been around for millennia, and people understood their conventions and uses. Moreover, "seeing America" was a well-established practice, with emerging modifications for the automobile age. So the launching of new travel guides for motorists, American Baedekers on wheels, raised certain expectations. Guiding and educating Americans would turn out to entail more contradictions and generate more conflicts than the cocktail party enthusiasts had ever imagined.

PART TWO

Guides for Travelers

THREE

Guiding Travelers

When the Works Progress Administration was in its infancy, travel guides were a top priority for just about no one. Roosevelt cared about jobs, about putting millions of unemployed Americans to work, period. Harry Hopkins cared about jobs too, including jobs for white-collar workers, professionals, and artists—hell, they had to eat too—and his assistant Jake Baker was especially concerned about these people. Henry Alsberg cared about the life of the mind, history, literature, encyclopedic reference works that would stand the test of time. He also cared about the Federal Writers' Project's survival, which meant protecting it from its many critics. And the Project's employees just cared about getting a paycheck.

Katharine Kellock did care about travel guides, however, and even though her colleagues were initially lukewarm to the idea, they came on board. Given the treacherous political landscape and the WPA's federal-state structure under which the Federal Writers' Project would operate, Kellock persuaded everyone that her proposal for American Baedekers was the means by which the Project could give impoverished writers something useful to do while keeping them out of trouble. Travel guides were politically unobjectionable, they could be pitched as spurs to increase tourism, and they would be seen as serving the growing number of Americans who owned automobiles and took vacations.

So the employees of the Federal Writers' Project would work on preparing travel guides. Problem solved. The next question: What was a travel guide anyway?

The contradictions intrinsic to guidebooks as a genre, together with the contradictory impulses of the men and women of the Federal Writers' Project, were to have an impact on American culture that no one expected or intended. To understand the consequences of setting writers to work on travel guides, one must understand two things: what a guidebook was (a genre question) and what travel in the 1930s was (a history question). This chapter addresses the first of these questions and the next addresses the second.

Ancient and Early Modern Guidebooks

In his comprehensive history of the genre, Nicholas Parsons locates the impulse to write guidebooks[1] in "man's desire to understand the world in which he lives, to explore the unknown, to create an intellectual order for an incoherent mass of data, to document, classify, and pass on to others the fruits of observation and autopsy."[2] Just as human guides are experienced and knowing, written guides promise to make the naïve traveler similarly wise. Travel guidebooks have never been just about travel, however. They have also been about knowledge, status, and social membership.

Guidebooks have been around since antiquity, when Greek writers tried to reconcile the landscapes that Homer had described with what people actually observed. Similarly, Christian guidebooks of the Middle Ages attempted to fit biblical geography to that which the pilgrim would encounter. The tension between text and experience, between on the one hand, what the guidebook writer thinks readers *ought to see and do*, and how they *ought to respond*, and on the other hand, what travelers *will see and do*, and how they *will respond*, is an old one. Premodern guidebooks also included practical advice; a tenth-century guide for Muslim travelers to Syria warned about which towns had good water and which ones did not (the waters of Tyre were said to cause constipation). The didactic function came out forcefully in the moral guides of the seventeenth century that aimed to set human souls on the straight path as they journeyed through life's temptations, *The Pilgrim's Progress* being the best known example.[3]

1. Again the reader should note that I am using travel guides, guidebooks (sometimes written as guide books), and guides interchangeably. All draw on the idea of someone more experienced escorting a newcomer through an unknown territory, as in Virgil guiding Dante through the Inferno. A guide or guidebook refers a travel guide first and foremost; other types of guidebooks have modifiers, as in a "field guide" to birds. I capitalize Guide when referring to a volume in the American Guide Series.

2. Parsons (2007): 4. I am basing much of the following discussion on Parsons's well-informed and amusingly told history of the genre.

3. Hunter (1966) suggests that in the late seventeenth and early eighteenth century, many Englishmen believed they saw a breakdown in traditional values and a decaying moral climate. They turned to guide literature, which had been flourishing in the seventeenth century, for direction. Guide literature, often aimed at youth, warned of the evils people faced from their own depravity and the temptations

Until the nineteenth century, travel guides appealed to niche readerships, specific types of travelers with specific purposes. There were guides for pilgrims journeying to the Holy Land, to Santiago de Compostela, to Mecca, and to Rome. There were guides for statesmen and diplomats, and others for the young noblemen who would someday take on these roles. There were guides for connoisseurs. All contained some mix of practical and educational functions; they directed travelers toward what they should see and instructed them on how they should respond, that is, on what should be their travel's impact on their intellectual, aesthetic, political, and spiritual development. Premodern and early modern guides established the genre's conventions: lists of must-see sights, road tours (late eighteenth-century road-books followed the post roads), and shopping hints. In the Jubilee Year 1300, guides to Rome advised pilgrims on where they could buy particular types of indulgences.

Guides, human or written, had never conceived of travel as being for pleasure alone. For the Greeks, travel was intellectual and literary; in the Middle Ages pilgrims aimed at spiritual elevation; for the young men of the Reformation era, travel was to increase learning, especially the arts of politics and statesmanship as practiced on foreign soil. Guidebooks directed the travelers' perception, attention, and evaluation. They taught them what to see and what to think and feel about what they saw.

The British were the world's travelers par excellence in the early modern period, and by the end of the seventeenth century, two changes were taking place that changed the meaning and demography of traveling Britons. First was a change in thinking about the purpose of travel, a shift from the study of politics to the study of culture. John Evelyn was an early representative of and advocate for this shift. In 1660 Evelyn was a founding member of the Royal Society, which supported scientific studies and the New Learning associated with Francis Bacon, and he had traveled widely in his youth. While agreeing that travelers should not indulge in "the sensuality and satisfaction of a private *gusto*," Evelyn advocated that the traveler investigate the fine arts and sciences. Late in life he wrote to a travel companion of his youth

> I frequently call to mind the many bright and happy moments we have passed together at Rome and other places, in viewing and contemplating the entertainment

---

of the world, and instructed them about how to avoid the dangers by submitting to God. Hunter argues that the guide tradition influenced Daniel Defoe's *Robinson Crusoe*, which was structured on the Christian pattern of "disobedience-punishment-repentance-deliverance." The tenth-century Muslim guide that warned about drinking the water in Tyre was Al-Muqaddesi's *Description of Syria, including Palestine* (c. AD 985), discussed in Parsons (2007): 63.

> of travelers who go not abroad to count steeples, but to improve themselves. . . . Whenever I think of the agreeable toil we took among the ruins and antiquities, to admire the superb buildings, visit the cabinets and curiosities of the virtuosi . . . [4]

Travel was about agreeable toil and improvement through exposure to different cultures, not about counting steeples.

The second change was that increasing numbers of young Britons from the mercantile and gentlemen classes, not just the aristocracy, were visiting the Continent, particularly France and, above all, Italy, in pursuit of culture. The two changes went hand in hand: Not every young traveler was going to be managing affairs of state, but anyone could increase his refinement and improve his taste. What became known as the Grand Tour, which reached its apogee between the Peace of Paris in 1763 and the Napoleonic Wars, followed a fixed route of going to Paris, down through France, through the Alps, and on to Italy. The British esteemed Italy in particular as being the source of Western European culture, both Latin and Renaissance; as Samuel Johnson put it, "A Man who has not been in Italy, is always conscious of an inferiority, from his not having seen what it is expected a man should see."[5]

Under the watch of tutor-chaperones, countless young Englishmen toured the Continent to acquire the breadth of knowledge and the refinement of tastes appropriate to their status. The Grand Tour was not confined to the British—Goethe made one, as did some Americans—but British wealth enabled a greater proportion of young men to take up this rite of passage than elsewhere. (Women travelers, though not unknown, were rare.) Affluent young adults, old enough to leave their parental households but young enough to have not formed households of their own, have always been avid consumers of experiences,[6] and their elders anticipated that the young men who took Grand Tours were to become "cultured" in both senses: gaining a firsthand look at cultural masterpieces and gaining the wisdom that would prepare them for professional and social leadership. They relied on "road-books" to lead them along specific post roads, "itineraries" to give them practical advice and sociological information about where they were going, and guidebooks to suggest what they might see and learn while they were there. Of course these youth often had quite different ideas about what kind of experiences they hoped to pick up during their continental travels, and consequently their beleaguered tutors

4. Parks (1947): 261; from Bray, *Diary and Correspondence*, 716–17.
5. Withey (1997): 7.
6. Weinberger and Wallendorf (2008).

and governors—popularly known as "bear-leaders"—worked strenuously to keep their charges away from both Catholicism and brothels.[7]

It wasn't just the privileged young bears that were on the move. During the eighteenth century educated Englishmen began discovering and exploring the British Isles, especially Scotland, and these journeys—like the Italian excursions on the Grand Tour—mixed travel and art. When Samuel Johnson and James Boswell traveled to the Scottish highlands, they were constantly writing. Both subsequently published an account of their travels, and their presentations of their shared trip were quite different: Johnson focused on the people, their history and economic conditions, while Boswell wrote about the travel experience itself, including the physical discomforts, and—inevitably—about Johnson. Neither seemed especially interested in the landscape. Their contemporary William Gilpin was interested in the scenery, but he saw it through the lens of art, seeking and analyzing views that were naturally picturesque.[8] Prior social and aesthetic interests thus framed the travel experience, sometimes obliterating the landscape itself. All three men felt compelled to render their experiences into art: writing in the case of Johnson and Boswell, writing and sketches in the case of Gilpin, who indeed maintained that sketching picturesque landscapes and using them as the basis for imagined compositions was one of the primary purposes of travel.

The pleasures of the Grand Tour came to an abrupt end with the Napoleonic Wars (1803–1815). Although continental travel for the British and others resumed after Waterloo, it was never the same. Steamboats and railroads made travel more accessible and ultimately launched the tourism industry epitomized in midcentury by Thomas Cook's excursions and "grand circular tours."[9] Once it was relatively easy for the English to tour the Continent, the once-in-a-lifetime quality of travel changed, as did its social exclusiveness. Now traveling was easy, predictable, and open to everyone.

Modern Guides for Modern Travelers

For most of human history, travel—in the sense of making a tour, going out and returning home (as opposed to migrating)—was something only

7. For histories of the Grand Tour, see Hibbert (1987) and Trease (1967).

8. Johnson and Boswell ([1775] 1984); Gilpin (1794).

9. Thomas Cook's package tours began as excursions for temperance societies and Sunday schools in the 1840s. His first grand circular excursion to the Continent, in which he personally conducted a tour of Switzerland, was in 1864. See Trease (1967) and Withey (1997) for discussion of the revolution in bringing travel to the middle class.

a minority of people did or even contemplated, people like merchants, explorers, pilgrims, intellectuals, soldiers, and privileged young men. Most ordinary people stayed put, or else they migrated to a new place and stayed put there. The Industrial Revolution was a revolution in travel as well, for it opened the possibility of taking a trip or making a tour to people of moderate means, to women and families, to the merely curious or mildly adventurous. Railroads and steamships, together with the affluence that industrialization created, put leisure travel within reach of the rapidly expanding middle class, first in England and soon after in Western Europe and North America. The modern traveler was no longer a privileged youth or a doughty explorer but a tourist, usually one with limits on both time and budget, who wanted to see more of the world and who expected some guidance on what to see and how to see it efficiently and safely.

The guidebook industry responded to the aspirations of this new market with a burst of innovation. Travel was opening up to both genders and it happened that the first professional guidebook writer was a woman, Mariana Starke. Daughter of an officer in the East India Company, Starke grew up in Surrey determined to become a writer, and in fact she wrote some not-very-successful plays set in India, although she herself had never been there. A spinster, she lived in Italy from 1792 to 1798 caring for an invalid relative and she used her experience to write a guide for English visitors. *Letters from Italy*, published in 1800, was hugely popular, eventually going through nine editions. The subtitle announces Starke's innovation:

> *Letters from Italy, between the years 1792 and 1798, containing a view of the revolutions in that country, from the capture of Nice by the French Republic to the expulsion of Pius VI from the ecclesiastical state: Likewise pointing out The matchless Works of Art which still embellish Pisa, Florence, Siena, Rome, Naples, Bologna, Venice, &c. With Instructions For the Use of Invalids and Families Who may not choose to incur the Expence* [sic] *attendant upon travelling with a Courier.*

Starke recognized, in other words, that not all travelers were rich young men fresh out of the university. Some were families, some were on a budget, some were frail, and some needed guidance on what artistic and cultural works were not to be missed. British travel to the Continent, which had been depressed during the Napoleonic War years, boomed after 1815, and Starke's insights about the emerging market and its needs grew even clearer. Her guidebooks provided practical advice about passports, luggage, and where travelers could find good value for their money. She also devised a system to help the visitor figure out which paintings and sculptures to see: one to four exclamation points indicated an artwork's cultural importance.[10]

Starke was an entrepreneur, a one-woman operation that revealed the guidebooks' booming market to the publishing industry's major players. The London firm of John Murray published one of Starke's later editions, *Travels in Europe between the Years 1824 and 1828 Adapted to the Use of Travellers Comprising an Historical Account of Sicily with Particular Information for Strangers in That Island* (1828). In spite of the long-standing success of Starke's series, however, John Murray III, third in line in the publishing family, was not satisfied with it, nor with the other guidebooks he used when traveling to the Continent. He began collecting "all the facts, information, statistics, &c., which an English tourist would be likely to require or find useful."[11] He published his first *Handbook* (small enough to fit in a hand or pocket), which covered Holland, Belgium, and North Germany, in 1836. Others soon followed.

Murray's *Handbooks* institutionalized the paradigm shift, which Starke had launched, from books guiding the wellborn traveler on a Grand Tour to books guiding the middle-class tourist on a self-improvement mission while on a budget. He continued Starke's practice of grading sights, architecture, and art by exclamation points, later changed to stars; this would become one of the genre's conventions. He presented his materials by routes, taking readers from one city to the next and drawing their attention to the sights and worthwhile stops along the way. The *Handbooks*, which Parsons calls "avuncular companions," began with practical information followed by extended essays on such matters as government, constitution and administration, religion, industry, agriculture, architecture, and the arts. Then came the tours, which filled most of the pages. The *Handbooks* blanketed England; by the end of the nineteenth century there was one for every English county, as well as for Scotland, the Continent, the British Empire, and beyond.

Murray's avuncular approach was an innovation in what we might call a guidebook's personality. Formerly guidebooks served as an authoritative tutor, while the traveler was a student, naïve and needing direction. Nineteenth-century travel created the tourist, the traveler as a consumer, and this social change set up a new relationship between guide and guided. Now guidebooks somehow had to retain their authority (I the Guide know more than you do and you need to know what I do, so I will teach you)

10. Starke did not invent this forerunner to the star system—according to Withey (1997) it had first appeared in Thomas Martyn's *A Gentleman's Guide in His Tour through France* in 1787—but she was the first to bring it to a wide readership.

11. Wind (1975): 51.

while catering to the desires of the tourist-consumer (I the Tourist want to see the high points, I want to be entertained, I want to have travel made easy and comfortable, I want to enjoy myself, and I want to get my money's worth). This shift in power from author-as-authority to traveler-as-consumer, with guidebooks themselves being one of the commodities, was a permanent change that has lasted until the present.

Popular as the Murray *Handbooks* were with the British, it was the German firm of Karl Baedeker that dominated European and American markets during the nineteenth and early twentieth centuries, dominated to such a degree that "Baedeker" became a generic term for travel guide, as we saw when Katharine Kellock advocated that the Federal Writers' Project employees "write Baedekers." In 1827 Karl Baedeker opened a bookshop in Coblenz, a traditional tourism center at the junction of the Rhine and the Moselle Rivers. The next year he bought a small publisher that had gone bankrupt, and on its list and selling well was the *Guide to the Rhine* by Professor Johannes August Klein. Baedeker decided to issue a new edition, which he himself would revise by supplementing Klein's historical approach with practical information about hotels, restaurants, boat schedules, and small towns worth a visit. The revised edition came out in 1835. Baedeker brought out his first independent volume, *The Rhineland*, in 1839, followed by *Holland* and *Belgium* the following year.

An admirer of the Murray *Handbooks*, which he sold in his shop, Baedeker adopted their small size, their organization by routes, and their star system of must-see sights; after starting out with tan covers, he even imitated Murray's red covers with gold lettering (figure 3.1). For years Baedeker prefaces made a point of acknowledging that many innovations that people attributed to the Baedeker guides were actually Murray's. Nevertheless, travelers regarded Baedekers as the superior series. Like Murray, Karl Baedeker did his own legwork, never describing anything he had not seen himself. "Accurate practical information was something of an obsession with him, and in this controlling sense he remained the 'author' of the guides, while the 'experts' were mere contributors and checkers."[12] Baedeker emphasized walking as the only way to get to know a place, and he wanted to help his readers be independent in their explorations. With their detailed and reliable maps and their regular revisions, Baedekers set the gold standard for travel guides.

After Karl's death in 1859, his three sons ran the company. The younger son Fritz presided during the late nineteenth-century glory days when the Baedeker firm put out a constant stream of guides, all filled with superb

12. Parsons (2007): 205

3.1 *Baedeker's United States*

maps and ground plans, all on extra-thin paper with marbled edges. The company began publishing guides in English in 1861, and from then on most Baedekers came out in French and English as well as German. When they had a choice, American and even British travelers preferred Baedekers to the guidebooks from their own countries. Travelers thought of the series as having been written by, as Mark Twain put it, one "'Mr. Baedeker,' an old and kindly friend, who knew the problems they were likely to run into and was always ready with wise, practical advice." Indeed, "Karl Baedeker" was the signer of every preface, a company practice that reinforced the notion that there existed a single, practical, detail-obsessed personality eager to help travelers and prevent them from making any mistakes.[13]

No single Karl-Baedeker-as-kindly-friend existed after the founder's death, of course. Different Baedekers had different authors, and while they were all standardized and of high quality, some were better than others. One of the very best ("magnificent" according to Herbert Wind, an expert on the publisher) was *The United States*, first published in 1893 and written by James F. Muirhead, a Scot who traveled the United States extensively and spent two-and-a-half years working on the guide. Revised editions of *Baedeker's United States* came out every few years, with the fourth and final one appearing in 1909. This then was the model that Kellock and the others had in mind when they urged that the Project writers be set to producing "American Baedekers."[14]

American Guides

There had been guides to America long before Baedeker. The new republic inspired men (and a few women) from Lewis and Clark to Alexis de Tocqueville to report on what they found, and travel narratives proliferated over the course of the nineteenth century. Early accounts often focused on nature, famously with John Bartram's botanical writings in the mid-eighteenth century and John James Audubon's ornithological studies in the nineteenth. The 1820s saw the birth of less strenuous and less studious travel when fashionable New Yorkers began taking steamboats up the Hudson to Saratoga Springs and west, via the Erie Canal, to Niagara Falls, and guidebooks offered the pleasure seekers both practical

13. Wind (1975) comments that once the guides began appearing in English, "it wasn't long before the English-language Baedekers became far more popular with both English and American travelers than any of the guidebooks published in their own countries" (58). "'Mister Baedeker,' an old and kindly . . ." from p. 64.

14. The First World War almost ruined the publishing house. Fritz Baedeker and sons got the company going again after the war, but it faced a range of new European competition including Michelin's *Guides Bleus* (Hachette), the *Blue Guides*, edited by James Muirhead's younger brother Findlay (Ernest Benn Ltd.), and *Touring Club Italiano*. Baedekers made a comeback—indeed some experts think *Egypt* (1929) is the finest guidebook ever published—but the firm never dominated the market as it previously had. Parsons calls *Egypt* "among the best, if not the best, guidebook ever compiled, with its 676 pages, its superb maps and plans (an area in which Baedeker was still head and shoulders above all competitors), the distinguished scholarship of its historical and cultural essays and its readable style" (212).

information and social reassurance. A Saratoga printer named Gideon Minor Davison published the first such guide, *The Fashionable Tour: or, A Trip to the Springs, Niagara, Quebeck* [*sic*], *and Boston, in the Summer of 1821*. Despite the subtitle, Davison's pocket-size book was not a travel narrative but a geographically ordered series of facts following a route that people of leisure had been traveling for a decade or more.[15] Two more guidebooks followed in 1825: Theodore Dwight's *Northern Traveller* focused on social etiquette and the tourist's encounter with society while Henry Dilworth Gilpin's *The Northern Tour: Being a Guide to Saratoga, Lake George, Niagara, Canada, Boston, &c. &c.* celebrated landscape and the tourist's encounter with the sublime. When Davison put out a second edition that same year, the "Tour" of the title had become an "Excursion," in other words, a luxury good, and what had been personal reminiscence four years earlier had become commercialized, a guidebook to be consulted by actual travelers rather than read by armchair travelers.[16]

Presently railroads began to open up more of the nation to the casual traveler, and train schedules became essential guidebook material. A popular example from 1844 was *The Picturesque Tourist: Being a Guide throughout the Northern and Eastern States and Canada: Giving an Accurate Description of Cities and Villages, Celebrated Places of Resort, Etc., with Maps and Illustrations*, edited by O. L. Holley. Along with engravings of picturesque sights like Niagara Falls that the tourist would encounter, this handsome guide gave detailed information on railroads, steamboats, canal packets, and stagecoaches, as well as the names and addresses of hotels (figures 3.2 and 3.3).

While Holley's volume was a stand-alone like its American predecessors, the first series that aimed to be comprehensive was initiated only two years later. *Appleton's Hand-Book through the United States*, published in 1846, tried to replicate the successful Murray's and Baedeker's guides. Appleton's initial volume covered the eastern United States and Canada

15. The travel historian Richard Gassan (2005) speculates that the book's "cheap printing standards point to the likelihood that the audience to whom the book was directed was less the 'fashionable' visitor to Saratoga Springs than to the striver, a newly wealthy traveler unfamiliar with the 'fashionable' routes and sites" (55).

16. See McKinsey (1985): 133–35. She notes that Davison

> seems intent on "selling" the various excursions and amenities available, and it is not surprising that a number of the many guidebooks that soon appeared to compete with Davison's were written by proprietors of various bridges, museums, or taverns. Each sought to prescribe "a judicious routine of observation . . . without loss of time or unnecessary toil," as if to sell a package deal. What must have been a lively competition among the numerous books is indicated by repeated assertions to the effect that "this is the only original, correct, and reliable work in the market" and claims to having directed the reader to "the most eligible view" of the rapids or the "best view" of the entire scene. Tourists are told time and again to "feast their eyes" on certain features as if they were to consume them, and they are guided to the best souvenir stands for genuine Indian artifacts and other curiosities" (133–34).

3.2 *The Picturesque Tourist*

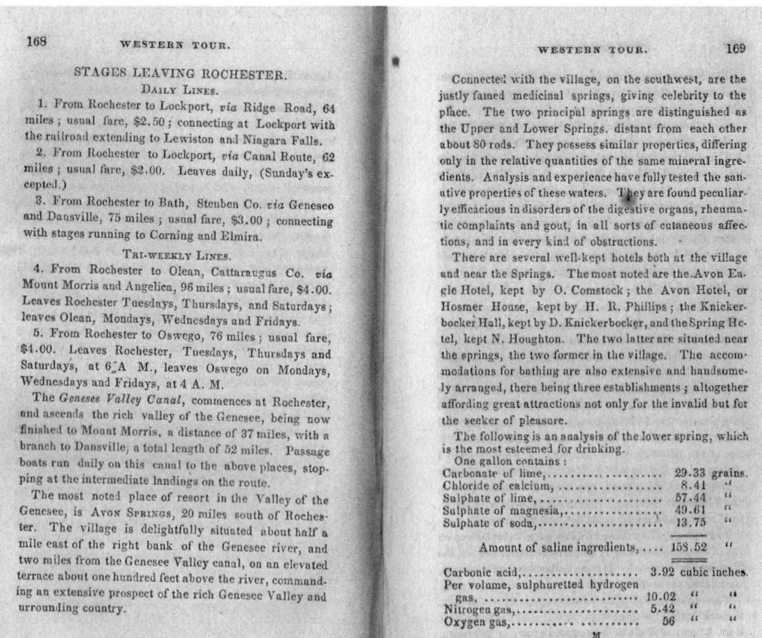

168 WESTERN TOUR.

STAGES LEAVING ROCHESTER.

DAILY LINES.

1. From Rochester to Lockport, *via* Ridge Road, 64 miles; usual fare, $2.50; connecting at Lockport with the railroad extending to Lewiston and Niagara Falls.

2. From Rochester to Lockport, *via* Canal Route, 62 miles; usual fare, $2.00. Leaves daily, (Sunday's excepted.)

3. From Rochester to Bath, Steuben Co. *via* Geneseo and Dansville, 75 miles; usual fare, $3.00; connecting with stages running to Corning and Elmira.

TRI-WEEKLY LINES.

4. From Rochester to Olean, Cattaraugus Co. *via* Mount Morris and Angelica, 96 miles; usual fare, $4.00. Leaves Rochester Tuesdays, Thursdays, and Saturdays; leaves Olean, Mondays, Wednesdays and Fridays.

5. From Rochester to Oswego, 76 miles; usual fare, $4.00. Leaves Rochester, Tuesdays, Thursdays and Saturdays, at 6 A M., leaves Oswego on Mondays, Wednesdays and Fridays, at 4 A. M.

The *Genesee Valley Canal*, commences at Rochester, and ascends the rich valley of the Genesee, being now finished to Mount Morris, a distance of 37 miles, with a branch to Dansville, a total length of 52 miles. Passage boats run daily on this canal to the above places, stopping at the intermediate landings on the route.

The most noted place of resort in the Valley of the Genesee, is AVON SPRINGS, 20 miles south of Rochester. The village is delightfully situated about half a mile east of the right bank of the Genesee river, and two miles from the Genesee Valley canal, on an elevated terrace about one hundred feet above the river, commanding an extensive prospect of the rich Genesee Valley and urrounding country.

WESTERN TOUR. 169

Connected with the village, on the southwest, are the justly famed medicinal springs, giving celebrity to the place. The two principal springs are distinguished as the Upper and Lower Springs, distant from each other about 80 rods. They possess similar properties, differing only in the relative quantities of the same mineral ingredients. Analysis and experience have fully tested the sanative properties of these waters. They are found peculiarly efficacious in disorders of the digestive organs, rheumatic complaints and gout, in all sorts of cutaneous affections, and in every kind of obstructions.

There are several well-kept hotels both at the village and near the Springs. The most noted are the Avon Eagle Hotel, kept by O. Comstock; the Avon Hotel, or Hosmer House, kept by H. R. Phillips; the Knickerbocker Hall, kept by D. Knickerbocker, and the Spring Hotel, kept N. Houghton. The two latter are situated near the springs, the two former in the village. The accommodations for bathing are also extensive and handsomely arranged, there being three establishments; altogether affording great attractions not only for the invalid but for the seeker of pleasure.

The following is an aaalysis of the lower spring, which is the most esteemed for drinking.

One gallon contains:

Carbonate of lime,	29.33	grains.
Chloride of calcium,	8.41	"
Sulphate of lime,	57.44	"
Sulphate of magnesia,	49.61	"
Sulphate of soda,	13.75	"
Amount of saline ingredients,	158.52	"
Carbonic acid,	3.92	cubic inches.
Per volume, sulphuretted hydrogen gas,	10.02	" "
Nitrogen gas,	5.42	" "
Oxygen gas,	56	" "

M

3.3 *The Picturesque Tourist* on stage coaches, springs, water quality

and featured practical information (travel, accommodation, currency), an overview of the United States, and a series of tours out of New York City, where the firm was located. The publisher usually organized guides by regions, as in the 1866 title *Appleton's Hand-Book of American Travel, the Southern Tour; Being a Guide through Maryland, District of Columbia, Virginia, North Carolina, Georgia, Florida, Alabama, Mississippi, Louisiana, Texas, Arkansas, Tennessee, and Kentucky*, which likely found its way into some carpetbags; a few were organized by cities. Appleton's series continued to appear throughout the nineteenth century.

In 1869 the transcontinental railroad opened the West to tourism, and that same year George Crofutt published the first guide for leisure travel by rail. *Crofutt's Great Trans-Continental Railroad Guide* gave train schedules, descriptions of and historical anecdotes about the towns that the railroad passed through (and advice as to which ones were worth exploring), maps, and engravings of some of the more dramatic views. Crofutt attended to travelers' pleasures, not just their needs. The 1879 edition, now called *Crofutt's New Overland Tourist and Pacific Coast Guide*, proclaimed itself "containing a condensed and authentic description of over one thousand two hundred cities, towns, villages, stations, government forts and camps, mountains, lakes, rivers, sulphur, soda and hot springs, scenery, watering places, and summer resorts." Crofutt was not alone in responding to the post–Civil War surge in leisure travel, so his 1879 preface tried to fend off rivals by claiming that

> from the first issue of our book, in 1869, imitators have been numerous; no less than *twenty-five* "guide-books," "Tourists' Hand-Books," and "Books of Travels Across the Continent," etc. etc., have been issued, most of which were compiled in the East—without their compilers traveling over one foot of the route or at least not spending more than a few days on the road—while we have spent the best part of every year since 1860 acquiring the information,—every item of which we are prepared to verify.[17]

We see here the influence of the Murray-Baedeker model: Authenticity and reliability came not from a publishing house but from an individual, an authority who could be trusted because he had traveled the routes himself.

Of course the real "American Baedeker" was, after all, the American Baedeker. Muirhead's 1893 *The United States, with Excursions to Mexico, Cuba, Porto Rico, and Alaska: Handbook for Travellers, by Karl Baedeker* (who had been dead for thirty-four years; nevertheless the cover simplified the title as *Baedeker's United States*) contained 494 pages, with seventeen maps and twenty-two city plans (figure 3.4), all preceded by a 99-page introduction that included essays by eminent authorities such as James Bryce, who wrote "Constitution and Political Institutions" (Bryce's masterpiece *The American Commonwealth* had just been published in 1888). Muirhead, who was Baedeker's editor in charge for all English-language books, continued to work on *The United States*, and when the fourth revised edition came out in 1909, it had grown to 724 pages with thirty-three maps and forty-one plans.[18]

Muirhead opened his preface by saying that "in response to repeated requests from British and American tourists, [the book] is intended to help the traveller in planning his tour and disposing of his time to the best advantage and thus to enable him the more thoroughly to enjoy and appreciate the objects of interest he meets with." Thus in once sentence he put together the old and the new, the discriminating traveler who appreci-

17. Crofutt (1879): Preface.

18. Herbert Wind (1975) refers to the 1909 publication as the second edition, although its title page says "Fourth Revised Edition." It may be that there had been printings with modest changes in the sixteen years following the initial publication.

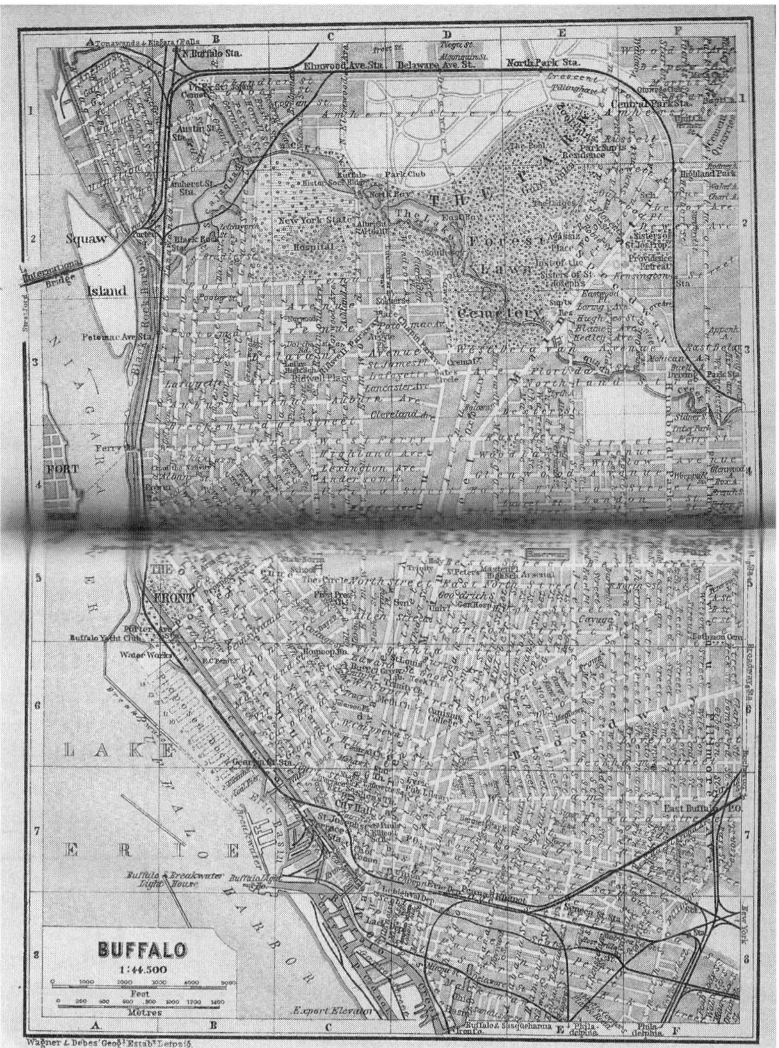

3.4 Plan of Buffalo, from *Baedeker's United States*

ates and the pleasure-seeking tourist who enjoys. Muirhead himself had "personally visited the greater part of the districts described," though he also thanked a professor who toured Yellowstone Park, the Grand Canyon, and California for the new edition; he thanked the railway companies as well. Thus the American Baedeker carried on the tradition of having an individual, authoritative voice.

Since it was Katharine Kellock's model (the Project should write American Baedekers) as well as her foil (the Project can do better), the 1909 edition of *Baedeker's United States* warrants a closer look. At 4 ½ x 6 ½ inches, the guidebook easily fits the hand. It is bright red, with *Baedeker's United States* embossed in gold on the spine and the front cover, and it has a gold ribbon attached to the inside top of the spine to serve as bookmark. The endpaper (pastedown and free sides) at the front lists the titles, contents, and publication dates of the twenty-nine other Baedeker's *Guide Books* currently available. A large, foldout colored map of most of the eastern United States to just beyond the Mississippi River (northern Maine and the southern parts of Georgia, Alabama, and Mississippi are missing, as is all of Florida) is set in before the cover page. Its counterpart at the back of the volume, set in just after the index, is a smaller scale map of the entire United States. Both are clear and detailed, showing railroad lines, towns, natural features, ocean depth, with the eastern United States including such details as lighthouses and Indian reservations. The map of the United States in the back shows the Baedeker mapmakers' cleverness by including a small insert of Switzerland to indicate scale, so a glance tells the European visitor, for example, that South Carolina is twice as big as that country.

The hundred-page introduction begins with practical advice on expenses, passports, the voyage from Europe, railways, hotels, restaurants, and the post office. A glossary informs the visitor that in America a cattle herdsman is called a "cowboy," and "chowder" is a kind of thick fish soup. A section on "General Hints" warns that while Americans are accommodating, the visitor should "reconcile himself to the absence of deference or servility on the part of those he considers his social inferiors" as well as the "dust, flies, and mosquitoes of summer, and (in many places) the habit of spitting on the floor."

Essays follow. In addition to Bryce on the Constitution, there is one on American politics, on Aborigines, on physiography (geological history), on "Climate and Climatic Resorts," on the fine arts, on sports, and on "Educational, Charitable, Penal, and Industrial Institutions." While all this might seem to be "going beyond the recognized functions of a guidebook . . . their general aim is to enable the traveller who studies them to give and intelligent appreciation to the political, social, industrial, and physical aspects of a great country that is much less accurately known by the average European than its importance warrants." Muirhead explains the star system (asterisks are "marks of commendation"), discusses how American hotels differ from European ones ("the comfort of an American hotel is, however, much more likely to be in the direct ratio of its charges than is the case in Europe"), and helpfully points out how each of the nine sections can be removed from the book as a whole.

What follows for the next 700 pages are descriptions of routes or individual cities, 120 in total. The comparatively short section on southern states, for example, contains the route from Washington to New Orleans, from Cincinnati to New Orleans, and from Chicago and St. Louis to New Orleans, each of these covering the railway lines and fares, the towns and sites along the way; later comes a section devoted to New Orleans itself, its station, its hotels, restaurants, tramways, places of amusement, geography and history, accompanied by a foldout street-by-street plan of the city. The guide contains thirty-three maps, forty-one city plans, and seven ground plans of museums and universities, and it ends with a detailed index. All in all, it's hard to imagine a more comprehensive or practical guidebook in such a compact format.

In spite of its many virtues—the combination of the instructional and the practical, the exquisite attention to detail, the extraordinary maps—*Baedeker's United States* had two deficiencies that, thirty years later, the Federal Writers' Project's "American Baedekers" would attempt to remedy. Neither seemed to be much of a problem in 1909, but one of them in particular would be very shortly.

First, the guide emphasized the Northeast and far West, while it virtually ignored the South and middle of the country. Over half the pages were devoted to New England, New York, Pennsylvania, and Washington, while the South and Midwest got only 13 percent each, and the interior was mentioned only in terms of the trains that passed through it. Philadelphia gets eighteen detailed pages and a city plan, while Atlanta gets half a page, the state of Mississippi gets less than a page, and New Mexico, not yet a state, doesn't even make it into the index (Texas had been a state since 1845 but it was given short shrift as well). While it no doubt was true that European travelers were more interested in New York, Boston, San Francisco, and Philadelphia than in the South or the Great Plains, nevertheless, the emphasis on the coasts and the neglect of the interior gave a highly skewed picture of the nation.

Second, *Baedeker's United States*, like all of the series, assumed that the traveler would be traveling by train. The emphasis on cities, the downplaying of states with few rail lines or stations, and the layout of the tours themselves, which followed rail lines rather than roads and ignored state boundaries, derive from that assumption. This model had served Karl Baedeker and his readers for seventy years, but by 1909 the travel-by-train assumption was about to become obsolete. In the future the typical leisure traveler would go by automobile.

This was what Kellock and her by-now-convinced colleagues envisioned: The Federal Writers' Project would produce guidebooks that were as comprehensive as the Baedekers *and* that suited American motorists of the automobile age. But was this a good idea? Were there any such travelers during the Great Depression? Were people driving around for pleasure trips? Was anyone taking vacations? The next chapter explores these questions.

FOUR

Seeing America

New Dealers would never have set writers to work on travel guides if travel itself had been out of reach for most Americans. Although jobs, any jobs, were the order of the day, the disconnect between helping the unemployed "without jobs or nest eggs, marching they don't know where" and helping the wealthy get the most out of their pleasure trips would have been politically impossible. The New Dealers were not fools, and they never would have embraced Kellock's proposal if they didn't believe that American Baedekers would be appealing to the average American family and voter.

From the vantage point of the twenty-first century, however, it is hard to bring Depression-era travel into focus. The vision of being on the road in the 1930s connotes either desperate families fleeing the Dust Bowl or heiresses in screwball comedies fleeing their assigned social roles. Both images were popular cultural tropes at the time, and both are misleading. Such tragic or comic depictions—*The Grapes of Wrath* versus *It Happened One Night*—dramatized the travel of people at the extreme top or bottom of the social spectrum, but they did not come anywhere near representing the routine quality of Americans pursuing entertainment and a change of pace as they drove the nation's highways.

This everyday reality was itself quite new. When the automobile came along, Americans had been enjoying leisure travel, by steamboat and rail, for less than a hundred years. Although the nation had always been unusually mobile thanks to colonization, immigration, ambition, and the pursuit of better land, travel for sheer pleasure, with no economic motivation, did not develop until the nineteenth century, well after the English had institutionalized the Grand Tour. Such travel required not just inventions and infrastructure but also a change in ideas about what travel for recreation meant. Automobile travel for the masses resulted from both a revolution in technology and a revolution in thinking.

Travel for Improvement and Enjoyment

For a long time Americans were suspicious of traveling just for the fun of it. Puritans distinguished between recreation (restorative, uplifting, enabling people to return to work with fresh zeal) and amusement (draining, exhausting, degenerate), and that distinction persisted. Leisure travel was for recreation, and thus it had to have a clear purpose. By the early nineteenth century, that purpose was usually the health of the body or the soul. Wealthy people traveled to spas or the seaside, both regarded as salubrious, while less wealthy ones traveled to religious camp meetings. No one regarded such travel as vacation—though no doubt people found the break in routine enjoyable—because it was not for amusement but for personal development. In that respect American travelers resembled their Grand Tour predecessors, and perhaps they shared a similar dash of hypocrisy.[1]

Tourism, whereby people who were not wealthy took trips for sheer pleasure and to see the sights, was coming to America nevertheless. Seeking out nature instead of culture first developed in England during the late eighteenth century, stimulated by landscape gardening and painting and by popular theories of the sublime and picturesque. The English began something entirely unprecedented: travel in search of scenery. Seeking edifying landscapes arrived somewhat later in America. While there had been some health resorts like Saratoga Springs—leisure travel being acceptable if in pursuit of health—it was not until the 1820s and '30s that natural wonders like Niagara Falls, the Hudson River valley, and the White Mountains drew visitors who simply wanted to see them firsthand.

Such travel could have never become popular without advances in transportation. Going about by horseback or on foot was fine for explorers, naturalists, and Methodist missionaries, but it was a more strenuous undertaking than most tourists were prepared for. It was the development

1. For much of this discussion I have relied on Cindy Aron's (1999) comprehensive history of American leisure travel. For a general history of the concept of being "on holiday," see Löfgren (1999). Löfgren notes a polarity between people who want to see the sights "setting mind and body in motion, producing memories" and those who want to get away from it all in "elsewhereland."

of canals, steamboats, and then railroads that opened leisure travel to the public at large. Even then, travel still required some degree of affluence and risk taking (it usually still does). It also seemed to call for some responsiveness to the "body of images and descriptions—a mythology of unusual things to see—to excite people's imaginations and induce them to travel."[2] Sublime places like the Catskills, Mammoth Cave, and Yosemite acted as holy shrines, and although America lacked places of religious pilgrimage, these sites worked the same way, inspiring awe just like the sacred mountains and grottos of more traditional societies. Set apart from reality, such places—Niagara Falls being the prime example—suggested transcendent meanings for the nation as a whole, not just for some particular religious sect. At the same time, just like those Roman sellers of indulgences mentioned in the previous chapter, entrepreneurs were quick to commercialize these spots. Thus tourists experienced the familiar emotional dissonance of sacred and profane, feeling both awe at the natural wonders and contempt for the people who profited from them or defiled them simply by being there (including, of course, their fellow tourists).[3]

Nature inspired tourists with awe, and so did historically significant places. In the latter part of the nineteenth century, history began to compete with, if not replace, nature. Civil War battlefields and monuments drew visitors in increasing numbers, and in some cases, notably Gettysburg, they barely waited for the fighting to end. Civilians crowded onto the battle sites almost immediately when the guns stopped; these included relatives seeking the dead, enterprising coffin makers, scavengers, and "swarms of tourists attracted by the hope of experiencing 'the sublimity of a battle scene' or simply, as one disgusted soldier put it, 'gratifying their morbid curiosity.'"[4] As time passed such tourism became aligned with what the historian Michael Kammen has called the "Party of Memory," the desire to keep the past and its sacrifices alive in the national consciousness.[5]

Although they visited resorts, battlegrounds, and natural wonders, most middle-class travelers did not include cities on their itineraries until late in the nineteenth century. American cities did not enjoy the historical

2. Sears (1989): 3.

3. As Americans' sacred places, such tourist sites "unify us, and provide us with a common experience which appears at once mythical and trivial and thus provokes us to both awe and irreverence" (Sears [1989]: 216). Despite the human defilement, Sears emphasizes the genuine awe travelers felt when confronted with such myth-embellished spots of national veneration. The Willey disaster in the White Mountains, and the pilgrimages to see the awful scene, offer a clear example; see Purchase (1999).

4. Faust (2008): 85.

5. Kammen (1991).

and cultural appeal of their European counterparts, so they did not fit the Victorian self-improvement-through-travel schema. By the end of the century this had begun to change. Transportation companies, fairs, and expositions (always set in cities), urban hotels that featured secure and refined spaces especially for women, a business community that supported the City Beautiful movement, and emerging tour companies all worked to make cities appealing to the nation's tourists. City guidebooks, photo view books, and urban sketches in magazines suggested that every city had a distinct personality and was worth getting to know. Such appealing personification encouraged travelers to take a more forgiving attitude toward any urban disorder they might encounter.[6]

As travel options multiplied, the idea of "taking a vacation" emerged as a form of therapeutic recreation for middle-class working people, not just for those who already possessed plenty of leisure. In her history of the concept, Cindy Aron identifies four types of popular vacations in the second half of the nineteenth century: stays at resort hotels; trips for self-improvement (Ocean Grove–type Christian summer communities, Chautauqua and many "chautauquas" outside of western New York); trips to Civil War battlefields and historical monuments, to natural wonders like Yosemite, to cities; and camping. Increasingly the middle class began to enjoy these forms of leisure travel. In the twentieth century vacationing expanded as a social practice, going from being something done largely by the white middle-class-and-up to being a mass phenomenon, something done by the working class, immigrants, African Americans, Jews, everyone.[7]

Some of the impetus for this came from social reformers who wanted to get vulnerable people out of the pestilent and crime-ridden cities and into the great outdoors. Progressive-era groups started to offer fresh-air programs for children and working-class women, modeled on the Fresh Air Fund for New York City children that had begun in 1877. However, it was not charity but business that institutionalized vacations for everybody. A few firms had begun offering two-week paid vacations for workers, and by the 1920s, reformers, social scientists, and journalists were promoting vacations as being good for productivity by reducing worker fatigue. Employers began offering various types of vacation plans. The First World War had spurred their interest, for with conscription and the cutoff in im-

6. As Cocks (2001) sums it up, "The brilliant, exciting, and thoroughly safe city that the guidebooks depicted and that growing numbers of tourists visited was the landscape of an emerging consumer culture" (207).

7. Many Jewish "Borscht Belt" resorts in the Catskills, for example, had their origins in farms owned by immigrant Jews in the early twentieth century. Resorts specifically established for African Americans, like Idlewild in Michigan and Lincoln Hills in Colorado, developed after the First World War, while Oak Bluffs on Martha's Vineyard goes back to the late nineteenth century.

migration, labor became a seller's market, so firms were trying new things to attract and retain workers. Paid vacations to workers were still the exception, however, and labor unions had little interest, pushing for shorter hours rather than for vacations. Nevertheless, by 1927, one quarter of the Teamsters Union had paid vacations, and in 1930 the Ford plant in Detroit gave a vacation with pay to its 100,000 workers for the last two weeks of July. With this the American vacation had arrived.[8]

The Automobile

If it had not have been for the automobile, the vacation movement might never have taken off. Baedeker and Murray signaled and fostered the nineteenth-century travel revolution, whereby ordinary people could travel easily via trains and steamers, but these people still needed plenty of time and they still were bound by schedules set by the railroad and steamship lines. The twentieth century brought the second revolution, whereby automobiles gave travelers new freedom, which required a new type of guidance. "Automobility" ended spatial dependence on train tracks and rivers and temporal dependence on timetables.[9] It also altered the form and proportions of the travel experience: Whereas leisure travel had been focused on cities and locations of specific historical or aesthetic significance, now *the road itself*—along with all the places previously glimpsed only out of a train window—swam into view.

At first only people of means could experience this new freedom. Edith Wharton's oddly apt title *A Motor-Flight through France* (1908) captures the sense of no limits that the affluent enjoyed in the early years of the century. Wharton and her companions, who sometimes included Henry James, toured France in a Panhard-Levassor that she bought in 1904. Her rhapsodic beginning was typical of the time:

> The motor-car has restored the romance of travel. Freeing us from all the compulsions and contacts of the railway, the bondage to fixed hours and the beaten track, the approach to each town through the area of ugliness and desolation created by the railway itself, it has given us back the wonder, the adventure and the novelty which enlivened the way of our posting grandparents. Above all these recovered pleasures must be ranked the delight of taking a town unawares, stealing on it by back ways and

8. This historical summary is based on Aron (1999).

9. The useful term "automobility," along with its verb, usually in the participle form "automobiling," had grown obsolete by the middle of the twentieth century, but recently travel historians have resurrected it; see, for example, Jakle and Sculle (2009) and Seiler (2008).

unchronicled paths, and surprising in it some intimate aspect of past time, some silhouette hidden for half a century or more by the ugly mask of railway embankments and the iron bulk of a huge station. Then the villages that we missed and yearned for from the windows of the train—the unseen villages have been given back to us![10]

Private clubs like the New York Automobile Club of America catered to people like Wharton, with membership a sign of social distinction. In 1900 a group of wealthy Rhode Island men founded the Rhode Island Automobile Club in Newport. Its bylaws described its purpose as "generally to maintain a social club devoted to the sport of automobilism throughout the country." Some fifty such clubs sprang up, and soon the members began to recognize that their associations could exert pressure for changes that would improve driving conditions. Thus in May 1902, nine regional clubs met in Chicago to form a federation, the American Automobile Association, to lobby for better roads.[11]

Early motorists conceived of the automobile as a means of returning to a past "hidden for a half century or more by the ugly mask of railway embankments." Trains seemed emblematic of industrial modernity, while the automobile gave access to a simpler time and way of life. In America the rediscovery of "some intimate aspect of past time" was as compelling as it was in Europe. Turn-of-the-century automobilists assumed the role of doughty explorers. They wrote a flurry of books describing their adventures and hardships on cross-country tours, with jaunty titles like *Transcontinental Trip in a Ford* (1915), *Family Flivvers to Frisco* (1927) *How's the Road?* (1928), *Modern Gypsies: The Story of a Twelve Thousand Mile Motor Camping Trip Encircling the United States* (1922), and *It Might Have Been Worse: A Motor Trip from Coast to Coast* (1919).[12] By the century's second decade, bohemian members of the middle class were taking to the highways under the romantic label of "gypsying," camping by the roadside and celebrating their freedom from train schedules or idle resort life.

The future lay not with the motor flights or gypsies, however, but with those whom Henry Ford called the "great multitude." When the Ford Motor Company brought out the Model T in 1908—pared down, affordable,

10. Wharton (1908): 1–2.

11. The original member clubs and their founding dates were: Chicago Automobile Club, 1900; Automobile Club of America, 1899; Automobile Club of New Jersey, 1900; Long Island Automobile Club, 1900; Rhode Island Automobile Club, 1900; Philadelphia Automobile Club, 1900; Automobile Club of Utica, 1901; Grand Rapids Automobile Club, 1902; and Princeton University Automobile Club, 1901. AAA Southern New England—History, http://secure.aaasne.com/public/news/aaahistory/history.html, retrieved January 24, 2010.

12. The titles are from *Autos across America*, a bibliography of early auto travel books put together by Bliss (1972).

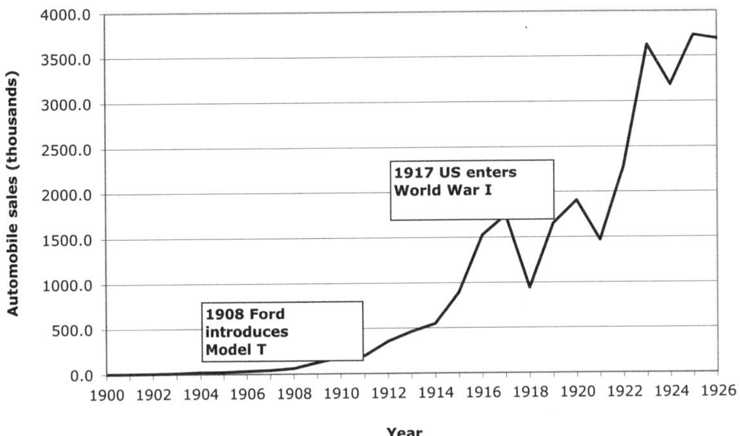

4.1 Automobile factory sales 1900–1926. *Source:* US Census Bureau, 1975, *Historical Statistics of the United States: Colonial Times to 1970,* bicentennial edition, part 2, series Q, 148–62, "Motor-Vehicle Factory Sales and Registrations, and Motor-Fuel Usage: 1900 to 1970," 716. These figures refer to new cars only; trucks and buses were counted separately, and used car sales are not included.

reliable—it changed the meaning of the automobile. The Model T flew in the face of the "pleasure car" concept whereby motoring was a luxury. Against the advice of his sales staff, Ford announced in 1908 that henceforth the company would manufacture only one model:

> I will build a motor car for the great multitude. It will be large enough for the family but small enough for the individual to run and care for. It will be constructed of the best materials, by the best men to be hired, after the simplest designs that modern engineering can devise. But it will be so low in price that no man making a good salary will be unable to own one—and to enjoy with his family the blessing of hours of pleasure in God's great open spaces.[13]

Ford realized his vision of mass automobiling by paying high wages to attract skilled workers and avoid turnover, by introducing assembly line production to lower costs, and by publicizing the Model T relentlessly. The result was that the cost of the Model T dropped every year, sales soared, and the middle class came to own the automobile in every sense.[14] Figure 4.1 shows the impact of the Model T on car purchases.

By the 1920s, the combination of cheaper cars, highway improvements,

13. Ford (1922): 73.

14. The Model T sold for $825 in its first year. By 1916 the price had dropped to $325. *Wikipedia,* http://en.wikipedia.org/wiki/Henry_Ford#cite_note-11, retrieved March 14, 2010.

and general postwar affluence had transformed auto travel from being a lark for wealthy pleasure seekers and less wealthy free spirits into being a work and leisure vehicle for middle-class families. The industry's marketing efforts changed the automobile's image from expensive toy to everyday necessity, for instance, by eliminating the term "pleasure car" from the corporate vocabulary.[15] Automobile associations both followed and facilitated the automobile's descent from the rich to the general public. The AAA federation and the regional associations produced guides, maps, and other aids for the growing ranks of motorists. New laws emerged, as cities and towns shifted from catering to pedestrians and merchants to catering to drivers. Institutionalization produced an entire industry of gas stations, auto camps, mapmakers, travel planners, automobile associations, souvenir manufacturers, hotels catering to motorists—and, of course, new types of guidebooks.[16]

Travel in the 1930s

Counterintuitive as it seems, during the Great Depression more and more Americans took to the roads on more and more vacations. Automobile travel had been increasing for years, and an elaborate infrastructure, consisting of better roads, auto camps, standardized highway signage, gas station maps, and guidebooks catering to motorists, was in place. For over a decade, motor flights for the rich and gypsy jaunts for the bohemian had given way to road trips for the general public.

Popular culture registered the change, as "automobiling" became commonplace. Gus Edwards and Vincent Bryan wrote the song "In My Merry Oldsmobile" in 1905, and Bill Murray recorded it for Columbia Records the following year. Other artists recorded it over the decades, including a 1927 double-sided version, with the song in a waltz on one side and a foxtrot on the other featuring jazz cornetist Bix Beiderbecke; General Motors sponsored this recording and gave it away at the 1927 Detroit Auto Show. By 1932 "Come away with me, Lucille, in my merry Oldsmobile" was so familiar that the Max Fleischer studios turned it into a slightly risqué cartoon that featured the same Bill Murray leading a sing-along of the song, twenty-six years after originally recording it.[17]

15. Norton (2008): 12

16. For changes in the hotel industry, see Jakle and Sculle (2009) and Sandoval-Strausz (2007). For how the auto changed cities, see Norton (2008).

17. See the Virtual Victrola, http://www.virtualvictrola.com/2009/04/in-my-merry-oldsmobile.html; for the video see http://www.youtube.com/watch?v=YwmGw_ZVMhU.

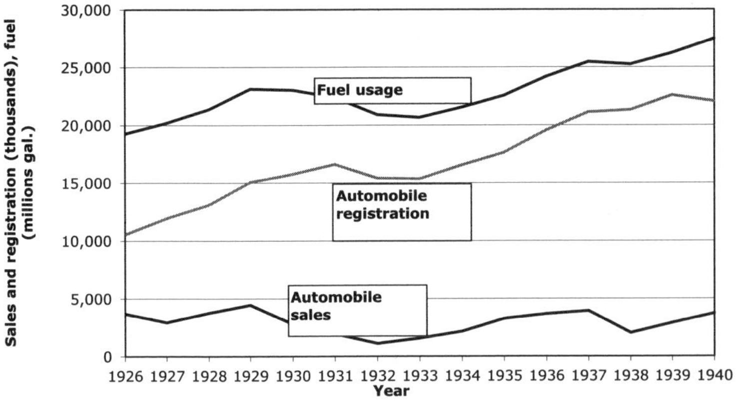

4.2 Automobile sales, registrations, fuel usage 1926–40. *Source:* US Census Bureau, 1975, *Historical Statistics of the United States: Colonial Times to 1970,* bicentennial edition, part 2, series Q, 148–62, "Motor-Vehicle Factory Sales and Registrations, and Motor-Fuel Usage: 1900 to 1970," 716.

In the 1920s after sales had recovered from the wartime drop, Americans were buying over three-and-a-half million cars every year, and in 1929 sales peaked at 4,455,000. While the Depression brought a sharp decline, the downturn was for sales of new cars, and *not* for driving itself. As figure 4.2 makes clear, after a brief slowdown in 1932 and 1933, automobile registration and fuel sales, both indicators of the amount people were using their cars, continued their upward trajectory. During the thirties Americans may have been driving older cars but they were driving more than ever.

Not only did they have cars, people had the time to take trips. This was not simply because they were jobless, for we should remember that most American workers were still working even during the Great Depression's worst years. (In 1935 when the Federal Writers' Project decided to go into the guidebook business, unemployment was at a horrendous 20 percent, but that meant that four out of five workers still had jobs.) And they were taking more vacations. "Between 1935 and 1940 the privilege of vacations with pay finally was extended to a majority of America's industrial labor force, ironically making the decade of the depression a period when vacationing became more rather than less widespread."[18] In the early years of the Depression the paid vacation movement had a temporary setback, but it quickly picked up again. A 1935 study by the National Industrial Conference Board indicated that two-thirds of the companies surveyed (177/274) had some sort of a vacation plan, while a 1937 study of 90,000 firms by

18. Aron (1999): 238.

the US Bureau of Labor Statistics showed that the number of plants and workers enjoying paid vacations had tripled since 1934.[19] In addition to the general trend that had been growing since the beginning of the century, firms worried about unionization (particularly after the 1935 Wagner Act) and about the radicalization of labor, and they saw paid vacations as one way of keeping their workers more content, and perhaps—in a nod to the old recreation view—more productive as well. Initially this was a top-down movement; unions for the most part did not press for paid vacations. By the midthirties, workers who had been exposed to all the advertising and promotional campaigns, began accepting the idea that vacations ought to be a standard part of their employment package. Indeed, by 1940 fourteen railway unions representing 750,000 workers demanded vacations with pay; by the time they got their vacation plan, over 50 percent of wage workers and 95 percent of salaried workers had paid vacations, which Americans now regarded as normal, not exceptional.[20]

Inevitably, scholars and policy makers began offering opinions on how people should spend their leisure time. Self-improvement and "constructive leisure" were preferable to "trivial" or "passive" activities, and newspapers gave advice about how to teach both adults and children to play. Vacations were said to be more important than ever during hard times; in 1932 the *Ladies Home Journal* urged readers to just "pack up your family and go!"[21] Even Eleanor Roosevelt recommended vacations that would give "a needed rest and change yet conform to the family budget." The press especially promoted "vacations put to intellectual and artistic uses," "mental growth," and vacations that produced "some new knowledge, some idea." All this, of course, was very much in line with the Federal Writers' Project's thinking about Americans seeing America.

Economic indicators reveal that tourism, especially by automobile, was growing throughout the thirties. Tourist spending in relation to national income averaged 2.96 percent during the 1920s. In the early and mid-1930s it averaged 3.94 percent, going to 4.37 percent in 1935.[22] Vacation spots like Niagara Falls and the Grand Canyon, which saw a decline in the early thirties, recovered by mid-decade; Yellowstone National Park, for example, saw more visitors in 1934 than in 1929, its previous highpoint.[23] In 1936 a survey conducted by *Fortune* magazine indicated that over half of

19. Aron (1999): 247.

20. Berkowitz (2001).

21. Aron (1999): 253; Eleanor Roosevelt quote following is from 254.

22. Berkowitz (2001): 185. Berkowitz gets this statistic from a *Harvard Business Review* article from 1937 (Julius Weinberger, "Economic Aspects of Recreation," *Harvard Business Review* 15 (Summer 1937): 448–63.) The data end at 1935.

23. Aron (1999): 238–40.

the respondents planned on taking a vacation that year. Even during the early years of the Depression, the amount of money people spent on vacation travel did not decline as much as the amount spent on other forms of recreation. Moreover, the *Fortune* survey showed that three-quarters of those who took vacations traveled by car.[24]

Not only did chambers of commerce, mayors' offices, and oil companies promote the "travel habit" during the Great Depression, but the federal government jumped in as well. Eager to encourage hitting the road and seeing the country, Washington expanded National Park Service authority over tourist attractions like battlefields and monuments; it made 1934 "National Parks Year"; six years later it proclaimed 1940 to be "Travel America Year"; and in 1937 it created a national tourist agency, the United States Travel Bureau (USTB) under Interior Secretary Harold Ickes, with funding and staff from both the Civilian Conservation Corps and the WPA. Though it was closed down when the Second World War started, during its brief life the USTB

> assumed the role of a national clearinghouse of valuable tourist-related information, issuing a series of newsletters, bulletins, events calendars, research reports, and promotional aids to travel agencies, transportation companies, tour operators, and members of the hospitality industry. It facilitated relations between the constituent parts of the nation's rapidly growing yet inchoate tourist industry by creating a National Travel Advisory Board consisting of executives and officials from transportation and travel-related businesses and organizations. It directly assisted tourists, establishing local offices in New York City, San Francisco, and Washington, where it held lectures, screened travel-related motion pictures, staged exhibits, and distributed travel literature for government as well and nongovernment tourist attractions. The bureau also sponsored a series of radio programs throughout the nation as well as created and coordinated special promotional campaigns such as the Travel America Year campaign proclaimed by FDR for 1940.[25]

Not surprisingly, in 1939 Katharine Kellock wrote radio scripts for the USTB that promoted the use of the American Guides as an aid for recreational travel.

Why did the federal government assume such an active role in promoting tourism? The historian Michael Berkowitz points to three factors. First, fearing both radicalism and right-wing populism, congressmen and administration officials believed that recreational travel would turn Ameri-

24. Aron (1999); Berkowitz (2001).
25. Berkowitz (2001): 203.

cans into better citizens. Second, both public and private officials hoped that travel would produce economic benefits. Third, many business and civic leaders sought the active participation of the federal government to bolster their local efforts. All of these factors played into the rationale for the American Guide Series as well.

The government was riding the boom, however, not causing it. Americans were on the road, and they were reinterpreting what "Americana" and "See America First" really meant to them.[26] Nothing demonstrates this as forcefully as the astonishing success of a new magazine called *Life*. Having already revolutionized the magazine industry when he founded *Time* in 1923 and *Fortune* in 1930, Henry Luce had come to believe that pictures could tell a story, not just accompany a text. The thirties were the great age of photo-documentary, and while the federal government was employing photographers to celebrate New Deal initiatives, Luce figured out a way of employing photographers to make money. He launched the first issue of *Life* on November 23, 1936, just in time for Thanksgiving table talk two days later, and it was an immediate hit. Although it soon would become famous for its war photography, *Life*'s first issue ignored the civil war in Spain, the Japanese in Manchuria, Hitler and Mussolini in Europe, and instead focused on America, especially the American heartland. On the cover was Margaret Bourke-White's photo of the spillway of Fort Peck Dam, a massive Public Works Administration project in eastern Montana that was then under construction. The feature article was on recreation at the Fort Peck site: "10,000 Relief Workers Make Whoopee on Saturday Night." The issue contained articles on celebrities—film star Robert Taylor and actress Helen Hayes—and on some French aristocrats' weekend of pheasant shooting. There were long photo features on the Regionalist artist John Steuart Curry and on Brazil. Shorter features included a piece on aeronautical engineers' attempts to develop planes that could fly at greater heights ("Over Weather"), one on a Chinese school in San Francisco, and one on black widow spiders. Advertisements for cars and automobile products were scattered everywhere. Just behind the cover was a full-page ad for Ethyl gasoline, followed by a full-page ad touting "First Pictures and Details about the new plymouth." The next ad was for piston rings, the next for car insurance, then an ad for Heinz, one for kitchen mixers, and another full-page ad, "Announcing the New Ford V-8 Cars for 1937." *Life*'s editors and advertisers conceived of their readers as car owners, travelers, and people with broad interests, interests that were largely American but went well beyond the East Coast.

26. For the history of the "See America First" concept, which promoted tourism as a "ritual of American citizenship" and a form of "virtuous consumption," see Shaffer (2001).

By the Second World War, tourism had become one of the nation's biggest industries, "as large as the automobile, petroleum, and lumber industries combined and 50 percent larger than iron and steel production."[27] Most of this growth was in auto travel, that is, family vacations on the road. Restaurants, gas stations, and motor courts proliferated. So did travel guides. Katharine Kellock's pitch was persuasive because everybody involved thought that the boom in travel offered a way to have writers doing something popular and even useful because they would be satisfying American motorists' demand for information.

Automobile Travel Guides

But was there actually such a demand? As Kellock and Alsberg saw it, Baedekers represented the travel guide as a genre, the gold standard, but Baedekers did not meet the needs of motorists. The Writers' Project, therefore, could seize the opportunity and produce travel guides that would fill the yawning gap between what was needed and what was available.

These New Dealers seemed oblivious to the fact that automobile guides had proliferated during the first third of the twentieth century, and by the 1920s they were aimed squarely at the general public. True, Baedeker had responded slowly and somewhat grudgingly to the new reality, not coming out with its first motoring guides until the 1930s and then not for the United States, but that was just one publisher. All sorts of entrepreneurs had been bringing out new guides organized explicitly around the needs of American motorists. These guides were less focused on cities, museums, and sights, the stuff of railway travel, and more on the road itself. They laid out routes, mileage, and what motorists would see along the way. They also featured advertisements, not just for hotels and resorts but also ads for gasoline, tires, and service stations.

For three decades the most prominent of these new guidebooks were the *Automobile Blue Books.* Founded in Chicago in 1901, Automobile Blue Books Inc. produced its guides by sending out teams of cars to scour the highways. The 1924 volume for New York and New England explained the company's methods:

> Blue Book cars start in the south in January and continue till snow stops them in the north about December. They select the best and shortest routes through towns and country where the most scenic and historic attractions abound. Every mile of road

27. Berkowitz (2001): 206.

data and other information in the Blue Books is gathered by our own trained *road scouts*. For 23 years the Automobile Blue Book has been the Standard Touring Guide of America and we aim to keep it so.[28]

They did keep it so by offering motorists detailed guidance on what they would encounter. Consider, for example, the 1924 *Automobile Blue Book*'s volume 1, which covered New York and New England ("Route 150—Boston to Swampscott, Salem, Ipswich, Newburyport, Mass., Rye Beach, Portsmouth, N.H., and Portland, Me.—128.2 m"), and begins by offering some general remarks: the roads are paved throughout, the route follows the shore, there is a shorter inland option for drivers in a hurry. It then gives a mile-by-mile itinerary and directions, for example, "Mile 2.7 Prospect St.; right over RR bridge. 2.9 End of street; right on Washington St. 3.3 Franklin St.; left from trolley." And so on for all 128.2 miles. If you happen to be coming *from* Portland to Boston, the next section has the steps all over again, only in reverse order. Meanwhile there is information along the way: a history and map of all the towns the motorist will pass through: Lynn, Ipswich, Salem, Newburyport, Portsmouth, Kittery, Biddeford, Saco, Portland. All this, and yet over half of the sixteen pages devoted to the route are taken up with advertisements for hotels, restaurants, garages, and gasoline stations. The *Blue Book* covered a total of 596 routes in this manner, plus set-in sections on New York City and Boston, a large map on a ribbon that served double duty as a bookmark, and information at the end on customs regulations between the United States and Canada. The driver with a *Blue Book* in the glove compartment did not lack for information.

Over and above the *Automobile Blue Books*, motorists could consult a huge array of other guides. The American Automobile Association published various guides over the early years including the *Green Books*, which imitated and competed with the *Blue Books*. Local and regional auto clubs produced their own guides. Railroads, resorts, and tourist destinations pumped out their own promotional materials. Associations certified that lodgings and restaurants were up to their standards. Some guides aimed at specific groups. One such guide was *The Negro Motorist Green Book*, which was launched in 1936 and listed accommodations—hotels, motels, tourist homes, restaurants—that African Americans could patronize "without encountering embarrassing situations."[29] Oil companies had been giving

28. Automobile Blue Books Inc. (1924).

29. *The Negro Motorist Green Book*, later called *The Negro Travelers' Green Book*. Victor H. Green, the editor and publisher, began the series in 1936. The guides (128 pages, paperback) offered "Assured protection for the Negro Traveler," according to the 1958 through 1961 editions that I have examined. The

away maps at filling stations since 1913. And various tourism brochures, often including maps, proliferated.[30]

All told, Americans who took to the roads during the thirties had plenty of written guidance. They were by no means dependent on the railroad-centric Baedekers of a quarter century earlier. Indeed, by the time the Federal Writers' Project began working on the American Guide series of guidebooks, the field of automotive travel guides was crowded. If the genre that the Writers' Project was entering was travel guides and specifically guides for motorists, it was a genre with a long history and a set of conventions about what a guidebook should contain. Moreover, there was a lot of competition in the field due to the number of Americans taking to the road and the number of services available to them. Thus although putting the writers on the government payroll to work on American Baedekers carried political advantages, it is not clear that anyone actually *needed* new travel guides, for there were more guides around than the motorist could possibly use.

It is quite possible that the New Dealers—urban, East Coast intellectuals who probably never took family road trips in the first place—did not realize how much competition was out there. Either that or they didn't care. They recognized that working on travel guides perfectly fulfilled the need for the Project employees to engage in a "socially useful" activity that kept them gainfully and peacefully occupied. Automobile travel was booming, and producing travel books showed the federal government was responding, even if private enterprise had responded much earlier.

In any event, the decisions made as Federal One was being thrown together were compromises and seat-of-the-pants choices. The American Guide Series hedged its bets. It ended up producing books that were hybrids, part travel guides for the motorist and part essays for the armchair traveler, the student, and the general reader. Given the mixed motives of the Guides' creators, this mixed outcome is not surprising. The results, however, were to transform the shape of American culture in ways that no one anticipated.

---

price was $1.25 in 1958, up to $1.95 in 1961. The booklets contained advertising. In the early years (e.g., 1949) the title was either *The Negro Motorist Green Book* or *The Negro Motorist Green-Book*.

30. For a history of the maps produced by oil companies, see Yorke and Margolies (1996). These maps had their heyday from the 1920s through the 1950s. Yorke and Margolies associate their disappearance with the rise of the interstate highway system, which made their detailed guidance less necessary.

PART THREE

Cultural Federalism

FIVE

Negotiating Federalism

For reasons that were political, not cultural or commercial, the Federal Writers' Project committed itself to writing travel guides. They called the enterprise the American Guide Series. The Project would eventually produce a Guide for every state, a couple of territories (Alaska and Puerto Rico), and cities both large and small. It would also churn out hundreds of pamphlets. By doing so, the Project would fulfill its essential charge of giving writers jobs doing something that seemed useful.

Washington wanted the Guides to be standardized, so the central office issued the *American Guide Manual* and then a series of eighteen supplements in 1935 and 1936 as it tried to ram home its changing model among the forty-nine different units.[1] Central office administrators stressed efficiency, a crisp and clear style, and attention focused on what they regarded as significant. The states, on the other hand, had their own priorities, their own ideas about what was significant, and sometimes their own styles as well. The wrestling between Washington and the states—carried out through letters, telegrams, field visits, hiring and firing, budgets, and the Washington editors' sharp blue pencils—gave the Guides their peculiar form and their peculiar blend of the conventional and the idiosyncratic.

This chapter looks at how the men and women of the Federal Writers' Project, both in Washington and in the state of-

1. NARA 69, Records of the Federal Writers' Project, Entry 11: Manuals and Instructions, 1935–39. The fifty units were the forty-eight State Projects plus New York City, which had its own unit.

fices, tried to carry out what they understood to be the Project's mission. The next chapter looks at the results.

The View from Washington

When he was tapped to head the Federal Writers' Project in the summer of 1935, Henry Alsberg was fifty-seven. He had taken a law degree from Columbia when he was twenty, got bored with law after three years, and studied literature at Harvard for a year (he got bored with that too). Instead of a career in either law or teaching, Alsberg spent most of his adult years as a journalist and intellectual rolling stone in bohemian-literary circles. He was a foreign correspondent in Europe, a secretary to the American ambassador to Turkey, and a relief worker for a Jewish social service agency in Russia; later he described his work there as traveling around the post-revolutionary countryside handing out money to Jews threatened with famine. During the twenties he based himself in New York and dabbled in theatre, both as playwright and director.

If Henry Alsberg was at home anywhere, it was in New York's radical-pacifist-intellectual community. Jerre Mangione, who worked in the Washington office and later wrote an invaluable, gossipy history of the Project, calls him a "philosophical anarchist": left-wing but not Communist, mistrustful of authority, and driven by enthusiasms that sometimes faltered before coming to fruition. Having no administrative experience whatsoever, Alsberg was hardly an obvious choice to head up a sprawling federal bureaucracy. Nevertheless, he had been on Jacob Baker's staff for a year editing two FERA magazines and a CWA compilation called *America Fights the Depression*. Baker had faith in Alsberg's honesty, vision, energy, and literary taste, and he never considered anyone else for the job.

The Project got off to a chaotic start. Alsberg threw together a staff dominated by—what else?—East Coast men whose worlds revolved around Columbia University, New York City, and the Boston-to-Washington axis. Since their first priority was to provide white-collar jobs, with the decision to write travel guides simply a stratagem for fulfilling this primary mission, it is not surprising that no one had given much thought to what a guidebook actually was or what type of guide the Project should produce. The original thinking was that there would be one book, following the Baedeker model in which an enormous amount of information would be stuffed into a single, pocket-size volume. The 1909 Baedeker was largely the product of one man's efforts, however, and that would never do for a jobs program. So the "Federal Project, No. 1" proposal described an organization that would be run out of twelve regional offices and that would produce guidebooks for the United States in five regional volumes. In addition, the Federal One proposal promised that the Project's employees would turn out WPA progress reports and an encyclopedia of government functions—exactly the sort of things writers detested doing.

George Cronyn, Alsberg's associate director who became the chief editor for the American Guides, and Katharine Kellock, originator of the guidebook idea who now bore the vague title of field supervisor, both vehemently opposed the five-book plan. It made little sense geographically, they argued, since the borders of many regions were unclear and some states would get short shrift. It made no sense culturally, for the regions would be too big for precise description. Nor did it make sense politically; a regional structure could not command support in Congress the way a state-by-state structure could. Cronyn and Kellock urged a separate guide for each state, and by October they had prevailed. Since the first edition of the *American Guide Manual* had been prepared for regional guides, it was obsolete by the time it was printed.

This critical decision—to organize the American Guide Series by state—inadvertently introduced a new way of thinking about American culture. Until that time most people thought of a region and its culture as referring to a broad swath of the nation, as in southern cooking or western tall tales, and while some regions like New England conveniently followed state lines, others like the Great Plains did not. Although Cronyn and Kellock based their arguments on practical administrative and political considerations, their success in getting their way meant that *there would now be forty-eight state-shaped molds into which cultural content would be poured.*

Once the region-versus-state question had been settled, disagreement remained regarding what would actually be in the Guides. Kellock's idea was to write travel guides, American Baedekers that were organized around tours that followed a state's highways and that laid out in detail the places to be found along the way. She envisioned the potential audience to be *tourists*, motorists seeing America. This was also the hope of the local business communities and state officials who supported the books, as well as congressmen looking to promote their states while pumping up the economy. The Guides would sit in glove compartments and be consulted when people were on the road.

Alsberg and Cronyn, on the other hand, had in mind something more like encyclopedic repositories of information, reference works. Thus they focused on essays that would offer informed and accessible coverage of the states' natural resources, history, social makeup, and culture. As we have seen, Baedekers themselves had introductory essays, but they were comparatively short. Alsberg and Cronyn wanted the Guides' essays to be extensive. They envisioned the audience to be *readers*: students, Americana buffs, and anyone else who wanted to explore the nation's diversity. They saw people using the Guides from their chairs, not from their cars.

The American Guide Series ended up containing both tours and essays. In a classic bureaucratic compromise, each State Guide was an awkward hybrid that aimed for both audiences.

Another debate was over whether or not the Guides should arrange their materials alphabetically. Early manuals put forth conflicting instructions, driving the state directors to distraction with all the changes in their marching orders. That is, if they paid attention at all: When the second manual emphasized uniformity and rigid page limits, Washington staffers—especially the irrepressible Kellock—assured the state directors they could safely ignore them.

Alsberg spent the fall of 1935 hiring directors for every state, a pressing issue given that the Project would officially launch on November 1. To persuade qualified people to head up state units of a new program with shaky funding and ill-defined responsibilities was hard enough, and friction between the Project and the state WPA offices made it even harder. Under the WPA, each state had an administrator who was in charge of that state's operations, including hiring and firing. Unlike the rest of the WPA, however, the state directors of the Federal Writers' Project reported to Washington, not to the state administrators. At the same time they had to depend on the state administrators for various kinds of assistance. This contradiction between centralized control and decentralized operation was to bedevil the Writers' Project endlessly.[2] Resentful over not being part of the decision-making process and not having control over the salaries, state administrators flooded Washington with complaints, and locally they sometimes retaliated with bureaucratic pettiness. In Idaho, when the administrator hadn't been consulted when Alsberg appointed Vardis Fisher to be state director, he refused to provide furniture for Fisher's staff, who had to work sitting on boxes.[3]

2. See McDonald (1969), ch. 9, "A Problem in Contradiction," for an extended discussion. Although Hopkins had ordered the state WPA administrators to give Alsberg "their fullest cooperation and aid," they did not make the decisions, nor were they always consulted; in some cases a letter from Jacob Baker informed the administrator only after an appointee had gotten his or her letter. This structure was true for all four Federal One projects.

3. Mangione (1972): 73. Despite such turf wars, those involved looked back on the centralized structure as critically important. As Penkower (1977), who interviewed many of the principals years later, sums it up,

> The fact that FWP state units remained under national jurisdiction meant that salaries, cuts, and the writing and publication of guide copy ultimately could not be tampered with for personal ends. As Florence Kerr [who became

Another problem was political interference. A state directorship was a plum patronage job, so politicians were loath to leave it all up to Washington. Appointing directors in states with powerful Democratic machines like Missouri and New Jersey was especially problematic, but trouble could arise in all sorts of ways. Nebraska's powerful senator George Norris was a liberal Republican who supported the New Deal and thus was someone to be carefully stroked. Norris had a newspaper publisher who was an important political ally, and the publisher had a mistress, Elizabeth Sheehan, so Senator Norris successfully pushed her to head the Nebraska Writers' Project. When Sheehan proved to be incompetent and was about to be fired, she appealed to her publisher-lover, who appealed to Norris, and Norris fired back that "as long as Nebraska had a writers' project, Miss Sheehan would have her desk." Unwilling to buck the senator but unable to get the Nebraska Project moving with Sheehan at the helm, Alsberg assigned her to work at home (she continued to draw her salary until the Project closed in 1942), while J. Harris Gable assumed the actual responsibilities of directorship.[4] While the details of this contretemps were more salacious than most, the outcome was typical: Alsberg was sensitive the Project's need for political backing, and he hated to fire people anyway, so he usually caved in.[5]

Confusion reigned for the first year, exacerbated by impossible deadlines. No one knew if the WPA would be funded after July 1, 1936, so when the Writers' Project officially began operations on November 1, 1935, Alsberg instructed that "State Directors should plan to have all state copy cleared by Washington not later than May 1, 1936." This thoroughly unrealistic demand brought forth a flood of half-baked, uninformed writing. Meanwhile the Washington staff itself bounced around, first assigned space in an old movie theatre where the organ pipes loomed over the file cabinets, and then under the crystal chandeliers of the McLean Mansion ballroom, where staffers used plaster casts of Greek statues as coat racks.

During the early months, a sixty-two-person staff in the Washington office developed procedures, wrote and rewrote manuals, and dispatched field representatives to get the states moving. Katharine Kellock

head of WPA's Professional and Service Projects Division in 1939] concluded years later: "Federalization saved the arts projects." (50)

4. Mangione (1972): 76–77.

5. Alsberg virtually never resisted political pressures, nor did he defend his own state directors. An egregious case of this took place in Minnesota, when State Director Mabel Ulrich tried to transfer some incompetent workers. The local branch of the Workers' Alliance, whose president was a Communist, threatened to strike in retaliation. Both Alsberg and Harry Hopkins buckled under pressure, Ulrich resigned, and the workers were reinstated as "writers." (Penkower [1977]: 184; for the state director's account, see Ulrich [1939]).

later recalled the organizational chaos: "Most titles of personnel were almost meaningless and changes were frequent. . . . All very erratic."[6] Associate Director George Cronyn was in charge of editorial matters and Assistant Director Reed Harris handled administration, an enormously important role in light of Alsberg's deficiencies. Table 5.1 gives a group portrait of the major staff members, who—like the New Dealers as a whole—were heavily northeastern, male, and holding degrees from Columbia or Harvard.[7]

Greater stability emerged in the summer of 1936. In July Harry Hopkins solved the problem of overlapping functions and clashing personalities by combining the two previous divisions into a "Division of Women's and Professional Projects." As we have seen, Baker had incurred the wrath of state officials—largely because it was his name on letters telling them to do things they didn't want to do—and they had been howling for his removal, so Hopkins moved Baker out and placed Ellen Woodward, who had been heading the Women's Division, in charge. A southerner, more diplomatic and less radical than Baker, she was acceptable to everyone. For the next two-and-a-half years, what McDonald calls "the golden age of the federal arts projects," Woodward gave Alsberg staunch support and a free hand.[8]

Nineteen thirty-six was an election year, however, and Americans were worrying about the vast amount of deficit spending that had characterized the early years of the New Deal. The decline in unemployment—from a high of almost 25 percent in the spring of 1933 to below 17 percent three years later—gave Roosevelt room to cut the WPA budget in general and the Federal One budget in particular. Two blows came in the summer: In July the budget was shrunk by a third, and in September Harry Hopkins rescinded the Federal One exemption whereby up to 25 percent of the Arts Projects' employees could be workers who had not been on relief (the WPA limit in general was 10 percent). Then in November the WPA budget was cut once again. Strikes and protests followed, especially by the highly politicized artists and writers in New York City, but pink slips went to about 4,000 Federal One workers. From that point on, the threat of layoffs hovered over the Project continuously.[9]

The tension between state and federal control boiled right from the

6. Kellock papers, "Rough Notes Made from Photostats of Personnel Records Cards," Folder #6, WPA Federal Writers' Project, Personnel Records.

7. The historian Christine Bold (1999) says that Baker had assembled "networks of East Coast, Ivy League intellectuals" (22), and it was actually even narrower than that.

8. Mangione (1972): 8; McDonald (1969): 164–68.

9. N. Taylor (2008), ch. 14.

Table 5.1 Federal Writers' Project Washington staff

Name	Position	Career prior to FWP	Born	Place	Gender	Ethnicity	Education	Notes
Abbott, Leonard D.	Research editor	Editor (*Literary Digest*), friend of Emma Goldman, old friend of Alsberg			M	W		Source: Mangione 1972
Alsberg, Henry Garfield	National director of the Federal Writers' Project		1881	New York City	M	W	BA and Law, Columbia University	Source: Mangione 1972; Penkower 1977
Baker, Jacob	FERA, PWA, CWA, head of WPA Professional and Service Projects Division	Industrial engineer	1895		M	W	No college	Source: Mangione 1972; Penkower 1977
Botkin, Benjamin	(Second) Folklore editor 1938–41	English professor at University of Oklahoma	1901	Boston, MA	M	W	BA, Harvard; MA, Columbia; PhD, University of Nebraska	Source: Hirsch 2003; "B(enjamin) A(lbert) Botkin," *Contemporary Authors Online* (Detroit: Gale, 2002), *Biography In Context* website, accessed Sept. 3, 2013
Brown, Sterling Allen	National editor for Negro affairs	Poet, English professor at Howard University	1901	Washington, DC	M	AF-AM	BA, Williams College; MA, Harvard	Grew up on Howard Univ. campus, father a religion professor; at Harvard studied lit, influenced by Frost and E. A. Robinson, incl. their regionalism
Browne, Waldo R.	Literary editor	Editor (the *Dial*, the *Nation*); old friend of Alsberg			M	W		Source: Mangione 1972
Cheever, John	Junior editor for six months, then transferred to the New York City Project	Writer	1912	Quincy, MA	M	W	Did not attend college	Major twentieth-century author

(*continued*)

Table 5.1 (continued)

Name	Position	Career prior to FWP	Born	Place	Gender	Ethnicity	Education	Notes
Colby, Merle Estes	Territorial editor; earlier assistant state director in Massachusetts		1902		M	W	Harvard	Wrote the Guides for Alaska, Puerto Rico, Virgin Islands
Coy, Harold	Executive editor				M	W		Source: Mangione 1972; Penkower 1977
Cronyn, George	Associate director, Federal Writers' Project, handled editing	English professor Univ. of Montana; had published two novels, anthology of Native American poems			M	W	Education unknown; editorial staff of *Columbia Encyclopedia*	Source: Mangione 1972; Penkower 1977
Gaer, Joseph	Field supervisor	Author (*How the Great Religions Began*); worked on California FERA writing project		Russia	M	W		Russian immigrant; source: Mangione 1972
Harris, Reed	Assistant director, Federal Writers' Project, handled administration	Journalist for *New York Journal* and *New York Times*			M	W	Columbia University (expelled for writing football exposé)	
Hettwer, Dora Thea	Executive secretary for Alsberg				F	W	Radcliffe and Harvard	
Kellock, Katharine	Field supervisor, then Tours editor	Relief supervisor for American Friends Committee; public health and settlement work	1892	Pittsburgh	F	W	Columbia University after war, studied history, social science, journalism	Source: Bold 1988

Lomax, John	(First) Folklore editor 1936–38	Folklorist, musicologist, educator	1867	Goodman, MS	M	W	Granbury Coll.; Univ. of Texas; MA, Harvard	Source: Hirsch 2003; *Wikipedia*
Mangione, Jerre	National coordinating editor	Journalist, worked for *Time* magazine in 1931	1909	Rochester, NY	M	W	Syracuse University	Source: Papers at University of Rochester library, http://www.lib.rochester.edu/index.cfm?page=3312#Early
McConkey, Darel	Field supervisor; later editor for city copy; in 1940 spent 6 months completing Utah Guide.	Columnist			M	W		
Morris, Lawrence	Field supervisor; later administrative assistant to Ellen Woodward	Former assistant editor of *New Republic*			M	W		
Rosenberg, Harold	Art editor	Poet, essayist, editor of *Art Front*; had worked for Federal Arts Project	1906	New York City	M	W	CCNY; law degree from St. Lawrence	Claimed to have been "educated on the Steps of the New York Public Library"
Royce, Morton	Social-ethnic studies editor (hired 1938; left Project 1940)	Social worker; interested in European ethnicity	1896	South Dakota	M	W	Two doctorates from Columbia University	Source: Hirsch 2003; Mangione 1972; introduction to *The Bohemian Flats* (FWP 1941)
Seidenberg, Roderick	Art and architectural editor	Architect; designed New Yorker hotel; old friend of Alsberg			M	W		Source: Mangione 1972
Woodward, Ellen S.	Replaced Baker, head of WPA's Women's and Professional Projects Division		1887	Oxford, Mississippi	F	W	San Souci, female seminary, Greenville, SC	

start. In December 1935 the anthropologist Paul Radin, the new California state director, and Hugh Harlan, Los Angeles supervisor, openly defied the charge to write guidebooks and kept working on studies begun earlier under FERA. Alsberg sent Cronyn out to fire both of them for insubordination. Furious local reaction to the dismissals, plus Harlan's complaints to his old Grinnell classmate Harry Hopkins, resulted in Harlan getting his job back and Radin being shifted to a research editor position that allowed him to do exactly what he wanted to do. While the California Project was back on track, Alsberg had learned his lesson: Firing the politically well connected would be all but impossible.[10]

Less overt forms of insubordination at the state level, encouraged perhaps by the contradictory messages coming out of headquarters, abounded. One state director wrote to another: "Congratulations on your new position. Don't take it seriously. It is not intended that we should achieve anything but only that we should put the jobless to work so they will vote for Roosevelt."[11] While few state directors were this openly cynical, their outlooks rarely coincided with that of the gung-ho New Dealers back in Washington.

The View from the States

While the view from Washington was exceedingly well documented (as was true for New Deal programs in general), the view from the states was less faithfully recorded and evidence scattered.[12] Reconstruction of what people in the State Projects were thinking depends on inference from the correspondence, from the press, which tended to support local views, and from the memories of people involved. We begin with the state directors who, alas, left few accounts of their experiences. The first step is to figure out who they even were.

The State Directors

Although the Federal Writers' Project lasted only a little over seven years, operated in full view of the media, and left detailed records in Washington and in the states, it is surprisingly difficult to come up with a list of

10. Mangione (1972): 68–69; Penkower (1977): 43–44.

11. Mangione (1972): 79.

12. This is the case for the secondary sources as well; for example, McDonald (1969) acknowledges that his interviews depended on Washington insiders and so his report skews toward the federal perspective.

the state writers' project directors.[13] A great deal of churning took place, especially at the beginning—directors appointed in late 1935 who were gone by early 1936—and after mid-1939, when the Project became the Writers' Program and shifted to state sponsorship. Even the highly productive years of 1937 and 1938 saw a lot of coming and going. Directors left the Project in order to take up better opportunities or because they were disgusted. They were fired for drunkenness, for incompetence, and for politics. Some of the incompetents were not fired at all, as in Nebraska, and sometimes assistant directors or state editors did all the actual work. Sometimes there was a crisis and an acting director was appointed, who might or might not have ever been named director.

I have managed to identify 116 state directors, including some whose tenures were very short and some who stayed on for the entire life of the Project. I have not included "acting directors" unless the record shows that they eventually became directors. Table 5.2 lists these state directors and what I have been able to find out about them.

Few directors were themselves prominent writers. Only twenty-one got mentioned in the Literature essays, and of those who did, eighteen showed up only in their own state's Guides. Georgia state director Samuel Tupper, for example, brought out a novel in 1934 called *Old Lady's Shoes* that depicted Atlanta in the Depression, following an earlier Atlanta-set novel *Some Go Up* (1931); the Georgia Guide mentioned both, but Tupper appeared nowhere else. Another southerner was Lyle Saxon, a New Orleans journalist and author who had written extensively about the city and who directed the unusually productive Louisiana Writers' Project. Saxon's energies focused strictly on Louisiana, and only that state's Literature essay mentioned him.

Three regionalist state directors received multiple mentions. Illinois director John Frederick, from Iowa, founded the *Midland* magazine in 1915 while still a student at the University of Iowa. Part of the little magazine movement, the *Midland* published writers from outside the Northeast who could not break into New York publishing circles. It focused on midwestern regionalists, publishing emerging writers such as James Farrell (author of the *Studs Lonigan* trilogy) and Sherwood Anderson (*Winesburg, Ohio*). Frederick moved through a number of teaching positions in the Midwest, taking the *Midland* with him until it ceased publication in 1933, and the Literature essays in three Guides—Illinois, Iowa, and Michigan—mentioned him. Out west, Montana state director Harold Merriam grew

13. None of the standard histories (McDonald, Mangione, Penkower, Bold) construct such a list; historians (McDonald and Penkower) and English professors (Mangione and Bold) do not tend to make lists and count things as much a sociologists do.

Table 5.2 State Writers' Project directors

Name	State (Directorship)	Year born	Place	Gender	State Guide (mentions him or her)	Notes
Adams, Bristow	New York	1875	3 (DC)	M		Cornell professor of agriculture, forester, journalist
Babcock, Bernie	Arkansas	1868	3 (OH)	F	Arkansas	Journalist and writer; novels about Lincoln; *Soul of Ann Rutledge* (1919)
Barrington, Lewis	DC			M		*Handbook of Am Museums* (1932); *Historic Restorations of the DAR* (1941)
Beckner, Col. Lucien	Kentucky	1872	1 (KY)	M		Geologist
Bell, U. R.	Kentucky, Missouri	1891	1 (KY)	M		Executive, journalist, writer
Billington, Ray Allen	Massachusetts	1903	3 (MI)	M		
Bjorkman, Edwin	North Carolina	1866	5 (Sweden)	M	North Carolina	Author, critic, and translator
Bowles, Ella Shannon	New Hampshire	1886	1 (NH)	F		
Bridges, J. M.	Virginia					
Briggs, Gordon F.	Indiana		3 (NY)	M		
Brown, Charles E.	Wisconsin	1872	1 (WI)	M		Archaeologist and historian
Browning, Frank A.	Virginia			M		
Burns, La Vega W.	West Virginia					
Caldwell, Katharine Hilliker	DC		3 (WA)	F		Editor and writer, film writer during 1920s
Cassidy, Ina Sizer	New Mexico	1869	2 (CO)	F		
Chadbourne, Horace	Montana			M		
Chittenden, Mrs. Cecile R.	Michigan			F		
Christenson, Mart	Wyoming			M		Journalist
Cleavenger, Morris	Colorado			M		Journalist, wrote for *Rocky Mountain News*
Colby, Merle	Massachusetts	1902	3 (WI)	M		
Conley, Philip J.	Maine	1912	1 (ME)	M		
Corse, Carita Doggett	Florida	1891	1 (FL)	F	Florida	Historian; *Turnbull and New Smyrna Colony* (1919), others on FL history
Crane, Byron	Montana			M		
Cunningham, William	Oklahoma	1901	1 (OK)	M	Oklahoma	*Green Corn Rebellion*, *Pretty Boy*
Davis, John Frank	Texas			M		Journalist and writer
Derby, John B.	Connecticut			M		English professor at Yale, Dartmouth
Dickerson, Mr.	Kansas			M		

Dillard, Carolyn P.	Georgia			F		
Doten, Dana	Vermont			M		
Douglass, Eri	Mississippi			F		
Du Von, Jay	Iowa	1909	3 (IL)	M		
DuBose, Louise J.	South Carolina	1901	2 (GA)	F		
Dunton, James G.	Ohio	1899	1 (OH)	M		
Eckenrode, Hamilton James	Virginia	1881	1 (VA)	M	Virginia	Historian, bio Jefferson Davis, novel *Bottom Rail on Top* (1935)
Eckman, Jeannette	Delaware	1882	1 (DE)	F		A Western Kentucky University library publication says she was a local historian. http://digitalcommons.wku.edu/cgi/viewcontent.cgi?article=1013&context=dlsc_fac_pub.
Edmonds, T. J.	Oregon			M		
Egan, James W.	Washington			M		500 stories, 2 novels (5-10-36 press rel)
Elder, Charles	Tennessee			M		
Ellingwood, R. Richard	Maine			M		
Evans, Harold C.	Kansas			M		Acting director
Finger, Charles J.	Arkansas	1871	4 (ENG)	M	Arkansas	Adventure tales, e.g., *Highwayman* (1923); Newbery Medal (1925)
Fisher, Vardis	Idaho	1895	1 (ID)	M	Utah	Prolific writer, *Children of God*, set in UT
Foster, Austin P.	Tennessee	1859	1 (TN)	M	Tennessee	*TN, the Volunteer State* 1923, w/ J.T. Moore
Frederick, John T.	Illinois	1893	3 (IA)	M	IL, IA, MI	Founding ed. of the *Midland*
French, Paul Comly	Pennsylvania	1903	1 (PA)	M		Journalist, from old Quaker family
Fuhlbruegge, Irene	New Jersey			F		
Gable, J. Harris	Nebraska	1902		M		
Graf, Harry	Ohio			M		
Harlan, Hugh	California			M		Historian, wrote *History of the Olympic Games* (1932)
Hatcher, Harlan	Ohio	1898	1 (OH)	M	Ohio	*Tunnel High* (1931), *Central Standard Time* (1937)
Hawks, Mrs. Muriel E.	Massachusetts			M		
Heidel, Mrs. L.A. (Teresa)	Vermont			F		
Herbert, James C.	West Virginia	1875	3 (PA)	M		
Hill, Victor	Rhode Island			M		
Hoke, Travis	New York City	1892	3 (MO)	M		
Holcomb, Gene	Missouri			M		

(*continued*)

Table 5.2 (continued)

Name	State (Directorship)	Year born	Place	Gender	State Guide (mentions him or her)	Notes
Hopper, James	California	1876	5 (France)	M	California	Short stories; journalist and educator
Howe, Maurice L.	Utah			M	Utah	*Miles Goodyear* w/ Kelly
Hutchinson, Viola	New Jersey			F		
Isbell, Egbert R.	Michigan	1898	1 (MI)	M		
Johns, Orrick	New York City	1887	3 (MO)	M	Missouri	Poetry and prose; *Time of Our Lives* (1937)
Johnston, Ross B.	West Virginia			M		
Jordon, Arthur (or Jordan)	Maine			M		
Key, William O.	Georgia			M		Journalist with *Atlanta Constitution*
Kline, Burton	New Jersey	1877	2 (PA)	M		Journalist
Kresensky, Raymond	Iowa	1897	1 (IA)	M	Iowa	Published in regional reviews
Lockridge, Ross	Indiana	1877	1 (IN)	M		Writer, educator (son, same name, wrote *Raintree County*)
Loewenberg, Bert James	Massachusetts	1905	1 (MA)	M		Historian, educator
Lyons, John. J. "Leo"	Wisconsin			M		
McCoy, Samuel Duff	New York City	1882	3 (IA)	M		NYC assistant director, some reports say director
McDaniel, William R.	Tennessee			M		
McKown, Dallas	Arkansas			F		
Merriam, Harold G.	Montana	1883	3 (MA)	M	MT, WY	Ed., *Northwestern Verse* (1931), edited regional literary magazine *Frontier and Midland* (1921–39)
Miller, Alexander Q.	Kansas	1905		M		Journalist
Montgomery, Mabel	South Carolina			F		
Morgan, Dale L.	Utah	1914	1 (UT)	M		Wrote Mormon histories
Morse, Jarvis M.	Rhode Island and Connecticut	1899		M		Historian, wrote about early Connecticut, professor at Brown
Newsom, J. D.	Michigan	1904	8 (China)	M		
Nusbaum, Aileen	New Mexico	1889		F	New Mexico	"Zuni Indian Tales" (1926)
Parker, Geraldine E.	Missouri			F		
Parkman, Mrs. Harrison	Kansas			F		
Pierce, Alvin B.	Washington			M		
Powers, Alfred	Oregon	1887		M		
Radin, Paul	California	1883	8 (Poland)	M		Anthropologist

Reese, Lisle	South Dakota	1910		M		
Richardson, Eudora Ramsay	Virginia	1892	3 (KY)	F	Virginia	*Life Alexander H. Stephens* (1932), *The Woman Speaker* (1936)
Richmond, Roaldus	Vermont	1910	1 (VT)	M		
Rollins, George A.	Illinois			M		
Santee, Ross	Arizona	1889	3 (IA)	M	AZ, IA	Writer and artist; "Cowboy"
Sassaman, Grant	Pennsylvania			M		
Saunders, A. M.	Maryland			M		
Saunders, B. W.	Wisconsin			M		
Saxon, Lyle	Louisiana	1891	1 (LA)	M	Louisiana	Bio. of Lafitte, novel *Children of Strangers*, set in Lafitte Country
Schlasinger, Ethel	North Dakota	1913	1 (ND)	F		
Shaw, Harry	NYC	1905	3 (SC)	M		
Sheehan, Elizabeth	Nebraska			F		"Poet & short story writer" May press release; mistress (Mangione 1972)
Shipton, Clifford K.	Massachusetts	1902	1 (MA)	M		Historian, archivist
Singewald, Karl	Maryland	1886	1 (MD)	M		Geologist
Spring, Agnes Wright	Wyoming	1894	2 (CO)	F	Wyoming	Monograph on WY history, from list
Stender, John L.	West Virginia			M		
Thompson, Jim	Oklahoma	1906	1 (OK)	M		
Tupper, Samuel Jr.	Georgia	1904	1 (GA)	M	Georgia	Novelist *Some Go Up* (1931), *Old Lady's Shoes* (1934), both set Atlanta
Ulrich, Mabel	Minnesota	1876		F		
Van Devort, T. D.	Nevada			M		
Van Olinda, Walter K.	New York City			M		
Wainger, Bertrand M.	New York	1902		M		
Wells, John W.	Kansas			M		
Westall, Dorris	Maine			F		Journalist
White, Charles Earnest	New Hampshire			M		
Williamson, David E.	Nevada			M		
Windhusen, Anne E.	Washington			F		
Young, William F., Jr.	Michigan			M		

up in Wyoming and, after studying at Harvard and Oxford, became a professor at the University of Montana. There he founded *Frontier and Midland*, a magazine that lasted from 1920 to 1939 and featured western writers, especially young ones, including A. B. Guthrie Jr., Wallace Stegner, and Weldon Kees, so it is not surprising that Merriam and *Frontier and Midland* got mentions in both the Wyoming and Montana Guides.[14] The third director appearing more than once was Arizona state director Ross Santee, another Iowan, who came to Arizona in his midtwenties and who wrote realistic fiction about the West. Both the Iowa and the Arizona Guides mention him and his highly regarded 1928 novel, *Cowboy*.

The typical state director was a man in his midforties, an editor, journalist, or educator born in the state itself or nearby. The oldest was Austin P. Foster. Born in 1859, Foster had a long career as an editor and historian, and he was well into his seventies during his brief tenure as Tennessee's state director. Swedish-born Edwin Bjorkman, a novelist, poet, critic, editor, and translator, was in his early seventies and had only lived in North Carolina for ten years when he came to head the North Carolina Project. He and W. T. Couch, his asssistant director lured away from the University of North Carolina Press, made a strong team and remained in charge. At the other extreme a half dozen or so state directors—including Jay Du Von (Iowa), Lisle Reese (South Dakota), Roaldus Richmond (Vermont), Philip Conley and Dorris Westall (both in Maine), Ethel Schlasinger (North Dakota), and Dale Morgan (Utah)—were only in their twenties. Most directors however were born in the 1880s or 1890s. They were part of a generation that saw the United States go from an assemblage of diverse, mostly agricultural states and territories to an industrial nation and international power. As they were becoming adults they had experienced the social transformations wrought by the telephone, the automobile, urbanization, world war, women's rights, and mass migration from eastern and southern Europe and, for African Americans, from the South to the North. No generation had witnessed a broader set of changes impacting the everyday lives of Americans.

Almost one quarter of the state directors, 27 out of 116 or 23 percent, were women. (As we shall see, this is identical to the percentage of female authors mentioned in the Literature essays). All directors were white. I know the birthplaces of fifty-three of them: twenty-seven were born in the same state where they became director, with another five born in the same region; sixteen were born outside of the region, and five outside

14. Information from University of Montana Creative Writing Program, http://www.cas.umt.edu/english/creative_writing/Merriam-FrontierAward.html.

of the United States. Many of the initial appointments didn't last long. Sometimes the problem was drink, sometimes incompetence, sometimes politics. New York State's opaque story of whistle blowing and political intrigue, told in appendix C, exemplified both the revolving directorships during the early months and the political pitfalls in that fraught era.

Washington and the States

During the early months, the State Projects were mainly concerned with hiring, always with Washington looking over their shoulders. Desperate writers applied by the thousands, but many found the "means test" by which an applicant had to prove he or she was a pauper to be degrading. Even worse, unemployed writers who had somehow managed to avoid going on relief were thus ineligible; the Authors League complained bitterly that the very people whom the league's emergency fund had assisted were thereby frozen out of the federal jobs.

A second structural problem was the immense geographic disparity in available talent. Although Alsberg envisioned professional writers on the Project, most professionals lived in cities, New York above all but also Chicago, Boston, Philadelphia, Los Angeles, and San Francisco.[15] Since the WPA's charge was to create jobs in every state, however, that's the way the Federal Writers' Project was set up. This meant that the number of Project jobs available in New York City did not come close to meeting the local need, while states like Montana and Alabama had nowhere near enough professional writers to staff the State Projects. Qualifications were very relaxed in such places; a common quip was that applicants in the hinterlands could qualify even if their only previous writing experience was forging checks.

The Authors League of America, Authors League Fund, and Writers Union all protested the geographic dispersion. We have previously seen the letter the Authors League Fund head wrote to Harry Hopkins fuming about "the means test, together with the stupid arrangement by which each state has been given a certain amount of money regardless of whether the state has writers or not."[16] The writer had a point: The Writers Union reported that New York City had 3,500 writers officially registered as destitute, while the Project's quota was only 447. Nevertheless, every state had to come up with its own destitute writers.

Outside of New York, state directors and WPA administrators respon-

15. "Probably half of the project's actual [i.e., professional] writers would come from New York City, Chicago, Boston, Philadelphia, and Los Angeles" (Penkower [1977]: 58).

16. Mangione (1972): 97–98.

sible for the actual hiring quickly recognized that the definition of "writer" had to be generous. The Federal One proposal had called for "writers, editors, historians, research workers, art critics, architects, archeologists, map draftsmen, geologists, and other professionals, . . . although a major part of the personnel will be made up of writers exclusively." The practical Reed Harris wrote to one WPA administrator that a writer might come from "almost any other occupation that involved an understanding of the English language and some training and observations in the preparation of records."[17] Sometimes a prospective employee was the genuine article. No account of the Project fails to mention its important or soon-to-be-important writers including Conrad Aiken, Nelson Algren, Saul Bellow, John Cheever, Ralph Ellison, Zora Neale Hurston, Studs Terkel, Margaret Walker, and Richard Wright; as this list indicates, the support that the Project afforded to African American writers is especially notable.[18] Regardless of race, however, few Project writers had talent of this caliber or even much experience. The Minnesota state director described her applicants:

> There were preachers, lawyers, executives, and editors mostly of country papers or small trade journals (older men these); there was a graduate from the University of Edinburgh and a Ph.D. from Munich, a girl from the Paris Sorbonne, a colored woman physician, and a writer of vaudeville skits; there was a publicity man whose salary "before his nervous breakdown" had been, he claimed, ten thousand dollars. . . . All had "written a little," usually adding, "not much published, you understand, but at college I used to get awfully good marks in English." . . . It was tacitly conceded that for emergency purposes the designation *writer* might be interpreted with considerable latitude.[19]

At its November 1935 launching, the Federal Writers' Project had 4,016 employees, and by early 1936 it had over 6,000. It peaked in April of that year, and its average was 4,500–5,200 over the life of the Project.[20] Man-

17. Penkower (1977): 58–59.

18. Black writers were concentrated in New York City (Claude McKay, Ralph Ellison), Chicago (Richard Wright, Arna Bontemps, Katherine Dunham), and Louisiana. In Washington Sterling Brown was editor for *Negro Affairs*, though he was more successful with content than with personnel. In the South discrimination kept many qualified black writers off the project, and overall the numbers are less impressive than the Hurston/Ellison/Wright constellation might suggest. Penkower (1977: 67) cites one report of February 1937 that indicated there were 106 African Americans working on the Project, out of a total of 4,500, an unimpressive 2 percent.

19. Ulrich (1939): 654, 655.

20. "A Brief History of the Federal Writers' Project" is in the Katharine Kellock papers in the Library of Congress Manuscript Division; she apparently wrote it sometime after August 1939. It says that the employment figures peaked at 6,686 in April 1936. With it is a one-page memo called "Writers" that

gione estimated that up to 40 percent of FWP employees were women.[21] This may be a bit high; a list of the Washington staff at one point compiled by Katharine Kellock shows forty-two men and eleven women. Since the WPA's average monthly employment was 2,060,000, a mere 0.25 percent of WPA workers were on the Project.

Wages were higher for Writers' Project workers than for manual workers and were adjusted to the regional cost of living. New York City professionals got $93.50–$103.50 monthly, while their counterparts in Mississippi and Georgia got $39.00.[22] To men and women who had been out of work for years, the paychecks meant everything. They worried constantly, especially after the summer of 1936, about funding cuts and getting "pink slips" or being "403'd" (laid off). Illinois state director John Frederick said that although his project was full of radical writers, their protests and demands seldom interfered with their work because "a good 80 percent of the workers were so dependent on their monthly checks and so grateful for them that they would do nothing that could conceivably endanger them."[23] State Project offices seethed with anxiety, which turned out to be justified. After sharp cuts in WPA funding in 1937, the New England units, which had finished their State Guides, were all but closed down, and staff levels were cut everywhere.

State Project writers were motivated, but many grew demoralized by criticism. Unlike the other Arts Projects that immediately began turning out concerts, plays, and art classes, the Writers' Project produced no visible results for well over a year, so it was easy for the press to label their work as boondoggling. Much of the criticism was partisan, coming from anti–New Deal newspapers like the *Chicago Tribune*, *Baltimore Sun*, and *New York Herald-Tribune*. The editorial sniping died down once the State Guides began to come out, but it would be months before this happened. So state staffs were worried about being fired, were confused by changing signals from Washington, were attacked by the local press, and were filled with, and sometimes led by, people of talent and dedication but also people who were drunks, layabouts, political hacks, and mediocrities. Nevertheless they had to turn out copy, and they did.

At peak employment in late 1936 and early 1937, a typical State Writers' Project would have a staff of a hundred or so workers. The director, along

updates the figures; it gives the employment figures as follows: May 1935, 2381; April 1936, 6686; August 1939, 3366; August 1941, 1900. This first must be an error, for the Project didn't exist until August; in "A Brief History" she says the Project had 2,381 in 1935, no month, so presumably this is toward the end of the year. In any event Kellock's upper figure is in line with Mangione's.

21. Mangione (1972): 88.

22. Figures are from Penkower (1977), ch. 3.

23. Mangione (1972): 84.

with an assistant director and various editors, would be in the central office, usually located in the state's largest city rather than the state capital. Many states had district offices as well; for example, Massachusetts had six, each with a district supervisor. Employees would fan out, gathering information, interviewing people, scouring newspaper archives, and mapping highways. They would feed their field notes into the district supervisor, who vetted them and sent them on to the central office, where more experienced writers and editors would transform them into acceptable copy. In the preface to *Vermont: A Guide to the Green Mountain State*, State Director Dana Doten described the process:

> A score or more of research workers scattered throughout the State were engaged for over a year in gathering data and in forwarding it to Montpelier. A handful of editors in the central office sifted and checked and revised this accumulation. A still smaller group took the results in hand and in mind and went out on the road, covering every foot of the tours (in some cases driving over sections three or four times), and returned to piece together the mosaic of the tour descriptions. A great amount of independent research by the editors was, of course, also required before any final copy could be produced. And the contributions of voluntary assistants and consultants (of which, fortunately, almost every town furnished generous examples) had to be incorporated. But even then it sounds simpler than it was.

Since the writers themselves were a heterogeneous lot characterized by their poverty rather than by their depth of local knowledge, the "voluntary assistants and consultants" were critically important. Central office editors would seek help from local authorities: professors, librarians, historians, state officials, business leaders, and local residents with long memories. The preface to *Maine: A Guide "Down East"* gives a sense of the range of experts:

> Thanks are also due the following for expert advice and assistance in their special fields: H. L. Baldwin, of the Boston and Maine Railroad; Alexander M. Bower, Director of the L. D. M. Sweat Museum, Portland; Philip J. Brockway, Placement Director at the University of Maine; Freeman F. Burr, State Geologist; Judge Benjamin F. Cleaves, Secretary of Associated Industry; Harry B. Coe, of the Maine Publicity Bureau; Cressey and Allen Music Company, Portland; William S. Crowell, Maine W.P.A. Director of the Division of Operations, Portland; Mrs. Fanny Hardy Eckstorm, Brewer; Judge Edward K. Gould, State Historian; Professor Orren C. Hormell, of Bowdoin College; Captain Alfred E. Mulliken, of the State Planning Board; Dorothy Hay, of the Maine W.P.A. Art Project; Arthur H. Horton, Curator of the Portland Society of Natural History; Colonel Henry W. Owen, Bath; the late Professor Edward H. Perkins, of Colby College; John

Calvin Stevens, Portland; George J. Stobie, State Fish and Game Commissioner; Professor William J. Wilkinson, of Colby College.

Two things about the Maine list stand out. First, it is almost entirely male, with only two women among the eighteen names mentioned. Second, it is tilted toward the private liberal arts colleges (Bowdoin and Colby) rather than the state university, and toward Portland, Maine's largest city. Thus a New Deal project in a rural state that had a woman director nevertheless shows the usual biases toward the elite, the male, and the urban.

When a state director decided that a section of copy was ready for review, or when Alsberg demanded to see some product, the copy went to Washington. There George Cronyn and the other editors would have at it. The manuscript, marked up and with accompanying (often scathing) editorial comments, would go back to the state, and the cycle would repeat. The first deadline for all states to send their copy to Washington was May 15, 1936. When the copy arrived, the Washington editors were dismayed by its poor quality.[24] The Washington staff saw this was not going to be easy, but by then the Project had a longer time horizon. Throughout the life of the Project Alsberg demanded that every part of every Guide get approval from Washington. Each manuscript went to Alsberg and Cronyn, who passed it on to various editors in the DC office. They wrote comments, and Alsberg or Cronyn sent a letter back to the state director with the general comments and edited manuscript pages.

The letters that passed between the Washington and state offices amount to a perpetual tug-of-war for control over the final product. Beyond quality of writing, at issue were comprehensiveness, judgment, and the central office's incessant demand for the Guides to be standardized. Ray Billington, the Massachusetts state director and a liberal who had been bedeviled by the radicals on his own staff, later recalled: "Scarcely less annoying than the Communist irrationality was the attitude of Washington officialdom. I think back on those days as a continuous battle with Alsberg and his staff. Of course they were right. We wanted to create a guide for Massachusetts that would mirror the situation in the state. . . . Washington wanted and had to have a standard pattern. How we fought each decision aimed at uniformity!"[25] Minnesota's Mabel Ulrich blamed Washington's naïveté, which "complicated matters considerably for the States, especially as the [Washington] editorial staff made up with

24. As Penkower (1977) reports, "Workers gave little thought to proportion and balanced accounts. Chicago, Detroit, and Baltimore overshadowed the rest of their respective guides. Colorado's history essay devoted one paragraph out of twenty-two pages to post-1894 events" (80).

25. Mangione (1972): 86.

enthusiasm for its lack of experience. All had a vital interest in proletariat warfare, a deep suspicion of chambers of commerce, distrusted all statements not found in their often-outmoded source books, and were undoubtedly overworked. To their inexperience must be charged the false starts and many of the fantasies that drove many a State director to the verge of lunacy."[26]

One of the original state directors who had seen his Guide through to completion, North Carolina's Edwin Bjorkman, was more diplomatic. His preface to *North Carolina: A Guide to the Old North State* (1939) included a description of how the project had operated over the previous three-and-a-half years:

> The Federal Writers' Project of North Carolina was started in October 1935, with headquarters in Asheville, and district offices were established later in seven other cities of the State. The project was primarily designed to provide work for unemployed writers, journalists, and research workers. Little by little—from books and periodicals, from chambers of commerce and State departments, out of the memories of kindly disposed individuals, and by actual travel over all the main highways—the workers collected and sent to State headquarters between one and two million words of roughly transcribed source material.
>
> By a long and arduous process of sifting, elimination, and condensation, this enormous mass of material was gradually reduced to the desired essentials. Then followed the no less difficult task of arrangement, formulation, revision, and thorough checking for accuracy. Out of all this cooperative effort has emerged the present volume. (viii)

Such an organization and procedures were roughly the same in every state. The soul of discretion, Bjorkman makes no mention of the conflict with Washington.

The View from New Jersey

Tracing the life of an individual State Project reveals the political and operational challenges. New Jersey's first director was Burton Kline, a Harvard-educated journalist who had been special assistant to the secretary of labor during the Harding, Coolidge, and Hoover administrations. He didn't last more than a few weeks, and the reason for his swift departure seems to have been political; an innuendo-strewn account in the *Newark Ledger* said that both the New Jersey and New York Projects were "honeycombed

26. Ulrich (139) 656.

with Reds."[27] Be that as it may, as of February 1936 the new director of the New Jersey Project was Irene Fuhlbruegge, a former leader of the New Jersey League of Women Voters and the wife of a social science professor. Over and above keeping an eye out for radicalism, she labored mightily to allay the suspicions of the business community and fend off the notorious Hague machine's attempts to use the Project for patronage jobs; she was never entirely successful at any of these attempts, but it wasn't for lack of effort.[28] Despite these local problems as well as the general ones of conflicting directions from Washington and uncertainty about funding, Fuhlbruegge was enterprising, and the New Jersey Project produced a steady stream of publications, including one—*Matawan 1686–1936*—that came out when the Project was less than a year old.

Correspondence between Washington and Newark (as elsewhere, the Project office was in the largest city rather than in the capital, Trenton) gives a glimpse of how each side tried to manage the vexed relationship. On January 22, 1936, Burton Kline, the original state director, wrote to Alsberg to thank him for sending sample briefs that were "uniformly bully," and promising to "send you some humdingers" in return. At the close he added, "Incedentally [*sic*], I owe you a grovelling apology for having sassed the boss when I saw you last. There was no excuse for the outburst, and I sincerely regret it, especially since I have had nothing but unfailing courtesy and helpfulness from yourself." This exchange gives some idea of what Alsberg had to deal with and suggests there may have been editorial as well as political reasons why Kline didn't last long.

On May 26, 1936, Fuhlbruegge wrote to Alsberg about the poor quality of most local histories ("people would be better off if they didn't read them"). In response to his request that she cover New Jersey folklore, she airily asserted that there wasn't any:

> I do not believe we have any folklore, other than the old wives' tales and superstitions, which are universal. However, because I am always open to proof, I have sent your outline of folklore to each district asking that they make a special effort to get stories concerning any of the topics enumerated. Mr. Arthur B. Reeve of Trenton responded with a story about the "Jersey Devil," this famous personage being said to appear in certain South Jersey counties before each war. No one else with whom I have had

27. *Newark Ledger*, November 29, 1938.

28. See Mangione (1972). Frank Hague was the mayor of Jersey City for thirty years (1917–47) and the boss of the state's Democratic machine at all levels. He was effective, flexible (he organized a huge rally for FDR in 1932 despite having previously supported Al Smith), and notoriously corrupt. Case in point: In 1937 Jersey City had 160,050 registered voters despite having only 147,000 adults of voting age (Jersey City University, "Jersey City, Past and Present," http://www.njcu.edu/programs/jchistory/Pages/H_Pages/Hague_Frank.htm).

> contact seems to have heard of this monster and I am somewhat of the opinion that perhaps this is another of Mr. Reeve's creations.[29]

She also told Alsberg that since there was scant information on Indians, "an introductory essay of a few paragraphs" should do. All this flew in the face of Washington's stipulation that every State Guide should include an essay on folklore and one on Indians. Alsberg and Cronyn gave the essays top priority, and as New Deal liberals, they wanted plenty of social history, not just accounts of great men and battles; while they were not particularly focused on Native Americans, "a few paragraphs" would not suffice. Washington got what it wanted: *New Jersey: A Guide to Its Present and Past* ended up with a chapter on "Archeology and Indians" and another on "Folklore and Folkways," though such standardization came at the expense of what the locals considered important.

In August 1936 Alsberg sent a list of questions to every state asking about, among other things, publication plans, whether they had placed employees in private industry, well-known writers, and the number of Negroes employed on the project. Fuhlbruegge replied a week later: New Jersey had no plans for publication of its Guide, though some local guides were being sponsored by towns; five Negroes were gathering "a résumé of negro activities"; five published writers worked on the project; and although twenty-four project employees had found jobs in the private sector, "we do not feel that we have been in any way responsible for this employment" (such frankness must have been discouraging to the folks in Washington).

Lack of funds was a nagging problem, as when Fuhlbruegge asked about getting "printed cards on New Jersey books" from the Library of Congress for free (she had been discussing setting up a catalog of New Jersey materials with the New Jersey Historical Society), and Reed Harris wrote back saying the library would not reduce its price. Equally vexing were the bureaucratic strictures. A flurry of letters went back and forth in early 1937 when Harris chastised Fuhlbruegge for allowing her name to appear on some of New Jersey's school publications. Anonymity, along with an insistence that Project publications were collective efforts not individual ones, was something of an obsession with the Washington office. "I am sorry that this point ever had to be raised," Harris wrote, "but it is really true that feelings are pretty strong on such matters and Mr. Hopkins, himself, on occasion expressed interest in having publications done as anonymously

29. Fuhlbruegge showed a surprising ignorance in this case, for the Pine Barrens of southern New Jersey had been giving rise to stories and sightings of the Jersey Devil since at least the eighteenth century. In the end she must have been convinced, for the Jersey Devil, also called the Leeds Devil, made it into the New Jersey Guide for two full pages.

as possible, as far as individuals are concerned."[30] Fuhlbruegge was suitably apologetic, suppressing any hint of irritation.

Complaints from New Jersey's business community never abated. The November 30, 1937, newsletter of the Camden Chamber of Commerce reported the general feeling that "most of the descriptions of New Jersey communities would hardly be pleasing to their citizens and seem to have been written by disgruntled and embittered writers who have gone out of their way to dwell, in sarcastic language, upon unpleasant incidents [no doubt referring to labor conflicts] while ignoring worthwhile institutions and accomplishments of which our communities are so justly proud." Fuhlbruegge defended the project against such "unfair impressions," but the battle was ongoing.[31] Mayors demanded to see preliminary copy, a request Fuhlbruegge refused. Objections of this type, while not crippling in themselves given the state director's firm hand, laid the groundwork for the congressional charges of subversion that were to come.

In spite of uncertainty and opposition, the New Jersey staff was wildly energetic, developing library projects, city and county histories, school pamphlets, and children's books as well as the New Jersey Guide. One result was *Stories of New Jersey*, a series of school bulletins; the first was on Stephen Crane and the second on Robert Louis Stevenson, two New Jersey–connected authors (Stevenson spent some time on the Jersey coast). In 1938 the project published a compilation of these bulletins. More controversially, nine New Jersey writers from District Six in Morristown, working (or so they claimed) on their own time, put together a little magazine called *6 x 9*. They intended it to be a periodical, although only one issue ever materialized, and they sent a copy to Alsberg, who was not impressed, comparing it to an undergraduate literary magazine. He had a point—poems with lines like "Narcotic moons and anesthetic stars / Subdue meek pulses" give some idea of the literary quality—but Alsberg's real concern was that the Project needed to show it was working on socially useful projects rather than facilitating creative writing on the taxpayers' dime. Even worse, "narcotic moons" came from a poetic tribute to Tom Mooney, a labor agitator imprisoned twenty years earlier for involvement in a San Francisco bombing; Mooney's (possibly wrongful) conviction was a cause célèbre among radicals of the twenties and thirties.[32] A poetic tribute to an anarchist was the last thing the Federal Writers' Project needed.

30. Letter from Reed Harris to Irene Fuhlbruegge, February 18, 1937.

31. Letter from Irene Fuhlbruegge to Loyal D. Odhner, Secretary, Camden Chamber of Commerce, December 7, 1937.

32. Arnesen (2007): 1336; *Wikipedia*, http://en.wikipedia.org/wiki/Thomas_Mooney, retrieved April 21, 2011.

When some copy generated strong protests from both Atlantic City's public schools and its Chamber of Commerce, Fuhlbruegge complained to Alsberg that the problem was that the Newark Public Library, one of the sponsors, insisted on local approval for each city essay, and Fuhlbruegge argued that there was no way a local approval requirement could result in a "good book."[33] But that, of course, was the problem: Local views on what was "a good book" were often at odds with those of the Project. Case in point: Having revised her dismissive views on Indians, on May 19, 1938, Fuhlbruegge sent Alsberg two copies of *Stories of New Jersey*, Indian Series, Bulletin 1, "The Creation Myth." A state board of education official expressed alarm because the creation myth, which involved a turtle rising from the waters to create land, might raise questions about sex. Fuhlbruegge quotes him as saying:

> There are three subjects which the State Board of Education never permits to be discussed in New Jersey public schools: religion, sex and communism. . . . You do discuss creation and to little children that means where babies come from. It is my belief that by issuing this bulletin you will have started off on the wrong foot in many localities. The State Board of Education does not have time to take care of complaints so we, therefore, make every effort to avoid any criticisms.[34]

Fuhlbruegge suggested that Alsberg use the story to illustrate the headaches raised by the Project's requirement of local sponsorship, but such buy-in at the state level was simply a political necessity.

Fuhlbruegge's tortured relationship with Washington came to a head in August 1938 when she sent Alsberg her letter of resignation. As she told the story that November, Alsberg spent three months trying to persuade her to reconsider, but she was unmoved; "My resignation was given after deliberate thought for two reasons: politics in the New Jersey W. P. A. and inefficiency in the Washington office of the project."[35] By politics she was specifically referring to the pressure to hire politically connected (i.e., Hague machine–connected) writers instead of competent ones. The *New York Herald-Tribune* summed up her explanation:

> Supplementing her statement Mrs. Fuhlbruegge, whose husband is a professor at the University of Newark, said that for almost three years she "tolerated and tried to minimize" the political hold over the W. P. A. in New Jersey [the Hague machine, which controlled the state's Democratic Party] and did the best she could in spite of

33. Letter from Irene Fuelbruegge to Henry Alsberg, May 18, 1938.
34. Letter from Irene Fuelbruegge to Henry Alsberg, May 19, 1938.
35. *New York Herald-Tribune*, November 30, 1938.

it. The situation become so acute before the recent election that it was impossible to continue she said. She cited instances in which she was forced to drop competent, well-qualified writers to keep under the quota because she was unable to dismiss persons who were incompetent but who had political connections.

Since last summer, when the W. P. A. regional office here started certifying W. P. A. enrollees, no one, however competent, could get on the Writers' Project, unless he was "right politically," Mrs. Fuhlbruegge charged. This condition, she alleged, left the project with such a dearth of competent writers that it was unable to function efficiently and turn out the work required. She had a choice of accepting "writers" who could not write or accepting none at all, she said.

The state WPA administrator distanced himself ("It's strictly a matter between Alsberg and Mrs. Fuhlbruegge"). So did Washington: Alsberg and other WPA officials had no comment for the *Herald-Tribune*, and "one W. P. A. spokesman, informed that Mrs. Fuhlbruegge had alleged that politics made it impossible for her to continue, asked 'So what?'" Fuhlbruegge insisted that the "politics" that drove her out were local New Jersey patronage politics. However with the coming election, the reduction in the Project budget, quotas following the 1937 recession, and the Dies Committee's relentless rooting around for subversion, national-level politics seem clearly to have played a role.

Martin Dies Jr. was a Democratic congressman from Texas. Although he had been an early supporter of the New Deal, by 1937 he had joined up with southern conservative Democrats and Republicans in opposing the administration.[36] The 1920s and '30s had seen a series of congressional committees investigating radical and "un-American" activities. Some pro-Nazi rallies in the spring of 1938, combined with the long-standing alarm about Communism, spurred House approval of Dies's resolution to appoint a new investigative committee to monitor Nazi and Communist threats. The Special Committee to Investigate Un-American Activities (at the time everyone called it the Dies Committee, and later it became the House Un-American Activities Committee) had seven members: two Republicans, three conservative Democrats, and two liberal Democrats.[37] Enormous publicity surrounded the committee hearings, which some-

36. Dies was "particularly troubled by the administration's apparent sympathy for sit-down strikers in the automobile factories of Flint and Detroit, Eleanor Roosevelt's persistent advocacy of anti-lynching legislation and other human-rights issues, the court-packing scheme of 1937 that would have added administration supporters to the U.S. Supreme Court, and FDR's attempt to purge the party of anti-New Deal southern Democrats during the 1938 primary elections" (O'Reilly [2000]).

37. The Republicans were J. Parnell Thomas of New Jersey and Noah Mason of Illinois; the conservative Democrats were Harold Mosier of Ohio, Joe Starnes of Alabama, and Dies; the liberal Democrats were Arthur Healey of Massachusetts and John J. Dempsey of New Mexico.

times veered into anti-Communist hysteria. Parnell Thomas of New Jersey focused on the WPA and especially on the Arts Projects. Federal One administrators, and Alsberg in particular, didn't expect the committee's aggressiveness and were unprepared.

In late summer the Dies Committee began holding hearings, some secret, in which disgruntled employees and others testified regarding subversion in the Writers' Project, and some of them cited the New Jersey Project as a prime case. "Representative Dies, chairman of the House committee investigating un-American activities, [charged] that State guides compiled by the Federal Writers Project contained 'propaganda and appeals to class hatred.' The New Jersey guide was said by a committee witness to be 'the most flagrant of all.'"[38] A few days before Fuhlbruegge's resignation went public (but weeks after she had submitted the letter), Chairman Dies charged that "the New Jersey section of The American Guide, principal work of the Writers' Project, contained propaganda and inflammatory material."[39] Fuhlbruegge always denied that the Dies Committee's investigation had anything to do with her decision, just as she denied earlier newspaper reports that she had been dismissed, but the timing suggested otherwise. She held a press conference on November 29 to clarify that she had resigned and not been fired.

Fuhlbruegge had long complained about Washington interference. Though she claimed her resignation was triggered by having been forced to retain two incompetent "political leaders" and dismiss two men doing "excellent work," she went on to criticize the Washington editorial control bitterly.[40] A very different version of the story appears in the *Newark Ledger*, however, under the headline "Mrs. Fuhlbruegge Ousted from Writers' Project." The *Ledger* reported that she was "ushered out of her job . . . in the wake of Dies Committee charges that her project was the worst Communist nest of WPA writers in the country."[41]

One can speculate that the scenario was something like this: By summer of 1938 Fuhlbruegge was exhausted. Pushed to the brink by losing

38. *New York Times*, November 30, 1938.

39. *Newark Evening News*, November 29, 1938.

40. *New York Times*, November 30, 1938.

41. *Newark Ledger*, November 29, 1938. According to this version of events, Fuhlbruegge had sent Alsberg a letter of resignation in August because she wanted "to retire because of temporary poor health," and Alsberg was using the convenient letter to dismiss her now. The paper describes Fuhlbruegge as formerly "active in civil and political [activities] and in the trade union movement," thus implying she was a radical. It also reported that when she was confronted with the Dies Committee charges about "appeals to class hatred . . . statements [that] criticized our system of government and that the tenor of them was incendiary, she snapped: 'Don't be ridiculous!' and refused further comment." (That part sounds plausible.)

control over which workers should be dismissed, she impulsively resigned but was in fact ambivalent. Alsberg was equally ambivalent: The New Jersey Project was a pain in the neck, but it was also productive and its many publications helped justify the Project overall to an increasingly skeptical Congress. During the fall he encouraged her (perhaps not wholeheartedly) to remain, and she wavered. When the Dies Committee began its probing, she decided she needed to get her own version of events out there. She gave the November 29 press conference and made her resignation effective a few days later.

Of course the whole affair was red meat to the anti–New Deal press. The *Macon (GA) Telegraph* headlined the story "Politics in WPA" and reported Fuhlbruegge's comment that "no one could get on the pay roll unless 'politically right.'" It ended with a jab: "But there must be a mistake somewhere. Harry Hopkins says there is no politics in WPA."[42]

Whatever the truth of the matter, Fuhlbruegge was out and Viola Hutchinson was now in charge, but New Jersey's problems were by no means over. In early 1939 as *New Jersey: A Guide to Its Present and Past* was going to press, the political heat on Alsberg was intense. The New Jersey Guild Associates, a writers' union, wrote a foreword to the Guide that apparently apologized for soft-pedaling the state's labor history. Viking Press did not want to include it, and in a letter of February 2 the firm's president told Alsberg that the foreword was "especially unwise in its present form. It is apologetic in tone, it suggests omissions far more serious than those actually existing, and it invites hostile criticism from any number of sources."[43] Alsberg concurred. On April 5 Hutchinson sent Alsberg a revised foreword. Her letter contained the damning-with-faint-praise remark that "although the social scene could have been better portrayed by including a few facts (especially in reference to strikes) that were adjudged unsuitable for this volume, there can be no doubt that the Federal Writers' Project has done an excellent piece of work."[44]

Yes indeed, for in spite of everything, *New Jersey: A Guide to Its Present and Past* was "one of the best in the American Guide series," according to Jerre Mangione. The Project also produced a slew of other books—*Bergen County Panorama*; *New Jersey: A Profile in Pictures*; *Old Princeton's Neighbors*; *The Swedes and Finns of New Jersey*; and so on—thereby putting New Jersey among the most prolific states, along with California, Illinois, Iowa,

42. *Macon (GA) Telegraph*, December 2, 1938.

43. Letter to Alsberg from HKG (signature is indecipherable), president of Viking Press, February 2, 1929.

44. Letter from Viola Hutchinson to Henry Alsberg, February 5, 1939.

Massachusetts, Ohio, Pennsylvania, as well as New York City.[45] The New Jersey Project was a mess, but its legacy was commendable.

It was from such insecurities as New Jersey faced, insecurities that were bureaucratic, political, and financial, that the American Guide Series emerged. In light of the problems that beset the central and state offices of the Project, the quality of the books themselves is something of a miracle. The next chapter will examine the State Guides that came out of all the chaos.

45. Others included *Entertaining a Nation: The Career of Long Branch*; *Livingston: The Story of a Community*; *Matawan 1686–1936*; *Monroe Township, Middlesex County, New Jersey 1838–1938*; *New Jersey* (American Recreation Series); *Princeton's Fire Fighters, 1788–1938*; *Proceedings of the New Jersey State Constitutional Convention of 1844*; *The Records of the Swedish Lutheran Churches at Raccoon and Penns Neck, 1713–1786*; *Ridgefield Park Fire Department*; *Stories of New Jersey: Its Significant Places, People and Activities*; *The Story of Dunellen*; and *The Story of Wyckoff*—an impressive record.

SIX

Describing America

The people so often sleepy, weary, enigmatic,
Is a vast huddle with many units saying:
    "I earn my living.
    I make enough to get by
    and it takes all my time.
    If I had more time
    I could do more for myself
    and maybe for others.
    I could read and study
    and talk things over
    and find out about things.
    It takes time.
    I wish I had the time."

CARL SANDBURG, *THE PEOPLE, YES*

The Federal Writers' Project would give its employees time to "find out about things," and to write about them for the country as a whole. Describing America was not easy, nor could it be done quickly. While the other three Arts Projects immediately started turning out concerts and art classes and plays, the Writers' Project had nothing to show for months. Since the Project was driven by the need to come up with something (anything!), its first publications were less than compelling. In 1936, when Federal One was less than a year old, the Pennsylvania Project managed to bring out the twenty-four-page *3 Hikes through the Wissahickon*, New Jersey produced *Matawan, 1686–1936*, and the Arkansas Project claimed first place with its *Guide to North Little Rock*. Not everyone was impressed. When a beaming Alsberg showed the Little Rock pamphlet to New York City's WPA administrator, an Arkansas native, the latter responded, "Who in the hell wants a guide to North Little Rock? Don't you know it's the asshole of the world?"[1]

Once the State Guides started coming out in 1937, the American Guide Series finally could be seen offering something useful and Alsberg could breathe easier. Over the next five years the states took up a wide range of projects over and above the State Guides. Many resulted in publications, while others fell by the wayside when the Second World War started. There are various estimates of how many people worked on the Project—6,500 at the outset is the usual figure—and how many works came into print. If we consider only the books and pamphlets that appeared over the life of the Project, somewhere around 600 publications is a reasonable guess.[2]

The State Guides always held top priority—Alsberg recognized that pamphlets on Matawan or the Wissahickon, let alone North Little Rock, weren't going to impress anyone—and they required the most extended effort. During the two-and-a-half years from the beginning of 1937 until the reorganization of mid-1939, that effort was at its peak. This chapter looks at the Project's unfolding and at the State Guides that were its crowning achievement.

The Short Life and Long Death of the Federal Writers' Project

At the beginning of 1936, every State Project had its project office set up, state directors in place, and writers (sometimes that term should be in

1. Mangione (1972): 89. Penkower (1977) reports that *3 Hikes* actually came out first.

2. Given the constant churning, employment figures are estimates, but most commentators agree that even at its height, the Federal Writers' Project was modest in size, never topping 7,000 employees. Ray Allen Billington, who had been the Massachusetts state director, wrote in 1961 that within six months of its launching some 6,500 workers were employed on the Writers' Project; in comparison there were 16,000 on the Music Project, 12,500 on the Theater Project, and 5,000 on the Arts Project (Billington [1961]: 468). Forty-seven years later Nick Taylor repeats the 6,500 figure (N. Taylor [2008]: 297).

As for the number of publications, it is impossible to come up with a final count of publications from the Federal Writers' Project. Some works were mimeographed, some were recorded as published but never were, and some continued to come out after the Project itself had closed down (indeed they still do). Merle Colby's final report of 1942 lists several hundred unpublished manuscripts, a few of which have been published in the years since. The bulk of materials, including pamphlets and ephemera as well as records, remained in the state repositories. Some were lost altogether; the story is that when nobody paid the storage fees for the Maine Project files, they were thrown into the Portland harbor. In Project records as in much else, the abrupt disruption of the Second World War meant that there was no final accounting. Mangione (1972) lists publications by state and comes up with "more than four hundred." Selvaggio (1990) lists the publications that booksellers Arthur Scharf and Schoyer's Books had on record; their combined holdings offered the most complete collection that had been assembled. He comes up with 730 titles, including a few "After Hours" projects like *American Stuff*, plus six catalogs, but this list includes some duplication, and of course does not capture more recent publications.

scare quotes) hired. A few pamphlets began trickling out. Funding was assured until the summer, but not beyond. In light of the relentless journalistic and congressional carping about the WPA in general and the Writers' Project in particular, Alsberg was feeling the pressure to show more substantial results. Specifically, he needed to be able to produce some State Guides. Both Washington and the State Projects were learning on the job. Once the flow of contradictory manuals and the turnover of state directors slowed down, a handful of states managed to finish the work of putting a book together.

The first three Guides were instructive, for each managed to exemplify what Washington desperately did *not* want the American Guides Series to be: idiosyncratic, boring, and radical. Idaho (as in idiosyncratic) came in first. The director of that state's Writers' Project was Vardis Fisher, an Idaho-born writer from a pioneer Mormon family and an English PhD from the University of Chicago who had taught at Utah and NYU. A headstrong libertarian, Fisher grudgingly supported the New Deal, though later he would turn against it. Having recently returned to Idaho to write and farm, Fisher seemed a good choice for state director, although at the time he claimed that he was appointed because Idaho had only three real writers—Ernest Hemingway, Ezra Pound, and himself—and he was the only one who was unemployed. One biographical source describes him as "temperamental and obstinate," while his *New York Times* obituary in 1973 quoted an early review: "Proud, immensely learned . . . fiercely opinionated and belligerently prejudiced, Mr. Fisher seems like a sort of literary Savonarola from Idaho, fiercely denouncing the vanities of an idolatrous generation."[3] Inevitably, Fisher was going to make sure that the Idaho Guide was done *his* way. And done quickly too, which was achievable since he did most of the fact gathering and writing by himself.

Fisher frustrated central-office efforts to rein him in. Alsberg wanted the Washington, DC, Guide to come out first in order to cultivate congressional favor and appease those who saw boondoggling in the Project as a whole, but Fisher finished the Idaho Guide and was ready to publish with a local press. Alsberg and Cronyn tried to slow things down with various editorial quibbles and reminders that government employees could not insert personal judgments into the text, most of which Fisher chose to ignore. He also ignored the directive that all State Guide tours should

3. "Temperamental and opinionated" comes from the *American National Biography Online* (ANBO) article on "Vardis Alvero Fisher": http://www.anb.org.turing.library.northwestern.edu/articles/16/16-02010.html?a=1&n=fisher&s=10&d=10&ss=18&q=24. "Proud, immensely learned . . ." comes from a *New York Times* obituary, July 11, 1968, "Vardis Fisher, 73, Novelist, Is Dead." The obituary writer is quoting Orville Prescott's 1953 review of Fisher's book, *God or Caesar: The Writing of Fiction for Beginners*.

move from east to west and from north to south, a directive that vividly illustrates the New York–centric vantage point of the project as a whole. No one travels Idaho north to south, Fisher remarked, so he calmly organized the Idaho tours from south to north. Resisting all the efforts to hold back publication (once he got a supervisor from the Washington office too drunk to carry out his mission), Fisher succeeded in bringing *Idaho: A Guide in Word and Picture* out in January 1937, the first State Guide in the series. Alsberg was furious, though somewhat mollified by the rave reviews the Idaho Guide received, and he continued to refer to Fisher as "the bad boy of the Project."

"Boring" came four months later when *Washington: City and Capital* lumbered onto the desks of DC notables. Huge (1,141 pages, five-and-a-half pounds) and stuffed with details about the various units of the federal government, it is safe to assume that no one has ever read the entire volume. Even Harry Hopkins said it would make a nice doorstop. The size of the book belied any notion of it being a usable guidebook for tourists (especially compared to the pocket-size Baedekers), but it was what it was: proof that the Federal Writers' Project was actually *doing something*. Alsberg sent copies to every senator and congressman, every cabinet member, every governor, and every WPA administrator; while the other State Guides had to be published by commercial houses, in the case of *Washington: City and Capital* the Government Printing Office was the publisher so money was no object. The Guide flattered the Washington high-and-mighty by giving exquisite attention to the intricacies of their legislative and bureaucratic procedures, thus helping to sweeten potential critics. Alsberg also sent copies to journalists, and the press response was surprisingly favorable. "Extend this method to all America," wrote R. L. Duffus in the *Sunday Times*, "and it is apparent that we shall have something useful now and in time still to come. . . . Perhaps these guides, taken together, will enable us for the first time to hold the mirror up to all America." Doorstop or not, *Washington: City and Capital* allowed Alsberg to achieve his objective of producing "something useful" and giving the Project breathing time to develop the series.

He was going to need it, for "radical" was on the way. In August *Massachusetts: A Guide to Its Places and People*, the first of the four New England Guides published in 1937, came forth in a blare of publicity. Henry Alsberg and Ellen Woodward traveled to Boston to present a copy to Governor Charles Hurley as news photographers captured the moment. The celebrations abruptly stopped the next day, however, when a local newspaper reported that the Guide gave more attention to Sacco and Vanzetti than it did to the Boston Tea Party or the Boston Massacre. Other critics immediately scrutinized what they saw as a pro-labor orientation, charges of subversion and Communist influence flew, and the governor and local politicians did a U-turn and called for censoring the objectionable passages. Defenders of the Guide responded vigorously and Hopkins refused to take the matter very seriously, but the furor had an impact: The Washington office hired a censor (Louise Lazell, bearing the euphemistic title of "policy editor") to look for problematic material in the copy. The second printing of the Massachusetts Guide softened its pro-labor stance and rewrote some of the objectionable material (without anyone actually admitting they had done so), but the association of the Writers' Project with radicalism and Communism stuck and would haunt the Project.[4]

Despite such shaky beginnings, the other New England Guides came out smoothly and to good reviews. By the end of 1937 there was a sufficient body of work that pundits could pronounce their blessings on the entire series, and many did so. Lewis Mumford wrote a much-cited review in the October issue of the *New Republic* that called the Guides "indispensable" and "the finest contribution to American patriotism that has been made in our generation." Despite the generally favorable press and the quieting down of anti–New Deal critics of the series, however, the Project like the rest of the WPA felt the slash in congressional appropriations. Funding for all of the Arts Projects was cut by 25 percent in July 1937. Strikes in New York City and elsewhere protested the cutbacks, but to no avail.

The following year should have been a very good one for the Project, and it started out well. The State Projects were now humming along. Eight more Guides came out—the two remaining New England Guides, Delaware, Mississippi, and four from the Midwest (Iowa, Minnesota, North Dakota, South Dakota)—so now every region of the country except the Far West had a guidebook to show from the Project. Local newspapers praised the results. With the tangible, readable, popular Guides in evi-

4. Christine Bold (2006) excoriates the Project officials in Washington and Boston for submitting to pressure and censoring their own first volume without ever admitting it. She charges that the secrecy went on for decades, with even Jerre Mangione denying that changes had been made for the second printing, despite their obviousness to anyone who compared the two versions, as she did. Penkower (1977) makes vague references to changes for the second "edition" (significantly, the 1938 publication called itself a second *printing*, not edition, and as such there was no implication of any changes in the text). Even after citing examples of self-censorship, he maintains that the Guides "struck a successful balance between radical propaganda and chamber of commerce boosterism" (114). In an appendix Selvaggio (1990: 166–68) lists some of the changes. For example, in Tour 19: From Boston to Bourne, under the section on the town of Braintree, the original Guide had on page 587: "Here in 1920 occurred the holdup and murder of a paymaster for which Sacco and Vanzetti were executed (see dedham)." This sentence disappeared in the so-called second printing (really, revised edition) and the substitution read: "Increasing numbers of people employed in Boston, to which Braintree's excellent transportation makes it easily accessible, have established homes here." Such changes lend support to Bold's opinion that the "successful balance" was really a capitulation.

dence, the charges of boondoggling faded. Charges of incompetence and/or corruption continued, as in the New Jersey case discussed in the previous chapter, but for the most part they were contained at the local level, with Alsberg and his staff scrambling to replace state directors and appease the powerful. And while there was plenty of sentiment against the federal government interfering in state affairs, and against the New Deal in general, the State Writers' Projects gave the impression of local control (more than there actually was), so this complaint had died down as well. So what could go wrong?

By the last half of 1938, plenty. In an early sign of trouble, Reed Harris, Alsberg's invaluable right hand who oversaw the Project's administration, abruptly resigned. Harris believed that the continued radicalism of the New York City office would destroy the Project, and he regarded his boss's hands-off approach as naïve and potentially fatal. In this he was prescient, for of the three persistent lines of criticism—boondoggling, big government, and subversion—it was the third that would prove deadly. As we have seen, Martin Dies, the congressman from Texas, was chairing the House committee charged with rooting out subversives from government positions. Right from the beginning, the Dies Committee (which would become the House Un-American Activities Committee in 1946) zeroed in on the Arts Projects, especially the Theatre and Writers' Projects. During the committee's hearings in the fall of 1938, it brought in Project employees, usually people who had been disgruntled or fired, who testified that the Writers' Project was riddled with Communists and that writers were instructed to approach their topics from a "class angle." Ellen Woodward, Alsberg's boss, stoutly denied these charges when called to testify in early December. Both she and Alsberg, whose testimony followed hers and who was more inclined toward appeasement, pointed out that, under the WPA rules, employers were forbidden to inquire about an employee's political preferences, and they maintained that while there had been trouble with radicalism in New York City, New Jersey, and a few other offices, such problems were rare and were largely in the past. Their testimony did not change any minds, and in fact the nation approved of the Dies Committee's work; as Jerre Mangione, who saw the attack from up close, recalled it, "most Americans were either indifferent or unsympathetic to the problems of unemployed actors and writers, generally regarding them as loafers and troublemakers."[5] Alsberg dismayed his colleagues with his testimony, which they regarded as inept and excessively deferential. It certainly failed to quell suspicions about the federal government coddling feckless and possibly radical writers.

5. Mangione (1972): 290.

The Writers' Project may have been doomed by the attacks of the Dies and (later) Woodrum Committees, but even without them it would have fallen victim to the shift of national attention from unemployment to Europe.[6] In the late 1930s, New Deal interventionism was giving way to debate over and preparations for war. Harry Hopkins, the face of New Deal to many Americans, had directed the WPA for three-and-a-half years. Now legislators were bent on reining it in, the number of workers was falling, and Hopkins, who could see that his "dream of a twenty-year WPA" was not going to be realized, began looking for something else. When Roosevelt offered him a cabinet post as secretary of commerce, Hopkins accepted and resigned as works progress administrator on December 23, 1938. FDR named Colonel F. C. Harrington as his replacement. Federal One had lost its strongest and most politically savvy defender.[7]

As 1939 opened the House Appropriations Committee, chaired by Virginia senator Clifton Woodrum (a Democrat like Dies), had the Writers' Project, and even more the Theatre Project, in its sights. The fact that the Writers' Project was smoothly turning out books and pamphlets, including ten or so State Guides each year that won praise just about everywhere, did not change the situation. The WPA as a whole was in trouble and, with Hopkins gone, it could no longer hold on to its independence. In April Congress reorganized the WPA, changed its name to the Works Projects Administration, and made it a subsidiary of a parent agency known as the Federal Works Agency.

Colonel Harrington, Hopkins successor as WPA head, had little use for the Federal One programs and did not try to defend them. The Emergency Relief Act of 1939 eliminated the Theater Project altogether and moved the other three arts programs to the states, requiring state sponsorship of up to 25 percent of the costs. This was the beginning of the end. The Federal Writers' Project became the Writers' Program, with control now vested in the states, and the much-reduced Washington, DC, office staff served largely as advisors. Alsberg struggled to keep his job, but July brought the inevitable when Colonel Harrington fired him. Alsberg's replacement was John Dimmick Newsom, who had headed the Michigan Writers' Project. Less of a visionary, Newsom was a better administrator than Alsberg had been, and he committed himself to finishing the job of getting the State

6. Clifton Woodrum, a Democrat, was on the Committee on Appropriations. In 1939 he chaired a subcommittee that investigated the Federal One programs and recommended their restructuring.

7. Hopkins was also contemplating a run for the presidency and therefore considering buying a home back in Grinnell, "the idea being to run as an Iowan and a Midwesterner, and not as the eastern bureaucrat he had been these many years." This summary comes from N. Taylor (2008); "The idea being . . ." is from p. 417.

Guides out. Over twenty had been published, others were well along at this point, but their remained over a dozen that were coming along more slowly—Alabama, Arkansas, Colorado, Indiana, Louisiana, Michigan, Missouri, Oklahoma, South Carolina, Utah, Washington, West Virginia, Wisconsin, and Wyoming—and a few of these were problematic cases that Newsom and his reduced staff had to shepherd along to completion. In the end they all made it, with *Oklahoma: A Guide to the Sooner State* becoming the last State Guide to reach the public (it actually came out in January 1942, despite its 1941 publication date). Map 6.1 shows the five-year rollout, which indicates a general progression from the northeastern states to the South and West.

By the time the Oklahoma Guide came out, the attack on Pearl Harbor had finally hurtled America into war. The Writers' Program became Writers' Unit of the WPA War Services Subdivision, Newsom resigned and joined the army, books and pamphlets lay unfinished, and the program turned out its lights. As Mangione summarized, "The Writers' Program had begun to die months before the war came; the war simply administered the coup de grace."[8] But by the time that happened, the Federal Writers' Project / Writers' Program's finest achievements, the State Guides of the American Guide Series, were in the hands of journalists, travelers, educators, libraries, and the public at large.

The Guides as Material Objects

When the State Guides are lined up on a shelf, they all look pretty much the same—except for *Idaho*, which sticks out literally and figuratively. The book that Vardis Fisher rushed into print stands nine-and-a-quarter inches high, while all the others are eight inches. That the other forty-seven State Guides shared a standard size is remarkable given that there were fifteen different publishers involved. Dismayed by the bulky and inelegant *Washington: City and Capital*, Henry Alsberg did not want the Government Printing Office to get its hands on any more volumes in the series; in addition to the doorstop problem, he recognized that commercial publishers knew something about design and marketing that the GPO didn't. So he

8. Mangione (1972), a member of the Project's staff, dismisses Dies as a rabid headline seeker and regards both him and Woodrum as southern Democrats motivated by an anti–New Deal agenda. Penkower (1977) is more temperate, pointing out that there indeed was subversive and Communist influence in some of the Project offices, notable New York City (Mangione agrees), Minnesota, Washington (state), and New Jersey. Both Mangione and Penkower insist that political tampering had no impact on the Guides, and while they indeed were written from a liberal viewpoint that eschewed boosterism, the charge that they promoted a class-based analysis is unfounded.

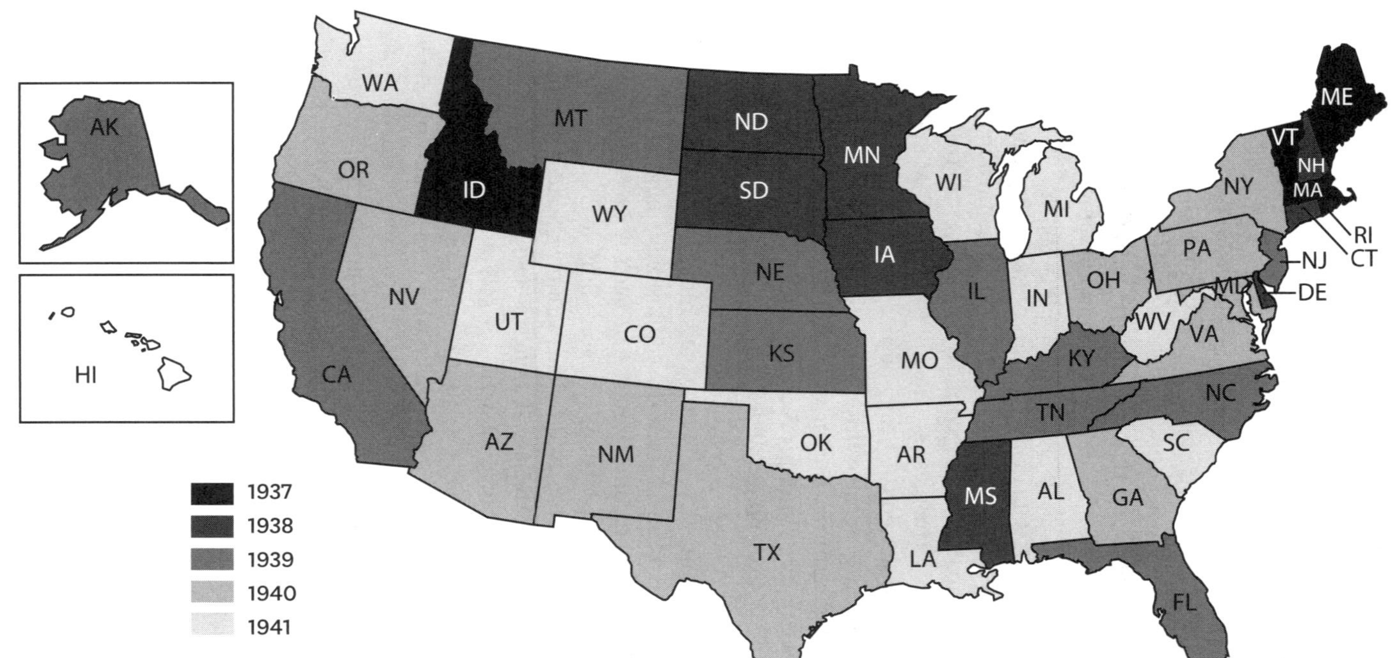

Map 6.1 State Guides by year of publication

hired Jerre Mangione, gave him the title of national coordinating editor, and charged him with lining up prestigious publishing houses for the future Guides. Mangione, whose reminiscences in *The Dream and the Deal* are required reading for anyone interested in the Project, described his job as serving essentially as a literary agent.

A legal problem arose at once: Federal law required that the GPO publish anything written by a federal agency. Vardis Fisher had gotten around this by having a nonfederal government official (Idaho's secretary of state) sponsor the project and then contracting with Caxton, an Idaho publisher. Bad boy or not, Fisher's work-around became standard operating procedure, and part of Mangione's job was lining up the local sponsors, these usually being state or city officials or local nonprofit organizations like historical societies; given that the federal government backed the Guides, these sponsors were confident of recovering their initial start-up expenditures. "The greatest value of the system," Mangione recalled, "was that it transferred the heavy burden of publication expenses from the shoulders of the taxpayer to that of the publishers. This unforeseen marriage of government and private enterprise enhanced the prestige of all parties concerned and proved to be the most potent single factor in keeping the Writers' Project alive."[9]

New York publishers brought out most Guides, with Oxford University Press publishing eleven, Viking Press nine, and Hastings House eight. Some regional publishers got involved; Boston's Houghton, Mifflin published all six New England Guides, Chicago's A. C. McClurg published the Illinois Guide, and Portland, Oregon's Binford and Mort brought out the Oregon, Washington, and Nevada volumes. State university presses published the North Carolina, Georgia, and Oklahoma Guides, while Alabama, both Dakotas, and Idaho were one-offs published by local firms.

In spite of the contradictory directives at the Project's outset, a nonconforming first book by a maverick state director, multiple publishers, publication dates spread over five years, and completely different writing and editorial staffs at the state level, the Guides turned out remarkably consistent in format. Each had three sections: Essays, Cities, and Tours. It is fair to say that Alsberg was most keenly interested in the Essays, Kellock in the Tours, and the residents of the state itself—including the State Project writers and the business community—in the Cities (because most of them lived there). Regardless of whether a state was predominantly urban or rural, the three sections were divided in a fairly standard way, with about a quarter or so of the pages going to the Essays, another quarter

9. Mangione (1972): 221.

to the Cities, and close to half to the Tours. The proportions varied somewhat depending on how many cities the state had. Maine, a notably rural state, had a breakdown of 114 pages of Essays, 84 of Cities, 204 of Tours; it had a fourth section of 39 pages on Sports and Recreation (because they were published early, the New England states sometimes slipped out of the uniform format.) At the other extreme, neighboring Massachusetts, a predominantly urban state, had roughly the same number of pages devoted to Essays (125) and Tours (224) as Maine had, but over three times as many (280) pages on Cities. Western states typically devoted more space to Tours than eastern ones; Montana, for example, had 125 pages of Essays, 60 pages of Cities, and 224 of Tours. Appendix D: "Contents of the 48 State Guides" gives the page breakdown for each State Guide.

The length of the Guides roughly corresponded to the size of the states. Most big books came from big states. New York was the largest state according to the 1930 census, and *New York: A Guide to the Empire State* was the longest State Guide; moreover the Guide gave relatively scant space to New York City, which had a separate organization and produced its own two volumes. Most states in the top ten in terms of population—New York, Pennsylvania, Illinois, Ohio, Texas, California, Michigan, Massachusetts, New Jersey, and Missouri—were in the top ten Guides in terms of pages, with Pennsylvania and Missouri just below. The same held at the other end of the distribution: Small states produced small Guides. Nevada was the smallest state and *Nevada: A Guide to the Silver State* was the shortest of all forty-eight. Vermont, North Dakota, and Idaho were all small states with short Guides.

Within the general pattern one finds some anomalies. A few small states wrote disproportionately large Guides. Wyoming had a tiny population, second only to Nevada, but its Guide ranked thirty-fifty of the forty-eight. Delaware was even more striking; the third smallest state, its Guide muscled in at twenty-fifth in size. And some medium-size states wrote huge Guides. Louisiana was the outstanding case, for while it ranked only twenty-second in population, *Louisiana: A Guide to the State* was the second-largest Guide, coming in at 746 pages to New York's 782. Virginia was another state with a lot to say, for while it ranked twentieth in population, *Virginia: A Guide to the Old Dominion* was the sixth-longest Guide. The opposite is also true, for states like Ohio (fourth in population, fourteenth in size of its Guide) and Indiana (eleventh in population, twenty-seventh in Guide size) had shorter Guides than might have been expected. Regional stereotypes of midwestern modesty and southern braggadocio are hard to resist.

Given the Washington-imposed standardization, we can speak of the

"Average State Guide."[10] This Average Guide is 560 pages long. The table of contents divides the book into four parts. In our Average Guide, "Part I, Essays" covers 154 pages and makes up 28 percent of the book. "Part II, Cities" is 127 pages or 22 percent.[11] "Part III, Tours" accounts for 236 pages, 43 percent of the book; there are an average of eighteen tours described, many broken down further into Tour 15A, 15B, and so on. "Part IV," the remaining 8 percent and an average of 43 pages, comes from the appendix and index. (See appendix D for a state-by-state breakdown.)

A Guide presented visual as well as textual clues to the state's character through its dust jacket, photos, and maps. Since different publishers were involved, these elements were somewhat less uniform than the contents per se. Most of the dust jackets featured photographs, usually of some familiar tourist attraction; New York State's Guide had Niagara Falls, Kentucky some grazing thoroughbreds, Maine a lighthouse. Cover photos lacked credits or labels, so while a Mainer might recognize the lighthouse as the Cape Neddick (Nubble) Light, the Maine Guide did not identify it. Some of the covers featured industry instead of scenic spots; Ohio featured a tire factory photo and Pennsylvania had a blast furnace. A few of the dust jackets eschewed photography for art: John Steuart Curry's painting *Landrush* on the Oklahoma Guide, a print of a farmer holding wheat on Nebraska, a cartoonish pelican on Louisiana. It's surprising that there weren't more, for one might have expected the Arts Project to be involved, but apparently that didn't happen. Some covers juxtaposed the state's past and its future; Wyoming's cowboy turns on his horse to look up at an airplane flying overhead.

All of the State Guides had photos, and although a few books scattered them throughout, the standard format was to arrange the photographs in eight thematic groups. The Maryland Guide's photo sections were typical: History; Architecture; Industry and Commerce; Education and Religion; Baltimore; Sports and Recreation; Agriculture; and In the Counties. For Pennsylvania it was History; Coal, Iron, and Steel; Industry, Commerce, and Transportation; Education and Religion; Philadelphia; In the Cities; The Farmlands; From the Delaware to Lake Erie. Although it may not be surprising that Pennsylvania had two sections devoted to cities, so did

10. The following calculations are based on the forty-eight State Guides. They exclude *Washington: City and Capital* and the New York City guides. The DC and New York City Guides contain Literature essays that I include in my coverage of these essays, but their distinctive structures makes them inappropriate for this discussion. The reverse point is that I am including the four Guides that do not have Literature essays—Idaho, Nevada, and the Dakotas—because they generally followed the Washington-set format. This data for this section is in Appendix D: "Contents of the 48 State Guides."

11. This is slightly misleading, for two books (Idaho and Nevada) have no section on Cities; removing these, the average for the Cities section is 132 pages, or 23 percent.

overwhelmingly rural South Dakota: Introducing South Dakota; Pioneer Trails; Cities of the "Middle Border"; Cities Built by Gold; The People and Their Schools; Ranch, Range, and Badlands; Heights and Depths of the Black Hills; and Ghosts of the Past.[12] The photographic insistence on cities everywhere, as well as the insistence on industry in nonindustrial states like New Mexico and Maine, is another indication of what the Columbia- and Harvard-educated northeasterners thought a proper state ought to contain.

Every Guide had maps in one form or another. Most were for driving rather than walking, and even the city maps had nothing like the detail that the Baedekers offered. Thirty-nine of the guides had folding maps of the state's main highways set in a pocket inside the back cover.[13]

What the Guides Had to Say

Most Guides had both a foreword and a preface, and this front matter, undoubtedly ignored by most readers, vividly displayed the essential confusion about the series' mission. Were the books intended to be working travel guides, encyclopedic reference works, or armchair reading? Was the readership expected to be residents of the state or outsiders? General readers, students, potential travelers, local boosters, or actual tourists? As we have seen, the Federal Writers' Project itself had not decided the matter—its charge was "Jobs!" not "Books!"—so those who wrote the front matter were free to offer their own interpretations of what the Guides were and for whom.

If a governor wrote the foreword, the keynote was boosterism. *Alabama: A Guide to the Deep South* (published in 1941, it was one of the last to appear) had a foreword by Governor Frank M. Dixon that extolled Alabama's "happy blending of the old and the new" and proclaimed that "although we take pride in what it [the Guide] shows, we are not yet satisfied. When

12. South Dakota was one of four states whose urban population was below 20 percent in the 1930 census. Two of the other four, Mississippi and North Dakota, had photos scattered through the Guide, not organized thematically. The fourth, Washington, had its photos grouped as The Coast; History: The Indians; The Dams; Agriculture; In the Cities and Towns; Industry, Commerce, and Transportation; Lumbering; In the Mountains. The sixth and seventh sections might also seem to give a misleadingly urban and industrial slant to a state where only 6 percent of the people lived in cities.

13. The nine states without separate maps were Arizona, Arkansas, Colorado, Idaho, Louisiana, Missouri, Texas, Utah, and Wisconsin. With the exception of the always-exceptional Idaho, these Guides were all published late—Arizona and Texas came out in 1940, the rest in 1941—and the exclusion of the maps may have been due to the pressure to finish the job; also at this point it would have been a decision made by the state's Writers' Program rather than one made in Washington, so the pressure for standardization would have been less intense.

our land closely resembles Paradise we will rest content with Alabama." According to Ohio's Governor John W. Bricker, his state was not a heavenly but a political gem: "It is my keen desire that this book shall record the story of the state for all generations to come, and serve as an inspiration to those who consecrate their lives toward the improvement and the perpetuation of our representative system of government. Here in Ohio, representative government has worked. Our people are happy and successful and, above all, proud of their state."

While the governors touted their respective states, Harry Hopkins touted the WPA itself. Having missed his chance to introduce the Idaho Guide, Hopkins used his foreword to the New England Guides (and two other early ones, Mississippi and North Dakota) to promote the Federal Writers' Project in particular and the Works Progress Administration in general by celebrating how they were employing people in ways that were useful, productive, professional, and collective:

> *Massachusetts: A Guide to Its Places and People* is one of the volumes in the American Guide Series, written by members of the Federal Writers' Project of the Works Progress Administration. *Designed primarily to give useful employment to needy unemployed writers and research workers*, this project has *gradually developed the ambitious objective of presenting to the American people a portrait of America*—its history, folklore, scenery, cultural backgrounds, social and economic trends, and racial factors. In one respect, at any rate, this undertaking is unique; it represents a far-flung effort at *co-operative research* and writing, drawing upon all the varied abilities of its personnel. All the workers contribute according to their talents; the field worker collects data in the field, the research worker burrows in libraries, the art and literary critics cover material relevant to their own specialties, architects describe notable historical buildings and monuments; and the final editing of copy as it flows in from all corners of the state is done by the more experienced authors in the central offices. The *ultimate product, whatever its faults or merits, represents a blend of the work of the entire personnel*, aided by consultants, members of university faculties, specialists, officers of learned societies, oldest residents, who have volunteered their services everywhere most generously.
>
> A great many books and brochures are being written for this series. As they appear in increasing numbers we hope the American public will come to appreciate more fully not only the *unusual scope of this undertaking*, but also the *devotion shown by workers*, from the humblest field worker to the most accomplished editors engaged in the final rewrite. (Italics added.)

In the Guides that followed Massachusetts, Hopkins remembered to say something about the state in question and not just the series: for example,

"Through every vicissitude of progress New Hampshire remains unchanged New Hampshire. To a peculiar degree her landscape and climate seem to be responsible for the spirited character of the New Hampshire man, as self-reliant now as in pioneer days."

While Hopkins addressed his foreword to *New Hampshire: A Guide to the Granite State* to the state's residents in flattering terms (spirited, self-reliant), his foreword to *Mississippi: A Guide to the Magnolia State* was quite different. In this case Hopkins seemed to assume that the Mississippi Guide's audience would be outsiders, not locals: "Here is a book which *takes us vividly into the South*. . . . To the visitor Mississippi offers . . . This Guide . . . could have been written only from self-knowledge. . . . It is the modest yet proud statement of *their accomplishments* by the people of this Gulf State" (italics added). Once again we see a powerful example of the view from the Northeast that was so prevalent among the New Dealers: New Hampshire men and women were people who might actually read their State Guide and in any case were people whom the New Dealers could relate to, while Mississippi was exotic, a place to be visited and marveled at (and, the implication was, Mississippians were not readers).

Hopkins was not the only one who vacillated over who the Guides' audience actually would be. In addition to their encomiums about the state and her citizens, different forewords aimed at different sets of residents and visitors. Logically, four types of people might pick up a State Guide:

1. State residents who toured around their state
2. State residents in general
3. Nonresidents who were visiting the state or planning to
4. Nonresidents who were not planning to visit the state but were curious about it

Forewords shifted among these four potential readerships. Governor Ralph L. Carr of Colorado spoke to (2) and (3): "Any Coloradoan who reads it will know his State better, and any stranger who turns its pages cannot but be filled with a determination to see and to know our country of mountain and plain. We invite you to enjoy this book and then to come to Colorado and see for yourself the things which it describes." His counterpart in Connecticut envisioned only travelers, (1) and (3): "Connecticut has a wealth of interest and beauty for the traveler, be he a resident or a visitor. . . . This Guidebook will help its readers not only to find their way through valleys and over hills, but also to understand what lies back of all they see." Texas focused on visitors (3): "Texas is a friendly State and genuinely welcomes the traveler from far or near. Within her borders he will still find the freshness and ruggedness of 'A Home on the Range' and all the comforts and conveniences of the most modern American cities. . . . We greet the visitors as they bring suggestions and views which, combined with our own, result in mutual helpfulness and pleasure. The men and women of the Lone Star State, through their Highway Commission and Department, extend to all good people the hand of friendship." And the foreword for Kentucky did not envision travelers at all but students and information seekers, category (4): "These guidebooks will find place in schools, colleges, and libraries; and private individuals will consult them for information available elsewhere only in world-of-mouth tradition or obscure archives and files. For these volumes are more than simply guidebooks: they are wide-angle reference books as well." Kentucky's image of its Guide's audience was unusual, and it turned out to be prescient.

A preface followed the foreword. Written by the state director (the title changed to state supervisor in the volumes that came out after mid-1939, when the Writers' Program devolved to the states), prefaces were more intimate and they gave a sense of the actual work involved in putting the Guides together. Samuel Tupper introduced *Georgia: A Guide to Its Towns and Countryside* by noting the State Project's early confusion: "No one knew exactly where to start. . . . It became evident that we must be a little of everything—farmer, map maker, historian, architect. We traveled broken roads, struggled out of ditches, shivered in frigid old houses . . . shouted questions at deaf caretakers and puzzled over the peals of mirth our questions sometimes evoked" (vii). Here we see the familiar motif of the clueless outsider encountering the savvy local. In the Federal Writers' Project, this trope operated at many levels.

Prefaces acknowledged the experts and consultants who helped. In retrospect, it seems ironic that these people had names and affiliations presented while the Project writers themselves remained anonymous, but anonymity and the presentation of collective rather than individual effort were the intention all along. In the preface to *Texas: A Guide to the Lone Star State*, J. Frank Davis names some forty experts who were consulted for various sections and mentions "2,914 local consultants and volunteer associates, a listing of whose names the limitation of space prevents, [who] gave of their services as called upon, in the interest of completeness and accuracy." Thus he identifies the experts and enumerates the consultants, but the faceless employees of the Project itself go unremarked; it is as if there were people making voluntary contributions who got credit, and people working for a paycheck who didn't. Indeed Davis's first paragraph emphasizes this eclipse of the writers:

> Much of the labor that has gone into the making of this book is not immediately apparent. The reader, by adding the tour and side trip distances, can discover that more than fifteen thousand miles of Federal, State and county highways were traversed and carefully described by workers, and from a mere skimming of its pages will observe that all the larger cities and hundreds of lesser towns and villages have been the scene of their efforts. The succinct form of the completed volume gives little indication, however, of the vast quantity of field copy—more than twelve million words—from which selection and condensation had to be made, or the research embraced in the consultation of hundreds of books and periodical files and the interviewing of authorities upon many subject in all parts of the State.

The "workers" evaporate, leaving behind the labor, the field copy, the research, the experts, and the active "reader." The spirit of collectivism thus led to the symbolic obliteration of the workers themselves.

After the prefaces came General Information, starting with travel and moving on to other things that tourists might want to know. The subsections were largely but not entirely the same from one Guide to another. *Utah: A Guide to the State* had a typical set: Railroads, Bus Lines, Air Lines, Waterways, Highways, Traffic Regulations, Accommodations, Climate and Equipment, Photography, Recreation Areas, Fishing, Hunting, Liquor Regulations, Poisonous Plants, Poisonous Reptiles and Insects, Water. *New Mexico: A Guide to the Colorful State* wanted to make sure its visiting hunters and fishermen knew the rules, so its general information section consisted of Railroads, Airlines, Busses, Highways, Motor Vehicle Laws, Accommodations, Climate and Equipment, Recreational Areas, Fishing, Trout Fishing, Fish and Game Laws, Big Game Hunting, Open Season for Hunting, Birds, Waterfowl, Licenses, Limits, No Open Season, Prohibited, General Service for Tourists, Boating, Winter Sports. Massachusetts featured a more urban list—Railroads, Highways, Bus Lines, Airlines, Waterways, Traffic Regulations, Accommodations, Climate and Equipment, Information Bureaus, Recreation, Transportation—although the Guide did manage to work in the usual warnings about poisonous snakes.

Several things about such conceptions of "General Information" are notable. First, the sections seemed designed entirely for out-of-state tourists. Information that state residents might want, such as town populations or school holidays or emergency phone numbers, was absent.

Second, readers today will be bemused by how state highway laws differentiated between in-state and out-of-state drivers, as in the assumption that outsiders unaware of local laws might be surprised to learn that in Michigan, "no person under 14 yrs. of age, or person under the influence of intoxicating liquor or narcotic drugs, shall operate a motorcar." Driving conditions were a concern as well; the Arizona Guide advised motorists, "Do not leave trunk highways without a full supply of gasoline and oils, and without information on distance to the next filling station." The Florida Guide reassured visitors that "nonresident owners or operators of motorcars have the full use of Florida highways."

Third, although supposedly for tourists, the General Information sections gave almost no practical information about where visitors might eat or sleep. Massachusetts claimed a section on Accommodations, but in its entirety it read:

> State is well provided with hotel accommodations. Accommodations in private houses are also available in nearly all towns. Tourist camps are located in all parts of the State. Municipal ordinances require rigid enforcement of rules on sanitation and hygiene. Most of these establishments are privately owned, but there is every evidence of their being orderly and well regulated. As most of the camps are within easy reach of trading centers, food supplies as well as emergency clothing are quickly obtainable.

All good to know, but of limited helpfulness to the tired family approaching Worcester and looking for a place to stay the night. *Florida: A Guide to the Southernmost State* devoted exactly two lines to accommodations: "Acceptable living quarters and meals for transients in all sections of Florida. Prices generally higher in winter," while it gave twice as much space to warnings about critters and, of all things, nuts: "Do not enter bushes at sides of highways in rural districts. Snakes and redbugs usually infest such places. Do not eat tung nuts; they are poisonous. Do not eat green pecans; in the immature stages the skins have a white film containing arsenic." *Delaware: A Guide to the First State* said, "Hotels and boarding houses, both white and Negro, in nearly all towns; city of Wilmington has also Y.M.C.A. and Y.W.C.A.," while *Indiana: A Guide to the Hoosier State* advised: "Hotel accommodations scarce in Indianapolis during last week in May because of Memorial Day 500-mile Auto Race, and Labor Day because of State Fair. Accommodations scarce in South Bend, LaFayette, and Bloomington on week-ends during the football season." While such general information may have been vaguely useful, other travel guides like the *Automobile Blue Books* were recommending specific hotels and including advertisements so travelers could compare their features and prices. Travelers using the American Guides, on the other hand, were on their own.

After General Information came the Calendar of Events, a list of festivals that made one thing clear: Even during the Great Depression, Americans loved to celebrate. Typical items included agricultural fairs (the Alfalfa Festival in Fessenden, North Dakota), Pioneers or Old Settlers Festivals in the West, Old Home Weeks in New England, sporting events (fox hunts in Virginia; Gulfport's Mackerel Rodeo in Mississippi), and ethnic holidays (fiestas in New Mexico, the Negro Song Fest in Mississippi, and Czechoslovakian Independence Day in Masaryktown, Florida). Every state had its distinctive events. In addition to various winter carnivals, Michigan had five different smelt festivals; in addition to the Mark Twain Festival, Missouri held the National Egg Laying Contest. New Hampshire's Calendar of Events included county fairs, Methodist camp meetings, Laconia's Annual Sled Dog Derby, and an Annual Old Home Week in August celebrated by eighty towns.

Finally after all of this preliminary material, the Guides came to the main event, the sections for Essays, Cities, and Tours. As we have seen, Washington administrators insisted on standardization: all forty-eight states, all the same dimensions, all with the same three-part structure. While the Essay sections averaged only a little over a quarter of the Guides, the space given to them varied. Louisiana and Missouri, both long Guides (second and twelfth) devoted the most pages to the Essays, but shorter Guides followed them: Idaho (forty-fourth in size overall), Utah (seventeenth), and then the long Guide for Virginia (sixth). Most of the Guides with the shortest Essay sections were short themselves, but Massachusetts and Connecticut, both among the longer Guides (tenth and eighteenth in size) had relatively short Essay sections. The percentages reveal the emphasis more clearly. At 44.5 percent Idaho had by far the greatest percentage of pages devoted to the Essays. The reason is simple: It had no Cities section, so virtually all of the rest of the Idaho Guide was composed of Tours. Of the seven Guides that devoted more than one-third of their pages to Essays, Nevada also had no Cities section and Wyoming's and New Mexico's were minuscule. The other three—Rhode Island, Alabama, and Nebraska—had average City sections but shorter-than-average Tour sections, so the extra pages had gone into the Essays.

Given the breadth of the Essay section topics, there is no obvious reason why one state should have devoted more energy to the Essays than another, but we would expect more urban states to have longer Cities sections. America was growing increasingly urban. At the turn of the century 40 percent of the population lived in cities, but the urban proportion grew steadily: 45.8 percent in 1910, 51.4 percent in 1920.[14] In the 1930 census

14. US Census Bureau, *Statistical Abstract of the United States 1930*, vol. 1, Area and Population, "No. 39.—Urban and Rural Population, by States," 46.

the United States population was 56.2 percent urban, but of course this varied wildly: 92 percent of Rhode Islanders and 90 percent of Massachusetts residents lived in cities, while out west only 6 percent of people in Washington State were urban, with 17 percent in North Dakota and 19 percent in South Dakota. Several southern states were extremely rural as well: Mississippi was just 17 percent urban, South Carolina and Arkansas just 21 percent.[15]

As with the Essays, some but not all of the Guides follow the expected pattern for their Cities sections. Massachusetts, Illinois, New Jersey, Texas, Connecticut, and Michigan all devoted more than 200 pages to the Cities. Most were indeed urban states, but Texas was the exception; with only 41 percent of Texans living in cities, it was a rural state right along with Maine, Louisiana, and Iowa, but the Texas Writers' Project produced a long Cities section. South Dakota, Arkansas, Montana, North Dakota, New Mexico, and Wyoming all gave Cities less than 80 pages, and Idaho and Nevada left them out altogether; all of these were very rural states. The percentages tell roughly the same story. Massachusetts, second only to Rhode Island in its percentage of city dwellers (90 percent) tops the list, with 41.5 percent of its Guide devoted to the Cities section; other urban states like Illinois, Connecticut, New Jersey, Michigan, and Ohio follow closely. But then come some anomalies: Texas, again, and Alabama, only 28 percent urban but devoting an unusually high proportion of its Guide—almost a third, higher than Rhode Island—to its Cities.

Tours were quirky. They constituted the largest section in all but three Guides (Massachusetts devoted more pages to Cities, Rhode Island and Alabama to Essays) and the average Tours section, 236 pages, amounted to 43 percent of the Guide and contained eighteen different tours. The number varied, in part due to the nature and number of the highways. Mid-Atlantic states had the most: New York led with forty tours and New Jersey, one of the smallest states, had thirty-seven, though much-larger Pennsylvania managed to get by with only twenty. Vermont had the fewest, seven tours, so size mattered, although tiny Rhode Island came up with eleven. Some states in the West had surprisingly few tours, which followed the few long highways in those sparsely inhabited regions; thus Nevada had only eight, Washington nine, North Dakota, Utah, and Oregon ten apiece. Most of the nine states that devote over half their pages to Tours were the big western states: South Dakota, Nevada, Colorado, California, Montana, and Idaho, with the Nevada and Idaho Guides being helped along by the

15. US Census Bureau, *Statistical Abstract of the United States 1940*, vol. 1, Area and Population, "No. 11.—Population, Urban and Rural, by States: 1910 to 1930," 8.

fact that they contained no Cities section. The other three are the not-so-big northern New England states: Vermont, Maine, and New Hampshire. On the other hand a few big western states like Arizona and Texas gave less space to Tours than average.

In addition to the three main sections, a few Guides contained a fourth section devoted to parks and wilderness areas, like South Dakota's six-page section on the Black Hills, New Hampshire's ten pages on the White Mountains, or Utah's whopping eighty-two pages on Parks and Primitive Areas. Most states just include the national and state parks as part of their Tour sections.[16]

Overall one finds a rough conformity between the characteristics of a state and those of its Guide, though there were plenty of oddities and exceptions. Every State Guide had its own story of how it was composed, and they varied in terms of both the state characteristics (having a more urban population encouraged but did not force a State Project to give greater emphasis to cities) and the concerns and enthusiasms of the writers and editors (apparently the Texas Writers' Project editors were just wild about Texas cities). Some state directors were able to get their way, either because Washington respected their judgment (Lyle Saxon) or because they bulled on through despite Washington (Vardis Fisher), while most, like New Jersey's Irene Fuhlbruegge, had to wrestle out compromises with the DC staff.

The Essay sections followed a standard sequence that moved the reader from nature through history through economic development to culture. *Kansas: A Guide to the Sunflower State* was typical. It opened with a short essay on "The Contemporary Scene" by William Allen White, a well-known newspaper editor and writer (he was one of the founders of the Book-of-the-Month Club) called the "Sage of Emporia." White was a leader of the Progressive movement and a liberal Republican who supported the New Deal, so he had been a natural choice to introduce the book. He sets up his essay by admitting that Kansas appears "flat and uninteresting . . . a rectangle of prairie grass with no more need for a guide book than is met by its highway junction signs." However that "slanting slab of prairie sod" is split in the middle, two types of soil, two different rainfalls, corn in the East and wheat in the West. This division has social implications. Farms in the East are small, 100 acres or so, and grow more corn, while those in the West are large and grow wheat. In the East farmers live on their farms ("the little farm with its garden, its diversified crop, its chickens, its calves, its pigs"); in the West they live in towns and do their farming with ma-

16. In calculating the percentages I have included these in the Tour section even if they were in a separate section. I have separated them out in Appendix D.

chinery. White suggests that these differences produce different kinds of people with different economic and political interests: "The eastern Kansas farmer is a thrifty, cautious, diligent descendant of the New England puritan, physically and spiritually. The western Kansas farmer is a gambler, a go-getter. . . . In our politics, western and western Kansas often find antagonistic interests."[17] Thus in two-and-a-half pages White manages to give his state's geological, economic, and social profile. He also gestures to the future of the state and, implicitly, the future of its Guide. At the close of his essay he says, "In these latter days of the mid-third of the century, oil is coming into western Kansas and to transform its civilization entirely." Western Kansas had undergone multiple boom-and-bust changes, while the East had grown incrementally, and White sees this continuing with oil refiguring the West's politics and social outlook. Notice the "latter days of the mid-third of the century." *Kansas: A Guide to the Sunflower State* came out in 1939, very *early* in the middle third of the century. White, who died in 1944, assumed that the Guide would find readers for decades, and he was speaking to these future readers.

Kansas: A Guide to the Sunflower State sets out its Essays in the mandated nature-to-culture order:

- Natural setting and conservation
- Archeology
- Indians
- History
- Agriculture
- Transportation
- Industry, Commerce and Labor
- Folklore
- Education
- Religion
- Sports and Recreation
- Journalism and Journalists
- Literature
- Art
- Music and the Theater
- Architecture

17. The urban population of Kansas was growing steadily—30 percent in 1910, 35 percent in 1920, just short of 40 percent in 1930—but you'd never know it from White's essay. US Census Bureau, *Statistical Abstract of the United States 1940*, vol. 1, Area and Population, "No. 11.—Population, Urban and Rural, by States: 1910 to 1930," 8.

Other Guides followed roughly the same sequence. *New Hampshire: A Guide to the Granite State* also began with a short introduction called "The Merriest of the Puritans" by Cornelius Weygandt, an English professor at the University of Pennsylvania who summered in, and wrote about, New Hampshire. Weygandt's take on the state was romantic: New Hampshire maintained a Puritan essence, leavened by a Merry England drollery, which absorbed newcomers from French Canada and southern Europe. Old timers and newcomers shared pride in the White Mountains, the good farming of the Connecticut Valley, and the lumbering. "It is a State of hundreds of ponds and of thousands of granite ledges. It is a State of remote farms, and of old villages of white-painted houses under high elms. It was a State of little industries, and the signs point to a return to those industries along its many rivers with water-power waiting to be harnessed to man's service. The gospel of work has been held to in New Hampshire. The gospel of laughter has not been forgotten." The Guide's essays then follow the usual progression from nature to history to economy to culture:

- New Hampshire's natural setting
    - Geography, topography, and climate
    - Geology
    - Wild life
    - Natural Resources
- The Indians
- History
- Government
- Industry, Commerce and Labor
- Transportation
- Agriculture
- Racial Elements
- Education, Religion
- Architecture
- Literature
- Newspapers and Radio
- The Arts
- Folklore

Like the Guides as a whole, the Essays feature Washington-imposed standardization with some variation sneaking through. (See Essays in the State Guides, www.press.uchicago.edu/sites/griswold/.) An introductory essay like those of White and Weygandt typically opens the section. Then follows an essay on the Natural Setting, one on Indians (often combined with Archeology, although sometimes Archeology gets its own essay), and one on History. Next the section turns to economic life, with essays on Agriculture, Transportation, and Industry, Commerce, and Labor, these last three usually but not always combined. Social life follows, with essays on Folklore and Folkways, Education, Religion, and Journalism. Finally comes culture: Literature, The Arts, Music, Theater, and Architecture; usually these are separate essays, but sometimes they are grouped under "Arts."

If we look at the American Guides' standard Essay sequence with twenty-first-century eyes, we find their Washington-mandated order to be racist, sexist, and materialist. The racism is explicit: Indians come just after nature and before history. The sexism is implicit: There are no essays on women or women's issues (women had gotten the right to vote less than twenty years earlier), nor any on domestic life. And the materialism is built into the sequence and follows a simple Marxian model: The economy derives from a base of natural resources and their historical exploitation, and culture derives from the economy.

While the standard essays showed up in most Guides, a few others cropped up fairly regularly. Most common was Government or State Government, which appeared in thirteen Guides. This hints that the Guides were not only aimed at tourists: How many visitors to Arizona really wanted to read up on its state government? Also popular was the awkwardly designated "Racial Elements"; there were ten of these, plus four more with slightly different names like "Ethnic Group" and "The Racial Make-up of Connecticut." "Racial Elements" essays came from all over, but the seven essays on "The Negro" were all from southern states. African Americans in other states were discussed, if at all, under "Racial Elements," although some states with ethnicity essays had virtually no Negroes (Maine, Montana, Oregon), and one state, Maryland, had essays on both "Racial Elements" and "The Negro."

More idiosyncratic are South Carolina's essay on "Gardens," Nevada's on "Mining and Mining Jargon," Wisconsin's on "The Cooperative Movement," Kentucky's on "The Kentucky Thoroughbred," and Michigan's on, somewhat surprisingly, "Marine Lore." Some of the earlier Guides used imaginative chapter titles: Maine's agriculture essay was "The Maine Farm," followed by its transportation essay, "From Waterways to Airways." Finally and most germane to the present study, four of the Guides—Nevada, North and South Dakota, and Idaho—lacked any Literature essay whatsoever; the first three successfully convinced Washington that they didn't have any literature, while out in Idaho, State Director Fischer just went ahead without it.

Impressive as the essays' coverage was, disquisitions on the Wisconsin Cooperative Movement, New Hampshire's Industry, Commerce and Labor, or Arkansas Literature were by no means typical components of travel guides. Such essays remind us of the two, not-necessarily-compatible goals of the State Guides: guiding travelers and guiding readers. The essays, and perhaps especially the Literature essays, were aimed squarely at *readers*, as the Project understood them. Indeed one begins to suspect that the Guides served readers better than they served travelers. Claims of American Baedekers notwithstanding, the American Guide Series fit uneasily into the travel-guide genre; while they constituted vast repositories of information, their on-the-road usefulness was less than Harry Hopkins might have imagined. With this in mind, the next chapter will consider reading and readership of the 1930s.

PART FOUR

Readers and Authors

SEVEN

Guiding Readers

Whom were the State Guides of the American Guide Series actually *for*? As we have seen, they were for Congress, to mollify its members. They were for the press, to show that the Federal Writers' Project was actually doing something. They were for state governors and mayors and Chambers of Commerce, to flatter them by bringing out their state's unique qualities and to assure them that these unique qualities ought to be and would be brought to the attention of the nation. They were for writers, to keep them in jobs and out of hot water. None of this could be admitted, however. Travel guides had the great virtue of allowing the Project to claim, with some plausibility, that they were being written *for* the American public.

As we have seen, the Project conceived of this public in two quite different formations. First, the public was a collection of travelers and would-be travelers, all of those automobile-owning citizens who might hit the road in search of America. For over a century, guidebooks had helped Americans experience what they should experience and avoid what they should avoid, comfortably and conveniently. Automobiles were replacing trains for leisure travelers, but they still needed guidebooks. Travelers were tourists, consumers, who wanted to spend their time on the road efficiently, to see the sights, and to get good value for their travel budget. The State Guides were for them.

Second, less obvious but more important in the opinion of Alsberg and Cronyn, the public was a collection of readers, all of those students and armchair travelers and people with broad curiosity about their nation. The Guides would tell America about itself, would make Americans aware of their diversity as intrinsic to their common experience, thus contributing to the progressive goal of melding regional distinctiveness into a united whole. Few people would travel very many of the highways described in such detail in the Tours section of the books, but almost all Americans could read. The State Guides were for them.

Just as the Baedeker model influenced the State Guides' formats, so did the Project leaders' assumptions about readers. Most critically, the Guides gave much more space to their elaborate Essay sections than other travel guides did. Baedeker's 1909 *United States* devoted 11 percent of its pages to introductory essays, *The Connecticut Guide, What to See and Where to Find It* gave only 4 percent, and other guides such as the popular *Automobile Blue Books* had no essays whatsoever (table 7.1). In contrast, as we saw in chapter 6, the State Guides devoted about a quarter of their pages to essays. This was something quite new.

The American Guides did not key their essays to the Tours or Cities, so the Essay sections were aiming at readers, not travelers. This was true for the Essays in general, and it was even truer for the Literature essays. It would not be obvious to most Americans that South Carolina or Arizona travel guides should have a Literature essay in the first place, especially not one on a par with their essays on History or Agriculture. (*Baedekers' United States* had nothing of the sort.) Indeed the need for a Literature essay was not obvious to many state directors, who objected along the lines of, "we don't have much literature out here." But it was obvious to Alsberg and his staff. Their northeastern outlook assumed that a proper state would have a unique culture, that this would include a unique literature, and that people would want to read about it. Minnesota's Mabel Ulrich recalled:

> We were completely baffled by the tendency of all federal editors to regard us as inhabiting a region romantically different from any other in the country. "This is not unique to Minnesota. What we want are the customs and characteristics that differ sharply from those of any other state." . . . When we protested mildly that we and our local advisers had firsthand knowledge of our state, we were told that we were too near it to get a proper perspective.[1]

In the minds of the Washington officials, Minnesota and every other state must have a distinctive literary tradition. The Literature essays were to record this tradition—which in fact was often assembled for the first time for the Guides—to inform and instruct curious readers who, sharing the

1. Ulrich (1939): 656.

Table 7.1 Travel guides and their contents

	Pages	Essays	Cities	Tours	Maps	Stars	Hotels	Dining, shopping	Advertising
BAEDEKER'S UNITED STATES 1909	814a	90 pages (11%)	Part of tours	724 pages (89%)	33; large end maps	Yes	Yes	Yes	None
AUTOMOBILE BLUE BOOK 1924	794	No essays	In routes; 2 inserts (Boston and NYC)	695 pages (88%); the rest is index	Dozens, incl. folded index map in plastic map holder	No	Ads	Ads	Extensive, with photos and drawings throughout
MIXER'S ROAD GUIDE ND STRIP MAPS 1926	Pages not numbered[b]	No essays	Part of tours and index	Entire book is tours and index	Half the book is strip maps	Yes	Yes, text and ads	Yes, text and ads	Extensive, with photos and drawings throughout
AUTOMOBILE GREEN BOOK 1932–33	964	No essays	Historical Section on cities 48 pp. (5%)	916 pages (95%)	47 sections and 100 city maps; folding map in back pocket	Yes	Yes, text and ads	Yes, text and ads	Extensive, with photos and drawings throughout
AAA WESTERN TOUR BOOK 1939	640 Descriptive section (362); Route section (278)	No essays	In Descriptive section	278 pages (43%)	Many; city maps and strip maps in Route section; folding map in back pocket	No	Yes, detailed descriptions	Only hotel dining	Few: Ethyl Gas, Coca Cola, Ontario Travel, Lincoln Hwy, AAA
MAINE (AMERICAN GUIDE SERIES) *1937*	476	113 pages (24%)	84 pages (18%)	205 pages (43%)[c]	Key to tours on front endpapers; 8 city maps; folding map in back pocket	No	No	No	None
NEW YORK (AMERICAN GUIDE SERIES) *1940*	782	177 pages (23%)	198 pages (25%)	340 pages (43%)[d]	Key to tours on front endpapers; 18 city maps; folding map in back pocket	No	No	No	None
COLORADO (AMERICAN GUIDE SERIES) *1941*	511	102 pages (20%)	92 pages (18%)	270 pages (53%)[e]	Key to tours on endpapers; 6 maps—3 city, 2 park, 1 state	No	No	No	None

[a]*Baedeker's* opens with cii (102) pages, twelve of front matter and the rest an "Introduction" made up of seventeen essays. This is followed by 120 tours divided into twelve regions—for example, Region V, "Southern States," has eighty-eight tours, "From Washington to Richmond," eighty-nine, "From Richmond to Norfolk and Old Point Comfort," ninety, "From Washington to Louisville," and so forth—amounting to 724 pages. Since the front matter is not usually included in page counts, I am taking the length to be 90 (102 minus the front matter) + 724.

[b]The first half of the book is strip maps; the second half is an alphabetical index with places.

[c]The other 72 pages (15 percent) include an (atypical) fourth section on Sports and Recreation, a Chronology, Selected Reading List, and Index.

[d]The other pages, over 8 percent, are the appendices and index.

[e]The other pages, over 9 percent, are the appendices and index.

federal editors' romanticism, would be interested in learning about how one state's prose and poetry differed from another's.

Alsberg and his staff recognized that people were reading more than ever. Again we remember that the Great Depression did not depress everything. We have seen that automobile travel, already booming in the twenties, continued to grow through the thirties; people may not have been buying new cars, but they were driving the cars they already owned more than ever. Most people still had jobs, and more of these jobs were offering paid vacations, so couples and families hit the road. Some of the wealthier may have been driving around the country in lieu of a more costly European sojourn, but most tourists were responding to the increasing ease of auto touring, the proliferation of motor camps and tourist cabins, and the encouragement given by government and industry.

A similar combination of frugalness and persistent growth was true for reading. Americans cut back on purchases of books, magazines, and newspapers, but that didn't mean that they cut back on reading. During the 1930s Americans had less money to spend on recreation, but while the total expenditures for leisure dropped, the drop was uneven. Sales of radios, records, and musical instruments declined precipitously and did not recover until after the Second World War. Theatre going suffered a similar fall and slow comeback. At the other extreme, motion picture and spectator sports dropped less and both had fully recovered by 1940. Reading materials present a mixed picture. Expenditures for books dropped to 60 percent of the pre-Depression level and did not recover until after the war. Newspaper and magazine sales, on the other hand, did not drop much and by 1939 they had surpassed their 1929 level. And library memberships went way up. So although people were buying fewer books during the thirties, they had not stopped reading—on the contrary, the evidence suggests that they were reading more than ever before.[2]

Alsberg, his Washington editors, and the state directors all knew this. They were men (mostly) of letters, and they operated in a print-saturated milieu. Reading retained its century-long position as the principal means by which people entertained and informed themselves, and the Project directors took for granted that people read. They specifically took for granted that Americans possessed prerequisites for reading: literacy, available reading materials, and the incentive to read. If these prerequisites were in place, if America was indeed a nation of readers, than writing guidebooks that might appeal to readers as much or more than they did to travelers

2. US Census Bureau, 1975, *Historical Statistics of the United States: Colonial Times to 1970*, part 1, series H 878–893, "Personal Consumption Expenditures for Recreation: 1909 to 1970," 401.

would have been a perfectly rational move. In order to assess whether it was or not, we need to look at the evidence.

Literacy

By the 1930s America was closing in on universal education. Only 57 percent of children ages five to seventeen attended public schools in 1870; by 1928 that percentage had steadily risen to over 80 percent, and it continued to grow during the Depression.[3] Another 10 percent went to private or parochial schools.[4] The type and amount of education children got varied from one region to another. In heavily Catholic New England, which also maintained an elite prep school tradition, close to one quarter of students went to private or parochial schools, whereas only 3 percent did in East South Central states. And some southern states lagged overall; Mississippi had only about 70 percent school enrollment. Overall, however, most American children were getting an education; in 1930 90 percent of children between five and nineteen were in school.[5] African Americans lagged behind whites in school enrollment; girls and boys, on the other hand, were virtually identical.[6] The vast majority of youth finishing their education could read. Their parents, by and large, were literate as well; the 1930 census counted only 4.3 percent of Americans over the age of ten (3 percent of whites, 16.4 percent of Negroes) as being illiterate.[7]

Not everyone could read, however. Race and geography had an im-

3. US Census Bureau, *Statistical Abstract of the United States, 1930*, 5, Education, no. 118, "Summary of Public Elementary and Secondary Schools: Continental United States," 107. In 1928 81.5 percent of the five to seventeen population was in public school. By 1938 the figure was 84.4 percent. US Census Bureau, *Statistical Abstract of the United States, 1940*, 5, Education, no. 133, "Schools, Public Elementary and Secondary—Summary for Continental United States: 1870 to 1938," 108.

4. US Census Bureau, *Statistical Abstract of the United States, 1930*, 5, Education, no. 124, "Elementary and Secondary Schools, Public and Private: Enrollment and Attendance," 112–13. In 1928 there were 25,179,696 students attending public schools; 21,268, 417 of these were in elementary school and 3,911,279 were in high school. An additional 2,576,157 were in private and parochial schools.

5. US Census Bureau, 1975, *Historical Statistics of the United States: Colonial Times to 1970*, part 1, series H 412–432, "Kindergarten, Elementary, and Secondary Schools and Enrollment: 1870 to 1970," 368.

6. US Census Bureau, 1975, *Historical Statistics of the United States: Colonial Times to 1970*, part 1, series H 433–441, "School Enrollment Rates per 100 Population, by Sex and Race: 1850 to 1970," 370.

7. US Census Bureau, 1975, *Historical Statistics of the United States: Colonial Times to 1970*, part 1, series H 664–668, "Percent Illiterate in the Population, by Race and Nativity: 1870 to 1969," 382. See also US Census Bureau, *Statistical Abstract of the United States, 1940*, 1. Population—Illiteracy. No. 47, "Illiteracy of Persons 10 Years of Age and Over, by Race, Nativity, and Sex, by Geographic Divisions: 1930," 53. The census defined illiteracy as "inability to write in any language, regardless of ability to read." Among city dwellers 3.2 percent were illiterate; for rural dwellers the figure was 6.0 percent. The most illiterate were rural African Americans (and in 1930 three quarters of Negroes lived in the country), where a full 29.2 percent of adults were illiterate.

pact on literacy, and so did recent immigration. In 1930 although only 2 percent of white Americans with native-born parents were illiterate, 11 percent of foreign-born whites could not read.[8] People who lived in the country were twice as likely to be illiterate than city dwellers. Still, even among these lagging groups, the vast majority of adults could read and write.

During the Great Depression, despite all of the hardship and dislocation, literacy continued to improve. Illiteracy dropped to less than 3 percent by 1940. All groups showed improvement: Now only 9 percent of the foreign-born population was unable to read, and the illiteracy rate for Negroes had dropped to under 12 percent. While the proportion of foreign-born illiterates had been relatively stable at around 10 percent for decades, Negroes showed a dramatic improvement in every decade since 1870, when fully 80 percent were illiterate. While only a little over 1 percent of native-born whites could not read in 1940, pockets of illiteracy persisted in places like Appalachia.[9]

Literacy varied by region as well. Just 2 percent of adults in East North Central or Pacific states were illiterate in 1930, and even fewer were in West North Central, whereas close to 10 percent in South Atlantic and East South Central were. Race was not the whole story; even among native-born whites, 6.3 percent of East South Central adults were illiterate, compared with a national average of 3 percent for the same group.[10] In 1934 FERA reported on "six rural problem areas"—these being Appalachian-Ozark, Eastern Cotton Belt, Western Cotton Area, Lake States Cut-Over Area (northern Minnesota, Wisconsin, Michigan), Short-Grass Spring Wheat Area (northern Great Plains) and Short-Grass Winter Wheat Area (southern Great Plains)—in which disproportionately high percentages of people were on relief. They found that in some rural areas poor education had left people illiterate and particularly vulnerable to economic distress.

> The lack of schooling of a large proportion of the heads of relief families appears to be one reason for their being on relief, inasmuch as the least trained tend to be the first to be dropped and the last to be employed whether for wages in industry or as farm tenants or laborers. In all but the two Wheat Areas over 30 percent of the heads of families had less than 5 years schooling, and in the Eastern Cotton Belt 51% of the Negro heads

8. US Census Bureau, 1975, *Historical Statistics of the United States: Colonial Times to 1970*, part 1, series H 664–668, "Percent Illiterate in the Population, by Race and Nativity: 1870 to 1969," 382.

9. US Census Bureau, 1975, *Historical Statistics of the United States: Colonial Times to 1970*, part 1, series H 664–668, "Percent Illiterate in the Population, by Race and Nativity: 1870 to 1969," 382.

10. US Census Bureau, *Statistical Abstract of the United States, 1940*, 1. Population—Illiteracy. No. 47, "Illiteracy of Persons 10 Years of Age and Over, by Race, Nativity, and Sex, by Geographic Divisions: 1930, 53."

and 20 percent of the white heads of families had no formal schooling. As long as so large a proportion of the poorer classes lack sufficient education to manage intelligently their own affairs there will be need of public relief and social case work.[11]

As this last sentence indicates, such "problem areas" were of intense concern to New Dealers. An example of this concern comes from the Tennessee Valley Authority, the massive federal hydroelectric power project created in 1933. Arthur Morgan, who initially ran the TVA, provided workers in Norris (the new town and TVA administrative center) with a mobile library, but "he worried that those farther out cutting timber must also need books . . . 'Why not place a box of books beside the tool box and make the saw-filer its custodian?' The saw filers then played the role of librarian to their fellow woodsmen." Since the typical woodsman's education had stopped by seventh grade, children's books were in greatest demand.[12]

Librarians and educators scrutinized rural reading as well. James Hodgson undertook an investigation of 300 rural families in Indiana and Illinois and found, not surprisingly, that they spent less time and money on reading than urban families. Newspapers and magazines were commonly found in country parlors but "rural homes are very weak on books, particularly the current ones."[13] Yet contrary to some more superficial studies, Hodgson distinguished between farm families, who were considerably worse off than city folks in terms of reading (having less education, access to books, and—above all—time) and nonfarming rural families, whose reading wasn't much different from that of their urban counterparts. The problem was more an isolated farm problem than a rural problem per se.

Thus the United States had stubborn patches of illiteracy, specific groups that were educationally disadvantaged, and the New Deal targeted these groups for assistance. Nevertheless most people were literate, and indeed this was why people in the thirties saw illiteracy as a social pathology. Which it was, for by and large, Americans of all races, regions, and conditions could read.

Availability

Having the basic literacy skills does not guarantee that people will read, however. For people to become actual readers, as opposed to potential

11. Beck and Foster (1935): 2–3.
12. Shlaes (2007): 180.
13. Hodgson (1944): IV-4.

ones, books and magazines and newspapers have to be available. (Reading, we of the twenty-first century must remind ourselves, meant print on paper.) There were two ways for people to get hold of something to read: They could buy it or they could borrow it. So the question is, during the 1930s were printed materials available for purchase or rental?

Although book publication collapsed in the early thirties, the decline was not as great as might be expected, and production began to recover by 1935. In 1929 there were 10,187 titles published; four-fifths of these were new works and the rest new editions and reprints. The number of titles published declined to 8,092 in 1933 (the ratio of new works to reprints stayed about the same), and then began to move up again. The decline in titles was not dramatic, but the decline in copies printed was; this was cut in half in 1933 (from 214 million in 1929 to 111 million in 1933). From then on, as with titles, the numbers began to recover.[14]

The raw numbers conceal differences in the types of books that did come out. New fiction remained strong; there was almost no change in the number of new fiction titles published. For previously published fiction, new editions and reprints dropped to 61 percent of the 1929 numbers in 1933, but recovered to 84 percent by 1935. Sociology and economics as well as fine arts and music were above the 1929 levels every year; one library science professional speculated that "cultural interests rose in popular esteem as business activity fell off."[15] (And Alsberg believed that it was to these "cultural interests" that the American Guide essays, especially the Literature essays, would appeal.)

Magazines and periodical sales showed a similar pattern, reaching a low point in 1933–34 (though they dropped less than books) and begin-

14. Wilson (1938): table 54, "Gross Book Production, 1929–35," 198. A study by Douglas Waples at the University of Chicago shows the patterns:

	Total number of titles*	Total number of copies
1929	10,187	214,334,423
1930	10,027	—
1931	10,307	154,461,622
1932	9,035	—
1933	8,092	110,789,913
1934	8,198	—
1935	8,766	140,651,953

*New titles and new editions combined, ratio roughly 4:1.

"Number and Index Numbers of Books Produced: United States, 1929–1935," Waples (1938): 60.

15. Waples (1938): table 4, "Number and Index Numbers of New Book Titles and New Editions and Reprints, by Subject Categories: United States, 1929–1935," 64. "Cultural interests . . ." from 66.

ning to recover in 1935. Between 1929 and 1934 newspaper circulation dropped about 5 percent, but then picked up again. Magazines dropped more sharply, down 10 percent in the same four-year period, but then also turned around. This is a bit misleading, however, because magazines, unlike books or newspapers, had enjoyed a boom in the late 1920s, so while the Depression wiped out the increase, by 1935 magazine circulation was approaching its 1925 level. "The stronger resistance of magazines to depression may be due partly to loyalties born of habitual reading, to the sales pressure of advertisers which books do not enjoy, to the lower cost of magazines, to the variety and brevity of their articles (which make most magazines fit more moods than most books will fit), and to their easier availability."[16] No doubt magazines, like books, were passed along hand to hand during the years when their absolute purchases declined, while newspapers, because their value quickly decayed, may not have been shared to the same extent.[17]

Overall, therefore, print publication declined in the early thirties but then recovered by the middle of the decade. Reading materials were not scarce. Where did people get their hands on them? Again there were only two routes: purchasing and borrowing.

Purchasing Books

Buying books was a hit-or-miss proposition even before the Depression took hold. (This discussion concentrates on books; magazines and newspapers had wider distribution through newsstands, although here again urban readers would have had an advantage over their rural counterparts.) For years publishers had consistently identified the industry's biggest problem to be distribution. Since their emergence in the late nineteenth century, department stores, mail-order houses, supermarkets, and chain stores had rationalized most retailing, but bookselling remained chaotic.[18]

16. Waples (1938): 62.

17. Wilson (1938): table 63, "Number of Copies of Books, Pamphlets, Magazines, and Daily and Sunday Newspapers Produced in the United States, 1925–35," 226.

18. L. Miller (2006) has pointed out that booksellers have always been "reluctant capitalists," and not very successful ones at that. In contrast, the first American department store is thought to be Wanamaker's in Philadelphia, which opened in time for the centennial in 1876, although the department store idea was emerging in many places at the time, with Paris's Le Bon Marché often credited with being the first. American mail-order giant Montgomery Ward issued its first catalog in 1872; Sears followed in 1888. The A&P grocery chain already had 1,600 stores by 1915, increasing to almost 14,000 by the midtwenties. The first true supermarket, a Piggly Wiggly, opened in Memphis in 1916. Woolworth's, which along with A&P was one of the first successful chain stores, opened its first store in 1878.

Bookstores tended to be small, independent, and inefficient; not surprisingly, they were seldom profitable. They also were scare outside of large cities. People didn't need bookstores, of course—they could buy books at drug stores, gift shops, and department stores—but a 1930 survey indicated that there were only 4,053 book outlets of any kind in the nation. Half of the nation's small cities and two-thirds of its counties lacked even one retailer that sold books.[19]

Sharp differences existed across regions. The Far West and Northeast led the nation both in bookstores and in overall book sales, followed by the Midwest and then the Northwest. The Southwest and Southeast lagged far behind.[20] As we shall see, this regional pattern held for virtually every type of book and reading-related activity such as library services and the distribution of magazines and newspapers.

Subscription book clubs like Book-of-the-Month (founded 1926) and the Literary Guild (1927) put books in the hands of many committed middle-class readers, though not casual readers or poorer ones. The twenties and thirties were also the heyday for selling encyclopedias and other series by subscription, and this segment of the book industry was huge: In 1933 the $26 million in subscription book sales was higher than trade book sales ($25 million) and almost as high as school textbooks ($30 million), the largest category.[21] Encyclopedias sold well in some rural, low-density states—Kansas and Nevada were tops in sales per capita—although the pattern was inconsistent; Delaware, Rhode Island, and Illinois were also in the top ten. Encyclopedia firms themselves believed that their success depended more on the intensity of the sales effort than any particular state characteristics.[22]

Overall, institutions that made books and reading materials available tended to cluster together rather than compensate for one another. In other words, areas with plenty of bookstores had plenty of libraries with high circulations, and these same places had high rates of book club membership and subscription book sales. The West Coast and the Northeast were consistently highest in all reading indicators, while the South was consistently lowest.

19. L. Miller (2006): 30. This figure seems low; in 1935 *Publishers Weekly* estimated that there were 10,000 bookstores in the country, but they may have been including a wider range of retailers.

20. Wilson (1938): table 56, "Gross Number of Bookstores per 1,000,000 Population, 1935", 201; figure 56, "Regional Summary," 203; table 58, "Index of Book Sales," 207; and figure 60, "Regional Summary of Index of Book Sales," 209.

21. Wilson (1938): table 55, "Estimated Book Sales by Different Branches of the Book Industry, 1933," 199. The textbook and trade book figures are net wholesale prices, while the subscription books are retail.

22. Wilson (1938): 221.

Borrowing Books

Libraries flourished during the thirties. Depression or not, library staffs grew dramatically, far more than other professions. From 1930 to 1940 the number of professional librarians increased by 30 percent, whereas the overall number of professional and technical workers went up 16 percent and teachers—a profession which might seem to be comparable to librarians—increased a mere 4 percent. Moreover, while clerical workers as a category grew by 15 percent during the thirties, library attendants and assistants went up an astonishing 600 percent.[23]

This remarkable increase in staffing occurred because library patronage was booming. More people than ever were getting library cards, a trend that had begun in the twenties. Applications for the enormous New York Public Library system (forty-six branches, eleven subbranches), for example, peaked in 1931 and then slowly declined; by 1936 they were back at the 1929 level, but this was well above the level in 1925–28.[24] In his study of library access and reading in the 1930s, Louis Wilson found a similar pattern nationwide: "The income of public libraries decreased considerably from 1931 to 1934, while the demand for their services during the same period was greatly increased."[25]

Circulation was increasing even more than membership. In 1926 Americans borrowed some 226 million volumes from their public libraries. The figure for 1934 was almost double that—449,998,845—despite the drastic cuts in library budgets.[26] A study of circulation per user from 1908 to 1946 showed relative stability (15–16 books per user) until the early twenties, then an increase through the twenties and into the thirties; the circu-

23. US Census Bureau, 1975, *Historical Statistics of the United States: Colonial Times to 1970*, part 1, series D 233–682, "Detailed Occupation of the Economically Active Population: 1900 to 1970," 140–41. Some of the increase in clerical staff may have been due to WPA workers assigned to libraries. In 1938 the American Library Association reported that there were 18,000 men and women working on WPA library projects in thirty-eight states, New York City, and the District of Columbia, with an additional 12,000 working on book repair projects in school and public libraries (Chapman [1938]: 1). Much-studied Middletown showed the pattern in microcosm: While its expenditures for new books declined dramatically, its staff increased from nine to eleven in the early thirties and stabilized at ten by 1935. Lynd and Lynd (1937): table 42, "Circulation, Expenditures by Kind, and Size of Staff of Middletown Public Library, by Year: 1926–1935," 572.

24. Haygood (1938): 19. Haygood attributes the decline to "the murderous reduction of the city's appropriation for new books, periodicals, and binding, slashed from $271,909 in 1932 to $61,357in 1933." Perhaps so, but again we note that the applications remained higher than in the late twenties.

25. Wilson (1938): 94.

26. Circulation statistics are from Wilson (1938): 96 and 98. Waples (1938) similarly concludes that "much evidence suggests that the same depression which decreased the production of the more expensive publications also supplied many incentives toward reading which doubtless increased the number of readers (and the number of pages read) per book, magazine, or newspaper sold. Such incentives undoubtedly produced the peak of public library circulation recorded in 1933" (85).

lation peak was in 1933 at 23.1 books per user.[27] Robert and Helen Lynd's follow-up volume on Middletown in 1935, ten years after the original Middletown study, tells a locally detailed version of the same story: a sharply increased use of the public library, as indicated by membership and by book circulation, by the citizens of one small city. Between 1929 and 1933 library cardholders grew by 17 percent (the city's population grew by 3 percent during the same period), and the average cardholder went from reading eleven books per year to reading twenty. "Middletown reads more books in bad times and fewer in good times," the Lynds concluded, and that looks like it was true generally.[28]

People may have been borrowing books instead of buying them, but they were getting their hands on more books than ever, and not just from public libraries. Rental libraries, where the customer paid a small fee to borrow a book for a certain number of days, are all but forgotten today, but they were ubiquitous during the thirties. Sometimes called circulating libraries, the business of renting out books was usually a sideline at drug stores, newsstands, and small shops, although there were some stand-alone stores. Rental libraries burst onto the scene in the mid-1920s, flourished in the 1930s, and then disappeared after the Second World War. While retailers had been lending books for a small fee since the eighteenth century, the reasons for the explosive growth in the late 1920s and 1930s are somewhat mysterious. A commentator in 1934 attributed it to people's lack of purchasing power and need for cheap entertainment, which sounds plausible but it does not explain the takeoff in the twenties.[29] Others have pointed out the pressure from the chain stores on independent retailers who responded with innovations beyond their typical product line. Store owners also saw rental libraries as ways of luring people into their stores.

Librarians maintained their traditional preference for classics, serious literature, and nonfiction, and their disdain for popular fiction played a role in boosting the rental-library competition. In the 1930s especially,

27. Galbi (2007): table 1, "Reported Public Library Circulation in U.S. Cities with Population 200,000 Persons or More." During this period juveniles accounted for roughly a third of the circulation, whose share increased to 40 percent during the war. There was a slight fallback later in the decade and a sharper drop during the war years, though 1943 and 1946 still averaged over sixteen books per user. Looking at a longer period of time Galbi found relative stability in the circulation per user from the mid-nineteenth through the mid-twentieth century, but again reaching a peak in the thirties; for example, looking at four survey years, both adult circulation and juvenile circulation were higher in 1938 than in 1944, 1950, and 1955 (Table 11, "Estimating Adult and Juvenile Circulation Per User in Survey Years").

28. Lynd and Lynd (1937): 252.

29. Rassuli and Hollander (2001): 125. While the reasons for the explosion of rental libraries during the 1920s remain something of a mystery, their demise is better understood: Following the Second World War, the availability of inexpensive paperbacks spelled their end.

public libraries' reduced budgets reinforced the acquisitions librarians' disinclination to purchase detective stories and romantic or faddish bestsellers, and these were exactly the books that rental libraries stocked. In fact, the very ubiquity of rental libraries supported the culturally conservative argument that public libraries need not allocate resources to this type of reading. In 1935 *Publishers Weekly* estimated that there were 50,000 rental libraries in the United States as compared with about 10,000 bookstores.[30]

In addition to carrying the popular fiction that readers sought, rental libraries may have had a locational advantage, the corner drugstore being more accessible than the library branch. In urban areas women—and the rental libraries were largely patronized by women—did not have to encounter homeless people that frequented the public libraries; by some accounts the books from the rental libraries were cleaner as well. It does not seem to be the case, however, that rental libraries flourished in places where public libraries failed to meet readers' needs. On the contrary, a 1938 report found that "rental libraries exist in relative abundance where public library service is best; and that they do not exist in large numbers, relatively, where library service is poorest." It followed that rental libraries developed "not so much to substitute for the lack of [public] libraries, as to make available certain types of books at convenient places and under conditions which appeal to certain population groups."[31]

All evidence points to the same conclusion: Reading did not decline in the 1930s but, on the contrary, it increased. This makes perfect sense: Other forms of entertainment cost more while reading could be essentially free; most people did not need to learn new skills to engage in it; and many people had time on their hands. So the next question becomes, Who were the readers?

Who Was Reading?

New Dealers paid a lot of attention to reading, and they were of two minds. On the one hand they worried about those left-behind areas where people could not read or could not get hold of reading material, and they addressed this with the usual array of programs. There were programs to combat illiteracy, to bring books to rural areas, to build and improve

30. Rassuli and Hollander (2001). The *Publishers Weekly* figures are from Eppard (1986), quoted in Rassuli and Hollander, 125. The decline of the rental library seems largely due to the rise of paperback books, which met the demand for cheap fiction, as well as the postwar relaxation of public libraries' attitudes to the merely popular.

31. Wilson (1938): 212–13.

schools, to give assistance to libraries, and—always—to document and celebrate everything the New Deal was doing.[32] On the other hand, they held a second, contradictory assumption: At the same time that New Dealers worked to promote reading, they also assumed that everyone could, in fact, read. Pamphlets poured out of New Deal agencies. Extension and outreach workers handed out brochures. And of course the Federal Writers' Project's idea of useful work was to produce books.

Unlike the other arts program under Federal One, the Writers' Project required its beneficiaries to have mastered a particular skill: the ability to read. Audiences who went to Music Project concerts did not need to play or read music; students at the Arts Project's community classes did not need to have any prior art training; and no theatrical knowledge was necessary to enjoy or be enraged by one of the Theatre Project's productions. But for Americans to benefit from the American Guide Series, they had to be able to read.

This skill requirement went unremarked on within the Writers' Project, for after all most Americans could indeed read. The Washington administrators and editors were themselves from highly literate backgrounds—New York intellectuals and the like—and most had likely never known an illiterate person. Moreover the writers, the people that the project sought to employ, were literate by definition and most would have been readers by avocation. So in putting out a socially useful product that would justify its existence to Congress and the media, the Project simply assumed that people could read. If certain niches in the society did not have the skills to access the Guides, well, these people probably didn't travel much anyway—and in any case, there were WPA and other programs that were helping them join the cultural mainstream.

Along with the assumption that most Americans could read, the Project administrators had a more specific sense of who their audience would be, a sense based partly on data and partly on shared interpretations, the view from the Northeast. Their conception of readership shaped the Guides in general and the Literature essays in particular.

We have already seen one answer to the "who reads" question: City folks read more than country folks. A higher rate of illiteracy in rural areas was only part of the problem. In 1930 the United States, including the territories of Alaska and Hawaii, had a population of 123,125,284. Of these

32. See, for example, Chapman (1938) on the WPA library projects in rural areas. Chapman focuses on South Carolina and Kentucky, and he claimed that South Carolina had only three "satisfactory county library systems" and five bookmobiles in 1936; WPA programs raised this to forty county systems and thirty-six book trucks. An increase from three to forty in two years seems suspiciously dramatic, but there is no doubt that the WPA increased rural access to books.

56.2 percent lived in cities; the percent urban had grown steadily in each decade. Rural areas lacked libraries (often) and bookstores (almost always). Only one-third of people outside of cities had access to libraries. Moreover, access varied enormously from state to state; just about all the country dwellers in Delaware, Massachusetts, New Hampshire, and Connecticut had libraries, while in North Dakota, Missouri, Oklahoma, Illinois, Florida, Arkansas, and West Virginia, fewer than 5 percent did. Wilson summed up the librarians' concerns about rural readers: "Here, then, is America's greatest library problem, the problem of providing effective public library service for the one-third of the total population [it was actually closer to half] who live on farms and in the small towns and villages of rural America."[33]

A second, related answer: More educated people read and less educated ones don't. Education has always been the strongest predictor of reading, and its impact is linear: High school graduates read more than those with only elementary education, college graduates read still more, and generally reading increases with each year of education.[34] This applies both to work-related reading—reading as an essential job requirement marks the boundary between white-collar and blue-collar positions—and to leisure reading, which is what we mean when we describe someone as "a reader." In the twentieth century, school enrollment increased every decade, and the increase did not falter during the Depression.[35] The same was true for college and university education: The percentage of eighteen to twenty-four year olds enrolled in institutions of higher education increased every decade, and the increase continued through the 1930s, going from 7.2 percent in 1929–30 to 9.1 percent in 1939–40.[36] More and more people, in other words, had the educational skill to become readers.

A third answer to the "who reads" question: People read who have the time to read. In his classic study *The Rise of the Novel*, Ian Watt found that in eighteenth-century England, specific groups with leisure time, notably urban middle-class women and their household servants, made up the genre's ini-

33. Population figures are from US Census Bureau, *Statistical Abstract of the United States*, 1930, "No. 5—Population: Continental United States and Outlying Territories and Possessions, 1910, 1920, and 1930," 3, and from US Census Bureau, *Statistical Abstract of the United States*, 1940, "No. 9—Population for Urban Size Groups and for Rural Territory, 1910 to 1930," 9. Library access figures from Wilson (1938): 28–31. "Here, then, is America's greatest library problem . . ." is from 31.

34. For a review of the research on the relationship between education and reading, see Griswold (2008).

35. At the turn of the twentieth century, 71.9 percent of five to seventeen year olds were enrolled in school. This went up to 74.2 percent in 1909–10, 78.3 percent in 1919–20, 81.7 percent in 1929–30, and 84.4 percent in 1939–40. National Center for Education Statistics, (1993), table 8, "Historical Summary of Public Elementary and Secondary School Statistics: 1869–70 to 1989–90," 34.

36. National Center for Education Statistics (1993), table 24, "Enrollment in Institutions of Higher Education, by Sex, Attendance Status, and Type and Control of Institution: 1869–70 to Fall 1991," 76.

tial audience. In the nineteenth century higher rates of literacy, better lighting, and shorter working days for city dwellers led to a boom of mass reading and the rise of magazines, newspapers, and popular fiction. And in the early twentieth century shorter working hours and few entertainment options, especially for middle-class women, accelerated the leisure reading habit; on the other hand, limited free time depressed farmers' reading.

Putting these three answers together suggests that that the typical reader, then and now, lives in a city, has some education, and has work that does not burn up every waking hour. Groups that fit this profile in the 1930s (or any other time) included students, professional and white-collar workers, and housewives. These groups constituted the core of the "reading class." During the Depression the unemployed (who had more time than before) and blue-collar workers (who had less money to pay for alternative entertainment) may also have been reading more than usual. This then was the potential audience for the books that the Federal Writers' Project was producing.[37]

An extensive study of library use in New York City confirms this profile.[38] In January 1936 the New York Public Library collected surveys from just under 20,000 patrons. The NYPL covers Manhattan, the Bronx, and Richmond (Staten Island); Queens and Brooklyn have their own systems. The 19,595 completed surveys came from thirty-five branch libraries in Manhattan, ten in the Bronx, and five in Richmond. William Haygood, a researcher from the University of Chicago's Graduate Library School whose mentor was Douglas Waples, analyzed the survey results, along with those of smaller surveys in Baltimore, Denver, St. Louis, and South Chicago, all of which showed similar patterns of library patronage.

The age of patrons skewed toward the young, and specifically toward students; over 70 percent of circulation patrons were under thirty. Men used the library more than women overall (men constituted 55–56 percent of the readers in the branches, and 82–84 percent of the readers in the Reference collection), though some branches had 70 percent women. Education was key, as always; 73 percent of the Reference users and 46 percent of the branch users had some college education, this in an era when only 6 percent of men and 4 percent of women had gone to college.[39] Along the same lines some 59 percent of the Reference users and 14 percent of the branch users fell into the "Professionals" occupational category.

37. Less advantaged city dwellers read as well. A study of two Chicago neighborhoods (R. A. Miller [1936]) suggested that the poor read less, had less reading material available, and preferred "less reputable" materials such as detective stories and true-love magazines.

38. Haygood (1938).

39. National Center for Education Statistics (1993): 8.

Breaking down by borrowers' occupational groups, and looking at South Chicago and St. Louis data as well as New York, Haygood found that students dominated (45.7 percent of patrons), followed by housewives (13.9 percent), then clerks and stenographers (8.5 percent) and professionals (8.5 percent; as noted above, this percentage is higher, 13.6 percent overall, in New York). As for genres, fiction accounted for three-quarters of housewives' selections, and two-thirds for clerks and stenographers, whereas less than half (43 percent) of professional men's withdrawals were fiction. Interestingly the unemployed made up only 5.9 percent, about the same as unskilled laborers (5.7 percent). It appears that just having free time is not enough to produce readers, so the Depression's reading increase cannot be attributed to people out of work seeking to while away the hours.

The reading habit varied by region, and once again, the South fell behind the rest of the country. Another University of Chicago librarian, Louis Round Wilson, studied the "geography of reading" by focusing on library service and the availability of books and other print materials in the six regions of the country defined by Howard Odum (Northeast, Midwest, Southeast, Southwest, Northwest, and Far West) as well as the individual states in each.[40] He found a consistent regional pattern: On virtually every measure of reading, the Far West and Northeast led, the Southwest and Southeast lagged, and the Midwest and Northwest were in the middle. For example, Wilson ranked the states in terms of the percentage of people who had local libraries. The top five were Delaware, Massachusetts, New Hampshire, Connecticut, and California, all with close to 100 percent access, while the bottom were Mississippi, Georgia, North Dakota, Arkansas, and West Virginia, where only 12 percent of the population lived in a library district. The regional ranking overall was: Far West 87.2 percent; Northeast 78.3 percent; Midwest 72.0 percent; Northwest 46.9 percent; Southwest 36.0 percent; Southeast 35.1 percent.

There was a considerable urban-rural divide, with only 34.9 percent of the rural population having access. There was a racial divide as well; in the South where there were separate facilities for Negroes, only 18.4 percent of them had access. Library support, library resources, and the percent of people who were members (had a library card) fell along the same regional rankings. So did bookstores, book sales (here the Northeast was a bit higher than the Far West), and the distribution of magazines and newspapers. So did rental libraries, which flourished where public libraries were

40. Wilson (1938). Martin (1986) points out that Wilson, best known as dean of the University of Chicago's Graduate Library School, published his *Geography of Reading* as the culmination of decades of investigation of regional library access, research motivated by his perception of scarce library resources in the South in general and in his home state of North Carolina in particular.

most abundant; as we've seen, Wilson believed that rental libraries made available "certain types of books" for certain population groups, but they did not serve people who lacked public libraries. His views represented the professional librarians' disdain for the unabashedly commercial rental libraries and the books they stocked. Along similar somewhat snobbish lines, Wilson noted that "magazines of opinion and criticism are found to have a comparatively more extensive circulation in the Northeast and the Far West, whereas magazines of the more popular type rank comparatively higher in the Southeast" (239).

Wilson's outlook was progressive: Reading was good for democracy and if people couldn't read, that constituted a social problem demanding government action. The WPA indeed had many programs to facilitate reading, including, for example, assigning its employees to work in libraries. The WPA's most dramatic intervention was the packhorse library program in Appalachia.[41] During the Great Depression one-fifth of Kentuckians, concentrated in the mountains of the state's eastern half, were unable to read.[42] Even if they could read, they had no books; Kentucky had long scrimped on education and reading, spending only one-third of the national average per capita on libraries. Fully half of its counties, mostly in the East, had no public libraries. These mountain counties were impoverished and isolated; few households owned any print material at all except perhaps a Bible. Educators, librarians, parents, and local notables saw access to books as a crying need. Bringing books around by packhorse was the only way to reach potential readers living in the mountain hollows. In 1913 a coal baron named John C. C. Mayo had funded a mounted library in Paintsville, and although it did not outlive him, the idea took hold. In 1934 a clergyman offered to share books, and together with a FERA official, they restarted the packhorse library movement. The WPA eventually employed 107 packhorse librarians in Kentucky alone, and traveling libraries reached rural readers in Ohio, Georgia, South Carolina, Mississippi, and eventually throughout the South and remote areas of the Great Plains and New England.

The packhorse libraries assumed an unmet demand for books—and as usual, the WPA photographed workers on horseback handing books to smiling recipients on cabin porches—but sometimes the demand itself had to be cultivated. Edward Chapman's 1938 report "WPA and Rural Libraries" noted that the development of library services in South Carolina depended on

41. See Boyd (2007); N. Taylor (2008).

42. US Census Bureau, *Statistical Abstract of the United States 1930*, no. 52, 1.—Area and Population. "No. 29.—Percentage of Illiteracy: By States," 34.

> carefully laid plans. . . . The first step was to develop, county by county, a citizen interest in the library service project. The library project supervisors, aided by local WPA supervisors, personally interviewed local organizations and outstanding local citizens, presenting the proposed inception of county library service. As a result, in county after county, a citizens library movement was built.[43]

We see here the WPA whipping up the demand for a service that it would then proceed to supply to a grateful public. Chapman also offered a somewhat measured assessment of the packhorse libraries, which he says are operating "with reasonable success." The problem was not simply isolated people in challenging terrain but their "general distrust of any outside help." The WPA tried to hire "native mountain workers . . . familiar with the social usages of the section," and Chapman acknowledged that the program "has been and still is, largely, a house-to-house selling campaign, with substantial help afforded by word-of-mouth endorsement of the service to neighbors by families whose resistance to and distrust of 'foreign' help has been overcome."

Packhorse service books came from donations. "As can be expected," Chapman commented, "a great portion of these donated books is scarcely suitable or usable," although old magazines, "which would be considered worthless in an average public library," do serve a need in the Kentucky mountains. The most popular reading materials were religious books, magazines with illustrations, and books for children. On the other hand, "novels in general will not be read"; Chapman thought this was a carryover "from a time when the reading of novels was considered 'sinful' by the progenitors of these mountain folk. They do, however, take pleasure in reading the tales laid in their section of the country and in stories of the cowboy west." Note that Chapman distinguished between regional and western fiction, which these mountain folk liked, and "novels in general," which they didn't. Again we catch a whiff of condescension.

Intellectuals like Chapman and Wilson, progressive New Dealers, and the urban, East Coast, Ivy-educated literati who ran the Federal Writers' Project all shared a set of views, shaped by facts and by their experience, that ran like this:

- Most people read.
- People who didn't, should.
- The problem was one of access to reading material.
- Some regions were more benighted than others.

43. Chapman (1938): 2.

- Some reading material was better than others.
- Something should be done.

What Were They Reading?

We have seen the professional librarians' implied scorn for "certain types of books" and "magazines of the more popular sort," and the WPA's complacent assumption that outdated magazines, especially if they had pictures," were fine for mountain folk even if they would be considered "worthless" elsewhere. Federal Writers' Project officials shared this snobbishness. While everyone should be encouraged to read, the people could not quite be trusted to select their own reading materials and to know what was of value. Thus the Literature essays were not just histories but guides to the formation of taste.

One type of reading that the Project directors favored was proletarian literature. In the mid-1920s many American intellectuals, inspired by events in the Soviet Union and encouraged by Communist and left-wing cultural theorists, saw the future of the written word to lie in the voices of the stenographers and steelworkers and prisoners that Mike Gold had championed. The John Reed Clubs had sprung up to foster just such voices—those of young, unpublished writers with working-class credentials—and they formed an urban, radical subculture that provided these novices with a supportive community in hard times. Ironically the movement was throttled by the Communist Party's 1935 turn to an anti-fascist Popular Front, which mobilized established writers instead of tyros; by the opportunities being offered in the recovering culture industry, especially in films; and by the Federal Writers' Project itself. Michael Denning's history of the Popular Front gives the accounting:

> If Proletcult died, it was killed by the WPA and Hollywood. The early John Reed Clubs had campaigned for relief for writers and artists; when the Works Progress Administration established that relief, the alumni of the Reed clubs carried their proletarian aesthetics into the guidebooks and folklore collections of the Federal Writers Project. Jack Conroy, Margaret Walker, Chester Himes, Arna Bontemps, Jo Sinclair, Nelson Algren, Kenneth Rexroth, Richard Wright, Meridel Le Sueur, Ralph Ellison, Jerre Mangione: all worked on the project, and Mangione eventually wrote their history.[44]

44. Denning's (1997) masterful history argues for the continuing influence of the Popular Front and its proletarian culture predecessors in shaping American culture. In particular he argues that "the poets and fiction writers who had published in the proletarian magazines wrote tour guides and collected folklore on the Writers' Project" (78), giving Jack Conroy as an example. While, in reaction to the

Unfortunately, the enthusiasm that Project members had for proletarian literature was not actually shared by the proletariat. Louis Adamic, a Slovenia-born Socialist intellectual who wrote about labor and immigration, addressed the question of "What the Proletariat Reads" in his report based on a yearlong trip around the country interviewing workers. He spoke with "workers in industrial centers and in small mining and mill towns in the East, Middle West, and Northwest, but outside of New York I found almost no awareness of the fact that among the intellectuals in Manhattan, Chicago, and Hollywood there was considerable excitement about a thing called proletarian literature. . . . Worse yet, none of the workers outside of New York who had read one or more proletarian novels was entirely pleased with it or them." Case in point: Some factory girls in Flint, Michigan, had read Catherine Brody's *Nobody Starves* because they had heard it was about them. They intensely disliked it, telling Adamic it was untrue and that conditions there were not as bad as the novelist painted them. Bemused ("a two days stay in town, although the social conditions there were anything but good, inclined me to agree with them"), Adamic concluded that "in consequence of reading the novel, they probably are farther removed from class-consciousness, radicalism, and the revolution that ever before; that, therefore, it probably is fortunate, from the radical point of view, that the novel was not read by many other workers."[45]

In addition to what Mabel Ulrich had called their "vital interest in proletariat warfare," we have also seen that the Federal Writers' Project directors believed that each state had a culture that was, again in Ulrich's words, "romantically different from any other in the country." Readers, therefore, should be interested in reading authors who were from and/or wrote about their state. The two interests, proletarian writing and localism, sometimes coincided in what Denning calls "left-wing regionalism," rooted in radical literary magazines that came out of the Midwest and West Coast. Denning includes Meridel Le Sueur, Carey McWilliams, Kenneth Rexroth, Norman MacLeod, Constance Rourke, and B. A. Botkin in this group. Unlike in the case of proletariat literature, this belief was

Dies Committee's exaggerations, recent historians have emphasized Federal One's *lack* of radicalism, Denning emphasizes "the influence of left-wing politics and aesthetics on the artists and intellectuals of the [Federal One] projects" (80). "If Proletcult died . . ." is from 227.

45. Adamic (1934) further notes that proletarian literature has reached "only a tiny segment of the proletariat, which already is radical and, therefore, really in no great need of being propagandized any more." The factory workers' disdain notwithstanding, other authors esteemed Brody's novel. In April and May 1934 the *New Republic* ran two issues on "Good Books That Almost Nobody Has Read," for which the magazine asked prominent authors to name neglected books. Both John Dos Passos and Sinclair Lewis named *Nobody Starves*; Dos Passos called it "a good local story about Detroit factory workers" and Lewis said it was "a story of the depression without romance because it is too authentic to need 'romance.'" *New Republic* 78 (April 18 and May 23).

probably correct, for today's readers do tend to favor books from or about their own locales.[46]

Third, Alsberg and the Washington editors, highly educated and traveling in literary circles, favored what was conventionally understood as being quality literature. Thus authors who were going to appear in the Literature essays should be of some importance, either historically or in terms of literary value. (In the case of novels, literary value, according to the "expert readers" of the day, generally meant critiques of the middle class, while realistic novels *about* the middle class were what people were actually reading.)[47] The state directors, on the other hand, were more concerned with mentioning as many state authors as possible, especially contemporary ones. This led to frequent exchanges where Washington tried to whittle down what the states had come up with and get them to focus on the best, not the most. Typical was a letter from George Cronyn to Arkansas state director Bernie Babcock: "I believe that the main trouble [with the draft of the Literature essay] is the mention of a large number of authors whose reputations are not very well known even in the state. Moreover, it is not necessary to give such inclusive lists of publications. . . . It is better to mention only the most characteristic or outstanding lists with some appraisal of their value and literary quality or their popularity."[48] State directors had local incentives to ignore such advice, and many did.

In short, the Federal Writers' Project, especially when formulating the Literature essays, wrestled with a three-way tension among authors who were politically correct, authors whose work was any good, and authors who were from or wrote about the state. The Washington office favored all three, but often the three didn't overlap. State Projects focused on the third almost exclusively.

Arizona offers an example of how the different agendas could clash. Adolf Bandelier, a prominent nineteenth-century archaeologist who studied Pueblo cultures, wrote a novel about prehistoric cliff dwellers called *The Delight Makers*. Henry Alsberg urged it be included in the Arizona Guide, writing to Ross Santee, the Arizona state director, that "in *The Delight* Makers, a fictionized [*sic*] account of prehistoric Arizona, we have one of the finest novels of ancient life in America." Santee wrote back pointing out

46. For evidence showing readers favoring books from their same states or regions, see Griswold and Wohl (2015) and Griswold and Wright (2004)

47. Hutner (2009). Looking at the forgotten fiction of the 1920s and '30s that represented the middle class confronting modernity, Hutner asks, "Why do the books that fall out of favor inevitably treat the middle class, while revenge narratives against the middle class manage to survive? Novels may be popular for all sorts of reasons, but it seems that they cannot be great unless they assail the middle class" (63).

48. Letter from George Cronyn to Bernie Babcock, October 8, 1936.

that the novel was about New Mexico, not Arizona, that the author's preface made this clear, and that "no part of the book suggests Arizona."[49] Santee was absolutely correct on the facts, but he lost the battle nevertheless and the Arizona Guide repeats Alsberg almost word for word: "Adolf Bandelier's *The Delight Makers*, a fictionalized account of prehistoric Arizona, is one of the finest novels of ancient life in America" (137). (The New Mexico Guide locates the novel's cliff dwellers as living in the Rito de Los Frijoles region of north-central New Mexico" [p. 192]). Thus the federal view of what was, if not exactly proletarian, at least the life of the "folk" and of what was "romantic" trumped the state view of what was Arizonian.

Like others who pressed for their state's local viewpoint, Santee sometimes got his way, however. In May 1937 Santee wrote George Cronyn that he had received the edited essays and would make the changes requested, but indicated: "I certainly do object to having all the flavor taken out of a piece just because the terms are strange to someone who doesn't know a damn thing about it." In reference to terms like "[to] gentle a horse" and "[to] haze herds into corrals," Santee pointed out that these were "common terms in the Southwest and among cowboys." In a final paragraph he gave way to his irritation: "Anyway, whatever you say goes. But personally, I'm fed up. There's little enough flavor of Arizona in the book as it is. If the magazines were all edited from Washington I'd quit writing stories and pick something easy like digging post holes or shoeing horses. I've decided that's what I should be doing anyway." Cronyn wrote back suggesting the colloquialism be explained in a glossary, pointing out that "we have to remember that your readers will be tenderfeet." No glossary appeared, and horses were gentled, herds hazed in the final Arizona Guide.

Reading and regionalism came together in the American Guide series. The Federal Writers' Project assumed that most Americans were, or could be, readers—people who could read and read in some depth—and the American Guides were for them. These were no ordinary guidebooks, and in fact they were not very practical for travelers. They were for readers, curious people who wanted to know about Indians of western New York, the labor history of Buffalo, the architecture of the downtown, and not just folks who wanted to find a meal or a hotel. The attitudes of the Project's central office about reading and regionalism were particularly influential in the Literature essays themselves. This influence made itself felt in three ways: judging quality, providing sufficient depth, and defining who was regional. The next chapter looks at their decisions.

49. Letter from Ross Santee to Henry Alsberg, February 1, 1939.

EIGHT

Choosing Authors

In the 1930s America was a nation of readers more than ever. This being so, it is not surprising that the American Guides, under the guise of being for travelers, were even more *for readers*. Tourists could read Guides to know what to see along the road and what not to miss when they reached a town. Locals could read up on their state's cities, history buffs on their state's origins, students on their state's flora and fauna. Beyond these readerships, the Project directors believed that the cultural essays would appeal to the reading class, the people who turn to books to satisfy both their intellectual curiosity and their desire for entertainment, and that this appeal would transcend state lines.[1] Readers of the Literature essays in particular would learn about a given state's literary history and they would get guidance about which authors were important and, therefore, which ones they ought to read. In this, the federal government was asserting a cultural authority that it had never previously claimed.

As we have seen, Henry Alsberg and his Washington team decided early on that every State Guide would open with a set of essays on that state's history and culture, one of which would be "Literature." Since development of the arts signaled a society that had advanced beyond the raw frontier, it seemed plausible to them that by the 1930s each state should be able to specify and describe its own literature—as well as its own architecture, music, and art, each of which were covered in separate essays. Plausible but ironic as well, for nineteenth-century American literati had worked vigor-

1. On the characteristics of the reading class, see Griswold (2008).

ously and eventually successfully to support their assertion of having a *national* literature, a distinctive American voice that was not just a subset of English literature. Now that national literature was to be carved up, state by state.

Most states complied with the requirement, some grudgingly. States like Massachusetts took the complacent view that their literature pretty much *was* American literature. Others, especially in the West, argued, "We don't really have any literature out here," but their protests usually fell on deaf ears. Idaho managed to slip past the requirement by jumping the gun in publication, and Nevada, North Dakota, and South Dakota persuaded Alsberg and Cronyn that they simply were not large enough or old enough to have a state literary tradition, but every other Guide ended up with a Literature essay. Additionally, the two City Guides that did not overlap with any State Guide contained full Literature essays. New York City had its own Writers' Project entirely separate from the New York State Project, and in spite of constant political turmoil it managed to produce two volumes on the city, *New York City Guide* and *New York Panorama*. The Literature essay, entitled "Market Place for Words," was in the second of these; its title indicates the New York City Project's Marxist, words-as-commodities viewpoint. *Washington: City and Capital*, that bulky monstrosity that Hopkins though might best serve as a doorstop, had its own essay with the more prosaic title "Literature in Washington."

Alsberg, Cronyn, and the central office editors unleashed their perfectionism on the essays in general, and on the Literature essays in particular because they believed that critics, whose early reviews could make or break the Project, would focus on them. Critics, the reasoning went, would be unlikely to hit the highway in order to judge the accuracy of a particular tour, nor would they have an in-depth knowledge of the cities depicted in a Guide's middle section. Reviewers in the national media were usually neither tourists nor residents; they were, however, readers, and they would approach the Guides from a reader's point of view. So it followed that of the three sections in the Guides, it was the Essays—which by default would interest readers more than Cities or Tours would—that were key to winning critical favor. And since reviewers and commentators were themselves members of the reading class, being writers and members of local or national literary circles, it was the Literature essays that would carry the most weight with them. Cronyn expressed this very directly in a letter to the Alabama state director:

> We are concentrating every effort on making the Literature essays critic-proof for the reason that the *professional* book reviewers, being more familiar with literature guide

> books, are likely to catch mis-statements in this field. If a critic takes issue with literary judgment expressed in a State guide, he may be skeptical of the rest of the material, although he will know *less* about it. [Emphases in the original][2]

So if the Literature essays were critic-proof, perhaps the Guides would be too.

Once again the view from Washington and the view from the states differed, this time regarding who the Guides' readers would be and what they cared about. State Project directors cared about local readers: businessmen, politicians, and journalists. It was important to them that their Literature essays mention the city newspaper editor's wife who had once published a novel or the collection of poetry sponsored by the local Chamber of Commerce. As a rule they did not have literary credentials of their own, though there were some notable exceptions, and they were inclined to claim any important author who had passed through their state as a favorite son or daughter, no matter how brief the stay or how tenuous the connection. They were political beings, whose politics were local. Thus they had to make sure that the people in their state were satisfied, especially given that their positions were precarious. Ultimately they cared about keeping their jobs more than anything else.

The men and women at the Project's Washington headquarters had more canonical literary tastes, tastes that had been refined at Columbia and Harvard and then flavored by their particular fondness for proletarian writing. Since the entire Guide series depended on the idea that every state was distinctive, the Washington editors sought literature that expressed a regional voice, but it had to be *good* literature, as they understood it, or at least it had to be historically or politically significant. They were not concerned with appeasing every local notable who thought his spouse or child was an undiscovered genius. Like their state counterparts, the Project central administrators were political beings who had to curry favor, but it was favor at the national level—especially Congress and the New York media—not the state level. Ultimately they cared about keeping the Project alive more than anything else.

Culture was nobody's priority. Like the Guides as a whole, the Essays were the result of competing political and economic forces, not cultural aspirations. Nevertheless the Literature essays came to define each state's literary profile. They *cast* its literary culture in two respects: The Essays singled out the cast of players, authors who mattered in the state's cultural

2. Letter from George Cronyn to Myrtle Myles, Alabama state director, June 17, 1937.

history, and they cast the form—the themes and tendencies—of the state's literary heritage.

To demonstrate how the Literature essays accomplished both of these, we can look at New Hampshire's seven pages on eighty-four authors who were from or somehow related to the state. Two claims organized the essay. First was the assertion of a distinctive voice: New Hampshire writers were down-to-earth, "characterized by an essential practicality," especially in comparison with those theologians and Transcendentalists and other dreamers from Massachusetts. Second was the state's indirect but powerful contribution to American literature: Although New Hampshire had produced few literary stars, it had nurtured many through its editors, publishers, and artists' colonies.

Having set the themes, the essay moved briskly through the eighteenth century—no Jonathan Edwards or Hartford Wits here, but instead writers of useful books like dictionaries and school texts—and then through some mediocre poets of the nineteenth. It settled with some relief on Daniel Webster, giving two long paragraphs to his person ("He was a commanding figure, with his lofty frame, his menacing brow, his coal-black hair, his fiery eye, his perfect self-possession") and his political oratory. It ran through a few other early nineteenth-century figures—a bookseller-historian, a Unitarian divine, the founder of Tufts College—and devoted a full paragraph to Mrs. Sarah Josepha Buell Hale, "whose name is little known but whose work is in three ways an integrated part of American tradition": She promoted Thanksgiving as a national holiday. She edited *Godey's Lady's Book*, one of the first women's magazines, for forty years. And she wrote "Mary Had a Little Lamb."

The essay then took up Horace Greeley, editor and social reformer. A series of other nineteenth-century journalists and publishers followed. Women of the era were clustered into a paragraph that included novelists, poets, and Christian Science founder Mary Baker Eddy. Such treatment was routine: The Guides' Literature essays usually grouped male writers by genre, female writers by gender.

A full paragraph went to Thomas Bailey Aldrich, a prolific writer and editor of the *Atlantic* from 1881 to 1890; although most of Aldrich's career was in Boston, he was born in the New Hampshire seaport of Portsmouth and wrote about it in his autobiography, short stories, and *An Old Town by the Sea*. (Surprisingly, Aldrich does not appear in the Massachusetts Guide. Less surprisingly, since he had spent some of his boyhood years in New Orleans, the indefatigable Lyle Saxon included him in the Louisiana Guide.) Quickly running through some twentieth-century writers,

New Hampshire's Literature essay devoted about a third of its pages to visitors who had written about the state and to the Cornish and especially the MacDowell artists' colonies ("probably no other small community in America has sheltered so many noteworthy American writers, artists and musicians"). It ended on a triumphant note—New Hampshire literature vindicated!—with two fulsome paragraphs on Robert Frost.

Essays like New Hampshire's assigned authors to states, and in so doing, they cast American literature into state-shaped molds. This chapter looks at the forty-six Literature essays (forty-four from State Guides plus the two from *New York Panorama* and *Washington: City and Capital*) and at the authors they covered.[3] Taken as a whole, these authors made up the cast of a Depression-era variety show that we might call "Our Literature from Sea to Shining Sea." Under desperate conditions, the federal government produced the show. It opened in the late thirties, it received rapturous reviews, the audience loved it, and it has been playing ever since. This chapter looks at the cast members and the next one looks at the influence of the show's long run.

Authors

The sheer size of "Our Literature from Sea to Shining Sea" is impressive: The forty-six Literature essays mentioned 3,463 names. Because more than one state might mention the same author, the 3,463 names represented 2,785 individuals. Most of these were mentioned in only one essay, but 410 appeared in two or more. Table 8.1 breaks down the number of mentions and names those authors who appeared in five or more Guides.

Being mentioned in a state's Literature essay may or may not have indicated a close connection with the state. When we conceptualize "Minnesota literature," for example, we think of writers who were born in Minnesota, who wrote about the state, or who at least spent a fair amount of time there. F. Scott Fitzgerald (born there) and Sinclair Lewis (born there and wrote about it) would be obvious examples. So would the less familiar Ole Edvart Rolvaag. Born in northern Norway, Rolvaag immigrated to America when he was twenty, studied at St. Olaf College, became a profes-

3. These data do not include the handful of authors that were mentioned here and there in the four State Guides that lacked Literature essays, nor the writers discussed in the other City Guides beyond New York City and Washington, DC. There were a few of these—on New Orleans; Philadelphia; Portland, Maine—that contained essays on literature, but these were closer looks at cities that were already covered in their respective State Guides, so to avoid repetition, they are not included in the analysis.

Table 8.1 Authors mentioned in the Literature essays

Authors with 1 mention	2,375	
Authors with 2 mentions	278	
Authors with 3 mentions	71	
Authors with 4 mentions	27	
Authors with 5 mentions	17	Hervey Allen, Sherwood Anderson, William Cullen Bryant, Pedro Castañeda de Nágera, Theodore Dreiser, Benjamin Franklin, John Charles Frémont, Nathaniel Hawthorne, Sidney Lanier, Sinclair Lewis, Meriwether Lewis, Thomas Paine, Zebulon Montgomery Pike, Father Abram Joseph Ryan, Carl Sandburg, Henry Rowe Schoolcraft, Edmund Clarence Stedman
Authors with 6 mentions	8	Hubert Howe Bancroft, James Fenimore Cooper, Ralph Waldo Emerson, Robert Frost, (Francis) Bret Harte, Joaquin Miller, Francis Parkman, Owen Wister
Authors with 7 mentions	3	Edgar Allan Poe, Harriet Beecher Stowe, John Greenleaf Whittier
Authors with 8 mentions	3	Willa Cather, Hamlin Garland, Henry Wadsworth Longfellow
Authors with 9 mentions	1	Walt Whitman
Authors with 12 mentions	2	Washington Irving, Mark Twain
Total individual authors	2,785	
Total mentions	3,463	

Note: A "mention" refers to when a Literature essay in a State Guide mentions an author by name. An author with five mentions would be one named by five different Guides; for example, the essays in the Connecticut, Maine, Massachusetts, New Hampshire, and Pennsylvania Guides all mentioned Nathaniel Hawthorne.

sor of Norwegian there, and remained in Minnesota the rest of his life. One of his sons became the state's governor. While he wrote prolifically, it was Rolvaag's *Giants in the Earth*, a novel about Norwegian immigrants on the prairie, that won him critical and popular acclaim, even becoming a Book-of-the-Month Club selection in 1927. To develop an authentic sense of his characters' physical hardships and emotional isolation, Rolvaag spent a sabbatical year alone in a cabin he built by himself on a Minnesota lake.[4]

Rolvaag , Fitzgerald, and Lewis were clearly Minnesota authors, then, but the Literature essays were more capacious than that. German poet and philosopher Friedrich von Schiller, for example, appeared in both the Minnesota and Wisconsin essays, not because he ever set foot in America but because he wrote a poem based on Jonathan Carver's *Travels through the Interior Parts of North America, in the Years 1766, 1767, and 1768*. Similarly, John Stuart Mill showed up in the Rhode Island essay because he corresponded with that state's philosopher Rowland Gibson Hazard on

4. Biographical information on Rolvaag and other authors discussed in this chapter comes from a variety of sources but especially from the *American National Biography Online*. The citation for Rolvaag is Shirley Laird, "Rolvaag, Ole Edvart," *American National Biography Online*, February 2000, http://www.anb.org.turing.library.northwestern.edu/articles/16/16-01405.html, accessed April 7, 2013.

the subject of free will. Schiller and Mill thus became part of America's literary heritage as constructed by the Federal Writers' Project. While such oblique references are unusual, more common are European writers who wrote their impressions of America, visitors like Charles Dickens, Frances Trollope, and Harriet Martineau. As we have seen, like every other section of the Guides the Literature essays went through multiple drafts as they moved back and forth between the state and the Washington offices. Every author who appeared in a Guide's Literature essay was vetted at both levels, and everyone who made it into the final version, both Washington and the state in question agreed, was an author who was part of "Our Literature." For this reason, the analysis here includes every name mentioned in a Literature essay, regardless of how attenuated his or her connection to America or American literature might be.

So who were these authors? The Literature essays included literary giants and bestselling celebrities. They also included explorers, academics, diarists, politicians, theologians, and poets who wrote for their local newspapers. Thorstein Veblen rubbed shoulders with Anne Bradstreet, Herman Melville with Zora Neal Hurston, Emily Dickinson with Francisco Vázquez de Coronado, "A Lady of Louisiana" with "A Gentleman of Elvas." The Project, in other words, had an expansive and practical definition of literature and of whom the Project directors considered to be an author. Of course Project employees themselves were writers, at least according to the federal government, yet most of them did not produce or aspire to produce anything like "literature." Their working definition of literature seemed to be pretty much anything that got published.

Many writers turned up in more than one Literature essay. Five southern states, for example, mentioned Father Abram Joseph Ryan, a Roman Catholic priest and chaplain with the Confederate forces. Father Ryan served heroically—he succored prisoners during a smallpox epidemic in New Orleans when the other chaplains had fled—and he was said to have picked up a musket more than once. After the war he wrote elegies to the Lost Cause and became known as the "Poet of the Confederacy." The Literature essays of Alabama, Georgia, Maryland, Tennessee, and Virginia (but not, surprisingly, Louisiana) all mentioned him. Most of the authors who appear multiple times are more familiar to twenty-first-century readers. Washington Irving and Mark Twain top the list with twelve mentions each, Walt Whitman has nine, and Willa Cather, Hamlin Garland, and Henry Wadsworth Longfellow each have eight.

Although the number of mentions might seem to suggest an author's importance, insofar as it indicates how many State Projects wanted to claim him or her, it is an imperfect measure for several reasons. First, an author who had moved around had a better chance of being mentioned by several states than one who had stayed put. Emily Dickinson exemplifies the latter. Aside from Massachusetts, only Vermont's Literature essay mentions her, and only to say that local poet Frances Frost is similar, but only two mentions hardly indicate her literary importance; she just didn't ever leave Amherst. John Steinbeck appears only in the California Guide, despite having had bestsellers in 1937 and 1939; he had spent too much of his life in California for other states to stake a claim. Timing mattered as well: Steinbeck's success may have been too recent for *New York Panorama* (1938) to pick him up, in spite of the fact that he had worked in the city in the twenties and his politics would have appealed to the New York City Project.

Second, authors who had won a Pulitzer Prize, like John Gould Fletcher, or who had written a recent bestseller, like Hervey Allen, often got a boost in their number of mentions, especially if the book had been filmed. In 1933 a San Diego reporter named Max Miller, little remembered today, wrote *I Cover the Waterfront*, a thriller about dockland smuggling. The next year it was made into a movie starring Claudette Colbert, and it inspired a jazz standard covered by many artists including Billie Holiday and Louis Armstrong. Miller got four mentions based on that one book and its pop culture offspring (by way of comparison, Hemingway and Melville each got three).

Third, emerging authors sometimes received fewer mentions than today's readers might expect. Robert Penn Warren appeared only twice, for example; he had been one of the Agrarians and early New Critics and he had published his first novel in 1939, but his masterpiece *All the King's Men* and his three Pulitzer Prizes were to come later. Charlotte Perkins Gilman was a case of delayed emergence. A social reformer who called herself a "humanist" instead of a feminist, in the 1970s Gilman would become widely celebrated for her 1892 short story "The Yellow Wallpaper," one of the canonical works of second-wave feminism. But in the 1930s she was more obscure; only the Connecticut essay (she was born in Hartford) mentioned her, describing her as "poet, sociologist, and ardent champion of a freer and fuller destiny for women." Gilman had grown up and attended college in Rhode Island and she lived for many years in California and in New York City, but she appeared in none of those Guides, for her hour had not yet come.

The Project slighted some locally loved authors because the Washington editors did not regard their work as good literature. They shared Cronyn's concerns about the consequences if "a critic takes issue with literary judgment expressed in a State guide." Building "critic proof" essays meant sticking to authors approved by cultural authorities, including professors. In an early draft of Kentucky's Literature essay, someone on the State Project wrote that despite the state's lack of truly first-rate poets, "Theodore O'Hara's immortal elegy, 'The Bivouac of the Dead,' the greatest single poem to come out of Kentucky, should not be forgotten." Professor Grant Knight from the English Language and Literature Department at the University of Kentucky, who rewrote the essay, strongly disagreed, writing, "I suggest that if 'The Bivouac of the Dead' must be mentioned it be given a sentence . . . and that it not be described as immortal."[5] The editors concurred, and neither O'Hara nor his poem appeared in the essay, despite the fact that "Bivouac" had been honored by veterans for almost a century and appeared at the entrance to Arlington National Cemetery and many other military graveyards. The poem's sentimental militarism did not appeal to modernist literary tastes, and thus it could not be "good literature."

This scorn for the merely popular worked to the disadvantage of women authors in particular. Susan B. Warner's *The Wide, Wide World* (1850) went through fourteen editions in its first two years and is considered the first American bestseller. Warner wrote many other novels that went through multiple editions, yet only one Literature essay mentioned her. Damning with faint praise, the New York State Guide said:

> The pre-Civil War literary production of the State is more notable for quantity than quality. Susan B. Warner (1819–85) and Anna B. Warner (1827–1915), sister spinsters who lived on Constitution Island near West Point, under the pseudonyms "Elizabeth Wetherell" and "Amy Lothrop" wrote novels heavy with moral teaching and sugared with romance. The former's *The Wide, Wide World* was, after *Uncle Tom's Cabin*, perhaps the most widely read book in nineteenth-century America. (147)

Warner had been born in New York City and her second novel, almost as popular as the first, was set there, but *New York Panorama* did not deign to mention her; the radicals of the New York City Project were not impressed by sales, nor by Warner's theme of Christian piety. (Their intellectual forefathers hadn't been either. In 1850 George Putnam only agreed to publish *The Wide, Wide World* because his mother was enthusiastic about the manuscript. Putnam's initial print run was only 750 copies, but his mother's tastes were dead on.)

While popularity in and of itself could be damning, the Guides were

5. Letter from Grant Knight to Professor Clifton [?], October 13, 1938. On December 23, 1938, Bettie M. Henry, assistant state director, wrote to Henry Alsberg that she agreed with Professor Knight, saying the sentence was "not true and should be deleted."

especially dismissive if the popular author were a woman. After all Hervey Allen, who wrote the bestselling melodrama *Anthony Adverse*, managed to get five mentions. In contrast, Augusta Evans Wilson's blockbuster novel *St. Elmo* so captivated the public that towns, steamships, and a brand of cigars were named "St. Elmo," and Wilson earned more from her writing than any other American woman author until Edith Wharton. She did get a mention in the Georgia and Alabama essays (was the Deep South more open to women's sentimental writing?) but she was ignored in Texas (she spent much of her childhood there and her first published story was about the Alamo), in New York (her postwar publisher was there, she spent time there with her wounded brother, and a bootleg version of one of her novels was published there during the Civil War), and in Tennessee (her books were banned there by the Union Army, a fact that might have seemed worth a mention in that state's Guide).

Louisa May Alcott presents the most extreme case of giving short shrift to a major woman author. Born in Pennsylvania, Alcott grew up and lived her whole life in Boston and Concord. The Pennsylvania Guide mentions her only to remark that although she was born in Germantown, "none of her work is concerned with the place of her birth" (129). She also received a line in *Washington: City and Capital* to the effect that she "served as a nurse in the Union Hospital at Georgetown during the early Civil War period, gleaning thereby the material for her earliest published book, the collection of 'Hospital Sketches'" (it doesn't mention that her nursing experience there lasted only three weeks). Alcott came from a Massachusetts family of prominent social reformers. Literature essays in both the Massachusetts and the Connecticut Guides mentioned her father Amos Bronson Alcott, a leading Transcendentalist and utopian philosopher. *Little Women* was and remains one of the bestsellers of all time, and it, like most of her many novels, is set in Massachusetts. Louisa May Alcott was a prominent public figure all her life, deeply involved with her family's many social and philosophical concerns that in addition to Transcendentalism included abolition and women's rights. Her writing balanced sentiment, moral uplift, and a traditional view of women's familial obligations on the one hand with an assertion of women's intellectual and artistic freedom on the other (recent critics have focused in particular on these feminist views). Astonishingly, neither of the two Massachusetts essays mentions her.[6]

6. The Massachusetts Guide was unique in having two essays on literature. State Director Billington wanted a conventional essay, while the radical writers on the Massachusetts Project wanted to write about literature as a collective product, so the Guide ended up with "Literature" and "Literary Groups and Movements."

The Literature essays scorned morally didactic literature in general and popular religion in particular.[7] Bestsellers like *If Christ Came to Chicago* (1894) had been around for decades. In the 1920s, British religious fiction was hugely popular in the United States. Robert Keable (1887–1927) came over on several book tours for his blockbusters *Simon Called Peter* (1921), which was number five on the 1922 bestseller list, and *Recompense* (1924).[8] Another Englishman, H. W. Freeman (1899–1994), had a 1929 bestseller called *Joseph and His Brethren*. Neither Freeman nor Keable was mentioned in the Guides. Although widely read in America, Freeman and Keable were English, after all, so perhaps it is not surprising that they were left out. However, the Guides downplayed American writers of religious fiction as well. In the mid-1930s Lloyd Douglas (1877–1951) was America's most popular novelist. Son of a Lutheran pastor, Douglas grew up in Indiana and Kentucky, attended college and seminary in Ohio, and served as a minister in multiple states including Indiana; Ohio; Washington, DC; Illinois; Michigan; and California; as well as Montreal. His first novel was *Magnificent Obsession* (1929), a story of spiritual reawakening that found its audience and made number eight on the top-ten list in 1932 and fourth place in 1933; a second novel, *Forgive Us Our Trespasses*, came in at number six. Douglas moved to Los Angeles to devote himself to writing and had bestsellers in 1935, 1936, and 1939 (his most popular novel, *The Robe*, was not to come until 1942).[9] Given his prominence, we might expect to find him in half a dozen states' Literature essays, but only New York City and Indiana mentioned him. *New York Panorama* sniffs, "On the whole, it is probably in the higher realms of literature that New York's critical influence is operative. That influence obviously has nothing to do with the huge sales of such contemporary authors as Lloyd Douglas." And the Indiana essay mentions him only in a long list of "other contemporary novelists, dramatists, essayists and poets born or reared in Indiana. . . . Few of these have remained in their native State and fewer still have written of it." Nonfiction religious bestsellers were also ignored. Advertising executive Bruce Barton's book *The Man Nobody*

7. There is no evidence that any of the Washington Federal Writers' Project staff were religiously active. Mangione refers to himself as a lapsed Catholic (p. 18) and Alsberg, of Jewish background, seems to have been nonpracticing. Undoubtedly some of the writers on the State Projects were religious believers, but the Project paid no attention to religious belief or practice. The New Deal as a whole was resolutely secular, though some members like Frances Perkins practiced their faiths in their private lives.

8. Bestseller rankings are from Korda (2001), which relied on the data from *Publishers Weekly*.

9. Smith calls him the nation's most popular novelist. The bestsellers are listed in Korda (2001). Gary Scott Smith, "Douglas, Lloyd Cassel," *American National Biography Online*, February 2000, http://www.anb.org.turing.library.northwestern.edu/articles/08/08-00397.html, accessed July 16 2010.

Knows (1925), a portrait of Jesus as a salesman and topflight manager, stayed on the *New York Times* bestseller list for two years, but Barton does not appear in the Guides.[10]

Not explicitly religious or moralizing, Pearl Buck (1892–1973), who grew up in China, was immensely successful in both literary honors and sales. Her second novel was *The Good Earth*, about a Chinese peasant family; it topped the *New York Times* bestseller list in both 1931 and 1932, and it won the Pulitzer Prize in 1932. Buck herself won the Nobel Prize for Literature in 1938, only the third American and the first American woman to do so. Though Buck spent most of her first four decades in China, she was born in West Virginia, went to college in Virginia, had her retarded daughter hospitalized in New Jersey, got a Master's degree from Cornell University in New York, and lived in Pennsylvania from 1934 on. Given her celebrity, we might expect any or all of these states to claim her, but only Virginia did, and only in rather feeble alignment with Willa Cather. ("Though she [Cather] does not use Virginia scenes, her matured and careful art reflects the State in its sense of background and its leisured grace of style. Something similar may be said of the Far-Eastern novels of Pearl Buck, who is a Virginian by descent and a graduate of Randolph-Macon Women's College.") Pennsylvania, West Virginia, New York, and New Jersey were silent.

The New Deal progressives who ran the Writers' Project may have disliked overt sentiment, moralizing, and religion, and they may have been suspicious of writers who were just too popular to be really good, but what on earth did they have against Edith Wharton? When Wharton died in 1937, as her long obituary in the *New York Times* attested, she had been a literary star for decades. She had published thirty-eight books (according to the obituary—it was actually more), and many had received popular as well as critical acclaim. She had won the Pulitzer Prize in 1921 for *The Age of Innocence*; she was the first woman to win. Yale had awarded her an honorary doctorate of letters; again she was the first woman. Other honors abounded: In France, her primary residence after 1911, Wharton was an officer of the Legion of Honor, while back home she won the Gold Medal of the National Institute of Arts and Letters—once again the first woman—and she was a member of the National Institute of Arts and Letters and the American Academy of Arts and Letters. Her friends included luminaries like Henry James, Sinclair Lewis, André Gide, Theodore Roosevelt, and

10. Dennis Wepman, "Barton, Bruce Fairchild," *American National Biography Online*, February 2000, http://www.anb.org.turing.library.northwestern.edu/articles/10/10-00105.html, accessed July 16, 2010.

Bernard Berenson. Her writing had been translated into six films and at least two plays, one starring Katharine Cornell.[11] Yet only two Literature essays mentioned her, and one was the Nebraska essay that pointed out how Willa Cather (who seemed to be the universal touchstone) rejected her influence!

Wharton had a lot of states that might reasonably claim her, Nebraska not being one of them. She grew up in New York City, the setting for many of her best-known works such as *The House of Mirth* (1905) and *The Age of Innocence* (1920). Her family traveled extensively, spending summers in Newport, Rhode Island, and a few in Bar Harbor, Maine, and winters in Paris. Marrying in 1885, she and her husband lived in New York and Newport; Newport is the setting for much of *The Age of Innocence* as well as a play she wrote, *The Twilight of the God* (1899). When they tired of Newport, the couple designed and built a mansion called "The Mount" in Lenox, Massachusetts, which was completed in 1902. Edith lived at The Mount for the better part of a decade, and it was there that she wrote *The House of Mirth*. Her most widely read work was (and remains) *Ethan Frome* (1911), which takes place in western Massachusetts and is based on a well-known sledding accident in Lenox; this short novel is steeped in New England local color, as is its companion work *Summer* (1917). So although Wharton had lived in France for twenty-five years, most of her writing was set in America, and one might expect to find her in the Literature essays of New York—State and City—Massachusetts certainly, Rhode Island, and possibly Maine. Yet she appears only in *New York Panorama* and only in a single paragraph that is astonishing for what it fails to say:

> As for New York's moneyed aristocracy it was not until the early years of the present century that it began to inspect itself, in the novels of Edith Wharton. In *The House of Mirth* (1905) and later in *The Custom of the Country* (1913), Mrs. Wharton subjected the social group of which she was a member to a searching criticism within a distinctly class-limited set of values. The aristocrat had failed of being an aristocrat, and the fault lay with money, in the hands of the *nouveaux riches*; which was much the same point of view, with the same element of snobbishness in it, as that of Henry James in his fragmentary *Ivory Tower*. Mrs. Wharton finally, in her popular success, *The Age of*

11. The figure of thirty-eight books reported in the *Times*'s obituary was low, in fact. *Wikipedia* lists forty-seven in total: twenty-two novels (two of which, *The Buccaneers* and *Fast and Loose*, were published posthumously), twelve collections of short stories, nine works of nonfiction, three poetry collections, and one edited book. See "Edith Wharton, 75, Is Dead in France," *New York Times*, August 13, 1937, http://www.nytimes.com/learning/general/onthisday/bday/0124.html; "Edith Wharton," *Wikipedia*, http://en.wikipedia.org/wiki/Edith_Wharton; and Judith E. Funston, "Wharton, Edith," *American National Biography Online*, February 2000, http://www.anb.org.turing.library.northwestern.edu/articles/16/16-01745.html;accessed July 1, 2010.

Innocence (1920), was to take refuge in nostalgia for the 1870's, when "society" was truly "good," having not yet been corrupted by the newcomer from "the Street" with his facile millions and his ignorant disregard for the aristocrat's code of conduct. (171)

With no reference to the breadth and extent of her writing, nor to her many honors (Guide Literature essays rarely failed to mention Pulitzer Prizes), this paragraph was followed by one of equal length about the contemporaneous publication of Upton Sinclair's *The Jungle* and the coming of the new social realism.[12] Wharton fared even worse in the Massachusetts Guide, where she appeared not in the Literature essays but only when one of the tours mentioned "The Mount." Wharton failed to make any appearance at all in the Rhode Island or Maine Guides.

What are we to make of these cases of literary amnesia? Not to put too fine a point on it, Federal Writers' Project personnel, especially the Washington editors who had the ultimate say, were snobs. They exhibited three types of snobbery: literary, political, and gender. They were literary snobs in that they adhered to the conventional canon whenever they could; sheer popularity did not guarantee a place in the essays and might have been damning in some cases. They were political snobs in that authors known or being suspected of being conservative (holding "a distinctly class-limited set of values") got short shrift, while they accorded lavish discussion to the era's proletarian writers, most of whom have passed into oblivion. And above all they were gender snobs: In the pages of the Literature essays, women who were successful in terms of popularity or honor often met neglect or scorn.

Like the Guides as a whole, the Literature essays reflected the tastes of male, northeastern intellectuals. These men were modernists, dismissive of religion and sentiment. They were attentive to history and progressive politics. They were levelers: If big states had literatures, little ones must have them as well. They were snobs. All of these characteristics came to bear on what authors made it into the Literature essays, the essays that collectively defined "Our Literature, from Sea to Shining Sea."

Centuries

Literature essays covered writing from the Age of Discovery to the Age of the New Deal. Each century produced more authors worth discussing

12. Wharton appears one other time in *New York Panorama*, in the "Nationalities: New World Symphony" chapter's section on Italians, where she is included among a list of writers who introduced Italian culture to Americans (*NYP*, 96).

than the previous one, as appendix E, table 8.2 indicates. (Here and in the sections that follow I am indicating both the number of individual *authors* and the number of *mentions*, recalling that one individual author might receive multiple mentions in different State Guides.) "Century" in this analysis refers to when an author wrote (and, usually, published) his or her first major work. This means that an author who first wrote during the eighteenth century but produced the bulk of his or her writing in the nineteenth would be counted as an eighteenth-century author, so these few borderline cases nudge the count toward the earlier centuries. Nevertheless the picture is clear: Over half of the authors in the Guides began writing in the twentieth century, over a third in the nineteenth, and the remaining—less than 10 percent—were earlier.

Two points are noteworthy, the first being that unlike any other century, the nineteenth-century authors had a higher percentage of mentions (37.2 percent) than names (34 percent), indicating that more than one state wished to claim many of them. These authors had already demonstrated some degree of durability—either they were canonical or at least their significance had become conventional—whereas many twentieth-century authors were newly emerging and little known beyond their local area. Following the same logic, we might expect eighteenth-century and earlier authors to have received even more mentions, but they do not. It may be that the State Projects scrambled to come up with some early names but that many of these, such as minor New England theologians, were unknown outside their home territories.

Second, women constituted 22.7 percent of the authors overall, and their percentage increased steadily every century. No woman writing before the nineteenth century received multiple mentions. Women's percentage of mentions was lower than their percentage of individual authors, which indicates that they appeared in more than one State Guide less often than men did.

The years of the authors' births, summarized in appendix E, table 8.3, tell the same story: The typical author was born in the latter half of the nineteenth century. The increased size of the literary market, beginning with the explosion of magazine publishing in the mid-nineteenth century and followed by the growth of inexpensive fiction (dime novels, railway novels, cheap books) and periodical outlets for poetry, meant that more people could aspire to write professionally. No doubt there was a recency effect as well, with contemporary authors or those who wrote in the recent past being more familiar to the writers on the Project.

Gender

We have already seen in table 8.2 that less than a quarter of the individual authors were women. Women were less likely than men to receive multiple mentions, as table 8.4, in appendix E, shows, and moreover, the women who do receive multiple mentions have fewer on average than men do.[13] Only two women, Willa Cather and Harriet Beecher Stowe, received over four mentions.

In addition to the two fundamental reasons—there were fewer women authors in the first place and those there were got slighted in the essays—other factors contributed to women's lower rate of mentions. Many Literature essays included early explorers like John Frémont, Pedro Castañeda de Nágera (one of Coronado's soldiers who recorded his expedition), and Meriwether Lewis, and these were all men. Furthermore, women were less likely to move around the country and win attention in multiple states. Women who moved about were typically following their husbands and thus were less likely to develop their own writing careers; it is notable that some of the most frequently mentioned women writers like Willa Cather were married only to their art.

Indeed, Willa Cather was just the type of author who garnered multiple mentions: She moved around a great deal, she was a regionalist who wrote about several different areas of the country, and she wrote about ordinary people (though she did receive some left-wing criticism in the thirties for writing escapist rather than social-realist novels). The eight Guides that mentioned Cather showed the variety of frames through which states viewed an author whom they claimed as one of their own.

- *Colorado: A Guide to the Highest State* notes that two novels, *The Lost Lady* and *Song of the Lark*, "have major scenes laid in Colorado."
- *Illinois: A Descriptive and Historical Guide* quotes an article H. L. Mencken wrote in 1920 on Chicago as "The Literary Capital of the United States" in which he includes Cather as part of the "Chicago palatinate."
- *Nebraska: A Guide to the Cornhusker State* celebrates Cather in general and her Nebraska-set novels in particular. *O Pioneers* was "a memorable example of the modern regional novel," *My Antonia* was "acclaimed by critics as a great novel of the Middle West," and her career is summed up with, "Few writers have so skillfully evoked a place or an atmosphere as Miss Cather has succeeded in doing

13. Women who are mentioned in more than one Guide received a total of 171 mentions, while men who are mentioned more than once received a total of 917 mentions. Therefore these women average 2.3 (76/171) mentions compared to the men's average of 2.7 (334/917) mentions.

in her subtle and admirable prose," despite the unsettling comment that in her later novels like *Death Comes for the Archbishop* she "seems unable to find the elements of a satisfying philosophy in the modern world, and to depend increasingly on the religious and cultural ideals of an earlier society." [This final note is indicative of the Project's discomfort with traditional religion while at the same time promoting "modern" regionalism.]

- *New Hampshire: A Guide to the Granite State* includes her among the four Pulitzer Prize winners who had stayed at the MacDowell Colony, a residential retreat for creative artists.
- *New Mexico: A Guide to the Colorful State* claims that among New Mexico writers "many nationally known names are included, indicating that New Mexico's literature, although regional in character, is not merely regional in interest or in quality. Some of these authors were of established reputation before coming to New Mexico or writing about it; as for instance the late Mary Austin . . . or Willa Cather, whose *Death Comes for the Archbishop* was the result of a literary sojourn."
- *New York Panorama* noted that Cather and many other regional writers had come to New York City to find a publisher "and New York, being not merely the market place but the editorial workshop, somehow feels that they belong to her."
- *Pennsylvania: A Guide to the Keystone State* notes that Cather "undertook her first literary work when she was head of the English department of the Pittsburgh Central High School and at the same time was doing editorial work for the *Pittsburgh Leader*."
- *Virginia: A Guide to the Old Dominion* asserts: "Among Virginia-born novelists . . . Willa Cather is perhaps best assured of lasting favor. Though she does not use Virginia scenes, her matured and careful art reflects the State in its sense of background and its leisured grace of style." [This claim sounds a bit desperate.]

The case of Cather again raises the issue of regionalism. In states that claimed her, we see both an attempt to claim a regional voice (Virginia's "leisured grace of style") and an attempt to say that a state's literature is somehow better than typical regionalism (New Mexico's works that "though regional in character, are *not merely regional* in interest or in quality"; Nebraska produced the "*modern* regional novel"). The thirties were both the heyday of regionalism and the heyday of a strident modernism that rejected the regional.[14] *New York Panorama*, a product of the most politically radical Writers' Project and staunchly aligned with both the proletariat and the cultural avant-garde, handled the issue of Cather's regionalism (and it was hard to write about her without referring to it) by

14. Sometimes the same person was pulled in both directions, Jackson Pollock being a familiar example.

bringing her to New York City and, by implication, into modernity. After a discussion of nineteenth-century regionalism, the essays goes on:

> The regional theme had its day and passed, tending to merge in the end with the Genteel Tradition [a pairing that would align Cather with Wharton and dismiss both]. One thing it revealed was the fact that America henceforth was too large and varied a country to be subjected to the cultural sway of, or even to take its prevailing literary tone from, New York, Boston, Philadelphia, or any other single center of population. The later and *less conscious regionalists* of the 20th century, such as Sherwood Anderson, Willa Cather, and Zona Gale, were to go on writing of the Nebraska, Ohio, or Wisconsin that they knew. They were also to keep their places of residence in the hinterland; yet like so many of the earlier sectional writers, they were to come to New York to make their publishing arrangements and to enjoy occasional intervals of recreation. And New York, being not merely the market place but the editorial workshop, somehow feels that they belong to her. (Italics added)

Note the convoluted logic: Regionalism was passé, but the newer regionalists got away with it because they were unconscious. Although they perversely continued to write about and live in "the hinterland," they had the redeeming good sense of coming to New York to publish and to play [no recreational possibilities in Wisconsin, apparently]. Moreover, by coming to the urban "workshop," they could almost be considered honorary proletarian writers.

Ethnicity

If women were somewhat thin on the ground in the Literature essays, ethnic minorities, including African Americans, Native Americans, Hispanics, and Asians, were even thinner, though perhaps the more important point is that they were there at all. Minority citizens were not scarce in the nation itself—in 1935 "Negroes and other" (it was not until 1960 that the nonwhite minorities were counted separately) accounted for 10.2 percent of the population[15]—but minority authors accounted for less than 4 percent of authors mentioned in the essays, as appendix E, table 8.5 shows. Asians were totally absent, other minorities underrepresented. A few states were exceptions: In both the Arizona and California Guides, Hispanics accounted for 15 percent of the Literature essay mentions, and

15. The estimated total population in 1935 was 127,250,000, of which 12,941,000 were Negro and other. US Census Bureau, 1975, *Historical Statistics of the United States: Colonial Times to 1970*, "Series A 23–28. Annual Estimates of the Population, by Sex and Race: 1900 to 1970," 9.

in Oklahoma, Indians, as they were invariably called, made up 10 percent of the authors.

Each minority presents a different picture. Native American authors, few and far between as they were, predominantly (and perhaps surprisingly) came from the twentieth century. But not all of them: Both the Iowa and the Wisconsin Guides mentioned Chief Black Hawk, the Sauk leader who fought the United States in both the War of 1812 and what became known as the Black Hawk War in the early 1830s and who published his autobiography in 1833. Black Hawk to the contrary notwithstanding, most of the Native American authors mentioned were contemporary, and while most of these wrote historical or fictional works about tribal history, they included the beloved humorist Will Rogers and the playwright Lynn Riggs, whose *Green Grow the Lilacs* ran on Broadway in 1931 and became the basis for the Rodgers and Hammerstein hit *Oklahoma!* a decade later.[16] Another self-identified Native American who did not write in the usual genres was George Todd Downing (1902–74), a Choctaw who wrote detective novels.

To the Project, Hispanics were part of the nation's literary history but not part of its literary present. Most Hispanic names refer to explorers and conquistadors or to their chroniclers, people like Luis Hernández de Biedma, the "King's factor" appointed by the Spanish court to accompany Hernando de Soto on his 1539 expedition to La Florida (all of southeastern United States) and keep a record. De Soto died in 1542, a year before the expedition straggled back to Mexico with fewer than half of the original 640 men. One of them was Hernández de Biedma, who dutifully wrote up his account and sent it to the king the next year. It wasn't published until the nineteenth century however, so only the Arkansas Guide mentioned Hernández de Biedma (calling him Luys de Biedma). Another survivor was the Portuguese "Gentleman from Elvas," whose account came out in 1557 as *True Relation of the Hardships Suffered by Governor Hernando de Soto and Certain Portuguese Gentlemen During the Discovery of the Province of Florida: Now Newly Set Forth by a Gentleman of Elvas*. Although no one knows who the Gentleman from Elvas was, he appeared in four of the Literature essays—for Arkansas, Florida, Louisiana, and Texas—all of which the expedition visited.

Only five Hispanics were contemporary. Two were members of an

16. Both Rogers and Riggs demonstrate the constructed nature of ethnic identification. Rogers was born in Indian Territory (later Oklahoma) to mixed-race parents who both identified as Cherokee; although he figured himself to be only one quarter Cherokee, he famously quipped: "My ancestors did not come over on the Mayflower but they met the boat." Riggs was one-sixteenth Cherokee but his mother made sure he had the land rights associated with the Cherokee Allotment (Dawes Act of 1887).

eminent New Mexico family, the Oteros, that traced its lineage back to the eleventh century. Miguel Antonio Otero (1859–1944) had been territorial governor of New Mexico from 1897 to 1906; in the 1930s he published a three-part memoir about the Southwest during the frontier days, along with *The Real Billy the Kid* (1936). His niece, Nina Otero-Warren, campaigned for women's suffrage and held prominent positions in state government; a Republican who had unsuccessfully run for the House in the twenties, Otero-Warren directed literacy education programs for New Mexico's Civilian Conservation Corps and the WPA. She wrote about her ancestry, childhood, and family hacienda in *Old Spain in Our Southwest* (1936), a popular success that remains in print. Another New Mexican was Elfego Baca, a colorful sheriff and U.S. marshal from territorial days who was the subject of Kyle Crichton's *Law and Order Ltd.* (1928). Two came from other states: Enrique Alferez, a Mexican-born Louisiana sculptor designed the "Fountain of the Winds" at New Orleans's Lakefront Airport and worked for the WPA; the Louisiana Literature essay says he collaborated with Hermann B. Deutsch on *The Wedge: A Novel of Mexico*, although the Library of Congress indicates Deutsch as the sole author. Ambrose Gonzales, a South Carolinian journalist of Cuban descent who collected stories in the Gullah dialect made it into that state's essay.

African Americans, on the other hand, stood firmly within the twentieth century. Three literary giants-to-be, Richard Wright, Margaret Walker and Ralph Ellison, were Project employees (Wright and Walker in Chicago, Ellison in New York); at the time they were in their twenties and had not yet emerged. A fourth was already well known: Zora Neale Hurston, who worked for the Florida Project, got a full and admiring paragraph in the Florida Guide (Ernest Hemingway got the same amount of attention on the previous page) that remarked on her masterpiece, *Their Eyes Were Watching God* (1937), as well as an earlier novel and two nonfiction works.

The Florida Literature essay was unusual in that it focused on Negro writers as a category. The two-paragraph section began: "The Negro's part in Florida literature has progressed from the simple recording of slave days to thoughtful self-expression." The first author discussed, oddly enough, was white: Jonathan Walker, jailed and branded for slave stealing in the 1840s, wrote the *Trial and Imprisonment of Jonathan Walker, at Pensacola Florida, for Aiding Slaves to Escape from Bondage* (1845), which became a favorite with Abolitionists and inspired a poem by John Greenleaf Whittier. The essay discussed John Wallace, a state senator during Reconstruction who wrote *Carpetbag Rule in Florida* (1888), and James Weldon Johnson, "gifted and versatile . . . as lawyer, poet, musical comedy composer, diplomatic official, author, editor, orator, and educator." The second paragraph turned to Hurston, noting that she lived in "Eatonville, Florida's only incorporated Negro town," and that her four books appeared in five years; each book gets exactly one sentence. The general impression given by the essay was that African American authors like Hurston and Johnson were phenomena, prodigious and strange.

The most striking aspect of how the Literature essays treated African American authors is how many failed to discuss them at all. One might expect that Deep South states could not manage to come up with many Negro authors, although even these varied: Alabama (7 percent of the essay's author mentions were Negroes) did better than Mississippi (0 percent), and Georgia (6 percent) better than North Carolina (3 percent). What is more surprising was that urban northern states with leftwing Projects were oblivious to the African American literary presence. Neither Massachusetts, the center of abolitionism and long the home of Frederick Douglass, nor Illinois, where Richard Wright and Margaret Walker were working on the Project, could find any Negro authors worth mentioning. Nor could New Jersey. And in New York City, which gave America the Harlem Renaissance and the "New Negro" movement before it, and which produced important writers and editors of the twenties and thirties including Claude McKay, Jean Toomer, Countee Cullen, Jessie Fauset, Charles S. Johnson, and of course Zora Neale Hurston, the Project could only come up with a single African American author, Langston Hughes, out of the 163 names it mentioned.

By the standards of the twenty-first century, the Federal Writers' Project was remarkably unconcerned with being inclusive. The Literature essays underrepresented women and they drastically underrepresented minorities. On the other hand, they did include them; women and ethnic minorities may not have been present proportionate to their share of the population or even to their presence in the world of literature, but some were there, fixed in "Our Literature from Sea to Shining Sea." This in itself was remarkable. As we shall see, compared with other early and mid-twentieth-century attempts to define American literature, the Literature essays' diversity, minimal as it was, was an innovation and a step in the right direction.

Places

The American Guide Series came out not in regional volumes, as originally had been proposed, but state by state, and most of the materials that a State Guide covered were congruent with the borders of that state.

Cities and Tours fell neatly within state lines. Essay topics like History, Agriculture, Industry, and Architecture were somewhat more regional in character, but a Guide could discuss them in terms of how they pertained to that particular state. Literature was different, however, for like anyone else, authors moved around. An author might be born in one state, establish a career in other states, write about other states, spend time in still other states; authors were not in any sense contained. This gave the State Projects considerable leeway in selecting who would represent that state's literature. The results were as follows.

Place Born

The vast majority of the authors mentioned in the Guides were born in America. Of the 14 percent born elsewhere, about half came from the British Isles, most of the rest from continental Europe. Appendix E, table 8.6 shows the patterns for both individual authors and author mentions.

American-born authors were in State Guides that were either close to home or far from it. Over two-fifths (43.7 percent) were born in the same state as the Guide in which they were mentioned (e.g., born in Wisconsin and mentioned in the Wisconsin Guide's Literature essay), while a similar proportion (44.6 percent) were born in an entirely different census division (e.g., born in Wisconsin [East North Central division] and mentioned in the California Guide [Pacific division]). Map 8.1 shows the census regions and divisions. Only a little over a tenth of the authors appeared in a Guide from a different state within the same division (e.g., born in Wisconsin [East North Central] and mentioned in the Illinois Guide [also East North Central]).

There might be a couple reasons for this pattern of very close / very far. First, authors who stayed close to home would have had an advantage with their state's Writers' Project; in some cases the authors actually worked on the Project, and in any case they were apt to be known to Project workers. People who had roamed far from home, on the other hand, might have been more successful, better known overall (i.e., well known enough to earn a Guide mention), than those who remained strictly local. If this thinking is correct, we would expect to find that bestselling authors received disproportionately more mentions in Guides from states out of their home division (the Wisconsin-born author in the California Guide pattern), for they or at least their fame was likely to have traveled (the Edith-Wharton-in-Nebraska pattern). This turns out indeed to be the case. Of the bestselling authors of the 1920s and 1930s who made it into the Literature essays, 52 percent were mentioned in Guides from a different

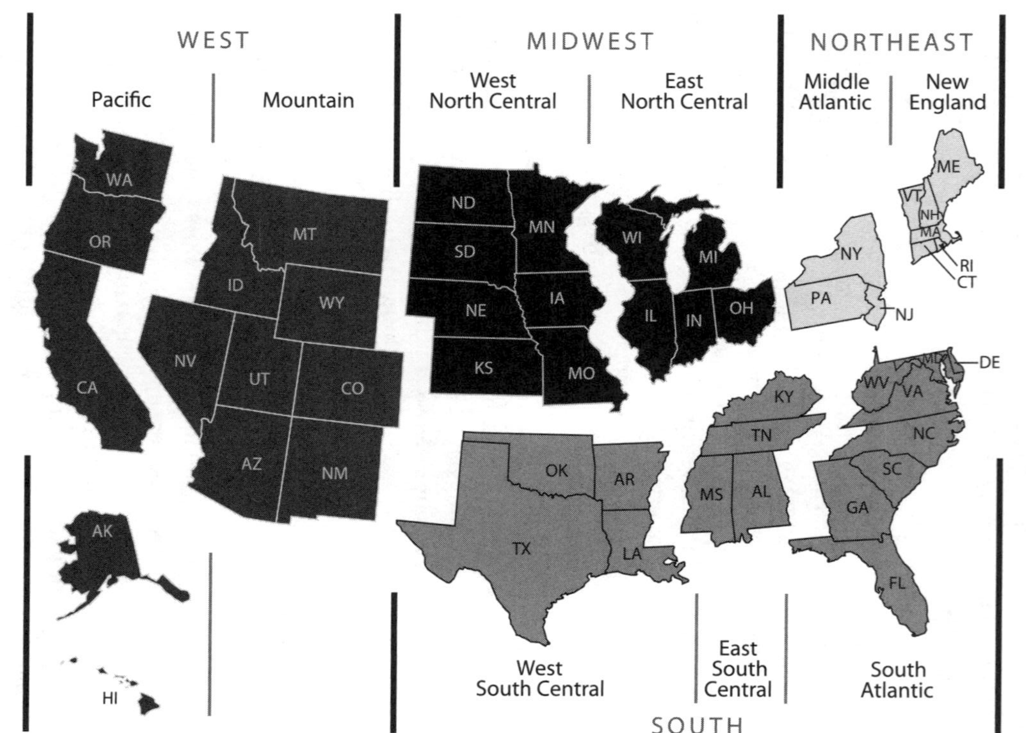

Map 8.1 US census regions and divisions

division, as opposed to 45 percent overall. The percentage from Guides within the same division but a different state was almost the same as overall (10 percent) so it was the same-state mentions that had given the most ground (38 percent as opposed to 44 percent overall).[17] Thus we have two different types: local literati and successful authors who had left home.

Second, only three divisions had major publishing centers: Middle Atlantic above all (New York City and Philadelphia), but also New England (Boston) and East North Central (Chicago). Therefore writers from other divisions who left home to pursue literary careers had to leave their home division, not just their home state. If this thinking is correct, we would expect to see a higher ratio of "2s" (different state in the same division) to "1s" (same state) in New England, the Mid-Atlantic, and East North Central than in the other six divisions, for in these three divisions an aspiring writer could head for a metropolitan literary center without actually leaving his or her home division. As appendix E, table 8.7 shows, this is exactly what we find; the ratio of 2s to 1s for the three divisions with publishing centers is 2.8/1, while for the other regions the ratio is 4.7/1. In those three divisions, successful authors could remain fairly, if not strictly, local.

State Born

Comparing states where authors were born relative to which State Guides they were mentioned in reveals how some states produced authors for export, others for local consumption.

Appendix E, tables 8.8 and 8.9 show the states in which the authors were born, the first by individual authors and the second by author mentions. Table 8.8 is straightforward: thirty-seven authors were born in Alabama, twenty-three men and fourteen women, and the Alabama authors account for 1.6 percent of the total 2,292 authors born in the United States (cf. table 8.6). Table 8.9 refers to Guide mentions, not individuals, and should be read as follows: there were twenty-four Alabama-born writers mentioned in the Alabama Guide, six Alabama-born writers mentioned in the Guides from other East South Central states (Kentucky, Mississippi, and Tennessee), and nine Alabama-born writers mentioned in Guides from states outside the East South Central division, making a total of thirty-nine mentions of Alabama-born writers, or 1.3 percent of the total 2,908 US-born author mentions.[18]

17. Bestsellers come from Korda (2001).

18. Note that the state-of-birth count does not pick up authors mentioned in a State Guide who were born in another state; if the Alabama Guide mentions an author born in Georgia, that author does not show up in the Alabama count. To take an extreme example, a long essay like Louisiana's

When we compare the mentions to the individual authors, we find that usually the two tell the same story. States that produced a lot of authors account for a lot of author mentions, and the reverse. For example, Michigan accounts for 2.4 percent of the author births and Michigan authors account for 2.4 percent of the mentions. Most of the time the birth states and the mentions are within a couple tenths of a percent of one another.

Some variations do occur, however, and they indicate which states were especially productive of American authors well known outside their home states and which states were especially parochial in their literatures. In nine states the difference between percent of total authors and percent of total mentions is 0.3 or greater. Six of these—Indiana, Massachusetts, Missouri, New Jersey, New York and Pennsylvania—are states where the percent of mentions is higher. That means, for example, that 2.7 percent of US-born authors came from Indiana, but Indiana-born authors account for 3.3 percent of the mentions. Massachusetts is the most extreme case (6.8 born, 7.7 mentions), for it gave birth to many authors who show up in other State Guides. Three southern states show the reverse pattern, where the percent of authors born in the state is higher than the percent of mentions. Louisiana is the outstanding example, where 2.8 percent of the individual authors were born in the state but they make up only 2.3 percent of the mentions; this is due to the unusual length and comprehensiveness of the Louisiana essay. Alabama and South Carolina have milder versions of the same pattern. These states' authors were known locally but not beyond.

Overall we might think of states as exporting or retaining authors (i.e., in terms of author mentions): Massachusetts was an *exporter*, Louisiana a *retainer*. A look at four middle-of-the-country, middle-of-the-alphabet states, Indiana through Kentucky, shows the range of possibilities. Kansas is typical: Almost half the mentions are in-state, slightly more are in a different division, and a handful stay in the West North Central division. We can visualize this as actual movement—a novelist born in Kansas either stayed in Kansas, moved to New York, or moved next door to Nebraska—and for the most part this is roughly correct, as long as we remember that some mentions do not involve actual moves or even visits (Nebraska mentioned Edith Wharton although she never went there). Indiana had more authors staying within its own division than Kansas did, no doubt because

---

Guide mentions many authors born out of state, and they don't appear under Louisiana (they would be counted under the states or countries where the authors were born); on the other hand, Louisiana-born authors are mentioned in only five other State Guides, one in the same West South Central division and four outside.

of publishing and journalism opportunities that Chicago afforded. Iowa showed an unusually high number of in-state mentions, indicating the thoroughness of the Iowa Writers' Project in identifying local writers; in this respect Iowa resembled Louisiana. And Kentucky authors typically left both the state and the division, this being due to general migration patterns out of Appalachia and to a lack of publishing opportunities in the East South Central division. So Iowa was a retainer of authors, Kentucky an exporter.

Authors and State Populations

Some states claimed lots of authors in their Literature essays, others only a few. Louisiana named the most, 192, reflecting the extraordinary commitment of its director, Lyle Saxon, as well as its complex literary heritage. Kentucky, larger than Louisiana in population, named only thirteen; the English professor who wrote Kentucky's essay valued depth rather than breadth.[19] Appendix E, table 8.10 shows the number of authors each essay mentioned and ranks them, comparing states' author ranks with states' population ranks as of 1930.[20] States where the rankings are separated by more than ten places are highlighted. The states fall into three clusters; call them the Balanced (white), the Boastful (light gray), and the Bashful (dark gray). The Balanced states' Literature essays named authors in numbers roughly proportional with the size of the state itself. Big states like Pennsylvania and California naturally had lots of authors to discuss, as did New York City, while small states like Vermont and Delaware naturally had just a few.

The Boastful states' essays set forth vastly more authors than the state's size would seem to have warranted. Louisiana heads the list in terms of the number of authors it mentioned, though it is in the middle (twenty-second) in terms of its actual population. New Mexico was even more egregious: a puny forty-fifth in terms of size, a mighty eighth in terms of the number of authors it featured. The Pacific Northwest seem to have been

19. Grant Knight, professor in the English Language and Literature Department at the University of Kentucky, wrote the Literature essay. He devoted a full paragraph to five of the Kentucky authors and two paragraphs to James Lane Allen. This was unusual; more often the people who wrote the Literature essays (who were usually writers in the State Projects, not English professors) tried to cram in as many names as possible without much discussion of any one in particular, but Knight's approach was the opposite.

20. Not every state produced a Literature essay (forty-four did) and we have two additional essays, one from New York City and the other from Washington, DC, making a total of forty-six "states." I have simply left out the four no-essay states (Idaho, Nevada, North Dakota, South Dakota) from the population ranking. The census includes New York City in the New York figure, of course, so I have indicated both as number 1 in population.

prone to boasting, as were some other western states like Utah, Oklahoma, and Wyoming.

But not, surprisingly, Texas. Bashful states like Texas could not seem to find many authors to write about, regardless of how big they were. Illinois was the third-largest state, and its state director an English professor and a regionalist, but the Illinois Project could only come up with eighty-six authors. Kentucky, a middling-size state, only came up with thirteen. The Upper Midwest was especially reticent: Ohio, Michigan, Wisconsin, Indiana, and Minnesota all named far fewer authors than one would expect from states of their size. A unique combination of factors influenced each state's essay. Nevertheless, as we have seen earlier, regional stereotypes about, in this case, bragging westerners (and Louisianans) and modest midwesterners seem apt.

Genres

State Projects had to face a fundamental question: What counted as literature?[21] Their answer: Literature was whatever the Literature essays ended up mentioning. (This has also been the working definition for the present analysis.) The essays discussed authors and works that went well beyond what people typically think falls in the category of "literature." We now turn to genres, specifically, to how the Literature essays connected the authors they discussed with forms of writing that readers would recognize, forms that they claimed to be literature.

Exploring this topic raised some methodological issues. I assigned "genre" to be *how the Literature essay in question categorized the author*. This meant that different State Guides might have assigned the same author to different genres. For example, most people would think of H. L. Mencken as a journalist first and foremost—he wrote for the *Baltimore Sun* for forty-two years after seven years at another Baltimore paper, and he edited the *American Mercury* for close to ten years—and indeed that's how the Maryland Guide treated him. But the New York City Guide positioned him as a literary critic, responding (a bit defensively) to Mencken having named Chicago as the nation's "literary capital." Even more defensive was the Virginia essay's counterpunch to Mencken's put-down of the South as the "Sahara of the Bozarts." So Mencken's genre was "Journalism" in the Mary-

21. The question of what was literature, specifically how literature could be distinguished from pornography, had been in the news, for in 1934 the US Court of Appeals had lifted the ban on James Joyce's *Ulysses*, in place since 1921.

land Guide but "Criticism" in the New York City and Virginia Guides, and I coded him accordingly.

When Americans think of "literature," they usually think of fiction, poetry, and drama. This definition, historically fairly recent, has been conventional since the nineteenth century. It covers what is taught in a typical English or comparative literature course. It is what the National Endowment for the Arts asks about in its comprehensive studies of "who reads literature."[22] Usage often tilts toward the high end—romance novels or doggerel are not "really literature" in the eyes of many people—but the category of literature itself typically begins and ends with these three.

The Literature essays expanded this definition dramatically. Appendix E, table 8.11 shows that only half (49.9 percent) of the authors mentioned in the essays were associated with one of the three conventional genres. Fiction accounted for only a little over a quarter of the total. Poetry just about tied with history for second place, well behind fiction, and drama was almost insignificant. Beyond these three, the essays discussed a very mixed bouquet. Travel narratives, theology, journalism, political oratory, archeology, children's books—the essays herded all of these into literature's capacious fold.

Thus the answer to the question of "what is literature?" was cheerfully democratic, not to say promiscuous. Literature was anything that either the state directors or the Washington editors thought to be suitable in terms of their overlapping agendas of celebrating the state's history and culture, standardizing the Guides, showing that every state had its own distinctive voice, and keeping the writers employed and safely occupied. A closer look at the genres discovers two unexpected consequences of this relaxed definition of literature. One involves gender and ethnicity, while the other involves geography.

Expanding the number of genres included as "Literature" worked to the *disadvantage of women authors*. As the subtotals indicate, women authors made up almost a third of the three traditional literary genres but only 12 percent of the others, and in several—publishing, political, theology, criticism, humor—they were negligible or totally absent. I believe this is because, unlike the three traditional genres, the expanded-definition genres usually require some type of institutional position. Most theologians are ordained clergy; most travel writers are explorers funded by governmental

22. The NEA studies of who is reading literature and "the role of literature in the lives of Americans" are based on surveys that ask participants if, "during the previous twelve months, they had read any novels, short stories, plays, or poetry in their leisure time" (National Endowment for the Arts 2004, 2009).

agencies or commercial enterprises; most political discourse comes from elected officials. Publishers work for firms, journalists for newspapers, and critics and philosophers for universities. So while a women may write a novel or poetry while remaining firmly ensconced in the domestic sphere (and she may likewise write children's books, the one nontraditional genre in which women are well represented), in the past she was much less likely to write history, journalism, literary criticism, travel journals, theology, or political theory because she lacked an institutional base of support.

Though it hurt women, the expansion of the definition of what was literature worked to the *advantage of Hispanic and Native American authors* in making it into the essays. As appendix E, table 8.12 indicates, these minority authors were concentrated in the nontraditional genres; only 6 percent (3/49) of the Hispanic mentions came from the traditional literary genres, and less than a third of Native Americans (7/22). African American authors, on the other hand, were like whites in that just under half of their mentions come from the three traditional genres, though they were much more likely to be poets than novelists; 34 percent (20/59) of African American mentions were for poetry, compared with 17 percent overall. All three minority groups wrote in the historical genres, recording the experience of their own people, and Hispanics were especially strong in travel writing because they had documented early Spanish expeditions.

The second discovery is geographic. Every state had its own unique influences stemming from its history and from the tastes and imaginations of the Project writers, so comparing the genre patterns by the nine census divisions is crude. Nevertheless, a rough picture emerges in appendix E, table 8.13: The Northeast, especially the census divisions of Middle Atlantic and East North Central, had a more conservative definition of literature, one favoring the three traditional genres of fiction, poetry, and drama, than did the rest of the country.

The concept of a "cultural hearth" gives a helpful way to think about this. Historical geographer D. W. Meinig defined a cultural hearth as "an area wherein new basic cultural systems and configurations are developed and nurtured before spreading vigorously outward to alter the character of much larger areas."[23] Although the traditional genres were not new, the idea of cultural centers establishing and institutionalizing specific cultural patterns seems apt. For the United States since the eighteenth century, the cultural hearth had been the Northeast, notably New York, Massachusetts, Pennsylvania, Illinois, Ohio, and New Jersey. This cultural hearth turns

23. Meinig (1986): 52.

out to have been culturally conservative, for as table 8.13 shows, these divisions, especially Middle Atlantic and East North Central, had high ratios of traditional to nontraditional mentions. (New England was somewhat less traditional because its essays included large numbers of sermon writers and philosophers.)

On the other hand, the farther away from the northeastern cultural hearth the division was, the less strict the boundaries of literature were. The divisions of East South Central, Pacific, and especially Mountain have low ratios, their State Projects being more inclined to look outside those standard three genres when deciding what should be included as literature. One would expect West South Central to be in this group; the only reason it is not is because of the size and therefore impact of the Louisiana essay and Lyle Saxon's conservative sense of what was literature. Fully 56.8 percent of the Louisiana Guide mentions refer to one of the three traditional genres, so the ratio of traditional to nontraditional is 1.4 to 1, the same as Middle Atlantic. If we look at the other three states in the West South Central division, we find that only 37.3 percent of the mentions refer to fiction, poetry, and drama, the ratio being .6 to 1, the same as Mountain, so these three fully fit the away-from-the-Northeast-means-less-traditional pattern.

Gender and Place

Just as places outside the Northeast were more catholic in their sense of what was literature, they were also more open to women writers. This finding might appear surprising. We have already seen in table 8.4 that the Literature essays did not pay an inordinate amount of attention to women authors (22.7 percent of the authors, 20.9 percent of the mentions). We have seen that women tended to write in the conventional genres of fiction, poetry, and drama, and we have seen that the census divisions outside of the Northeast were less conventional than the northeastern cultural hearth. So we might expect that women would do best in the Northeast.

However the tendency of places outside the Northeast to exhibit greater inclusiveness and diversity was true in the case of women authors as it had been with genre. Appendix E, table 8.14 compares the ratios of male to female authors in each census division. The three northeastern divisions—Middle Atlantic, East North Central, and New England—all have higher than average ratios, as does East South Central. And all of the non-northeastern divisions except for East South Central have lower ratios. Once again the cultural periphery—roughly speaking, the states farthest from New York City—showed the greatest inclusiveness, thereby expanding the definition of what was literature and who was a writer.

Accidental Diversity

The overall picture is clear and robust: Writers in states that were some distance from the northeastern, New York–centered cultural hearth were less apt to display the conventional understanding of what counted as literature and who counted as authors. This greater inclusivity, resulting in greater diversity, was not anyone's intention. We have no reason to believe that the state directors in the Rocky Mountains or Great Plains were any more concerned with gender and ethnic inequalities, or any more preoccupied with expanding the definition of literature, than their counterparts in the Northeast. The greater diversity of their State Guides was the result of the geographic structure of the Project, which itself was the result of political decision making under duress and of the desire to give jobs to people in every state.

Two structural elements, both of which we have seen repeatedly, shaped the cultural geography of the American Guide Series. First, the Federal Writers' Project organized the series by states, not by what people considered more natural cultural regions like "the Great Plains" or "Appalachia" or "the South." Given that almost all the Guides had Literature essays, that organization had an equalizing impact: Oklahoma had its "Literature" just like Pennsylvania, Arizona just like Massachusetts. Second, although the essays were drafted locally, they were vetted in Washington, vetted by the East Coast, male, white, left-of-center, Columbia-and-Harvard-educated, inside-the-Beltway-before-there-was-a-Beltway editors.[24] Nothing got mentioned that these editors didn't regard as worthy. So the Guides as a whole, and the authors that made it into the Literature essays, resulted from the fraught combination of a dispersed geography of production with a centralized geography of taste.

The result was accidental diversity. In spite of the fact that no one promoted or even cared about cultural diversification, the Guides pre-

24. The "Beltway," which Washingtonians are said to be inside of, is Interstate 495, which circles Washington and which was completed in 1964. During the New Deal Americans outside the Beltway-to-be would refer simply to "Washington" or "government" (as in "government work") to connote the same sense of federal officials whose parochialism is that of a company town and who are out of touch with the rest of the country.

sented diversity in spite of themselves. And while no one thought about whether the Guides would have any cultural influence or any influence at all beyond providing jobs and promoting tourism, this accidental diversity was to have a profound impact on how Americans saw their culture, "Our Literature, from Sea to Shining Sea." This impact is the subject of the following chapter.

PART FIVE

Casting Culture

NINE

Defining Literature

Through the American Guide Series, the Federal Writers' Project displayed and encouraged a broader definition of American literature than ever before. The Literature essays expanded the nation's conception of its culture, in terms of what kinds of people had produced it, what sort of works it contained, and where those people and works had come from. Both the immediate impact of the essays and their enduring influence over seven decades and counting have taught Americans to view their literature, and indeed their culture, as characterized by a multidimensional diversity, a view that was unthinkable before the Guides.

This chapter looks at the works that defined American literature both before and after the State Guides. It shows that the Guides were not simply mileposts on the way, not just reflecting trends, but instead they were abrupt and sweeping in their inclusiveness. They introduced change and a capacious definition of American literature that would not firmly take hold for another half century. And they did all this by accident—unemployed hacks struggling with bureaucratic snafus, high-handed New Yorkers struggling with hinterland rubes, New Deal diehards struggling with red-baiting congressmen—and not by design. A mighty recasting of American culture was the farthest thing from anyone's mind, but that's exactly what they were doing.

Defining American Literature

Until the very end of the nineteenth century, scholars and readers conceived of American literature as being a younger, less-developed branch of English literature. Commentators pontificated on "Why a National Literature Cannot Flourish in the United States of North America."[1] Universities never taught it as a stand-alone subject. Discussions of American literature tended to be apologetic, sometimes viewing it as an expression of New England idealism or as a pale effort to replicate the Old World genres on new soil.[2]

Post–Civil War relief that the country had not fallen apart followed by the celebration of the nation's centennial encouraged a more positive evaluation of New World culture, along with a determination to assess just what cultural bonds Americans shared. This was not simply a matter of the wealthy starting to collect American-made antiques and the middle class joining them in a passion for colonial revival furnishings, although both took place. On the academic front, efforts began to define and make available an American literary tradition, and thereby to differentiate it from English literature. Volumes of American literary history and anthologies of American writers resulted, and while some of these were vast works suited for the library, others were more compact and were aimed at undergraduate and graduate students.

The four most prominent and widely used of these were (and are) informally known as Pattee, Parrington, Spiller, and Norton. One or another of these volumes has been on the desks of students for over a century, and their influence is immeasurable. This chapter looks at these four monumental definers of American literature and compares them with the definition that the American Guides' Literature essays delivered. It asks if the diversification in the conception of our literature was a gradual linear evolution or one marked by lurches and reversals, and it asks where the Guides fit in to the picture.

Fred Lewis Pattee and the New Literature

Fred Lewis Pattee (1863–1950) was the founding father of American literature as an academic discipline. A New Hampshire Yankee, Pattee studied at Dartmouth College and, having worked as a teacher and journalist, began

1. This was the title of an 1845 tract by Joseph Rocchieti, an Italian immigrant, who argued that religious fanaticism and unprincipled newspaper editors both worked against the development of a national literature.

2. Graff (1987).

his long career in the English Department of Penn State in 1894. A bundle of energy, in addition to his scholarship and teaching Pattee wrote poetry and three novels, toured the British Isles on bicycle, and worked as a Methodist preacher.

A handful of courses on American writers and works had begun cropping up in the late nineteenth century, and the time was ripe for someone to theorize the field. Two years after he arrived at Penn State, Pattee published an article asking, "Is There an American Literature?"[3] Acknowledging that European literatures were defined by language and that the idea of there being two distinct literatures in a single language was unprecedented, he asserted that the unprecedented was not the impossible and "the time has come to study American literature, apart from the English product, as if it were a distinct entity." Pattee's case was at once pedagogical (the demand for textbooks devoted to American writing was increasing), historical (the pace of change during the nineteenth century—agricultural abundance, westward expansion and immigration, inventions like the cotton gin and steamboat, the conflict over slavery leading to the Civil War—had "developed an American spirit that makes us vastly different from every other people"), and philosophical: "It seems to me that it may be laid down almost as an axiom that when a distinct nation has acquired a distinct personality and has produced writers and writings *sui generis*, reflecting the soil, the spirit, the individuality of that people, then that nation has a distinct literature, no matter what may be the language in which it is written."

Since this position was controversial, Pattee set out to defend it with *A History of American Literature since 1870*. Originally published by Century in 1915 and reissued by Appleton-Century in 1933 (another reprint came out in 1968 from Cooper Square), *A History of American Literature* did not just transform the field: It created it. Writers of post–Civil War America, Pattee claimed, were no longer in thrall to English models as their predecessors had been. He argued that important writers came from outside of New England, and he included popular authors in his discussion; both of these were revolutionary moves. The book became the essential textbook for American literary studies, and over a quarter million copies were sold.[4] Building on the success of his first volume, Pattee followed up with two others that covered the years before and after his masterpiece; *The New*

3. Pattee (1896).

4. This figure is reported by Penn State's College of Liberal Arts, http://www.la.psu.edu/cla-alumni/centennial/fred_lewis_pattee.shtml, accessed August 4, 2011. See also Robert L. Gale, "Pattee, Fred Lewis," *American National Biography Online*, February 2000, http://www.anb.org.turing.library.northwestern.edu/articles/16/16-01266.html, accessed August 4, 2011.

American Literature (1930) updated the coverage from 1890 to 1930, while *The First Century of American Literature* (1935) covered the period from 1770 to 1870.

These three boundary-setting books defined the field for the new century. "American literature" became pretty much what Pattee said it was, and in some respects he was quite radical. Not only did he stress the independence and broad geographical range of American literature in general, but he argued that literary criticism should include historical and biographical analysis and should take account of popular writers as well as those with higher literary ambitions, for indeed their popularity indicated something about the American "distinct personality." In this regard, Pattee was less snobbish than the Federal Writers' Project editors. For example, in 1797 "A lady of Massachusetts" (revealed decades later to be Hannah Foster) published *The Coquette*, a novel based on a Connecticut scandal that involved forbidden passion, adultery, an illegitimate pregnancy, and the tragic end of a woman gone astray. Not surprisingly, *The Coquette* became a bestseller and remained one for decades. Unimpressed by mere popularity, the Massachusetts Guide did not deign to mention it. But Pattee did, calling it "the best of the seduction novels" that marked a new era of feminine fiction.[5] On the other hand, Pattee's own literary tastes were conservative. He favored writing that demonstrated sincerity and naturalness, he championed regionalists like Hamlin Garland and Mary E. Wilkins Freeman, and he was skeptical of modernists and writers he considered affected; in one essay he dismissed Emily Dickinson's reputation as "a sentimentalized myth."[6]

In the preface to his first volume, Pattee declared that American literature began with Washington Irving's *Sketchbook of Geoffrey Crayon*, which was serialized in 1819 and 1820. He divided the century into three periods—the Knickerbocker Period, the New England Period, and the National Period—and the latter, beginning after the Civil War and the subject of the book, was "our first really national period, all-American, autochthonic. It was not until after the war that our writers ceased to imitate and looked to their own land for material and inspiration." Pattee included only authors who "did their first distinctive work before 1892," and he explicitly focused on poetry, fiction, and essays, largely excluding history (which "all too often . . . has been presented in a colorless, journalistic form that bars it forever from consideration as literature" [416])

5. Pattee (1935): 90.

6. Pattee (1937) regarded Dickinson's poetic gifts as modest and suggested that she had been ill served by biographers who romanticized her "Lady of Shallot" life and by editors who were insufficiently discriminating; "great need is there in her overgrown garden for vigorous weeding" (197).

and drama (in his view, none of any literary value had yet appeared). His second volume took up the story where the first left off, though he limited the coverage to writers whose first work appeared before 1920. Its preface claimed:

> The volume is built upon the general thesis that the thirty or forty years since the 1890 decade constitute a distinct and well-rounded period in American literary history, that literature during this single generation of marvelous change departed so widely from all that had gone before that it stands alone and unique, that the soul of it and the driving power of it were born in the new areas beyond the Alleghenies, and that during its thirty or forty years was produced the greater bulk of those writings that we may call distinctively our own, work peculiarly to be called *American* literature. (vii)

And the third volume covered the century before 1870. By the time he wrote this, Pattee had expanded his thinking in two notable directions. First, he brought in a variety of genres beyond the initial three; for example, now he had several chapters on magazines and one on "gift books and annuals." Second, he devoted a chapter to women authors, "The Feminist Fifties," which covered not only Harriet Beecher Stowe but also the writers for *Godey's Lady's Book* and bestselling authors like Susan Warner, Fanny Fern, and Emma (usually identified by her initials, E.D.E.N.) Southworth. While Pattee did not entirely disagree with Hawthorne's complaint about these constituting a "d___d mob of scribbling women," he included them nevertheless, for they were part of "our own."

After reviewing the backgrounds of the three other definers of the American canon, I will compare Pattee's definition of American literature, along with those of Parrington, Spiller, and the Norton anthology that Nina Baym edited, with that of the American Guide Literature essays. In the case of Pattee, 1,265 individual names appear in his index for all three volumes. For this analysis I have drawn a 20 percent sample, 253 names, as the comparison set.

V. L. Parrington and the Progressive View

Twelve years after *A History of American Literature* came the second effort to delineate American literature: V. L. Parrington's *Main Currents of American Thought*. More theoretically ambitious than Pattee, Parrington aimed for a comprehensive intellectual history based on a Marxian analysis of the struggle between conservative and liberal ideas. Although his economic determinism later seemed dated, Parrington's three-volume masterpiece was widely acclaimed at the time of its publication; the first two volumes came out in 1927 and won that year's Pulitzer Prize for history, with the third appearing in 1930, a year after his death.[7]

Vernon Louis Parrington (1871–1929) grew up and began his teaching career in Kansas, where Populism strongly influenced his thinking. After studying at Harvard, which he later claimed to have detested, Parrington taught at Emporia, the University of Oklahoma, and the University of Washington. Over his career he moved steadily to the left, asserting in 1918: "I become more radical every year." Although just what he meant by radical was never entirely clear (his original drafts of *Main Currents* used the term, but Parrington substituted "liberal" for "radical" in the final version), it entailed a focus on economic influences shaping history and culture. Parrington idolized William Morris, favored realism, and voted Socialist. At the same time he was anything but predictable, and his biographer emphasizes the "conflict between two contrasting modes of explanation, between economic determinism and the history of ideas, [that] would become markedly apparent in *Main Currents*."[8] Though Parrington was an English professor all his life, Richard Hofstadter grouped him with Frederick Jackson Turner and Charles A. Beard as the "Progressive historians." Parrington's interpretation, "one of the most influential and highly regarded texts in literature, history, and American Studies" for decades,[9] presented American thought from the colonial period to the 1920s as a struggle between

> the humanitarian philosophy of the French Enlightenment, based on the conception of human perfectibility and postulating as its objective an equalitarian democracy in which the political state should function as the servant to the common well-being; and the English philosophy of *laissez faire*, based on the assumed universality of the acquisitive instinct and postulating a social order answering the needs of an abstract "economic man," in which the state should function in the interests of trade. (Parrington [1927–1930]: vol. 1, xxiii)

The former was Jeffersonian, the latter Hamiltonian, and Parrington left no doubt where he stood.[10]

7. Parrington's reputation declined somewhat as the century wore on. Midcentury critical giant Lionel Trilling called his base-superstructure assumptions "crude." According to Jaap Verheul (1999), Parrington was one of the "mythic founders" of American Studies, though he thinks the degree to which Parrington was a revolutionary and intellectual isolate has been exaggerated. See H. Lark Hall, "Parrington, V. L.," *American National Biography Online*, February 2000, http://www.anb.org.turing.library.northwestern.edu/articles/14/14-00464.html, accessed August 4, 2011. See also Levy (1995).

8. H. Lark Hall (1994) has written the only full biography of Parrington; the quotation is from 193.

9. Hall (1994), Preface, p. vii.

10. Alfred Kazin described the partisanship of *Main Currents* as "an eloquent democratic humanism cheerfully indiscriminate in its allegiance rather than a grim class loyalty" (from *On Native Grounds*, quoted in Hall [1994]: 236). Urging a "reconstruction" (rehabilitation) of Parrington's achievement,

Parrington's class-based analysis influenced many intellectuals of the late twenties and thirties, the heyday of the proletarian literature movement. It also corresponded to the thinking of the Federal Writers' Project editors, who themselves championed both proletarian writers and the connection between literature and context, although they were less doctrinaire. David Levy, who reviewed Parrington's biography, commented that "in explicating the economic and political influences on American literature . . . he produced a work that was in perfect harmony with the advanced thought of the 1930s."[11] Moreover, Parrington's intellectual history coincided with the expansionist definition of literature that the Project inevitably produced, if not encouraged.

Again I have taken a sample for comparison with the American Guide essays and with the other three defining works. One thousand and four names appeared in the index of Parrington's three volumes. The analysis here is of 201 authors, a 20 percent sample.

Robert Spiller and the Canon at Midcentury

After the Second World War and roughly a decade after the American Guides had been published, Robert Spiller's monumental *Literary History of the United States* emerged to become the new standard laying out the American canon. First published in 1948, *Literary History* went through a series of editions and reprints over the next twenty-six years, the latest in 1974. Every student of English or of American Studies had a copy of "Spiller" on his or her desk.

Robert E. Spiller (1896–1988) spent most of his career around Philadelphia, first at Swarthmore College and then at the University of Pennsylvania, where he had received both his bachelor's and doctoral degrees. He began his scholarly life studying British culture—his first book in 1926 was on Americans in England after the American Revolution—before turning to American literature, and he taught comparative seminars like "American-European Cultural Relations" and "International Aspects of American Literature." In the 1930s Spiller, along with other scholars in-

---

a sympathetic Russell Reising (1989) suggests that Parrington's commitment to focusing on what he described in the introduction to volume 1 as "the broad path of our political, economic, and social development, rather than the narrower belletristic; . . . forces that are anterior to literary schools and movements, creating the body of ideas from which literary culture eventually springs" (xvii) has led commentators to miss the shrewdness of his literary analyses themselves. For example, Parrington gave little attention to Edgar Allan Poe because "the problem of Poe, fascinating as it is, . . . [is] outside the main current of American thought," but then went on to give a brief but thoughtful analysis (Reising [1989]: 158).

11. Levy (1995): 666.

fluenced by Parrington and by the progressive historians, pushed back against the emergent orthodoxy of the New Criticism, which demanded that the critic analyze texts and their formal properties without regard for their social contexts.[12] Though no radical, Spiller thought that context had something to offer to students of literature. Indeed, he believed that literature and history were inextricable, a core tenant of American Studies as a discipline that he helped to institutionalize. In the postwar period he was president of the American Studies Association, and he led the movement to establish American Studies programs internationally and to see the field in a global context. [13]

Spiller was the lead editor of the *Literary History of the United States*, whose four editors, three associate editors, and forty-eight contributors were "historians and critics rather than specialists in a narrow sense." Spiller and colleagues opened the preface as follows: "Each generation should produce at least one literary history of the United States, for each generation must define the past in its own terms," and the editors aimed at providing that history for the mid-twentieth century. The text filled two volumes, with a third for the bibliography. Every chapter had its individual author, and while they were unsigned in the text, a list of the authors responsible for each appeared at the end. Thus *Literary History of the United States* occupied a middle position between the stubborn anonymity of the American Guides and the personal voices of Pattee's and Parrington's volumes. The second edition of what was universally known as "Spiller," appearing in 1953, dropped from three to two volumes and added a "Postscript" chapter on the literature of the late forties and early fifties, but the content was unchanged. A decade later, "again the temptation to alter the main text [had] been resisted," so the eighty-one original chapters were the same as those that had come out fifteen years earlier, while the "Postscript" had evolved into two chapters that give more comprehensive coverage of postwar literature.

The present analysis used this 1963 edition, including the postscript and supplement, thus representing the definition of American literature in the middle of the twentieth century. The index has 1,462 names, and

12. Verheul (1999) argues that the revolutionary impulse in American Studies has been exaggerated, and that the trend toward interdisciplinarity had been happening well before Parrington and Spiller came along. Nevertheless, the movement helped broaden the cannon and give prominence to authors who had previously been neglected.

13. *American Quarterly* 19 no. 2 (1967) published an issue dedicated to Spiller, "past president of the American Studies Association and an internationally known pioneer in the American Studies movement, on occasion of his retirement, July 1, 1967, as the Felix E. Schelling Professor of English at the University of Pennsylvania." Skard (1967) emphasizes Spiller's international outreach, calling him the "Bridge-Builder and Image-Maker."

my analysis of a 20 percent random sample therefore covers 292 authors. It should be noted that the sample has picked up writers of the forties and fifties whose careers had not taken off when the American Guides' Literature essays were written.

Nina Baym and the Drive for Inclusivity

Revolutionary change to the very definition of American literature came in the 1970s in response to demands for cultural recognition first made by African Americans and then by other ethnic groups. Minority writers gained permanent admittance to the canon by the end of the decade. Even more dramatic change followed the outburst of hugely influential books by second-wave feminist literary scholars like Nina Baym, Sandra Gilbert, Susan Gubar, and Elaine Showalter.[14] From then on, women and minority writers have stood in the foreground of American literature.

Norton anthologies both registered and fostered this cultural revolution. No set of books has defined American literature for more readers. W. W. Norton is an independent and employee-owned American publisher, founded in 1923, that is known for publishing widely used college textbooks. *The Norton Anthology of English Literature* first appeared in 1962 and has gone through nine editions. Although its younger sister *The Norton Anthology of American Literature* (*NAAL*) didn't come along until 1979, it quickly became the standard work used in college courses, and it has gone through eight editions. The seventh, which provided the data used here, was published in 2007 in five volumes; a shorter version of this edition—though at 2,874 pages by no means short—came out in 2008. Nina Baym (born 1936), the English professor and critic whose scholarship helped break down the barriers to women into the American canon, was the general editor of this edition (and the eighth one as well).[15]

Baym laid out her thinking in her influential 1981 article "Melodramas of Beset Manhood: How Theories of American Fiction Exclude Women Authors." She contended that it was not simple bias but literary theory itself that had excluded women from the canon. In making room for

14. Although the intellectual ground of second-wave feminism had been prepared for two decades, the key literary manifestos clustered in four years. Nina Baym's *Woman's Fiction* came out in 1978, Sandra Gilbert and Susan Gubars's *The Madwoman in the Attic* came out in 1979, Elaine Showalter's *Toward a Feminist Poetics* also came out in 1979, and Baym's essay "Melodramas of Beset Manhood: How Theories of American Fiction Exclude Women Authors" appeared in 1981. These authors were later criticized by poststructuralists for acquiescing to the idea of there being a canon in the first place, a debate that does not concern us here (or persuade us in general).

15. The eighth edition came out in 2011, with Nina Baym again as editor in chief.

American literature as a scholarly field separate from English literature, twentieth-century criticism had isolated "Americanness" as the criterion for literary excellence.[16] While it was not altogether clear what this might be, what it seemed to exclude were universal human themes (mutability, mortality, love, betrayal, etc.) and specific, detailed portraits of various types of Americans ("wealthy New Yorkers, Yugoslavian immigrants, southern rustics"). Such themes and portraits, she pointed out, were the particular province of women writers. The American romance involved the "unsettled wilderness and the opportunities that such a wilderness offers to the individual as the medium on which he may inscribe, unhindered, his own destiny," while women and their domestic society were the hindrance that would hold the American individual back from this destiny. Baym argued that this theory of American essentialism blinded literary historians and critics, leading them to dismiss immensely popular authors like Hannah Foster (the bestselling "Lady from Massachusetts" whom Pattee had in fact discussed) and Harriet Beecher Stowe. Critics who set aside the standard canon built on such a theory would find loads of women writers right from the beginning.

The Norton Anthology of American Literature, canon definer par excellence, offered Baym and her coeditors a prominent vehicle for setting the record straight. Accompanying the seventh edition was an elaborate website especially for students, which discusses 154 American authors. Thirty-five percent of them are women, drawn especially from the nineteenth and twentieth centuries (appendix F, table 9.1).[17] For my analysis of this edition, instead of drawing a sample from the index as in the case of the three previous works, I have used the entire population of 154 authors that appeared on the student website.[18]

16.

Of course, the idea of Americanness is even more vulnerable to subjectivity than the idea of the best. When they speak of "most American," critics seldom mean the statistically most representative or most typical, the most read or the most sold. They have some qualitative essence in mind, and frequently their work develops as an explanation of this idea of "American" rather than a description and evaluation of selected authors. . . . But an idea of what is American is no more than an idea, needing demonstration. The critic all too frequently ends up using his chosen authors as demonstrations of Americanness, arguing through them to his definition. (Baym [1981]: 126)

17. While women are securely in place in college English courses, and on bestseller lists, the same is not the case for what remains of the canon itself. The Library of America sets as its mission to foster "appreciation and pride in America's literary heritage by publishing, and keeping permanently in print, authoritative editions of America's best and most significant writing." Library of America Author Index (2011); see http://www.loa.org/images/pdf/author%20index%20(May%202013).pdf. Only 15.5 percent of the ninety-seven authors listed in 2011 are women.

18. Note that while I am referring to the first three anthologies by their editors' names (Pattee, Parrington, Spiller), I am referring to the work Baym edited by the publisher's name (Norton). This is because Baym's volume was the latest in an established series; students invariably refer to works in the series as "Nortons" or "Norton anthologies" rather than by individual editors' names.

Comparisons

Pattee, Parrington, Spiller, and Baym set out to define and reconfigure the American literary canon. In essence they asserted that "this work or author *is* American literature," and, by implication, what they left out is not. Although they had different editorial and theoretical agendas and they were working at different times, they were all committed to casting a specific set of writers and works at the heart of the American culture.

The Federal Writers' Project directors and editors had no such commitment. They set out to provide jobs, pure and simple. Given the unpredictability of writers and of the US Congress, jobs writing guidebooks seemed safe; given that guidebooks usually had something to say about culture, essays on literature seemed appropriate. No one—not Henry Alsberg, not Harry Hopkins, not the state directors, not the workers—had any intention of reconfiguring the American canon. But they did.

What follows are comparisons among the *intended canons*, those drawn up by Pattee, Parrington, Spiller, and Baym and the *unintended canon*, the by-product of a WPA jobs program via the Federal Writers' Project. These comparisons help assess three related questions:

- In comparing Pattee, Parrington, Spiller, and Baym: Were there gradual trends toward inclusion over the course of the twentieth century, were there abrupt changes, or was their general stability?

The *NAAL* website was accessed for this analysis on January 13, 2012. http://www.wwnorton.com/college/english/naal7/welcome.asp. The website breaks down its coverage of 157 authors into five periods:

To 1820
1820–65
1865–1914
1914–45
Since 1945

The first division, "To 1820," has twenty-nine authors. Two of the "authors" are collective ("Stories of the Beginning of the World" and Native American Trickster Tales) and two are combined (John Adams with Abigail Adams; Judith Sargent Murray with Hannah Webster Foster); we have included each member of the pair as a separate author. The second has twenty-two authors, with one collective entry (Fanny Fern with Elizabeth Drew Stoddard). The third has twenty-one authors, including one collective author ("Native American Chants and Songs") and four pairs (Sarah Winnemucca with Zitkala-Sa, Charlotte Perkins Gilman with Theodore Dreiser, Bret Harte with Mary Austin, and James Weldon Johnson with Paul Laurence Dunbar). The fourth has thirty authors in total, twenty-six standing alone and two pairs (Thomas Wolfe with Richard Wright, and Sterling Brown with Langston Hughes). The fifth, "Since 1945," is divided between prose and poetry, having twenty-eight prose authors with two pairs (David Mamet with Sam Shepard, Louise Erdrich with Sherman Alexie) and twenty-seven poets with one pair (Louise Glück with Cathy Song). Many "authors" are historical figures like Hannah Dunstan or Christopher Columbus, who were not primarily writers. Under authors are collections like "Native American Trickster Tales."

- In comparing the Guides' Literature essays to the other four: How much did the Guides' unintended canon resemble the intended canons before or after? Did the Guides represent a point along a path of change, or did they stand apart as something different?
- In comparing the authors appearing in both the Guides and one or more of the other four: Were the authors that appeared in both the Guides and the other works different from the authors that appeared in just one place or the other?

Answering these questions will help assess whether the Literature essays of the American Guide Series were symptomatic of their time, ahead of their time, or offered something completely different in terms of their conceptualization of American culture.

Century

The sources we are looking at spread out over the better part of a century. Pattee's first volume appeared in 1915, the second and third in 1930 and 1935. Parrington's three volumes came out from 1927 to 1930. The American Guides were published between 1937 and 1941. Spiller's third edition came out in 1963 and the Norton seventh edition came out in 2007. Obviously the later works could include more twentieth-century authors than the earlier ones, but even the earlier ones showed surprising variation.

Compiled in the last half of the 1930s, the American Guides put forward a more contemporary cast of authors than did their counterparts. As we saw in the previous chapter (table 8.2), well over half (56.7 percent) of the Literature essay authors wrote during the twentieth century. Pattee's twentieth-century authors show up in his first two volumes, published in 1915 and 1930, and they account for a fifth of his authors overall (appendix F, table 9.2), while in Parrington's magnum opus the twentieth century accounts for a mere 6.5 percent of the total (appendix F, table 9.3). The authors in Pattee and Parrington who also appeared in the Guides were considerably more likely to be from the twentieth century than the ones who had not appeared in the Guides; this suggests that while the Guides may have been inclusive bordering on indiscriminate in their choice of twentieth-century authors, they did not miss the truly important ones. Three decades later, Spiller (appendix F, table 9.4) drew about a third of his authors from the twentieth century—in this case Guide authors were only slightly more up-to-date than the non-Guide—though of course Spiller had much more of the century to work with. It is not until we get to Baym and the Norton seventh, published in the early twenty-first century, that the percentage of twentieth-century authors (58.4 percent) is as high as the Guides (appendix F, table 9.1), which is remarkable given that Baym could draw from the entire twentieth century whereas the Guides had only the first three-and-a-half decades.

So in comparison with the four others' attempts to define the canon, American Guide Literature essays emphasized writers in the here and now. This foregrounding of the present over the past could be applauded for its relevance or deplored for its historical amnesia, but regardless, the Guides were the first to feature living writers. Culture was not confined to tradition, to what had happened; culture was what was happening.

Year Born

Comparing authors' birth years reveals some fine points beyond what the century analysis has shown. Over 5 percent of Parrington's authors were born in the fifteenth century or earlier, while Spiller and Norton's percentage was minuscule and Pattee included none from that far back (appendix F, tables 9.5–9.8). Given that Parrington aimed to write an intellectual history and not just a literary one, it is perhaps not surprising that he brought out an array that included King Solomon, Horace, and Hugh Latimer, an English bishop burned at the stake in 1555 for his Protestantism. The American Guides, on the other hand, included only three such premodern authors in their Literature essays (appendix E, table 8.3): Peter Martyr [Pietro Martire d'Anghiera] (Florida), Alvar Núñez Cabeza de Vaca (Florida, Louisiana, and Texas), and Friar Marcos de Niza (Arizona), all of whom chronicled the Spanish explorations of the New World. For Parrington, the influences on "American thought" went way back, whereas for the Guides, American culture began with America.

Gender

We saw in the previous chapter (appendix E, table 8.4) that less than a quarter of the authors mentioned in the American Guide Literature essays were women (22.7 percent of individual authors). Not impressive by later standards, the Guides' representation of women marked a considerable improvement over the leading literary histories that had been written before the State Guides appeared. Less than 15 percent of Pattee's authors were women (appendix F, table 9.2), and Parrington was even worse, with women accounting for less than 8 percent (appendix F, table 9.3).

Beyond the literary histories' relative neglect of women, these tables reveal two other points. First, the authors cited by Pattee and Parrington that later made it into the Guides had a higher female-male ratio than the ones that did not. This suggests that overall, and without any intention or consciousness of doing so (indeed, without any concern for gender whatsoever), the American Guide Literature essays presented a more inclusive conception of literature in terms of gender than did the canon-defining works that had preceded the Guides.

Including more women was *not* simply a long-term trend, however, and this is the second point. Pattee, the conservative Methodist who found Emily Dickinson a bit too unconventional, included twice the percentage of women (14.6 percent) as did Parrington, the radical who insisted on literature's relation to its social context (7.5 percent). Though more aggressive, Parrington's point of view was identical to that of the Federal Writers' Project's Washington editors (and indeed to that of the New Dealers in general), who were mostly left-of-center white men and who viewed inequality strictly in class terms, giving little thought to minorities and even less to gender. So the Guides did not represent a stage in a development toward greater gender inclusivity, but a move toward something unexpected. Moreover, as appendix F, table 9.4 shows, there was no trend toward including more women authors in the postwar years; Spiller (9.6 percent women) was not much more gender inclusive than Parrington and considerably less so than Pattee. Spiller also maintained the pattern whereby his Guide authors had a higher female-male ratio than those who were not in the Guides, though not by much.

The *Norton Anthology* is a different story altogether. Nina Baym and her team were determined to include women, who made up over one-third of the *Anthology* authors (appendix F, table 9.1). And here, in the reverse of the earlier pattern, the non-Guide authors were more female than those in the Guides. Norton's vigorous search to uncover overlooked women writers, who constituted 57 percent of the eighteenth-century authors included and an astonishing 80 percent of the nineteenth-century authors, went well beyond what the Guides had offered.

The gender story is simple: the three earlier works—Pattee, Parrington, and Spiller—paid no particular attention to representing women, while Baym was determined to do just that. In other words, there was no century-long trend regarding gender; instead, the *Norton Anthology* made a sudden, deliberate leap. The American Guides with their 22.7 percent women authors were more inclusive than the other pre-Norton histories, and while they were ahead of their time in bringing in women authors, unlike Norton they did not have this as an explicit goal—far from it. For the Guides, gender inclusivity was an unintended consequence of geographical necessity: States where professional authors were thin on the ground cast a wide net, and that net drew in women.

Ethnicity

American literature as defined by the American Guides was undeniably a white affair. We have seen that just under 4 percent of the Literature essay authors were nonwhite, with African Americans accounting for half, Hispanics slightly less, Native Americans even less, and no Asians (appendix E, table 8.5).[19] While this is unimpressive by today's diversity standards, the Guides were considerably more ethnically diverse than were the three other attempts—two earlier, one later—to define the American canon. Pattee's and Parrington's authors were 99 percent white, Spiller's 98 percent (appendix F, Tables 9.9–9.11). There did not appear to be any trend toward broadening the ethnic profile of American literature, and the Guides' 4 percent was ahead of its time.

As was true in the case of gender, instead of a slow incremental move toward diversity, it came with an abrupt lurch. In the last third of the twentieth century, teachers, anthologists, and literary gatekeepers overall began celebrating multiculturalism and making intensive efforts at ethnic inclusivity. Thus by the seventh edition of the *Norton Anthology*, fully 28 percent of its authors were ethnic minorities (appendix F, table 9.12). Ethnicity was just like gender: There was no gradual trend toward greater diversity; the Guides were more inclusive than other literary histories before and after; and dramatic change took place late in the century.

Place Born

The scholars who drew boundaries corralling who would be included in the American canon never required that authors be born in America. Just under 80 percent of Pattee's authors were native born, Parrington's were less than 60 percent, and Spiller's 70 percent (appendix F, tables 9.13–9.15). Once again there is no discernable trend. And once again the Guides were ahead of their time with their emphasis on native-born authors at 86.3 percent (appendix E, table 8.6), which is almost identical to Norton's 85.7 percent (appendix F, table 9.16).

Of course the reasons for varying degrees of nativism are different.

19. Two authors from the Guides' Literature essays were born in Asia—Rudyard Kipling was born to an Anglo-Indian couple in Bombay and Haniel Long to an American Methodist missionary couple in Burma—but both were white.

Parrington's intellectual history included many European philosophers and writers.[20] *The Norton Anthology*'s determined ethnic inclusivity included many Native Americans (American born by definition) and African Americans (usually, though not always, native born); in addition, Baym had many more decades of American authors to work with. Probably the most telling comparison is between the Guides and Spiller, for they covered roughly the same years (Spiller having a couple decades more than the Guides) and were not motivated by the explicit agendas of the other two. Compared to Spiller, then, the American Guides were simply more American.

More American, but also less Anglocentric. Of the Guide authors born outside the United States, half (51 percent) were from Britain or Ireland, over a third more (38.5 percent) were from continental Europe, and a little over 10 percent were from everywhere else. Though the numbers are too small to be reliable, we note that Pattee seemed even more Anglocentric, with two-thirds of his foreign authors coming from Britain or Ireland, and Parrington was also higher at 60 percent. Spiller is roughly the same as the Guides (56 percent), and in *Norton* a surprising three quarters of the non-American authors came from the British Isles. So overall the Guides were not only more American but also more catholic than the others in their nonnative authors' origins.

Division Born

Geography matters. Most definitions of American literature have stayed close to the "cultural hearth," and the Literature essays of the American Guides were no exception. In the previous chapter, appendix E, table 8.7 showed the uneven geographical profile of American Guide authors: 55.2 percent came from the East Coast divisions (Middle Atlantic, New England, and South Atlantic) and over half came from divisions with major publishing centers (East North Central, Middle Atlantic, and New England). See Appendix G for the breakdown of Census regions and divisions. Fred Pattee (appendix F, table 9.17) was even more East Coast–centric, with 73.6 percent of his authors coming from the three East Coast divisions, 82.7 percent from major publishing centers. Pattee's Guide authors were slightly less geographically skewed than the rest, though still more so than the Guide authors themselves. Parrington (appendix F, table 9.18) was the same: 83.3 percent from the East Coast, 78.9 percent

20. Levy (1995) notes that Parrington, during his early career in Kansas, confined his teaching almost entirely to British writers.

from major publishing centers; once again the authors mentioned in the Guides are less skewed though much more so than in the Guides themselves. Despite his origins in Kansas and career in the Pacific Northwest, Parrington showed no movement toward wider geographical horizons.

Spiller (appendix F, table 9.19) showed a modest tendency toward moving away from the East Coast and publishing centers. While three quarters of his authors are from publishing centers, the East Coast share has dropped to 70.8 percent, more than the Guides but significantly less than Pattee and Parrington. While the Guide authors are more so as usual, even Spiller's non-Guide authors are considerably more geographically diverse than Parrington's and somewhat more than Pattee's.

The *Norton Anthology* (appendix F, table 9.20) showed a move toward greater geographical spread, with 63 percent of its authors from the publishing centers and 60 percent from the East Coast. Baym's shift, while a move toward geographic inclusivity, was not nearly as dramatic as the moves she made in terms of gender and ethnicity. From Parrington to Norton, gender rose from 7.5 percent to 35.1 percent and ethnicity from 0.5 percent to 28.0 percent, but East Coast dropped only from 73.6 percent to 58.9 percent. Thus while branching out well beyond the Northeast, the most inclusive articulation of the American canon to date was less geographically inclusive than the Guides were as a whole.

Genre

In the previous chapter we saw that the genres mentioned in the American Guide essays broke down fifty-fifty, half being the traditional genres (fiction, poetry, drama) and half being other genres (appendix E, table 8.11). Pattee (appendix F, table 9.21) was even less conventional in this definition of American literature, with 56 percent of his authors being outside the big three. He especially favored literary criticism, likely due to his agenda of academic discipline building. Journalists were also higher in Pattee, as were most of the minor categories such as theology, publishing, and political writing, although he included fewer historical and far fewer travel writers than the Guides did.

Parrington had an even broader definition of who was part of American literary history; fewer than a third of the authors he mentioned were focused on fiction, poetry, and/or drama (appendix F, table 9.22). Parrington's emphasis was on political writers, who actually outnumber the traditional literary categories; he also gave unusual emphasis to theology and philosophy (13.9 percent), but was uninterested in travel writing, archeology and natural history, music, children's books, or humor. None of this is surprising, given he was writing an intellectual history. What is surprising is the fact that he gave history itself only about the same attention as Pattee did, and considerably less than the Guides did. Spiller returned to the norm of the Guides and Pattee, with a bit less than half (44 percent) of his authors from the traditional genres (appendix F, table 9.23). He had fewer history and travel writers, more theology, politics, and literary criticism, but none of these differences stand out.

The Norton Anthology (appendix F, table 9.24) is the opposite of Parrington: Fully three quarters of its authors wrote in the three conventional genres, with poetry being especially high at 35.3 percent. There is some travel, not much history (three quarters of *Norton's* historical authors are minorities), and very little of anything else. It appears that the intention to include women and minority writers encouraged a traditional definition of literature, since women and minorities have higher representation in fiction and especially in poetry (we saw this pattern with African American authors mentioned in the Guides) than they do in most other genres.

Baym had an intellectual agenda, which resulted in the *Norton Anthology* being very traditional in terms of genre while untraditional in everything else. Women and minorities brought their genres with them. Parrington had an intellectual agenda, which resulted in *Main Currents* being untraditional in terms of genre. Philosophers and political theorists brought their genres with them. The American Guides had no intellectual agenda. Whatever people wrote, traditional or not, that was literature.

Ahead of Their Time

The American Guides were ahead of their time. Their inclusivity was and continues to be striking. Prior to the lurch toward diversity that American literature took in the late 1970s, standard literary histories showed no trends toward including more women or more ethnic minorities, and very little movement out of the Northeast. As for genre, if anything the general movement was toward the increasingly conventional. In contrast, the State Guides were inclusive demographically, categorically, and geographically by necessity, because they had to come up with a decent number of authors in every state, but they were not inclusive by philosophy or intellectual agenda.

Indeed, it must be said that their attention to woman and minority authors was modest by late twentieth-century standards, though ahead of the other canon definers. Moreover, the Guides exhibited contradictory tendencies: By expanding their definition of "literature" to include cowboy songs, travel journals, political orations, and Puritan sermons, Project writers were broadening the vision of what texts counted, but this broadening tended to favor white male authors. Inclusion in terms of field and inclusion in terms of players are not the same, and the two counteracted each other to some extent.

Both inclusions were the result of geography, more specifically, geography meeting bureaucracy in the complete absence of any cultural agenda. Recall the constraints and their causes:

- Politics would organize the American Guide Series by state regardless of the fact that culture had hitherto been seen in terms of broad regions.
- Intellectuals directing what went into the Guides would feature essays regardless of their being largely irrelevant for travelers.
- Standardization would give almost every state Guide a Literature essay regardless of how much literature that state had produced.

So states had to come up with some literature. The result was that as the Guides moved outside of the Northeast, they became more diverse and inclusive, and more imaginative in terms of what American literature, from sea to shining sea, actually encompassed.

TEN

Using Books

Three things are clear. First, the American Guide Literature essays were more inclusive in terms of gender, ethnicity, and genre than were the other major definers of the American canon before the late twentieth century. Second, an abrupt, wide-ranging, and surprisingly uncontroversial expansion of the canon took place in the last third of that century. Third, the idea of a state having its own distinctive literature, a new idea in the thirties, is unexceptional today.[1] Is there any connection among the three?

If one were to hypothesize that the answer is yes, a modest claim might be that the Guides registered and reinforced popular opinion, representing what a broad swath of American readers thought to be worth including in "Our Literature." Popular taste has always been broader than academic or critical opinion—bestselling books scorned by reviewers but loved by the public, for example—and American popular culture has always favored writers and genres that were entertaining, inspirational, or realistic depictions of middle-class concerns, while cultural experts have dispar-

1. A simple demonstration of how literature rests comfortably in state-shaped boxes comes from Amazon.com: Searching Books for "Midwest literature" yields 44 titles, including *Midwestern Literature: Critical Insights* and *The Midwestern Pastoral: Place and Landscape in the American Heartland*, as well as some novels and the annual *Yearbook of the Society for the Study of Midwestern Literature*. Searching for "Illinois literature" yields 45 titles, including *Illinois Literature: The Nineteenth Century*; *Writing Illinois: The Prairie, Lincoln, and Chicago*; poetry collections; and a number of thrillers. "Indiana literature" returns 37 titles, Michigan 26, Minnesota 22, Ohio 18, Iowa 17, and Wisconsin 5. Changing the search terms produces similar results: "Midwest authors" brings up 6 titles; "Illinois authors" brings 59. "Midwest poetry" produces 111 titles; "Illinois poetry" produces 136.

aged the same.[2] The Guides' Literature essays could have been simply an expression of this more catholic view of what should be included in the American canon.

A stronger claim would be that the Guides reached readers and influenced their thinking directly. The Guides did not just register cultural change: They helped make it happen. The Literature essays contributed to a climate of expansiveness that allowed the diversification and canon opening, which would come to a head in the 1970s, to take hold, and in which the idea of state literatures made sense. The Guides, in other words, recast American literature in the minds of Americans by including more types of authors and more types of works, and by putting them all in state-shaped boxes.

In order for this stronger, direct-impact argument to be on the mark, Americans would need to have actually read the essays. Henry Alsberg would have to have been right after all: The Guides would have to have ended up being for readers, not (or not only) for tourists. The essay sections, more than the tours, would have to have been what was valued and secured.

The Federal Writers' Project sold Congress and the American people on the idea of setting writers to the task of producing Guides by maintaining that such Guides would be worthwhile and socially useful. So the question becomes, how did people actually use them? Once the Guides made it to publication, did Americans use them as travel guides, as reference books, or as both? This question is key, because if the Guides functioned primarily as on-the-road travel guides, there is little reason to think that their essays had any particular cultural influence. On the other hand, if people used the Guides as reference books, they would have had exactly such influence, for they would have defined what aspects of a state's history, economics, and culture actually mattered. Thus in order to claim that the essays had cultural impact, one would need to show that they were read, that they continued to be read, and that Americans understood the Guides to be not so much handbooks for occasional road trips but reference books of lasting usefulness.

This chapter will offer evidence in favor of this stronger claim that the Guides reached readers and shaped the way they thought. First, it will show that the Guides were used primarily as collections of essays to be read and consulted in the home or library, and not as travel guides to be read and consulted on the road. Second, it will show that the Guides have en-

2. Recall Hutner's (2009) argument that during the period from 1920 to 1960, realistic, nonformulaic fiction about middle-class lives was hugely popular, was dismissed by intellectuals at the time, and has been largely ignored since.

dured and that they have continued to be influential. Third, it will suggest that one important channel through which their influence has flowed has been that of students using the Guides for research on their states.

Evidence Regarding Use and Impact

What do people do with books? It is never easy to assess whether a book has been read or not, what it has been used for, where it has been, or what impact it has had. Figuring such things out is even more challenging in the case of a series of books like the State Guides that reached geographically scattered readerships by intention. Nevertheless, five types of evidence can suggest how people use books and whether the books have been influential: (a) design utility, (b) material evidence, (c) initial popularity, (d) timing, and (e) endurance. Each of these offers clues regarding whether Americans used the Guides, just how they used them, and with what consequences.

Design Utility

By the 1920s, America was awash with travel guidance. As we saw in chapter 4, the automobile age had updated the Baedeker model. Oil companies and publishers competed for the motorist's attention. In addition to the ubiquitous advertising brochures and maps picked up at service stations, travelers had a choice of guidebooks, with the *Automobile Blue Books* being the most prominent.

So in considering the design utility of the American Guides, it is instructive to compare them with the competition, especially with the widely available *Automobile Blue Books* discussed in chapter 4. Let us imagine a motorist wanted to travel from Brunswick up the Maine coast to Woolwich along Highway 1. The 1924 *Automobile Blue Book*'s "Route 322—Brunswick to Rockland, Belfast and Bangor, Me—117.4 m." briefly describes Highway 1 as "a very pretty trip thru a rolling and hilly farming country, following the shore most of the way. Many fine views of the ocean and mountains." It then gives detailed directions by the miles from the starting point:

0.0 Brunswick, Pleasant & Main Sts. Northeast on Main St.
0.2 Fork at end of park; left.
0.3 4-cor. At Bowdoin college; left away from trolley onto Bath St.
restaurant: Right 6.5 leads to New Meadows Inn.
8.0 5-cor; bear right from trolley onto Lincoln St.

8.5 End of street; left onto Center St.
8.8 Bath, Center & Front Sts., end of street. Left onto Front St. hotels: Eamesholm; King Tavern; Phoenix. restaurant: Colonial Dining Room.
8.9 Ferry St.; turn right from trolley
9.0 Ferry over Kennebec River (toll 50c, 5c additional for each passenger). Leaving ferry, keep ahead.
9.2 Woolwich, end of street. Left across RR bridge and next right.

In the middle of the page is a one-paragraph description of Bath and Woolwich. The bottom half of the page contains advertisements for the five businesses mentioned, letting the traveler know that the Hotel Phoenix is quiet, homelike, and specializes in chicken dinners, while the King Tavern is open all year and hosts the local Rotary Club.

The American Guide volume *Maine: A Guide "Down East"* section on Bath and Woolwich is considerably longer, with two-and-a-half pages of small print. It gives much more information and focuses on industry and economic history, describing the operations of Bath Iron Works, for example, which the *Automobile Blue Book* never mentions, and offering a long description of the Kennebec River's trading role. Comparing the two guidebooks' short paragraphs on Woolwich offers a sense of how they differed:

Automobile Blue Book: Woolwich, Me. (pop. 880). Originally settled in 1638 by purchase of land from Indians by Edward Bateman and John Brown. Settlement destroyed in second Indian war; resettled in 1734. A special feature is the alewife fishery on Nequasset stream, owned and operated by the town.

Maine: A Guide "Down East": Woolwich (alt. 30, Woolwich Town, pop. 671), 1.2 m., is on the east bank of the Kennebec River opposite the city of Bath. Shipbuilding and fishing for shad and sturgeon were the early industries, now replaced by farming, dairying, and orcharding. The canning of corn, peas, and beans is here rapidly increasing in volume.

So the vacationer traveling with the *Blue Book* would learn about Indian wars and alewives, while the one traveling with the *Maine Guide* would learn about industries and that the canning operations processed three different vegetables. *Maine: A Guide "Down East"* has nothing to say about restaurants, service stations, or hotels, nor does it include advertisements that give some of this information. Most people taking a car trip want exactly the type of advice that the *Automobile Blue Book* contained and that the high-minded (and federal-policy handcuffed) *Maine Guide* left out: where to eat, where to sleep, where to fill up the tank, how much it would cost. Knowing that they do farming, dairying, and orcharding in Woolwich, while it makes for informative reading, does nothing for the driver who is low on gas and has a car full of hungry kids.

We have seen that the Guides—based on an awkward amalgam of travel guide for motorists, local celebration for boosters, and essays for students and scholars—were a solution to the problem of giving white-collar workers employment within a political structure of federalism and a political climate of anti-Communism. As such they were very successful. As practical travel guides, however, their design made them much less useful than their competitors. If vacationing families or traveling businessmen were interested in the history, culture, or economy of places they were driving through, and no doubt some were, then the American Guides would have been great to have in the glove compartment—but the motorist had better have had an *Automobile Blue Book* or some similar guidebook along as well.

Material Evidence

Next, consider the evidence from the books as material objects. The Baedeker and Murray guidebooks that had dominated the market prior to the automobile were handbooks; they were small enough to be carried in a traveler's pocket and held in one hand. *Baedeker's United States* (1909) was six-and-a-quarter inches high, four-and-a-quarter inches wide, and weighed fourteen ounces. With automobiles, this compact, lightweight size was no longer quite as necessary. An *Automobile Blue Book* was nine-and-a-quarter by five-and-a-quarter inches, and weighed a pound and a half. Long and slim, it could be held in one hand and would fit perfectly into the glove compartment (a Ford in the late 1930s, considered typical, had a glove compartment that was eleven inches wide and nine inches deep).[3] The American Guides were considerably bulkier (figure 10.1). They did not have the tall and slim shape of other auto guides; they could be held in one hand, but not for long given their considerable two-and-a-quarter-pound weight. They measured eight and a quarter by five and a

3. Glove compartments in the 1930s varied considerably in size, according to historians at three auto museums. The historian at the Henry Ford Museum, Matt Anderson, measured that of a 1939 Ford convertible, which he felt was a pretty typical automobile for that era. Its glove compartment measured seven inches high by eleven inches wide by nine inches deep at the opening. The box was trapezoidal in shape, so the height and depth both got a bit smaller as you moved deeper into the compartment. My thanks to Nancy DeWitt at Fountainhead Antique Auto Museum (http://www.fountainheadmuseum.com); John Jenza at the Society of Automotive Historians (http://www.autohistory.org/index.php/chapters/113-henry-leland-chapter); and Matt Anderson at the Henry Ford Museum (http://collections.thehenryford.org/).

10.1 Size and shape of three travel guides

half, so they too would fit comfortably in the glove compartment, though less comfortably in the hand. Unlike the other two, the Guides had no convenient ribbon bookmarks.

Bigger and more awkward than the competition, the Guides made a virtue of their size by having large, clear type. And anyway, they were intended for perusal in the car so they didn't need to be superlight or to be pocket-size. As for marking pages, people could just turn down the corners. So did people actually use them this way?

We start from a simple premise: Guidebooks that have seen service on the road show wear and tear. Lost or torn maps, lost or tattered dust jackets, loosened bindings, pencil markings, pages turned down, and stains are typical evidence of having been used during a trip. Guidebooks often acquire miscellaneous materials (set-in ephemera) on the road as well. Books used at home show less wear and tear, and are less apt to have picked other things up. Books from public libraries often don't have dust jackets and may have different bindings, though they may well have markings in the essays sections; in any case, they will usually not be used on the road.

Given these physical indicators of usage, how did the American Guides fare? One source of material evidence comes from the Complete Traveller, a New York City bookstore, closed in 2013, that specialized in rare travel books and was the largest retail purveyor of American Guides in the world. Arnold Greenberg, the proprietor of the Complete Traveller, told me in 2010 that the majority of the Guides that pass through his shop have their maps, and many have their jackets. Greenburg believes that most Guides were not actually used on the road, although he pointed out that he would tend to buy Guides that were in good condition. On the store's shelves were about 200 Guides, all either first editions or early printings. Virtually every volume had its map, and half or a little less had original dust jackets; for example, there were four first editions of the Oregon guide, all with maps, one with its jacket.

While Greenberg's stock may overrepresent Guides in good condition, with maps and dust jackets intact, the same would not be true of the market as a whole. In the summer of 2009 I looked up the books that were listed on Abebooks.com, the Internet home of the American Book Exchange and one of the two premier markets for rare and antiquarian books.[4] I looked up books that had "Federal Writers' Project" as author and that were first editions published between 1935 and 1945. There were 463 books listed, of which 175 were State Guides. I went through these to see how many had dust jackets and maps; if a map wasn't explicitly mentioned, I queried the seller. From this investigation I determined that 81 percent of the books on sale had their maps and 46 percent had dust jackets—proportions not very different from those in the Complete Traveller. From this I concluded that the majority of the Guides on sale in the early twenty-first century had never been used on the road.

What does a guide that has been used on the road look like? Until very recently, books have always been material objects and their physical condition registers their use, or lack thereof. The *Automobile Blue Book 1924* that I examined had two souvenir photos of the Carlton Bridge in Bath, Maine, which opened in 1927. So the set-in ephemera suggest that some traveler used the book several years after its publication, when the new bridge was still remarkable enough to warrant keeping its picture. The same volume had its bookmark with a large map set to the page on Bath. And in the front is a carefully cut-out rectangle of newsprint, about a half inch by two inches, that says "september, 1930." Might this have been stuck in the book to record the year of the trip?

Markings and ephemera give physical evidence about the lives and thoughts of those who have used them, and travel guides do so in specific ways. Some examples from the *Automobile Blue Books* I have picked up (one should bear in mind that guidebooks may be used for years after their publication dates):

4. The other would be eBay.com. Abebooks had the advantage for my research in that its rare-book sellers are professionals who know what information is relevant, e.g., the presence of a dust jacket or end map. The distinction between rare and antiquarian books is often blurred, but generally "antiquarian" refers to books that are a century old or more, whereas "rare" refers to hard-to-find books, usually of some value. Thus the first editions of the American Guides are still in the "rare" classification.

- *1910 Vol. 4. Middle West*. This book has lost its folding map. A memorandum page at the end has figures on it that look like expenses of some sort, perhaps gas.
- *1918. Vol. 1. New York State and Adjacent Canada*. This book, which contains a Kelly Springfield Tires bookmark, has a handwritten record by someone who took a 400-mile trip from Ottawa to Albany via Syracuse.
- *1919. Vol. 2. New England, Eastern Canada, Maritimes*. This book was published in conjunction with the Maine Automobile Association and contains extra materials about Maine. Some numbers (mileage?) are written inside the back cover.

All of these are bits and pieces, but in some cases a guidebook offers physical evidence that allows one to reconstruct a person's travel and, if pursued online, his or her life. My somewhat haphazard collection includes the *Automobile Blue Books 1923—Vol. 1 New England, New York, Southern Ontario, Maritimes*. At the front is a name and address: "Matthew Weber, 52 Division St., Salamanca, NY." Handwritten on the first page is, "State Road from Rochester to North Sterling turning left at Crocketts then dirt road to Nine Mile Creek." The book has a newspaper bookmark on page 576, which is a map of Rochester, and its spine is broken there. The corner is turned down on page 660, which has Salamanca. The foldout map in the back has been torn so it appears to have been used. I infer that Mr. Weber, who lived in Salamanca, traveled to Rochester.

Two years later Mr. Weber used a different book from a different series, the ALA (Automobile Legal Association) *Green Books*. The ALA was located in Boston and put out a periodical called *Automobilist* from 1919 to 1971. The *Green Books* are quite similar to the *Blue Books*, with the routes in both directions and advertising, so the two were competitors. *Green Books* feature large, foldout maps in a back pocket, interior maps of cities and regions, a "Historical Section" that lists cities and points of interest with a paragraph of description, a star system (places with stars are included in the "Historical Section"), and a "Golf Club Guide." Weber's copy was the 1925—*Automobile Green Book, Vol. 2, 1925. New York State Automobile Association. New York, New Jersey, Pennsylvania, Maryland, Delaware, District of Columbia, Central Canada and Florida, with Trunk Lines to New England and the West.* Again it has Matthew Weber's name and address in the front; it lacks the folding map; and it has a piece of paper stuck in the Rochester, New York, section referring to Arnett Boulevard and the trolley line. It reads, "Arnett Boulevard trolley line—Rugby intersection—Rugby runs into Chili?" A glance at Google Maps indicates that there is indeed an Arnett Boulevard, and Rugby Avenue does indeed run from Arnett into Chili Avenue. The nineteenth ward became a streetcar suburb; there was a trolley on Thurston Road. In the early decades of the twentieth century it was a prosperous middle-class residential neighborhood.[5] All this suggests that Weber used the *Green Book* to get around Rochester, perhaps to meet someone. Salamanca, south of Buffalo near the Pennsylvania state line, is 135 miles from Rochester. So just from the physical evidence it seems likely that Weber, who was not poor since he owned a car in the twenties, used the *Green Book* to find his way around that part of Rochester. A bit more Internet sleuthing reveals that Matthew Weber was a newspaper editor and publisher of the *Cattaraugus Republican-Press*, son of its founder, who was born in 1877 and was an active journalist at least into the 1930s. One of Salamanca's boosters as well as its newspaper editor, Weber wrote an article in 1912 called "Salamanca: New York State's Youngest but Pluckiest City."[6] So we can picture him in the midtwenties, a small-town notable driving through western New York in pursuit of stories, with his various travel guides to help him find his way around.

While such detective work is fun, I am going into all of this to drive home the point that books offer physical evidence about how they have been used. As the book historian and Harvard librarian Robert Darnton put it, "It is important to get the feel of a book, the texture of its paper, the quality of its printing, the nature of its binding. Its physical aspects provide clues about its existence as an element in a social and economic system; and if it contains margin notes, it can reveal a great deal about its place in the intellectual life of its readers."[7] Not to mention their travel lives.

The American Guides that I have collected, and I have at least one copy from every state, have almost none of this type of annotation. Most have no markings at all. A few came from library collections and have library stamps or envelopes for checkout cards. A few have a name or nameplate, and these can indicate something about the book's history. For example,

5. Amazon.com has a "product description" for *Rochester's 19*th *Ward (Images of America)*, put out by Arcadia Publishing: "Rochester's 19th Ward portrays one of the city's largest residential neighborhoods. The initial settlement, predating Rochester itself, was called Castle Town. It emerged around 1800 along the Genesee River, where boatmen poled flat-bottomed boats along a stretch of turbulence in the river known as the Rapids. Out of this desolate community developed a streetcar suburb, an elegant and vibrant neighborhood, designed for the modern 20th-century family. Fine homes, churches, shops, schools, and industries arose between 1900 and 1930, and the 19th Ward quickly became a prestigious address for doctors, professors, and skilled laborers." http://www.amazon.com/Rochesters-19th-Ward-Images-America/dp/0738539473/ref=sr_1_1?ie=UTF8&qid=1393338718&sr=8-1&keywords=rochester%27s+19th+ward.

6. Weber's article appeared in *Railway Life*, vols. 1–4, put out by the Buffalo, Rochester, and Pittsburgh Railway Company. http://books.google.com/books?id=1Rk9AAAAYAAJ&pg=RA4-PA13&lpg=RA4-PA13&dq=%22matthew+weber%22+salamanca+new+york&source=bl&ots=SDFz6NxCNL&sig=BIeGUtd4oZy-dQu9q1oq8oCI7V4&hl=en&sa=X&ei=5qQLU6KADerT0wHewIHwBg&ved=0CCwQ6AEwAQ#v=onepage&q=%22matthew%20weber%22%20salamanca%20new%20york&f=false.

7. Darnton (2009): 38–39.

Kentucky: A Guide to the Bluegrass State has a book plate with the name "Leland S. Page, Dec. 1939," which shows the book was purchased or acquired immediately upon publication. On the other hand my copy of *Montana: A State Guide Book* is stamped with Kenneth F. Veitch of Fernwood, PA 19050. Since ZIP codes (Zone Improvement Plan) came into effect in 1963, this means that Mr. Veitch put his name into the book (upon acquiring it? people usually put their names in books right when the get them) at least twenty-four years after its 1939 publication.

Even ex-library copies can hint as to how they had been used. Let me give two examples. My copy of *Minnesota: A State Guide* has stamps from two military libraries near Anchorage, Alaska: (1) US Air Force Library at Elmendorf AFB Alaska and (2) Post Library at the army's Fort Richardson in Alaska. It sounds like these libraries were merged into a single collection at some point (the two bases themselves were merged, but not until 2010, long after I had acquired the book). The volume has a checkout card with lots of due dates stamped on it. In addition to the checkout activity, the book has considerable wear and tear, suggesting it was heavily used, but there are no markings aside from an underlining of a sentence in the Historical Survey essay about the rapid opening of post offices in the nineteenth century. Since Minnesota is 3,000 miles from Anchorage, it is possible that one of those checkouts was for a road trip to the upper Midwest, but surely not all of them. Some military personnel were either engaging in some sort of research or just enjoying armchair travel to the lower forty-eight.

A second example: The copy I have of *Delaware: A Guide to the First State* came from the Detroit Public Library, which is stamped on the top and bottom of the pages. At the beginning of the essays section in the table of contents, someone has penciled in "Climate Vivian." The same hand has written "Linda" after Government, "Susan" after Agriculture, and "Susan" again after Folkways and Customs. This division of tasks indicates that at some point a group used the book for a project, probably girls working together on a school assignment.

Markings of any sort are few and far between. Of course it must remembered that one collection is not a random sample. The most beat-up Guides might not have lasted—but this would also be true for the *Blue Books* and *Green Books*, and these contain much more evidence of on-the-road use than the Guides do. At the very least we can say that neither an examination of the State Guides for sale nor an examination of a collection of them gives much physical evidence of the books having been used for road trips.

So our first two indicators—design utility and material evidence—suggest that the Guides may have not been used much for travel. That could be because they weren't used for anything. Perhaps they came out but were ignored, neither bought nor read. The WPA heavily promoted the series; a typical press release shouted "Attention Book Page Editors" and reminded them that "WPA American Guide Series, virtually completed, make valuable handbooks for summer tourists."[8] But what if nobody was paying any attention?

Initial Popularity

People were indeed paying attention, however, because from their first appearance, the Guides were hits. Local newspapers and radio stations praised their own state's Guide, and the critical response to the American Guide Series as a whole was glowing. Reviewing the Guides in the *New Republic*, Lewis Mumford asserted: "These Guidebooks are the finest contribution to American patriotism that has been made in our generation. . . . The Guides are indispensable toward creating that new sense of the regional setting and regional history, without which we cannot have an informed body of citizens." The Book-of-the-Month Club, then in its heyday, touted the Guides and offered them to its members.[9]

Reviewers praised even those volumes that had been slow in coming and problematic in content. Take Arkansas: From the very beginning, the Arkansas Writers' Project had been a problem child for the Washington office.[10] Because of an inept state director, whom Alsberg kept on for far too long, and the low skills of the staff, progress was slow, and *Arkansas:*

8. Library of Congress, file (WPA A 833), folder: American Guide Week, National Office (folder 1 of 2).

9. The April 1941 "Book-of-the-Month Club News," for example, announced the recent publication of the Colorado and South Carolina Guides. Library of Congress, Special Studies and Projects, Regional and National File (WPA A 834) Folder: American Guide Week, Colorado.

10. The original director was Bernie Babcock, whom Darel McConkey, in a Field Report of February 15, 1936, scorned as leading a nest of "militant feminists." Alsberg and his staff wrote numerous letters to her that were variously condescending, obsequious, and/or cajoling, as seen in this typical correspondence from March 1936:

March 31, 1936 HA to BB trying to get her moving. "I confess I am somewhat disturbed by the fact that we have received so little material from Arkansas in answer to our numerous requests. Most of the other states have responded very promptly. . . . We have not yet received your list of points of interest, list of historic and other buildings . . . state tour map. . . . Also we have received nothing of the introductory essays. Meanwhile, some of our other states are pretty nearly finished." And so on. She replies on April 4: "Dear Mr. Alsberg: I have nothing against you and would not for the world cause you any suffering." Then she asks him to look at an essay on paleontology, which he finds "far too technical," and closes with "While we are behind in sending you state copy I think the condition of the copy when you get it will repay the time used in perfecting it."

July 30, 1936 HA to BB, whom he addresses as "My dear Bernie: You see I am taking advantage of your permission to call you by your first name." A letter follows her visit to Washington, and he is being all charm: "I was sorry I didn't get a chance to talk to you more at length before you left. Perhaps I will get out to Arkansas and we then can spend more time together." He also encourages her to get him a copy of the final manuscript for the North Little

A Guide to the State was one of the last Guides to be published. Nevertheless, the local response was uniformly enthusiastic. "*arkansas: a guide to the state* wins praise of reviewer" shouted the headline in the *Arkansas Gazette*, which urged that the Guide be distributed widely. The headline for the *Fort Smith American* review proclaimed it a "Good Piece of Work" and went on to say it would be "permanently valuable." Glenn Green wrote in the *Arkansas Democrat* that the Guide was a "comprehensive factual directory" and "every business man in the state should have this volume on his desk. . . . Though it is not essentially a literary work, its practical value to the state should prove to be far greater than that of any single publication preceding it." A news article in the same newspaper announced that it was "now at long last available" and "while the guide has been designed primarily to give visiting non-residents a brief but entertaining story of the state's background [and] a more extensive description of its present . . . we believe the book should and will find a much more appreciative audience among Arkansans than outsiders." In this last point, he was absolutely correct.

A more pointed case of the insider-outsider motif appeared in a widely circulated review by John Selby:

> It would be nice if some of my friends in that most provincial of all American cities, namely New York, could be forced to read the first 126 pages of "Arkansas: A Guide to the State." It might for a time drive from their nostrils the stench of the subway, make them forget the cockroaches of Greenwich Village. . . . For somewhere in the Arkansas Writers' Project is tucked away a writer, or group of the same, with extraordinary ability. They have the ability to see a state and a people as a whole, without caricature, with appreciation of their differences and their characteristics as a folk, and to put this on paper [so] accurately that even a man whose horizon is the raddled back end of an apartment building might understand, and perchance marvel.[11]

Rock Guide, for "As you know, we are very interested in getting out some smaller publications to show the public samples of the kind of publication we are going to get out." [The first-name address does not last.]

But despite her incompetence, Babcock remained state director for three years; Penkower ([1977]: 52) says this exemplifies Alsberg's administrative shortcomings, particularly his reluctance to fire anyone. When Dallas McKown took over in early 1939 he was appalled at the state of the project. Writing to Alsberg on January 27 about the Tours section, he reported: "I have discovered that a great deal more of the file material than I at first thought is erroneous because it has either been taken from poorly chosen sources, or is misquoted, or plagiarized, or unidentified, or otherwise unsuitable for the purpose of preparing satisfactory tour manuscripts . . . plus the fact that very few of the Project workers have had anything approaching adequate training, experience, or aptitude as research workers or writers makes the preparation of manuscripts very slow and difficult." The book finally appeared in the summer of 1941, one of the last.

11. John Selby, "The Literary Guidepost," *Times*, Fairmont, West Virginia, September 21, 1941. Selby was apparently a reviewer for a number of newspaper, for the same article appeared as "About Books" in the September 19 issue of the *Post-Star* in Glens Falls, New York, and in the *Vindicator* of Youngstown,

And in an odd twist to the inside-outside theme, on December 1, 1941, the *Little Rock Gazette* reported that the *Milwaukee Journal* had devoted four columns to "Arkansas—Where Life Is Good," having "discovered Arkansas by reading the Arkansas Guide." The headline called it "Good Advertising for Arkansas," as indeed it was.

The Arkansas response was typical: Everywhere the Guides garnered accolades. The *Hartford Times* calling the Connecticut Guide "Distinguished," and that adjective summed up the response over all the states (at least after the early kerfuffle in Massachusetts). Sales were brisk; just about every public library in the country bought the Guides, as did city and state boosters, school libraries, and the public at large. In November 1941, just as the last volumes were appearing, the American Booksellers Association and a committee of publishers, with the cooperation of the WPA, celebrated American Guide Week (figure 10.2). With the theme of "Take Pride in Your Country," it featured displays in bookstores throughout the nation. WPA officials wrote to local Chambers of Commerce asking them to distribute the posters; libraries arranged displays; radio stations aired special broadcasts.

American Guide Week was the culmination of a five-year effort the Federal Writers' Project had spent winning over the public. One by one, in every state, the appearance of the Guides put to rest the griping about boondoggles and government interference. By the time the Guides had come out, anti–New Deal passions had cooled, the Depression had eased, and the country was focused on developments abroad. There was still skepticism about the Arts Projects overall and about subversion, but the Guides themselves had proved their worth. The success of the State Guides gave the Project (since mid-1939 the Writers' Program)[12] something of a second wind, and the self-celebration of American Guide Week tried to keep it going. States had unfinished projects that they had set aside in the push to complete the State Guides, so now that these were all out, and the critics had simmered down and the public was on board, renewed energy in the State Projects seemed to promise great things.

It was not to be. A month after American Guide Week the Japanese bombed Pearl Harbor and America was at war. No more motor jaunts, no more unemployment, and soon no more Writers' Project at either federal or state levels. America's entrance into the Second World War abruptly suspended many uncompleted books as the Project writers were moved

---

Ohio on September 21. These clippings are from the Collections of the Manuscript Division, Library of Congress.

12. See Timing section below. I will continue to refer to the "Project" in general, although this is not strictly accurate in light of the reorganization in 1939.

10.2 Poster announcing American Guide Week

into war work. By then, however, the State Guides had all made it into publication and into the public consciousness.

Timing

Although the Guides flowed in on a rising tide of good will, their timing could not have been worse. America's entry into the Second World War cut the Project short—suddenly, abruptly, chaotically, and long before the states had finished all they had set out to accomplish. Timing had an impact on the Guides themselves: Just when they were all out the door, the war effort put the brakes on tourism and automobile travel. The Guides had been conceived for prewar America. Postwar America was a very different place.

Well before Pearl Harbor, the end of the Federal One dream had been on the horizon. As the thirties drew to a close, America was preparing for war, and putting people to work was no longer the central concern of policy makers or the American public. Alsberg's dream belonged to an earlier era. A year after his firing, *Time* (whose founder and editor in chief Henry Luce was no friend of the New Deal) recounted the events in its usual adjective-laden style:

> Last year Congress decided to have a look at WPA's so-called Professional Projects—Art, Music, the Federal Theatre and Federal Writers. Well-founded rumors of radicalism among WPA artists and authors had long irked the legislators. After looking, Congress abolished the Federal Theatre, allowed the others to survive on condition they find local sponsors who would put up 25% of their expenses. To the surprise of nearly everybody, the States were so satisfied with WPA's writers that all 48 soon put up their 25%. [This of course was another indicator of the Guides' initial popularity.]
>
> About the same time it was decided that tousle-headed, slow-spoken, walrus-mustached Director Henry Alsberg seemed a little too pinko, talked a little too much about his indigestion, was a little too slow in getting production started on the Guide Books and other projects. He retired from the WPA. Alsberg and colleagues had started out to produce great Art. Congress by & large preferred results.[13]

Somewhere between wry and snide, the article nevertheless was essentially accurate. Afterward the Writers' Project carried on and brought out the State Guides, and the states had various other projects in the works, including a new American Recreation Series, a history of grazing in the West, a project on American regional foods, and numerous county histories and ethnic studies. America's entry into the war cut off all of these.

Such timing made it unlikely that the Guides would endure in the post-

13. "Books: WPAchievement," *Time*, August 12, 1940, http://www.time.com/time/magazine/article/0,9171,764376,00.html. At the time and since then the question of whether Alsberg resigned or was fired has been disputed. Colonel Harrington and the press claimed he had resigned, while Alsberg countered that he had been fired. On the basis of his interview with Florence Kerr in 1968, Penkower (1977) concludes that he indeed was fired (210–214). In any event the writing had been on the wall for months, and the reorganization of July 1 made it inevitable.

war period. While they were all in print by the time the war began, Americans had other things on their minds besides Pennsylvania and Oregon celebrating their unique qualities. Nor were wartime Americans taking many road trips using the State Guides, the *Blue Books*, or anything else, and almost a decade would pass before things returned to normal. It would not have been surprising if the Guides had just quietly disappeared into library shelves, relics of a New Deal era that suddenly seemed like ancient history. But that is not what happened.

Endurance

To exert any cultural influence, the Guides would have had to last after the disruption brought about by the war. They would have had to have a future years after the accolades and the reviews and American Guide Week were over and forgotten. Did they? What is the evidence?

If the State Guides had been used primarily as tour books, then we might expect their popularity to start out high and then decline as their contents became dated. Two historical upheavals would have first delayed this trajectory but then accelerated it. First, the Second World War depressed leisure travel for years. When it began to pick up again in the late forties, tourists might have grabbed older guidebooks, but only until the market produced new ones. Second, the Interstate Highway System, which President Dwight D. Eisenhower signed into law on June 29, 1956, made the Guides' maps and tours increasingly pointless, for motorists now could get from one place to another without using the old roads that the Guides had so carefully plotted. In using the interstates, they would also bypass the small towns and points of interest that the Guides had recorded. So while the Guides might have enjoyed a usage bump after the war as Americans hit the road again, by the 1960s they would have been obsolete.

On the other hand, if the State Guides' appeal rested on the essays and not on the tours, than the fact that the highway information was outmoded wouldn't have mattered. In fact, the liability of being old and prewar could become a virtue, even celebrated, if the Guides were sold as, for example, *The WPA Guide to 1930s New Jersey*. If readers and not tourists were the Guides' audience and market, then the problem of obsolescence would largely disappear.

This is exactly what happened. Readers found, and continue to find, the Guides to be valuable not for the tours but for the essays. Two types of evidence support this conclusion: first, the Guides' publication history and second, the Guides' persistence in public libraries.

Publishers have issued new editions and reprints of the Guides continuously over the past seventy-five years. Sometimes these are revised and updated, but more often the Guides are republished exactly as they were written in the thirties, perhaps with a new introduction giving their historical and institutional context, perhaps not. For example, Oxford University Press first published *Florida: A Guide to the Southernmost State* in 1939. Oxford released at least eight more printings through 1956. In 1976 Scholarly Press issued a new edition, as they did for many of the other Guides. In 1984 Pantheon came out with *The WPA Guide to Florida: The Federal Writers' Project Guide to 1930s Florida*, with a new introduction by John I. McCollum; Pantheon published many Guides in this format. In 2007 Native American Books Distributor reprinted the Florida Guide, and that same year Library Reprints came out with a CD-ROM version. And in 2013 Trinity University Press released *The WPA Guide to Florida: The Sunshine State*, along with copies of every other State Guide.

The Florida Guide's fourteen-and-counting appearances on the market were only a little higher than the average. Overall, the typical State Guide has come in a new format at least ten times; no Guide has had fewer than six editions or printings, and Mississippi tops the list with a whopping twenty. Table 10.1 shows the publication history of each state guide.[14] The Guides have had long lives, in print and in digital media, which continue to the present.

The second piece of evidence that testifies to the Guides' endurance comes from libraries: Ever since their publication, the American Guides have been on the shelves of public libraries throughout the United States. Despite the availability of newer material, they are still there today. And according to librarians and circulation records, they are still being used.

I wrote that last paragraph in Princeton, New Jersey, in 2014, so let's take that town as an example. The Princeton Public Library has four New Jersey Guides. There are two copies of the 1977 edition of *New Jersey: A Guide to Its Present and Past*; one of these is in the New Jersey collection, now shelved with Nonfiction, and it circulates, while the other is in the Reference collection and does not. The other two are of the 1986 volume put out by Rutgers University Press, *The WPA Guide to 1930s New Jersey*, and again one circulates and one is in the reference collection. There is no way of knowing how much the reference copies have been used; they appear to be worn but not worn out. The circulating copy of *The WPA Guide to 1930s*

14. The Library of Congress catalog and the listings on Amazon.com were the sources consulted.

New Jersey was added to the collection in 2000 and by 2014 it had been checked out ten times. *New Jersey: A Guide to Its Present and Past* entered the collection in 1999 and between then and 2014 it had been checked out thirty-three times. Not far away but serving a very different population, the Newark Public Library has thirty-eight copies of the New Jersey Guide, indicating a considerable degree of patron interest there.[15]

To examine library holdings at the state level, I needed a state with lots of counties (New Jersey has only 21), for that means lots of public library systems to give a broad picture of how the Guides have endured in libraries. I chose Kentucky because it has 120, an unusually large number (fourth after Texas, Georgia, and Virginia, and with a much lower population per county than these three). I was able to visit libraries in the eastern and central parts of the state, and I spoke with many librarians about local reading habits and about which patrons used the American Guides.

The Kentucky Writers' Project had been characterized by competence rather than brilliance. Its director was Dr. U. R. Bell, a Louisville journalist (the doctorate is an LLD from George Washington University) who had

15. The Princeton Public Library also has *The WPA Guide to New York City: The Federal Writers' Project Guide to 1930s New York / prepared by the Federal Writers' Project of the Works Progress Administration in New York City; with a new introduction by William H. Whyte* (New York: Pantheon Books, 1982). It has been checked out nineteen times since 1999. In addition, the library has a collection that Pantheon put out in 1985: *The WPA Guide to America: The Best of 1930s America as Seen by the Federal Writers' Project / edited by Bernard A. Weisberger; Selections from the American Guide Series, Written by the Federal Writers' Project of the Works Progress Administration, 1935–1941*. This volume has been checked out five times, suggesting that there may be more interest in the Project's depiction of particular places like New Jersey and New York than in its overview of the nation. The Princeton Public Library also has three other works that the New Jersey Writers' Project produced. First, it has two copies of *Old Princeton's Neighbors; Sponsored by the Borough of Princeton; Written and Illustrated by the Federal Writers' Project, Works Progress Administration, State of New Jersey*. Both of these are in the Princeton collection, both circulate, and both were checked out at different times in 2011. Second, it has one copy of *The Swedes and Finns in New Jersey . . . Written and Illustrated by the Federal Writers' Project of the Works Progress Administration, State of New Jersey; with an Introd. by Amandus Johnson . . . Sponsored by the New Jersey Commission to Commemorate the 300th Anniversary of the Settlement by the Swedes and Finns on the Delaware, D. Stewart Craven, Chairman*; this is in the Reference collection and does not circulate. Third, it has a copy of *Stories of New Jersey, Its Significant Places, People and Activities, Compiled and Written by the Federal Writers' Project of the Works Progress Administration for the State of New Jersey*. This volume is on the shelf in Nonfiction, NJ 917.49 Fed, and was last checked out less than a year ago, in May 2013. All of this demonstrates that the American Guide Series works, and the State Guides in particular, are not only available but that library patrons use them.

Princeton is perhaps not typical, for it is an affluent, well-educated suburb, so to see what an urban library serving a less-advantaged community might have, I checked the holdings of the Newark Public Library. The Newark Public Library consists of the Main Library and, as of spring 2014, seven operating branches. It has thirty-three copies of *New Jersey: A Guide to Its Present and Past*, and in addition five copies of *The WPA Guide to 1930s New Jersey*. Although I do not have circulation figures for Newark, such numbers again suggest considerable patron interest. Figures for Newark from http://catalog.npl.org/search/a?searchtype=t&searcharg=New+Jersey%3A+A+Guide+to+its+Present&SORT=D&searchscope=1&I3.x=43&I3.y=13, accessed March 28, 2014.

Table 10.1 State Guide editions and reprints

State	Region	Statehood	Authors mentioned	Year Guide published	Later editions or reprints	Total
Alabama	ESC	1819	46	1941	1949, 1959, 1973, 1975, 1984, 1992, 2000, 2007, 2007, 2013,2013	12
Alaska*	PAC	1959	0	1939	1942, 1943, 1944, 1950, 1959, 1973, 1976, 1981, 1991, 2007, 2013	12
Arizona	MTN	1912	34	1940	1949, 1956, 1966, 1972, 1989, 2007, 2013	8
Arkansas	WSC	1836	47	1941	1948, 1976, 1980, 1987, 2013	6
California	PAC	1850	100	1939	1955, 1967, 1972, 1984, 2012, 2013, 2013, 2013	9
Colorado	MTN	1876	57	1941	1943, 1945, 1946, 1948, 1951, 1958, 1959, 1970, 1973, 1987, 2007, 2007, 2013	14
Connecticut	NEN	1788	70	1938	1939, 1969, 1989, 2007, 2007, 2007, 2010, 2012, 2012, 2013, 2013	12
Delaware	SAT	1787	42	1938	1938, 1948, 1955, 1976, 1992, 2006, 2007, 2007, 2008, 2013	11
Florida	SAT	1845	85	1939	1939, 1940, 1944, 1946, 1947, 1949, 1955, 1956, 1976, 1984, 2007, 2007, 2013	14
Georgia	SAT	1788	108	1940	1946, 1954, 1976, 1981, 1990, 1992, 2007, 2007, 2013	10
Hawaii	PAC	1959	No Guide was written for Hawaii			
Idaho*	MTN	1890	0	1937	1937, 1950, 1961, 1968, 1973, 1976, 1999, 2007, 2007, 2012, 2012, 2013	13
Illinois	ENC	1818	86	1939	1947, 1972, 1973, 1974, 1983, 2007, 2011, 2013, 2013	10
Indiana	ENC	1816	45	1941	1945, 1947, 1961, 1973, 2007, 2013	7
Iowa	WNC	1846	68	1938	1941, 1945, 1949, 1959, 1973, 1986, 2007, 2007, 2010, 2012, 2012, 2013	13
Kansas	WNC	1861	81	1939	1949, 1976, 1984, 2007,2008, 2010, 2010, 2011, 2012, 2012, 2013	12
Kentucky	ESC	1792	13	1939	1942, 1947, 1954, 1973, 1996, 2007, 2007, 2010, 2012, 2012, 2013	12
Louisiana	WSC	1812	192	1941	1943, 1945, 1947, 1959, 1971, 1973, 2007, 2007, 2013	10
Maine	NEN	1820	50	1937	1970, 1972, 2007, 2008, 2010, 2012, 2012, 2013	9
Maryland	SAT	1788	88	1940	1941, 1946, 1948, 1973, 1976, , 1999, 2007, 2013	9
Massachusetts	NEN	1788	94	1937	1938, 1973, 1983, 2007, 2007, 2009, 2010, 2012, 2013, 2013	11
Michigan	ENC	1837	66	1941	1943, 1946, 1947, 1947, 1949, 1956, 1973, 2007, 2007, 2013	11
Minnesota	WNC	1858	32	1938	1947, 1954, 1972, 1985, 1989, 2002, 2010, 2010, 2013	10
Mississippi	ESC	1817	51	1938	1943, 1946, 1949, 1959, 1973, 1976, 1988, 2007, 2007, 2008, 2009, 2010, 2011, 2011, 2012, 2012, 2012, 2013, 2013	20
Missouri	WNC	1821	94	1941	1954, 1959, 1973, 1981, 1986, 1998, 2007, 2007, 2013	10
Montana	MTN	1889	52	1939	1946, 1949, 1955, 1973, 1994, 2012, 2012, 2013	9
Nebraska	WNC	1867	45	1939	1947, 1974, 1979, 2005, 2006, 2007, 2013	8

Nevada*	MTN	1864	0	1940	1957, 1973, 1991, 2007, 2007, 2013	7
New Hampshire	NEN	1788	84	1938	1947, 1974, 1989, 2007, 2007, 2011, 2012, 2012, 2013	10
New Jersey	MAT	1787	66	1939	1946, 1959, 1976, 1977, 1986, 1989, 2007, 2007, 2010, 2012, 2012, 2013	13
New Mexico	MTN	1912	101	1940	1945, 1947, 1953, 1962, 1974, 1984, 1989, 2007, 2007, 2007, 2007, 2013, 2013	14
New York	MAT	1788	69	1940	1946, 1947, 1949, 1955, 1956, 1962, 1962, 1974, 1989, 2007, 2013	12
New York City Guide**	MAT	NA	NA	1939	1939, 1946, 1957, 1968, 1970, 1972, 1974, 1976, 1982, 1992, 1995, 2007, 2010, 2012, 2012, 2013	17
New York Panorama*	MAT	NA	163	1938	1939, 1972, 1981, 1984, 2007, 2010, 2012, 2012	9
North Carolina	SAT	1789	63	1939	1944,1955, 1988, 2007, 2007, 2011, 2012, 2013	9
North Dakota*	WNC	1889	0	1938	1950, 1972, 1973, 1990, 2007, 2007, 2008, 2013	9
Ohio	ENC	1803	76	1940	1943, 1946, 1947, 1948, 1962, 1991, 2007, 2007, 2013	10
Oklahoma	WSC	1907	104	1941	1942, 1945, 1947, 1957, 1958, 1974, 1986, 2007, 2007, 2011, 2012, 2013, 2014	14
Oregon	PAC	1859	96	1940	1951, 1972, 1989, 2007, 2008, 2012, 2013	8
Pennsylvania	MAT	1787	105	1940	1946, 1947, 1947, 1949, 1950, 1950, 1957, 1963, 1976, 1980, 2007, 2007, 2013	14
Rhode Island	NEN	1790	69	1937	1973, 2007, 2007, 2007, 2010, 2012, 2013, 2014	9
South Carolina	SAT	1788	49	1941	1942, 1946, 1949, 1963, 1973, 1976, 1980, 1988, 1992, 2007, 2007, 2013	13
South Dakota*	WNC	1889	0	1938	1952, 1974, 1976, 1989, 2005, 2006, 2007, 2007, 2010, 2012, 2012, 2013	13
Tennessee	ESC	1796	69	1939	1945, 1949, 1959, 1976, 1980, 1986, 2007, 2013	9
Texas	WSC	1845	77	1940	1943, 1945, 1947, 1954, 1959, 1969, 1974, 1986, 2007, 2010, 2012, 2013	13
Utah	MTN	1896	83	1941	1942, 1945, 1954, 1955, 1959, 1972, 1982, 1982, 1998, 2007, 2013	12
Vermont	NEN	1791	26	1937	1966, 1968, 1973, 2007, 2012, 2013, 2013	8
Virginia	SAT	1788	134	1940	1941, 1946, 1947, 1951, 1952, 1956, 1964, 1972, 1974, 1980, 1992, 2007, 2013	14
Washington	PAC	1889	106	1941	1950, 1972, 1989, 2007, 2013	6
Washington, DC**	SAT	NA	72	1937	1939, 1942, 1976, 1983, 1989, 2007, 2009	8
West Virginia	SAT	1863	61	1941	1946, 1948, 1956, 1961, 1973, 1974, 1974, 1980, 2007, 2013	11
Wisconsin	ENC	1848	65	1941	1954, 1973, 1978, 2006, 2007, 2010, 2013	8
Wyoming	MTN	1890	79	1941	1946, 1948, 1952, 1956, 1966, 1973, 1976, 1981, 2007, 2007, 2013	12
Total authors mentioned			3463			564
					Average, 49 states (excl. Hawaii), plus Washington, DC and two New York City Guides (564/52)	10.8

*Did not have a Literature essay

**Not a state but had a Guide with a Literature essay

become friends with Cordell Hull during the First World War.[16] In the early months of the Writers' Project, Alsberg dispatched members of the Washington staff to report back on whether the various state offices were up and running. Field Supervisor Darel McConkey, who was not given to praise, reported back to Alsberg on January 27, 1936:

> Dr. Bell has shown considerable executive ability in lining up and finding people for his project in the state, he has a good grasp of the situation as it now stands, he is now ready to add N.Y.A. and volunteer people to complete his coverage of the state, and I feel certain he will turn in some good Kentucky Guide material. Colonel Beckner, Assistant Director, is a rare genius who has figured out what guide material is to be and since he is in charge of the editorial work, lending his vast knowledge of the state to the project, there need be little fear as to the final product.

This rare genius, a sixty-four-year-old lawyer, museum director, journalist, railroad man, and tobacco executive from Winchester, was not about to let the Washington boys tell him anything about Kentucky history. Responding to some editorial queries on June 25, 1936, Beckner wrote to Alsberg:

> The critic [an editor from the Washington FWP headquarters, possibly Cronyn] has questioned the expression "traveling in Kentucky," which occurs on page 2, line 15, and refers to La Salle's trip down the Ohio. He does not seem to know that every inch of the Ohio to low mark on its N. bank and from West Virginia to its mouth is in Kentucky; and, therefore, all travelers thereon were "traveling in Kentucky." We have been very careful of our statements and know our Kentucky, and must write its history as it is, not as someone who knows it not, thinks it should be.

Testy exchanges between Louisville and Washington were the least of Kentucky's problems. The Kentucky Writers' Project included six districts, with its central office in Louisville. In late January 1937 the Great Ohio River Flood inundated towns along the river from Pittsburgh to Cairo, Illinois; Louisville, right in the middle, was the hardest hit. Seventy percent of the city was underwater, and 175,000 people had to be evacuated.[17]

16. From Tennessee, Cordell Hull was an active Democrat (he chaired the Clay County Democratic Party at the age of nineteen) whom Tennessee sent to the House of Representatives for eleven terms, from 1907 to 1931 and elected to the Senate in 1930. Hull became Roosevelt's secretary of state in 1933, and he would continue in this position for eleven years, the longest time anyone has held that office. As FDR's confidant, he undoubtedly had a role in Bell's appointment.

17. "Fact Sheet: Ohio River Floods," prepared by the Kentucky Climate Center at Western Kentucky University by David Sander, Research Assistant, and Glen Conner, State Climatologist Emeritus for Kentucky. http://web.archive.org/web/20080604134934/http://kyclim.wku.edu/factSheets/ohioRiver.htm.

Nevertheless, the indefatigable Bell carried on, reporting to Alsberg on February 5:

> The water has been pumped out of our state office in Louisville and fires were [b]uilt Friday. We expect to be located again in our regular office on Monday February 8. I have been able to locate most of my best workers, especially editors. Some of the stenographers have not reported. Most of them are refugees who have been moved to other towns. One of them called me on long distance from a town down in the central part of Kentucky night before last. She said that her home had been completely covered with water and she was begging for her job as soon as she could get back to Louisville. We may be handicapped for stenographic help for a week or so. The editors have been working over the material for the State Guide Book in my apartment all this week and last week and they have three more tours ready for the typist. By the end of next week I am quite sure we will have a complete set of maps prepared for the State Guide Book ready for Washington. I will send them in under separate cover as soon as they are ready. I hope to be able to submit the "dummy" completed within the next two or three weeks.[18]

Not only was the Kentucky Project coping with floodwaters but, back in Washington, Henry Alsberg was fretting that the Kentucky Guide might end up being, of all things, dull! Alsberg wrote to Regional Director John Frederick that the latest draft was "notably lacking in mention of feuds, folklore and folk songs, mint juleps, wine, women and fine whiskey (the horses get some attention) and the like. The average tourist probably has an exaggerated idea of the importance of these subjects, but they do deserve some attention."[19]

In spite of tribulations from the Ohio River and from the Washington headquarters, the Kentucky Writers' Project brought out *Kentucky: A Guide to the Bluegrass State* in 1939. Kentucky was neither one of the first states to produce a Guide nor one of the laggards. Its Guide was relatively modest in size, smaller than the state's population might have warranted.[20] Although Alsberg had worried over whether the book would be sufficiently lively, apparently Bell produced enough feuds and whiskey to satisfy him; Alsberg came to rely on Bell's judgment and later sought his advice on the faltering Missouri project.[21]

The Guide's reception in Kentucky was enthusiastic. The *Sunday Lou-*

18. Letter from U. R. Bell to Henry Alsberg, February 5, 1937.

19. Letter from Henry Alsberg to John Frederick, June 28, 1938.

20. The state of Kentucky ranked seventeenth in total population according to the 1930 census. The Kentucky Guide, at 489 pages, ranked thirty-sixth out of the forty-eight State Guides.

21. Mangione (1972): 339.

isville Courier-Journal, the state's largest newspaper, headlined its review "W.P.A.'s Super-Guide to Kentucky" and praised its large type ("unlike the Baedekers which racked our eyes and fried our throats in the old days of cultural European tours"), its usefulness, and its wealth of curious information are "simply not to be had in any other one volume" (figure 10.3). Not just anybody wrote the review but Mary Caperton, actually Mary Caperton Bingham, the wife of media mogul Barry Bingham Sr., who owned the newspaper. The Binghams were stars of Louisville high society, active in philanthropy, cultural affairs, and Democratic politics; the *Louisville Courier-Journal* was a liberal voice in a conservative state. So the paper, predisposed to look favorably on this New Deal initiative, promoted the Guide through both the content of its review and the name on the byline. The more conservative press was positive as well, however; favorable reception was across the board. In his review for the *Lexington Herald-Leader*, Burton Milward praised the Guide for being "accurate, authoritative, well arranged, and generally well-written . . . an unusually worthwhile book," especially in comparison with the Project's earlier volume on Lexington that Milward dismissed as an error-ridden "fiasco."[22]

Off to a good start locally and nationally, since that initial launching the Kentucky Guide has been going strong for three quarters of a century and counting. At least twelve editions or reprints have appeared—the first in 1939, then again in 1942, 1947, 1954, 1973, 1996, 2007 (2), 2010, 2012 (2), and 2013—which suggests a steady and continuing demand (table 10.1).

Though Mary Caperton had ended her review by saying that "native Kentuckians should take great pride, not in borrowing and renting, but in buying" the Guide, apparently they have borrowed it plenty. Three quarters of the state's public libraries currently have some version of the Kentucky Guide in their collections. In its 120 counties, Kentucky has 119 public library systems (Ballard and Carlisle Counties have a combined system).[23] A county-by-county examination of these libraries in 2014 revealed that 88 of the 110 library systems, 74 percent, have at least one copy of the Kentucky Guide. Some have multiple copies; Woodford County in the bluegrass central region of the state, for example, has two copies of the 1947 edition and two copies of the 1996 edition. Many of these libraries have noncirculating copies in their Reference collections (in some cases

22. "University Staff Members Aid in Preparing Informative WPA Guide to State of Kentucky," review by Burton Milward, *Lexington Herald-Leader*, November 5, 1939, 29.

23. Kentucky ranks high in terms of its library professionals. It is one of twelve states, and the only one in the South, that has more than six American Library Association Accredited Master of Library Science librarians per 25,000 citizens. It is average or below in terms of library visits and circulation. See Swan et al. (2014), especially 51, 19, 21.

W.P.A.'s Super-Guide to Kentucky

Up-to-Date Facts Plus Quaint and Curious Fragments of Forgotten Lore

KENTUCKY, A GUIDE TO THE BLUEGRASS STATE: Compiled and written by the Federal Writers' Project of Kentucky. 489 pp. Harcourt Brace. $2.50.

Reviewed by Mary Caperton.

One of the most useful undertakings of the Federal Writers' Projects throughout the country has been the compilation of the American Guide Series. The Federal Writers' Guide books to the New England States have been available for several years, and their steadily mounting sales prove that they have met a long felt want. Now "Kentucky, A Guide to the Bluegrass State," compiled and written by the Federal Writers' Project of the Works Progress Administration for the State of Kentucky, and sponsored by the University of Kentucky, has just been published by Harcourt Brace and Company.

Shaker ceremonies. From the Harrodsburg Herald. Reproduced in "Kentucky: A Guide to the Bluegrass State." By the Federal Writers Project of the W.P.A.

Water Front in Louisville. From "Kentucky: A Guide to the Bluegrass State." American Guide Series.

"Kentucky," like the other books in the American Guide Series, is a good deal more than a guide book. Indeed, it seems happily unlike the Baedekers which racked our eyes and dried our throats in the old days of cultural European tours. The print is black and clear, and the type large enough to read comfortably in the back seat of a car going fast over a fair road. In it are chapters on the general background of Kentucky, its history, agriculture, labor, arts and architecture. Specialists, many of whom volunteered their services, read and criticised all copy prepared by the editorial staff. Information as reliable and as amazingly full as is available in this book is simply not to be had in any other one volume, or, in some cases, hardly to be had at all except by consulting old diaries and letters, and listening to the reminiscences of local story tellers all over the State. How many people know the tragic story of John Fitch, the inventor of the steamboat who, bitter and disillusioned, ended his life at Bardstown in 1798 with a dose of poison? Or, if they do know all about John Fitch's peculiarly harassing life, do they remember this quotation from his diary? "I know of nothing so vexatious to a man of feelings as a turbulent wife and steamboat building. I experienced the former and quit in season and had I been in my right sense I should undoubtedly have treated the latter in the same manner, but for one man to be teased with both, he must be looked upon as the most unfortunate man of this world."

There are two good maps in the guide book, and twenty tours in the course of which the whole State is very thoroughly covered. The many illustrations are conspicuous for their good taste and discrimination. The chapter on the architecture of Kentucky is a particularly good piece of work. It is very satisfying to be able to drive through the country and read as you run a competent history of many of the beautiful Kentucky Georgian and Greek Revival houses which stand back from the roads flecked by the shadows of their great protecting trees. The less traditional forms of architecture which, from one point of view, mar the landscape are, too, efficiently dealt with in a section devoted to Victorian Gothic and Romanesque as it was spewed forth in Kentucky—those great lowering mounds which Alexander Woollcott once called "Nobody's Byzantine."

The Kentucky Writers' Project and the director, Dr. U. R. Bell, deserve the highest praise for the work which they have accomplished. This is a book for the tourists who come to Kentucky in increasing numbers every year, and one which native Kentuckians should take great pride, not in borrowing and renting, but in buying.

10.3 "W.P.A.'s Super-Guide to Kentucky," from the *Louisville Courier-Journal*, November 5, 1939

in a special Kentucky Reference Collection). This rules out their use by tourists. Physical examination shows these books have been heavily used. So the question is, by whom and for what?

Librarians, in Kentucky and elsewhere, have told me that students doing research for papers and homework are the patrons who turn to the

Guides most often. This is not surprising in light of the fact that every state requires state history (including geography, economy, sociology, and culture) in the curriculum. These requirements begin in the elementary school years, and by the time a middle or high school student is working on independent research papers, many must write or choose to write about their own states.[24] The Guides are sitting in the library to help them. Or sitting in the cloud, with librarians, who now see themselves as providing access to information and not just to books, eager to help them find it. *The WPA Guide to Kentucky*, the edition of the Guide that the University Press of Kentucky published in 1996, is available on Google Books.[25]

Kentucky is by no means unusual. In an online discussion of state history classes, people schooled in every state except two reported their memories of these classes.[26] Some memories are fond: "California history was so much fun because we got to make our choice of Missions out of

24. While requirements vary, a typical pattern is for state-specific content to be mandated in the fourth-grade social studies curriculum and again at some point in the middle school years. For example, the Kentucky Department of Education specifies "the social studies content from Kentucky's Academic Expectations and *Program of Studies* that is essential for all students to know" at the elementary school level. The fourth grade, which focuses on the state, specifies the things students should know about Kentucky:

- constitution ("Students will identify the basic principles of democracy (e.g., justice, equality, responsibility, freedom) found in Kentucky's Constitution and explain why they are important to citizens today");
- history ("Students will describe various forms of interactions (compromise, cooperation, conflict) that occurred during the early settlement of Kentucky between diverse groups (Native Americans, early settlers");
- economy ("Students will describe scarcity and explain how scarcity requires people in Kentucky to make economic choices (e.g., use of productive resources—natural, human, capital) and incur opportunity costs");
- geography ("Students will describe how different factors (e.g., rivers, mountains) influence where human activities were/are located in Kentucky");
- regions ("Students will describe patterns of human settlement in regions of Kentucky and explain how these patterns were/are influenced by physical characteristics (e.g., climate, landforms, bodies of water)";
- environment ("Students will describe how the physical environment (e.g., mountains as barriers for protection, rivers as barriers of transportation) both promoted and restricted human activities during the early settlement of Kentucky"):
- culture ("Students will identify significant historical documents, symbols, songs and selected readings (e.g., state flag, United We Stand, Divided We Fall, My Old Kentucky Home) specific to Kentucky and explain their historical significance").

While such specific standards apply only to the fourth grade, Jennifer Fraker, social studies consultant at the Kentucky Department of Education, told me that "often schools will incorporate Kentucky-related content in the 6th grade as that tends to be more geography-related and then again in the 9th grade . . . later coverage (if and when) is left up to the discretion of the local school district" (e-mail to the author, March 26, 2014.)

25. http://books.google.com/books?id=IuGCoLRCN-kC&pg=PR21&dq=wpa+guide+to+1930s+kentucky&hl=en&sa=X&ei=neU7U8D_FaeW0AHtnIGYAQ&ved=0CDMQ6AEwAQ#v=onepage&q=literature&f=false.

26. http://ask.metafilter.com/150571/Which-US-states-have-state-history-classes, accessed March 15, 2014.

sugar cubes." Others are less so: "Every so often I wonder whether there might have been some better way to spend that year, since I have no need to recognize all of the New Jersey counties by shape." Regardless, the experience seems to be universal. Thus we see the ongoing need for librarians and teachers to help students with local history projects every year, and thus the ongoing life and relevance of the State Guides. Generations of students have learned about their states, including their state's literature, through the Guides.

What We Have Learned

The five types of evidence just presented support the earlier claims. People have used the State Guides less for travel and more for reading and reference. The Guides were popular from the beginning, and in spite of the disruption of the Second World War, they have continued to be popular. Students consult them as reference books. Librarians preserve and recommend them. Publishers reissue them. For almost eight decades the American Guide Series has unobtrusively been teaching Americans about their culture.

What the Guides did and continue to do is make plausible the idea that every state is unique, that each state has a distinct history and culture, and that each state has its own authors, its own voice, its own literary tradition. Generations of students, of researchers, of librarians, of teachers, and of ordinary people have come to absorb this idea—history and culture in state-shaped molds—just through the sheer presence of these books. The Guides reassured states outside of the Northeast, states like Alabama and Oklahoma and Utah, that yes, they too had a literature. And those who looked into what the Guides had to say about this literature found women, Native Americans, Hispanics, African Americans, theologians, cowboy poets, explorers, proletarian novelists, the talented, the connected, the obscure—a wildly diverse cast that, according to the federal government, made up the ongoing production of "Our Literature, from Sea to Shining Sea."

CONCLUSION

Casting American Culture

Once having marched
Over the margins of animal necessity,
Over the grim line of sheet subsistence
Then man came
To the deeper rituals of his bones,
To the lights lighter than any bones,
To the time for thinking things over,
To the dance, the song, the story,
Or the hours given over to dreaming,
Once having so marched.

CARL SANDBURG, *THE PEOPLE, YES*

American Guides has attempted to understand and explain the Federal Writers' Project's cultural impact by asking questions at three distinct levels. The substantive what-happened-and-why ones: What people in what context produced the State Guides of the American Guide Series? What made them the odd hybrids that they were? What was the depiction of American literature that the Guides' Literature essays presented? What impact did this presentation have on American culture? Second, the knotty methodological questions: How did people actually use the Guides? How can we ever tell what people do with books? What types of evidence—material, market, usage, other—can we assemble? Third, the theoretical questions: How does the shape of culture change? When does this change take hold, or in other words, under what conditions does the push and pull of different actors with different agendas result in lasting cultural shift? How does the dual casting metaphor—casts as shapes and casts as personnel—extend to culture more generally?

Most of the book has addressed the substantive questions, which are the sine qua non of empirical research. Issues of method and evidence came up along the way, and chapter 10 explored these explicitly. This final chapter will consider some more theoretical issues.

To recapitulate: The American Guides were compromises, Rube Goldberg make-dos constructed out of federalism and necessity. The Federal Writers' Project administrators dreamed up the American Guide Series to give out-of-work white-collar types something to do, to keep their radical tendencies in check, to make congressmen happy, to make local business interests happy, and—since the Project wasn't making anyone very happy anyway in the early days—to maintain a low profile until the Project proved its usefulness. Right from the start, the State Guides had split personalities. They were supposed to be travel books for the present, sitting in glove compartments and on back seats to help Americans See America First, and they were supposed to be collections of essays for the ages, sitting in libraries and studies to help Americans know about their history, economics, and culture.

Building this duality into the Guides was a brilliant stroke politically. The promise of producing travel guides solved the three-headed problem of keeping the writers out of trouble, keeping the states productively occupied despite grumblings from local WPA directors, and keeping Congress off the backs of the Project administrators. The promise of producing reference books brought the intellectuals and academics on board, both those inside the Project and the many more outside who worked as consultants and experts and general cheerleaders. Once the Guides began to appear, everyone found something to praise.

For Harry Hopkins, the job was done: The Federal Writers' Project had given work and paychecks to unemployed writers, thus helping them make it through the Great Depression. For Katharine Kellock, the job was done: In a short half-dozen years the Project had produced American Baedekers, travel guides to suit the age of the automobile. For the federal government, the job was done: Federal One was a one-off, Washington had never intended to support literary or artistic activity for long, and anyway there was a war to fight.

But for the disheveled, disorganized, politically naïve visionary who had directed the Project, the cultural work of the Guides was by no means done. Henry Alsberg had always intended the Guides to be for readers, for the students, the armchair travelers, the curious. They would be reference book that may or may not be used on the road but that would be available for the long haul, sitting in libraries and studies and bookshelves. He saw them as compendiums of what was known and what could be found out about America. Thus although he was a progressive, Alsberg's regionalism was documentarian: He sought to catalog and preserve American culture. Beyond comprehensive coverage, good writing, and attention to the experiences of ordinary Americans, however, Alsberg had no particular agenda. He only put out the American Guide Series in state volumes because George Cronyn and Katharine Kellock convinced him that this made political sense, and he didn't give much—make that any—thought to diversity. And yet it was in convincing Americans that culture came in state-shaped boxes and in opening American eyes to literature from diverse sources and places that the State Guides had their greatest impact. Alsberg would have been pleased but not surprised by the Guides' lasting influence, though he might have been surprised by the nature of that influence.

A Diverse Cast

The American Guides' definition of American literature, and indeed of American culture itself, was more diverse in every way—in gender, in ethnicity, in genre, in geography—than anything that had come before. This diversification was not the result of the Federal Writers' Project's intent to champion a more inclusive culture. It came from a series of politically strategic decisions, from bureaucratic organizational charts, and from petty tussles between high-handed East Coast intellectuals and stubborn you-can't-push-me-around locals. In spite of it being accidental, the unintended consequence of a jobs program, the Guides constituted the first major opening of a revolutionary democratization that, by the last quarter of the twentieth century, would transform American literary culture.

The Guides did not mark a point on some inexorable progression toward greater diversification. There were no long-term trends. Instead, the Guides' literary inclusivity was from the political-geographic necessity that moved the definition of American culture out of the hands of the northeastern intellectuals—which was ironic, given that the Federal Writers' Project was nothing if not a project of northeastern intellectuals.

Gender diversity offers a clear example. In their inclusion of women authors, the Guides were well ahead of other definers of American literature, both before and after, until the revolution of the 1970s. So how is it that women got the representation they did in the Guides? Certainly not because of intention: No one in the correspondence ever mentioned inclusion of women authors as a goal or even a concern. Project directors in Washington, who were ideologically oriented, were thinking about class, not about gender or race or any of the other diversity dimensions of today. Writers and editors in the states, who typically did not think in ideological terms, were just trying to fill up their essays. Nor was the inclusion of women because the state directors themselves were women. While almost a quarter of them were (chapter 5), states having women directors were not especially inclined toward including women authors in their Literature essays.[1]

Given the cultural elite's lack of interest in gender, one might expect the Northeast—home to the big cities, the publishers, the New Dealers, the radical intelligentsia, and the media—to be particularly unconcerned with including women in the literary pantheon. To assess this possibility, we need to see where women authors were and where they weren't. If our hunch is correct that the cultural centers were oblivious to women authors, then we would expect the three census divisions of the Northeast—New England, Middle Atlantic, and East North Central—to have lower representation than the six divisions of the South and West. Map C.1 shows that this is indeed the case. The Guides from all three of the northeast divisions have below-average numbers of women authors mentioned in their Literature essays, while the Guides of five out of the six non-northeast divisions have above-average representation of women.

A look at these gender ratios by state rather than by division gives a more nuanced picture (map C.2). We see that New England is a microcosm of the nation as a whole: The three northern states, outliers in terms of population and urbanization, favored women compared to the traditional cultural centers of Massachusetts and Connecticut. We also see that two of the four East South Central (Kentucky and Alabama) states favored women, but they were outnumbered by the two favoring men, therefore making the division an exception to the overall pattern. Moreover map C.2 shows that some of the larger states outside of the Northeast like California and Texas were conservative in terms of gender, whereas smaller "we don't have much literature here" states like Oklahoma and Wyoming and Oregon found plenty of women authors. Once again the key was necessity, not ideology: Project personnel in each of these states had to come up with a Literature essay so they scrambled around for any authors they could find. Geography and federal/state bureaucratic structure, not commitment to diversity, made the difference.

1. Twelve states had women directors during the time that the Guides were being written, and of these twelve, six were above the average of women authors and six were below. Alabama, Delaware, Maine, Minnesota, Virginia, and Wyoming had female state directors and above-average representation of women in the Literature essays, while Florida, Mississippi, Missouri, New Jersey, New Mexico, and South Carolina had female directors but below-average representation of women authors.

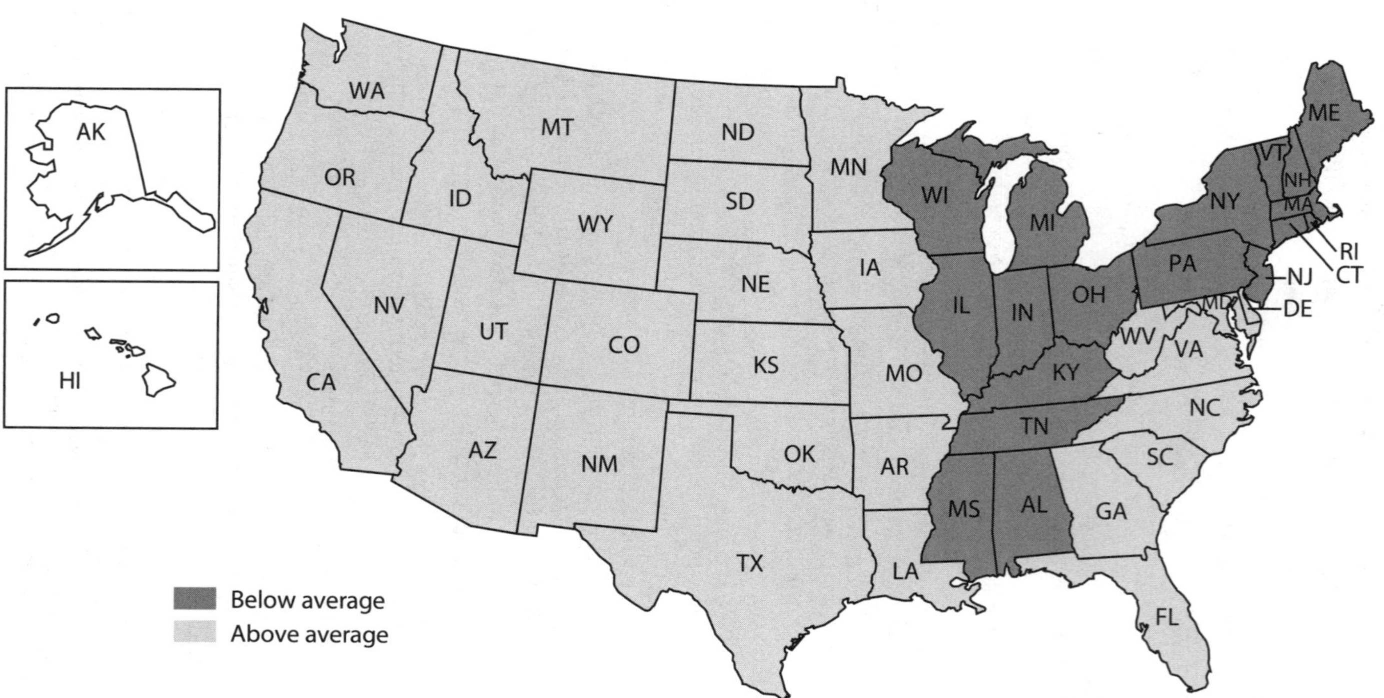

Map C.1 Ratio of female to male authors by division

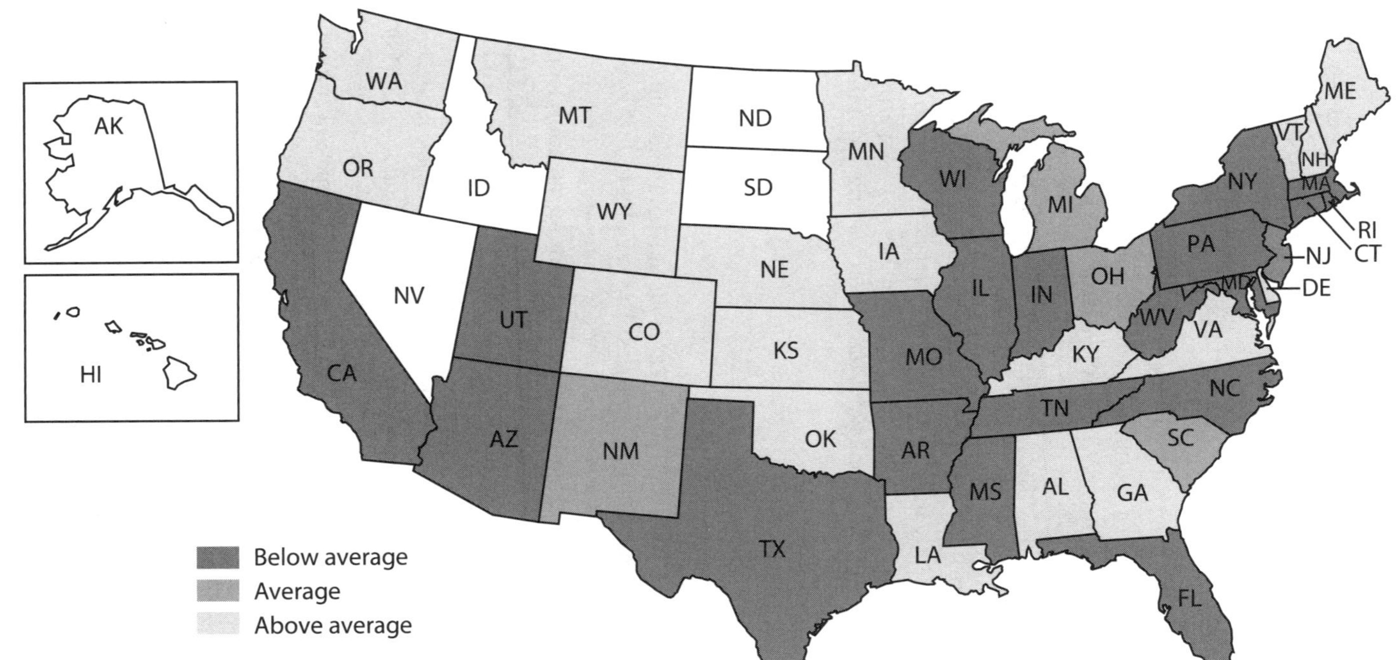

Map C.2 Ratio of female to male authors by state

Genre diversification shows the same basic picture (map C.3). States in the northeastern quadrant of the nation—those in the New England, Mid-Atlantic, and East North Central divisions—usually featured authors who write in the three conventional genres of fiction, poetry, or drama, while states to the south and, especially, to the west usually embraced more unconventional forms. Of course there were state-by-state exceptions. The Massachusetts essays, for example, included a number of theologians so they stand as an exception to the conservative New England pattern; outside of the Northeast, unusually knowledgeable and powerful state directors like William Allen White in Kansas and Lyle Saxon in Louisiana steered their essays toward the mainstream genres. Overall, however, the farther away from the Northeast, the broader the definition of American literature.

Again, diversity came from geography not ideology. Politics, Washington's desire for standardization, and local necessity wrought the newly expansive definition of American literature. And this expansive view is what students studying their states have been reading about in public libraries ever since.

In State-Shaped Molds

Until the Federal Writers' Project came along, state lines did not constitute meaningful literary boundaries. The key divide during the nineteenth century was that between American authors and British authors. By the century's end, the nation had gained cultural self-confidence. Both authors and readers became interested in literary expressions of specific American places—the vogue for local color stories and for Americana being well-known examples—but generally these places did not conform to state lines. Books like William Henry Venable's *Beginnings of Literary Culture in the Ohio Valley, Historical and Biographical Sketches* (1891) or Alexander Nicholas De Menil's *Literature of the Louisiana Territory* (1904) carved up American literature along geographic or historical lines, not state boundaries.

Organizing American Guides and the cultural essays therein by state made sense from a bureaucratic and political point of view, but it was illogical from a cultural point of view. State boundaries did not match cultural boundaries in most people's eyes. Southwestern fiction connoted a specific set of themes and a specific place character, but distinguishing between Arizona fiction and New Mexico fiction didn't add much. Nevertheless, after the Federal Writers' Project brought out its State Guides, the

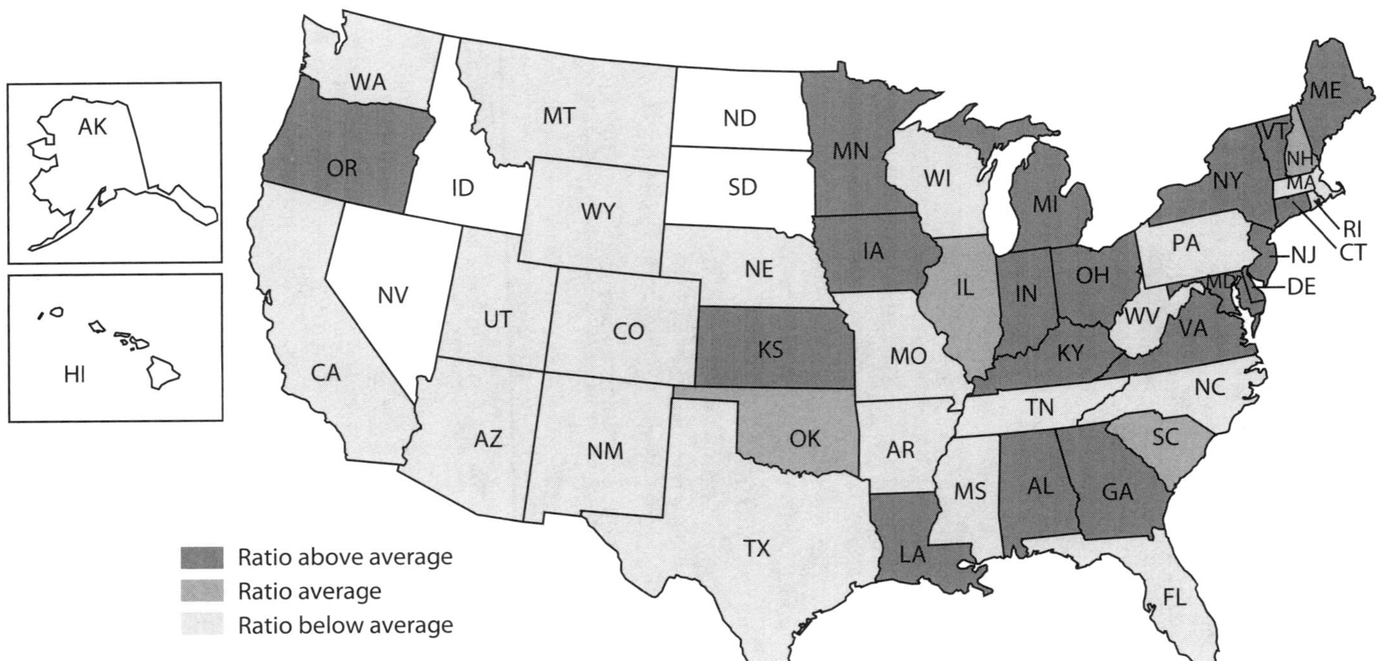

Map C.3 Ratio of conventional to unconventional genres by state

idea of individual states having their own characteristic cultures, including literatures, became more common. New Dealers, state bureaucrats, local boosters, East Coast intellectuals, politicians, desperate writers: All were accomplices in casting America's literary boundaries into state-shaped molds. And the readers, the high school students, the armchair travelers, the history buffs, the people interested in their states, and, yes, a certain type of tourist as well: These were the recipients of culture cast in these state-shaped molds.

The result was the normalization of the idea of states having distinctive literatures, or in other words, a recasting of regionalism away from geographic and historical boundaries and toward political ones. With the exception of the South, which has retained its cultural identity over and above the state lines, all other regions have given way to state forms. We feel no surprise at titles like *A Reader's Guide to Illinois Literature*; *Writing Illinois*; *Illinois Literature: The Nineteenth Century*; *Illinois Voices: An Anthology of Twentieth-Century Poetry*; or *Illinois Poets: A Selection.* And while for most Americans "the Midwest" probably still connotes more of a regional essence than "Illinois" does, in terms of literary packaging, the state mold dominates.

We can see this through a simple search on Amazon.com; searching "Midwestern literature" brings up 59 titles, "Midwest literature" brings up 1,185 (many of these are travel guides), and "Illinois literature" brings up 3,213. "Midwest poets" brings up 221, "Illinois poets" 800. "Midwest fiction" brings up 1,469 titles, "Illinois fiction" 2,269. And there is nothing unusual about Illinois or the Midwest. The same pattern is found for every region except the South:

- "New England literature" brings up 99 titles (top is *New England beyond Criticism: A Defense of America's First Literature*), and in light of the Massachusetts Writers' Project ignoring Louisa May Alcott, one is relieved to see that her *Collected Works* is third on the list;
- "Maine literature," 1,331 (top is *Maine Speaks: An Anthology of Maine Literature*);
- Massachusetts literature," 3,081 (top is *Goodnight, Massachusetts*, a children's book for young children modeled on *Goodnight, Moon*; there is one for every state);
- "New Hampshire literature," 848; "Vermont literature," 579; "Rhode Island," 512.[2]

2. These specific numbers come from a search of Amazon.com that I did on July 24, 2014. The titles were sorted by relevance. Some of the titles were, in fact, not relevant to literature in the conventional sense—travel guides, for example, or political histories—but this was true for every category, so the relative positions hold.

Of course there were some state collections of poetry and prose before the 1930s, and there continue to be regional collections, but classification by state is now normal and dominant.

Casting Culture

People often conceive of cultural change as a process either of evolution or of congealment. The evolutionary model of slow, cumulative change is older and more familiar. It envisions long-term trends—modernization, the division of labor, rationalization, intensifying conflict between social classes—that play out over time as earlier stages evolve into later ones. In some Hegelian versions, cultural change is the prime mover, but more often it is along for the ride, changing with or after more fundamental changes at the economic or social level. Two versions of this are Marx's observation that "the ruling ideas are the ideas of the ruling class"—class relations come first, culture follows and legitimates the class relations—and William Ogburn's cultural lag thesis, whereby "home, factories, machines, raw materials, manufactured products, food stuffs and other material objects" change, and the nonmaterial culture then adapts, catches up.

The congealment model, recently favored by cultural sociologists, is more postmodern in spirit, eschewing the search for trends or major historical narratives in favor of more random, episodic developments. The idea is that various cultural elements—materials, schemas, ideas, and symbols—are always swirling around. Some are innovations; some are leftovers from previous eras; the pieces don't fit together terribly well, and most of the time this isn't a problem. Although most cultural bits and pieces fall by the wayside, now and then some congeal into an identifiable form, and if this congealed form picks up economic, social, and political resources, it becomes institutionalized.[3]

The twofold casing of American culture described in this book corresponds neither to the evolutionary nor to the congealment models. There was no trend toward diversification. And there was no discernable movement toward seeing states as reasonable containers for regionalism. The Federal Writers' Project cast American literature with women and minori-

3. An influential statement of the congealment thesis comes from Jepperson and Swidler's (1994) discussion of the relative institutionalization of cultural elements: "Institutions such as marriage, markets, corporations, universities, or family are first and always cultural constructs, but they are constructs that have congealed, assembling resources . . . and commitments . . . around them. . . . They are indeed culture, but culture congealed in forms that require less by way of maintenance, ritual reinforcement, and symbolic elaboration that the softer (or more 'living') realms we usually think of as cultural" (362–63).

ties not because ideas about diversity were ascendant—that wouldn't happen for decades—but because Washington organized the American Guide Series state by state, and so the states out in the hinterland had to come up with some names for their Literature essays. The Project cast literature in state-shaped molds not because this made cultural sense but because it made political sense.

Nor did the new ideas about diversity and shapes congeal and then become fixed in institutions. Institutionalization came first. It was federalism and its political necessities that generated the new ideas, ideas about state culture, about what literature was, and about who wrote it. Institutional imperatives poured these ideas into the American Guides, where they got fixed, eventually becoming taken-for-granted elements in libraries, in curricula, and in American thinking, teaching Americans about the shape of their culture and about who was included in its cast of characters.

Form matters. In the present case, the form that matters is federalism. American federalism has not aimed toward a highly centralized culture like that of France or China, the centralization in both cases being strenuously achieved and maintained. Nor has it relaxed into a highly decentralized federalism like that of Switzerland or Nigeria, with different regions, different languages, and to a considerable extent different cultures, all loosely held together by the nation-state. The United States constitutes an unusual and often uneasy balance between the central and the local, between Washington and the states. This peculiar federal form gives the culture its state-shaped boxes and initiated the tug-of-war between Washington and the states that resulted in states bringing new characters and genres into the literary canon by pouring them into those state-shaped boxes.

Form matters more generally. A century ago Georg Simmel asserted that "the problem of sociology" was form, not content. He used competition as an example: Competition is a form, and parties might compete over various interests (content). Social analysis is like geometry, Simmel argued, and the goal is to abstract the form from various contents. The same is true for cultural analysis: Form influences content, the container both designating a schematic shape and shaping that which it contains.

Consider the sonnet for example. The genre's conventions accustom us to an idea or emotion expressed in fourteen-line packages, sometimes with a twist at the end (Shakespeare) and sometimes with a summation (Elizabeth Barrett Browning). A fourteen-line sonnet is an appropriate vehicle for some things—a striking metaphor, a crafted and polished passion—but not others; its formality makes it unsuitable for expressing uncontrolled rage, for example, while its brevity does not allow for narrative complexity.

So let us imagine that a culturally powerful actor like the National Endowment for the Arts decided to publish a series of contemporary poets, but for some reason, perhaps so the poems could fit on subway car cards as in the New York City Metropolitan Transit Authority's "Poetry in Motion" program, it mandated that all the poems should be sonnets. The legacy of the series would privilege a specific shape and a specific type of content in the American canon.

When proposing and implementing innovations, institutions specify the forms these innovations will take for reasons that usually are not cultural but practical, like the size of subway cards or the need to appease congressmen elected by states. These forms may have powerful, largely unintended consequences. An analysis that asks, Why that form? can help answer questions that are specifically cultural (e.g., Why do we think that states have distinctive literary voices?) as well as those that are more sociological (e.g., Why are these types of people included in or excluded from the canon?). *American Guides* has been my attempt to show the rewards of doing this type of analysis.

Appendix A: Organizations and Acronyms

AAA. American Automobile Association, formed in 1902 from a merger of regional automobile clubs

Authors Guild. After 1921 one of the two branches of the Authors League of America

Authors League of America. Oldest professional writers association founded in 1912. In 1921 the Dramatists Guild became a separate branch. During the 1930s Authors Guild and Authors League were used interchangeably.

Authors League Fund. Charitable branch of Authors League founded in 1917 to make loans to professional writers

CCC. Civilian Conservation Corps (1933–42), a federal jobs program for young men

CWA. Civil Works Administration (1933–34)

FERA. Federal Emergency Relief Administration, established May 1933

FSA. Farm Security Administration

FWA. Federal Works Agency, established by the Reorganization Act of 1939 to consolidate agencies under the executive branch. It included the (renamed) WPA.

FWP. Federal Writers' Project, one of the four Federal One arts programs

NIRA. National Industrial Recovery Act, June 1933

NRA. National Recovery Administration, under NIRA, code of standards for Industry (e.g., minimum wages, maximum hours), struck down by Supreme Court June 1935

PWA. Public Works Administration, established under the NIRA

PWAP. Public Works of Art Project, established by the Civil Works Administration in 1933 under the Treasury Department to decorate public buildings

RA. Resettlement Administration; became the Farm Security Administration in 1937

RFC. Reconstruction Finance Corporation, authorized by Title I of Emergency Relief and Construction Act (July 1932) to loan states money for relief

TERA. New York State's Temporary Emergency Relief Administration, headed by Harry Hopkins

UWA. Unemployed Writers' Association, a left-wing group pressuring Washington to employ writers

WPA. Works Progress Administration (1935–39); Work Projects Administration (1939–42)

Writers Union. Left-wing group that grew out of the UWA in 1934

Appendix B: Key Dates for the Federal Writers' Project, New Deal Relief Programs, and American Travel

1869 *Crofutt's Great Trans-Continental Railroad Guide* published
1893 Baedeker publishes *The United States*; second edition comes out in 1909
1901 *Automobile Blue Books* founded
1902 American Automobile Association founded
1908 Ford introduces the Model T
1913 Filling stations begin giving away free maps

New Deal

1932

July 21 Emergency Relief and Construction Act authorizes Reconstruction Finance Corporation to advance loans to states for relief and work relief

1933

March 4 Roosevelt's inauguration
May 12 Federal Emergency Relief Act (FERA) approved by FDR; it provided $500 million in outright grants to states for relief
November 9 FDR signs executive order creating Civil Works Administration (CWA), a temporary jobs program

1934

March CWA end, leaving FERA to provide work relief
April Unemployed Writers' Association becomes Writers' Union, under Communist Party influence

November Democrats gain seats in midterm elections
Thanksgiving Hopkins travels to Warm Springs to pitch new jobs plan to FDR

1935

January 4 FDR's State of the Union address calls for massive federal jobs program
January–April House passes emergency relief appropriations bill containing jobs program on January 24; Senate passes April 5: both houses pass Emergency Relief Appropriations Act April 8
April 28 FDR's seventh Fireside Chat introduces the Works Relief program (to become the WPA)
May 6 FDR by executive order establishes what is now called Works Progress Administration, picks Harry Hopkins to lead
June 25 WPA Professional and Service Projects Division submits formal proposal for Federal Writers' Project, which calls for guidebook for United States in five regional volumes, reports on WPA, encyclopedia of government functions, and some special studies; proposed project would last one year and employ 6,742 workers
July 25 Henry Alsberg, picked by Jacob Baker, officially appointed as national director of the Federal Writers' Project
August 2 Federal Project Number One, overseeing four arts programs, announced
September 12 Federal One get executive approval and six months of funding
November Historical Records Survey authorized as part of the FWP

1936

May Deadline for copy for five-volume *American Guide*; not met
July Baker replaced by Ellen Woodward to head WPA Division of Women's and Professional Projects, which included Federal One programs; budget cuts for WPA programs, including Federal Writers' Project; layoffs follow
August 13 Alsberg sends letter with series of questions about workers, who is a professional writer? and so on, to every state
October *3 Hikes through the Wissahickon* brought out by Pennsylvania project; pamphlet was first FWP publication
November More budget cuts and layoffs; Historical Records Survey severed from FWP, becomes free-standing part of Federal One; Roosevelt reelected

1937

January *Idaho: A Guide in Word and Picture* published
April *Washington: City and Capital* published
June–July Cuts in WPA rolls; picketing in New York City
August 13 Massachusetts governor Charles Hurley receives *Massachusetts: A Guide to Its Places and People* from Ellen Woodward, Allsberg's supervisor; the next day he condemns the *Guide* for its depiction of Sacco and Vanzetti trial and labor disputes

Fall New Hampshire, Maine, and Vermont Guides published; Lewis Mumford writes piece in the *New Republic* praising the American Guide series

1938

May 26 House of Representatives appoints Committee to Investigate Un-American Activities with Martin Dies Jr. as chair

July Reed Harris resigns as assistant director of the Federal Writers' Project

Fall Dies Committee hearings

December Alsberg, Woodward, and Hallie Flanagan testify before the Dies Committee

December Harry Hopkins resigns as WPA head, replaced by Col. F. C. Harrington

1939

March Alsberg writes to every state about the need to push as many projects to completion by June 30 as they can; asks for updates on projects that might be finished by then

April 3 President sends Congress reorganization plan that ends Works Progress Administration's independent status; changes its name to the Works Projects Administration, a subsidiary of a new agency: Federal Works Administration

June House relief bill ends Federal Theatre Project, transfers Writers' Program to states, requiring 25 percent local sponsorship

July Harrington fires Alsberg; his replacement is John Newsom

Fall Following German invasion of Poland, Newsom stresses program's relevance for war preparations

1940

Yearlong State Guides and other American Guide Series publications coming out; new projects being developed: America Eats, Hands That Built America, a history of grasslands and grazing, state recreation guides, miscellaneous pamphlets

1941

November 10–16 American Guide Week

December 7 Japanese attack on Pearl Harbor; United States enters Second World War

1942

January Last Guide (*Oklahoma: A Guide to the Sooner State*) published in January, though publication date is 1941

February Newsom resigns to join military; Merle Colby takes over program

May Writers' Program absorbed into War Services Subdivision of WPA

1943

April 8 Merle Colby presents "Final Report on Disposition of Unpublished Materials of WPA Writers' Program"

June 30 WPA officially dissolved

Appendix C: New York State's Directors

In the fall of 1935 Alsberg appointed Roland Palmer Gray, a folklorist, to be the New York State project director (New York City had a separate Project). Gray had edited a collection called *Songs and Ballads of the Maine Lumberjacks* that Harvard University Press published in 1924, which seems a questionable qualification for directing the New York State Project, and in any case things didn't work out. So on January 1, 1936, Alsberg appointed Bristow Adams to succeed him. Adams was a Stanford graduate (he founded the first college humor magazine in the West) with a long career in forestry and journalism, and he had been a professor in the Cornell School of Agriculture since 1914. His appointment to the project directorship must have been hasty; Gray had only been in office for two months, and we do not know who nominated Adams, why Alsberg asked him, or why he accepted. State directors were often academics—the requirement that incumbents should come from the relief rolls did not apply at this level—and perhaps after two decades at Cornell the sixty-year-old professor was ready for a new challenge.

Adams seems to have had a cordial relationship with the Washington office. On May 11, 1936, Alsberg wrote to him recommending

> a mine of delightful information on New York resorts, springs and so on in *The American Hotel* by Jefferson Williamson (Knopf, 1930). The

hotel history of New York State is of particular importance because of its influence on the standard of living of Americans. *Trumpets of Jubilee* by Constance Rourke will also give you valuable leads to little known material on New York State."[1]

It was unusual for Alsberg to make specific suggestions—he usually left this sort of thing to Cronyn—so this letter may indicate that he wanted to nudge the New York project along.

Twelve days later things took a bad turn. Adams telegraphed Alsberg to inform him that one of Washington's field supervisors, a man named Wallace Miller, was a fraud and a subversive. Under the headline "Communistic Activity in Writers' Project Charged," a central New York newspaper reported:

Professor Adams said that he telegraphed Henry G. Alsberg, federal director of the project, on May 23 "strongly" advising that "the man who calls himself Wallace Miller, Class of 1922, Stanford University" be removed "immediately from federal service for good of administration" and suggested that Miller's present and former activities "be investigated."

Professor Adams said he received a reply from Alsberg asking him to "specify" charges against Miller.

Professor Adams said he complied with the request.

Professor Adams said he later received a letter from Mr. Alsberg relieving him of his post, effective May 31.

Adams said he sent copies of correspondence with Mr. Alsberg to both Harry L. Hopkins, federal relief administration and Lester W. Hersog [Herzog], state works Progress Administration director.[2]

Apparently neither Hopkins nor Herzog was inclined to intervene. Then on June 2 the *New York Times* reported that "Union College Man Heads WPA Writers. Bertram Wainger Succeeds Bristow Adams of Cornell, Ousted as State Director." The story went on to say that

Bristow Adams, head of the Cornell University Press, coincidentally was dismissed as State Director by Mr. Alsberg, who explained that Mr. Adams was unable to give his full time to the project and that "administrative differences" made impossible proper development of the New York writers' program.

1. NARA 69, WPA, Federal Writers' Project, Editorial Correspondence, Box 37, Folder "New York—State Guide Miscellaneous."

2. *Citizen-Advertiser*, Auburn, NY, June 1, 1936.

> Mr. Adams had accused Wallace Miller, project field director, of communism. Mr. Alsberg said that this had nothing to do with Mr. Adams's dismissal, remarking:
> "Miller does not enter this affair."[3]

That seems unlikely. Some forty years later the Division of Rare and Manuscript Collections of the Cornell University Library put together a collection of Bristow Adams's papers, saying,

> In the early thirties [Adams] was made regional director for the Federal Writer's [*sic*] Project (WPA) in New York. He retained this position until he was dismissed by Henry G. Alsberg, for unsuccessful completion of work. Actually he was dismissed for charging Wallace Miller, who posed as a Stanford graduate, with being a communist and recommending his removal from the project. This affair got wide publicity and brought Bristow into the national headlines. Finally, in 1939, Bristow was given a reward for appreciation of service by the New York Press Association.[4]

While we don't know what was the basis for the "posed" and "actually," no doubt Adams's papers supported his own view of the matter. As for Miller, he was active as a field supervisor in early 1936 but then seems to have left the Project around the time of the Adams affair and disappeared from view. Things settled down in New York State from then on, and Wainger, the third director in six months, was still in charge when the New York Guide came out in 1940.

3. *New York Times*, June 2, 1936.

4. K. Lefferts, "Guide to the Bristow Adams Papers, 1853–1970, 1862–1957 (bulk)," Collection Number: 3205, Division of Rare and Manuscript Collections, Cornell University Library.

Appendix D: Contents of the 48 State Guides

State	Pages	Essays	% Essays	Cities	% Cities	Tours	# Tours	% Tours	Appendix and index	% Appendix and index	Sections, other	Cover
Alabama	442	156	35.3	128	29.0	117	15	26.5	41	9.3		Waterfall (photo)
Arizona	530	168	31.7	109	20.6	219	13	41.3	34	6.4		Cowboy riding in Grand Canyon (photo)
Arkansas	447	128	28.6	72	16.1	188	17	42.1	59	13.2		Hills, town, river (print)
California	713	176	24.7	138	19.4	370	18	51.9	29	4.1		Redwoods
Colorado	511	102	20.1	92	18.0	270	21	52.9	47	9.0		Mountains and pines (photo)
Connecticut	593	116	19.6	210	35.4	229	10	38.6	38	6.4		Colonial building
Delaware	549	164	30.0	152	27.7	200	16	36.4	33	6		Ship under sail
Florida	600	174	29.0	120	20.0	244	22	40.7	62	10.3		Palm trees and small sailboat
Georgia	559	144	25.8	124	22.2	250	17	44.7	41	7.3		Drawing of city and country, state seal
Idaho	431	192	44.5	0	0	221	11	51.3	18	4.2	The Primitive Area, A Trip into the Area, Buried Treasures, Ghost Towns, A Few Tall Tales, Origins of Names 71 pages, 16.5%	Collage of photos
Illinois	687	146	21.3	250	36.4	248	22	36.1	43	6.3		
Indiana	548	160	29.2	124	22.6	212	20	38.7	52	9.5		Trees and river
Iowa	583	166	28.5	154	26.4	224	17	38.4	39	6.7		*Agriculture*, mural by Richard Haines
Kansas	538	158	29.4	146	27.1	204	13	37.9	30	5.6		Farm scene
Kentucky	489	136	27.8	94	19.2	218	20	44.6	41	8.4		Thoroughbreds grazing
Louisiana	746	232	31.1	148	19.8	302	19	40.5	64	8.6		Pelican (drawing)
Maine	476	114	23.9	84	17.6	244	25	51.3	34	7.1	Sports and Recreation 40 pages, 8.4%	Rocky coast and lighthouse
Maryland	561	172	30.7	124	22.1	228	19	40.6	37	6.6		Sailboats on the water
Massachusetts	675	124	18.4	280	41.5	226	27	33.5	45	6.7		Church and green
Michigan	682	174	25.5	210	30.8	242	23	35.5	56	8.2		Lighthouse, pier, fishermen
Minnesota	523	150	28.7	128	24.5	208	20	39.8	37	7.1		Lake (photo)
Mississippi	545	162	29.7	120	22.0	224	17	41.1	39	7.2		Magnolia

Missouri	652	196	30.1	140	21.5	238	15	36.5	78	12.0		Steamboat
Montana	442	124	28.1	58	13.1	228	18	51.6	32	7.2		Mountains and Lake
Nebraska	424	144	34.0	110	25.9	144	13	34.0	26	6.1		Farmer holding wheat (print from wood engraving)
Nevada	315	110	34.9	0	0	176	8	55.9	29	9.2		Hoover Dam
New Hampshire	559	120	21.5	130	23.3	282	16	50.4	27	4.8	The White Mountains 10 pages, Sports and Recreation 18 pages, 5%	Birches and mountain
New Jersey	735	186	25.3	228	31.0	272	37	37.0	49	6.7		George Washington Bridge
New Mexico	458	170	37.1	54	11.8	196	18	42.8	38	8.3		Indian Pueblo
New York	782	178	22.8	198	25.3	340	40	43.5	66	8.4		Niagara Falls
North Carolina	601	134	22.3	138	23.0	292	33	48.6	37	6.2	National Park and Forest 8 pages, 1.3%	Three photos
North Dakota	371	108	29.1	58	15.6	172	10	46.4	33	8.9	Playgrounds 16 pages, 4.3%	
Ohio	634	164	25.9	190	30.0	242	23	38.2	38	6.0		Worker in tire factory
Oklahoma	445	122	27.4	94	21.1	196	16	44.0	33	7.4		John Steuart Curry's painting *Landrush*
Oregon	549	146	26.6	100	18.2	272	10	49.5	31	5.6		
Pennsylvania	660	178	27.0	174	26.4	260	20	39.4	48	7.3		Men working in mines, steel mills
Rhode Island	500	180	36.0	138	27.6	144	11	28.8	38	7.6		Shoreline
South Carolina	514	156	30.4	114	22.2	198	11	38.5	46	8.9		Palmetto trees
South Dakota	441	94	21.3	74	16.8	256	15	58.0	17	3.9	The Black Hills 6 pages, 1.4%	
Tennessee	558	176	31.5	110	19.7	232	16	41.6	40	7.2		TVA Norris Dam
Texas	718	156	21.7	214	29.8	296	29	41.2	52	7.2		
Utah	595	188	31.6	80	13.4	260	10	43.7	67	11.3	Parks and Primitive Areas 82 pages, 13.8%	
Vermont	392	74	18.9	82	20.9	214	7	54.6	22	5.6		Covered Bridge
Virginia	699	188	26.9	146	20.9	302	24	43.2	63	9.0		
Washington	687	162	23.6	142	20.7	330	9	48.0	53	7.7		
West Virginia	559	166	29.7	132	23.6	222	23	39.7	39	7.0		Mountain scene
Wisconsin	651	182	28.0	118	18.1	260	24	39.9	91	14.0		
Wyoming	490	170	34.7	44	9.0	224	13	45.7	52	10.6		Cowboy on horse, mountains, airplane

Appendix E: Authors

Table 8.2 Authors and mentions by century

a. Individual authors (2,785)

Century	Men	Percent men	Women	Percent women	Total	Percent in century
Sixteenth and seventeenth	70	97.2	2	2.8	72	2.6
Eighteenth	177	94.7	10	5.3	187	6.7
Nineteenth	789	83.3	158	16.7	947	34.0
Twentieth	1,118	70.8	461	29.2	1,579	56.7
Total	2,154	77.3	631	22.7	2,785	100.0

b. Mentions (3,463)

Century	Men	Percent men	Women	Percent women	Total	Percent in century
Sixteenth and seventeenth	89	97.8	2	2.2	91	2.6
Eighteenth	208	95.4	10	4.6	218	6.3
Nineteenth	1,095	85.0	193	15.0	1,288	37.2
Twentieth	1,346	72.1	520	27.9	1,866	53.9
Total	2,738	79.1	725	20.9	3,463	100.0

Table 8.3 Authors and mentions by year born

a. Individual authors (2,785)

Century	Authors	Percent of known
Fifteenth	3	0.1
Sixteenth	22	0.8
Seventeenth	72	2.7
Eighteenth	308	11.8
Nineteenth (1800–1849)	612	23.4
Nineteenth (1850–99)	1,365	52.1
Twentieth	238	9.1
Total known	2,620	100.0
Unknown	165	
Total	2,785	

b. Mentions (3,463)

Century	Authors	Percent of known
Fifteenth	5	0.2
Sixteenth	25	0.8
Seventeenth	82	2.5
Eighteenth	413	12.5
Nineteenth (1800–1849)	818	24.9
Nineteenth (1850–99)	1,679	51.0
Twentieth	269	8.2
Total known	3,291	100.1
Unknown	172	
Total	3,463	

Table 8.4 Authors by gender

a. Individual authors

	Multiple mentions	Single mentions	Total authors	Percent of authors
Male	334 (15.5%)	1,820 (84.5%)	2,154	77.3
Female	76 (12.0%)	555 (88.0%)	631	22.7
Total	410 (14.7%)	2,375 (85.3%)	2,785	100.0

b. Mentions

	Total mentions	Percent of mentions
Male	2,738	79.1
Female	725	20.9
Total	3,463	100.0

Table 8.5 Authors and mentions by ethnicity

a. Ethnicity of individual authors

Ethnicity	Authors	Percent of total	Female	Percent female
African American	50	1.8	7	14.0
Native American	19	0.7	2	10.5
Hispanic	38	1.4	1	2.6
Total minority	107	3.8	10	9.3
White, non-Hispanic	2,678	96.2	621	23.2
Total	2,785	100.1	631	22.7

b. Ethnicity of author mentions

Ethnicity	Authors	Percent of total	Female	Percent female
African American	59	1.7	7	11.9
Native American	22	0.6	2	9.1
Hispanic	49	1.4	1	2.0
Total minority	130	3.9	10	7.6
White, non-Hispanic	3,333	96.2	715	21.5
Total	3,463	99.9	725	20.6

Table 8.6 Authors and mentions by place born

a. Individual authors (2,785)

	Authors	Percent of known (2,656)
Total born in US	2,292	86.3
British Isles[a]	186	7.0
Continental Europe[b]	140	5.3
Mexico, New Spain	3	0.1
Canada	17	0.6
Other	18	0.7
Total non-US[c]	364	13.7
Total known	2,656	100.0
Unknown	129	(4.6% of total)
Total	2,785	

b. Mentions (3,463)

	Number	Percent of known (3,334)	Percent of US born (2,908)
Same state	1,270	38.1	43.7
Same division	342	10.3	11.8
Different division	1,296	38.9	44.6
Total born in US	2,908	87.2	100.1
British Isles, Ireland	212	6.4	
Europe	168	5.0	
Mexico	4	0.1	
Canada	18	0.5	
Other	24	0.7	
Total non-US	426	12.8	
Total known	3,334	100.0	
Unknown	129	(3.7% of total)	
Total	3,463		

[a]Of the 186 authors from the British Isles, 128 were born in England, 31 in Ireland, 21 in Scotland, and 6 in Wales.

[b]Of the 140 authors from the Continent, 46 were from France, 32 from Germany, 22 from Spain, 7 from Italy, 6 from Norway, 5 from Austria, 4 from Switzerland, 4 from the Netherlands, 3 from Denmark, 2 from Belgium, 2 from Sweden, and 1 apiece from Estonia, Greece, Hungary, Lithuania, Portugal, Romania, and Transylvania.

[c]Of the 18 "Other" authors, 6 were born in Russia, 3 in Jamaica, 2 in Haiti, and 1 apiece in Australia, Bermuda, Brazil, Burma, India, New Zealand, and Peru.

Table 8.7 Divisions and mentions

a. Divisions without major publishing centers								
Division of birth	1	%	2	%	3	%	Total	%
ESC	79	40	25	13	92	47	196	6.7
MTN	65	80	6	7	10	12	81	2.8
PAC	61	62	12	12	26	26	99	3.4
SAT	335	59	81	14	156	27	572	19.7
WNC	122	41	23	8	155	52	300	10.3
WSC	117	72	20	12	26	16	163	5.6
Total for six divisions	779	55	167	12	465	33	1,411	48.5

b. Divisions with major publishing centers								
Division of birth	1	%	2	%	3	%	Total	%
ENC	155	33	51	11	259	56	465	16.0
MAT	139	27	52	10	332	63	523	18.0
NEN	197	39	72	14	240	47	509	17.5
Total three divisions	491	33	175	12	831	56	1,497	51.5

c. Total of nine divisions							
Division of birth	1	%	2	%	3	%	Total
Total	1,270	44	342	12	1,296	45	2,908

Note: Refer to appendix G for the abbreviations and states included in the nine census divisions. *a*, Ratio of 1 (Guide mention in same state as birth) to 2 (Guide mention in same division as birth): 779/167 = 4.7 to 1. *b*, Ratio of 1 (Guide mention in same state as birth) to 2 (Guide mention in same division as birth): 491/175 = 2.8 to 1. *c*, Ratio of 1 (Guide mention in same state as birth) to 2 (Guide mention in same division as birth): 1,270/342 = 3.7 to 1.

Table 8.8 Birth state of individual authors

State of birth	Male	Female	State total	Percent of total (2,292)
Alabama	23	14	37	1.6
Arizona	1	0	1	0.0
Arkansas	12	8	20	0.9
California	22	8	30	1.3
Colorado	11	3	14	0.6
Connecticut	57	13	70	3.1
Delaware	23	7	30	1.3
District of Columbia*	3	3	6	0.3
Florida	10	3	13	0.6
Georgia	59	6	85	3.7
Hawaii*	1	0	1	0.0
Idaho**	4	0	4	0.2
Illinois	74	26	100	4.4
Indiana	50	12	62	2.7
Iowa	51	21	72	3.1
Kansas	19	20	39	1.7
Kentucky	36	13	49	2.1
Louisiana	45	19	64	2.8
Maine	38	10	48	2.1
Maryland	54	12	66	2.9
Massachusetts	127	28	155	6.8
Michigan	43	13	56	2.4
Minnesota	19	8	27	1.2
Mississippi	21	9	30	1.3
Missouri	44	21	65	2.8
Montana	1	6	7	0.3
Nebraska	18	9	27	1.2
Nevada**	1	0	1	0.0
New Hampshire	41	9	50	2.2
New Jersey	42	5	47	2.1
New Mexico	4	6	10	0.4
New York	150	45	195	8.5
North Carolina	60	5	65	2.8
North Dakota**	2	1	3	0.1
Ohio	70	16	86	3.8
Oklahoma	24	6	30	1.3
Oregon	15	8	23	1.0
Pennsylvania	115	21	136	5.9
Rhode Island	24	8	32	1.4
South Carolina	41	12	53	2.3

(*continued*)

Table 8.8 (continued)

State of birth	Male	Female	State total	Percent of total (2,292)
South Dakota**	1	1	2	0.1
Tennessee	39	12	51	2.2
Texas	27	8	35	1.5
Utah	20	10	30	1.3
Vermont	20	4	24	1.0
Virginia	97	37	134	5.8
Washington	18	11	29	1.3
West Virginia	19	6	25	1.1
Wisconsin	31	8	39	1.7
Wyoming	6	8	14	0.6
Total			2,292	

*Not a state at the time

**A state with no Literature essay

Table 8.9 Birth state of authors mentioned

State of birth	1	2	3	State total	Percent of (2,908)
Alabama	24	6	9	39	1.3
Arizona	1	0	0	1	0.0
Arkansas	10	7	7	24	0.8
California	17	4	18	39	1.3
Colorado	6	3	5	14	0.5
Connecticut	44	14	36	94	3.2
Delaware	29	2	2	33	1.1
District of Columbia*	1	1	5	7	0.2
Florida	10	1	5	16	0.6
Georgia	68	10	27	105	3.6
Hawaii*	0	1	0	1	0.0
Idaho**	0	2	2	4	0.1
Illinois	28	13	85	126	4.3
Indiana	34	13	49	96	3.3
Iowa	49	7	37	93	3.2
Kansas	18	4	24	46	1.6
Kentucky	9	5	48	62	2.1
Louisiana	61	1	4	66	2.3
Maine	33	11	25	69	2.4
Maryland	45	16	25	86	3.0
Massachusetts	48	38	137	223	7.7
Michigan	35	6	30	71	2.4
Minnesota	12	1	21	34	1.2
Mississippi	13	5	16	34	1.2
Missouri	28	8	57	93	3.2
Montana	7	0	0	7	0.2
Nebraska	15	1	14	30	1.0
Nevada**	0	1	0	1	0.0
New Hampshire	37	4	21	62	2.1
New Jersey	24	17	30	71	2.4
New Mexico	10	0	0	10	0.3
New York	62	22	184	268	9.2
North Carolina	44	15	16	75	2.6
North Dakota**	0	0	3	3	0.1
Ohio	35	14	67	116	4.0
Oklahoma	28	1	5	34	1.2
Oregon	20	3	3	26	0.9
Pennsylvania	53	13	118	184	6.3
Rhode Island	28	3	5	36	1.2
South Carolina	33	12	12	57	2.0

(continued)

Table 8.9 (continued)

State of birth	1	2	3	State total	Percent of (2,908)
South Dakota**	0	2	0	2	0.1
Tennessee	33	9	19	61	2.1
Texas	18	11	10	39	1.3
Utah	27	0	3	30	1.0
Vermont	7	2	16	25	0.9
Virginia	85	20	60	165	5.7
Washington	24	4	5	33	1.1
West Virginia	20	4	4	28	1.0
Wisconsin	23	5	27	55	1.9
Wyoming	14	0	0	14	0.5
Total	1,270 43.7%	342 11.8%	1,296 44.6%	2,908 100.1%	

*Not a state at the time
**A state with no literature essay

Table 8.10 Authors, rank, and state populations

State	Authors	Rank, number of authors	Rank, population in 1930
Louisiana	192	1	22
NYC	163	2	1
Virginia	134	3	20
Georgia	108	4	14
Washington	106	5	30
Pennsylvania	105	6	2
Oklahoma	104	7	21
New Mexico	101	8	45
California	100	9	6
Oregon	96	10	34
Massachusetts	94	11	8
Missouri	94	12	10
Maryland	88	13	28
Illinois	86	14	3
Florida	85	15	31
New Hampshire	84	16	42
Utah	83	17	40
Kansas	81	18	24
Wyoming	79	19	49
Texas	77	20	5
Ohio	76	21	4
District of Columbia	72	22	41
Connecticut	70	23	29
New York	69	24	1
Rhode Island	69	25	37
Tennessee	69	26	16
Iowa	68	27	19
Michigan	66	28	7
New Jersey	66	29	9
Wisconsin	65	30	13
North Carolina	63	31	12
West Virginia	61	32	27
Colorado	57	33	33
Montana	52	34	39
Mississippi	51	35	23
Maine	50	36	35
South Carolina	49	37	26
Arkansas	47	38	25
Alabama	46	39	15
Indiana	45	40	11
Nebraska	45	41	32
Delaware	42	42	48
Arizona	34	43	44
Minnesota	32	44	18
Vermont	26	45	47
Kentucky	13	46	17
Total mentions	3,463		

Table 8.11 Genres by author mentions

Genre	Male	Female	Percent male	Percent female	Total mentions	Percent of 3,463 total	Percent of 3,024 genres
Fiction	562	303	65.0	35.0	865	25.0	28.6
Poetry	429	159	73.0	27.0	588	17.0	19.4
Drama	47	10	82.5	17.5	57	1.6	1.9
Traditional genres	*1,038*	*472*	*68.7*	*31.3*	*1,510*	*43.6*	*49.9*
Historical	482	77	86.2	13.8	559	16.1	18.5
Folklore	24	9	72.7	27.3	33	1.0	1.1
Travel	276	25	91.7	8.3	301	8.7	10.0
Archeology, natural history	58	7	89.2	10.8	65	1.9	2.1
Journalism, editorial	214	23	90.3	9.7	237	6.8	7.8
Children's books	33	31	51.6	48.4	64	1.8	2.1
Music, songs	11	2	84.6	15.4	13	0.4	0.4
Theology, philosophy	75	3	96.2	3.8	78	2.3	2.6
Publishing	13	0	100.0	0.0	13	0.4	0.4
Political	69	2	97.2	2.8	71	2.1	2.3
Literary criticism	54	2	96.4	3.6	56	1.6	1.9
Humor	24	0	100.0	0.0	24	0.7	0.8
Nontraditional genres	*1,333*	*181*	*88.0*	*12.0*	*1,514*	*43.7*	*50.1*
Other, mixtures	216	33	86.7	13.3	249	7.2	
Unspecified	151	39	79.5	20.5	190	5.5	
Total	2,738	725	79.1	20.9	3,463	100.0	

Note: Ratio of traditional to nontraditional genre mentions: 1,510/1,514 = 1.0 (0.997).

Table 8.12 Genres by ethnicity

Genre	African American	Native American	Hispanic	Total minority mentions	Percent minority mentions
Fiction	9	3	1	13	10.0
Poetry	20	2	2	24	18.5
Drama	0	2	0	2	1.5
Traditional genres	*29*	*7*	*3*	*39*	*30.0*
Historical	13	7	13	33	25.4
Folklore	0	2	0	2	1.5
Travel	1	0	30	31	23.8
Archeology, natural history	0	1	1	2	1.5
Journalism, editorial	3	0	1	4	3.1
Children's books	0	0	0	0	0.0
Music, songs	2	0	0	2	1.5
Theology, philosophy	0	0	0	0	0.0
Publishing	0	0	0	0	0.0
Political	1	0	0	1	0.8
Literary criticism	0	0	0	0	0.0
Humor	0	1	0	1	0.8
Other, mixtures	7	0	0	7	5.4
Unspecified	3	4	1	8	6.2
Nontraditional genres	*30*	*15*	*46*	*91*	*70.2*
Total	59	22	49	130	100.0

Table 8.13 Genres by division

Division	ENC	ESC	MAT	MTN	NEN	PAC	SAT	WNC	WSC
Fiction	106	48	112	90	65	72	149	90	133
Poetry	65	28	64	40	93	53	140	53	52
Drama	4	1	7	10	7	2	9	8	9
Traditional genres	*175*	*77*	*183*	*140*	*165*	*127*	*298*	*151*	*194*
Historical	29	34	17	119	38	63	135	41	83
Folklore	5	1	0	14	0	5	0	4	4
Travel	16	17	9	67	11	48	47	32	54
Archeology, natural history	5	2	5	15	1	6	12	10	9
Journalism, editorial	28	9	55	9	37	17	40	26	16
Children's books	5	3	11	2	15	8	10	5	5
Music, songs	1	4	1	0	2	0	4	1	0
Theology, philosophy	0	2	11	10	40	1	6	5	3
Publishing	0	0	2	0	5	4	0	0	2
Political	9	14	2	3	9	1	28	2	3
Literary criticism	7	2	21	1	2	7	8	6	2
Humor	5	4	0	2	2	2	6	0	3
Nontraditional genres	*110*	*92*	*134*	*242*	*162*	*162*	*296*	*132*	*184*
Ratio of traditional/ nontraditional genres	1.6	0.8	1.4	0.6	1.0	0.8	1.0	1.1	1.1
Other, mixtures	32	10	40	17	48	8	44	21	29
Unspecified	21	0	46	7	18	5	64	16	13
Total	338	179	403	406	393	302	702	320	420

Table 8.14 Gender by division

Sex	ENC	ESC	MAT	MTN	NEN	PAC	SAT	WNC	WSC	Total
Male	274	150	339	314	314	234	547	248	318	2,738
Female	64	29	64	92	79	68	155	72	102	725
Total	338	129	403	406	393	302	702	320	420	3,463
Ratio of male/ female	4.28	5.17	5.30	3.41	3.97	3.44	3.53	3.44	3.12	3.78

Appendix F: Comparison of Canon Definers *Pattee, Parrington, Spiller, Baym (Norton), and American Guides*

Table 9.1 Baym (Norton) authors by century (this is not a 20 percent sample but the total on the NAAL website)

*a. Individual authors (154)**

Century	Men	Percent men	Women	Percent women	Total	Percent in century
Sixteenth and seventeenth	11	78.6	3	21.4	14	9.1
Eighteenth	9	69.2	4	30.8	13	8.4
Nineteenth	22	59.5	15	40.5	37	24.0
Twentieth	58	64.4	32	35.6	90	58.4
Total	100	64.9	54	35.1	154	99.9

b. Authors in American Guides (66)

Century	Men	Percent men	Women	Percent women	Total	Percent
Sixteenth and seventeenth	5	71.4	2	28.6	7	10.6
Eighteenth	6	100.0	0	0	6	9.1
Nineteenth	20	74.1	7	25.9	27	40.9
Twentieth	20	76.9	6	23.1	26	39.4
Total	51	77.3	15	22.7	66	100.0

c. Authors not in American Guides (88)

Century	Men	Percent men	Women	Percent women	Total	Percent in century
Sixteenth and seventeenth	6	85.7	1	14.3	7	8.0
Eighteenth	3	42.9	4	57.1	7	8.0
Nineteenth	2	20.0	8	80.0	10	11.4
Twentieth	38	59.4	26	40.6	64	72.7
Total	49	55.7	39	44.3	88	100.1

*Norton identifies three more "authors": Stories of the Beginning of the World, Native American Chants and Songs, and Native American Trickster Tales. These collective and anonymous authors are not included in the present analysis.

Table 9.2 Pattee authors by century (20 percent sample of 1,265 total)

a. Individual authors (253)

Century	Men	Percent men	Women	Percent women	Total	Percent in century
Sixteenth and seventeenth	3	100.0	0	0.0	3	1.2
Eighteenth	20	83.3	4	16.7	24	9.5
Nineteenth	148	85.5	25	14.5	173	68.4
Twentieth	45	84.9	8	15.1	53	20.9
Total	216	85.4	37	14.6	253	100.0

b. Authors in American Guides (86)

Century	Men	Percent men	Women	Percent women	Total	Percent in century
Sixteenth and seventeenth	3	100.0	0	0.0	3	3.5
Eighteenth	1	75.0	3	25.0	4	4.7
Nineteenth	44	83.0	9	17.1	53	61.6
Twentieth	21	80.8	5	19.2	26	30.2
Total	68	80.0	17	20.0	86	100.0

c. Authors not in American Guides (167)

Century	Men	Percent men	Women	Percent women	Total	Percent in century
Sixteenth and seventeenth	0	0.0	0	0.0	0	0.0
Eighteenth	17	85.0	3	15.0	20	12.0
Nineteenth	104	86.7	16	13.3	120	71.9
Twentieth	24	88.9	3	11.1	27	16.2
Total	145	86.9	22	13.1	167	100.1

Table 9.3 Parrington authors by century (20 percent sample of 1004 total)

a. Individual authors (201)

Century	Men	Percent men	Women	Percent women	Total	Percent in century
Before sixteenth	8	88.9	1	11.1	9	4.5
Sixteenth and seventeenth	22	95.7	1	4.39	23	11.4
Eighteenth	43	93.5	3	6.5	46	22.9
Nineteenth	102	92.7	8	7.3	110	54.7
Twentieth	11	84.6	2	15.4	13	6.5
Total	186	92.5	15	7.5	201	100.0

b. Authors in American Guides (45)

Century	Men	Percent men	Women	Percent women	Total	Percent in century
Before sixteenth	0	0.0	0	0.0	0	0.0
Sixteenth and seventeenth	1	100.0	0	0.0	1	2.2
Eighteenth	7	100.0	0	0.0	7	15.6
Nineteenth	26	86.7	4	13.3	30	66.7
Twentieth	6	85.7	1	14.3	7	15.6
Total	40	88.9	5	11.1	45	100.1

c. Authors not in American Guides (156)

Century	Men	Percent men	Women	Percent women	Total	Percent in century
Before sixteenth	8	88.9	1	11.1	9	5.8
Sixteenth and seventeenth	21	95.5	1	4.5	22	14.1
Eighteenth	36	92.3	3	7.7	39	25.0
Nineteenth	76	95.0	4	5.0	80	51.3
Twentieth	5	83.3	1	16.7	6	3.8
Total	146	93.6	10	6.4	156	100.0

Table 9.4 Spiller authors by century (20 percent sample of 1462 total)

a. Individual authors (292)

Century	Men	Percent men	Women	Percent women	Total	Percent in century
Sixteenth and seventeenth	25	100.0	0	0.0	25	8.6
Eighteenth	33	97.1	1	2.9	34	11.6
Nineteenth	128	90.8	13	9.2	141	48.3
Twentieth	78	84.8	14	15.2	92	31.5
Total	264	90.4	28	9.6	292	99.9

b. Authors in American Guides (109)

Century	Men	Percent men	Women	Percent women	Total	Percent in century
Sixteenth and seventeenth	5	100.0	0	0.0	5	4.6
Eighteenth	12	92.3	1	7.7	13	11.9
Nineteenth	51	91.1	5	8.9	56	51.4
Twentieth	30	85.7	5	14.3	35	32.1
Total	98	89.9	11	10.1	109	100.0

c. Authors not in American Guides (183)

Century	Men	Percent men	Women	Percent women	Total	Percent in century
Sixteenth and seventeenth	20	100.0	0	0.0	20	10.9
Eighteenth	21	100.0	0	0.0	21	11.5
Nineteenth	77	90.6	8	9.4	85	46.4
Twentieth	48	84.2	9	15.8	57	31.1
Total	166	90.7	17	9.3	183	100.0

Table 9.5 Pattee authors by year born (20 percent sample of 1,265 total)

a. Individual authors (253)

Century	Authors	Percent of known
Fifteenth	0	0
Sixteenth	2	0.8
Seventeenth	2	0.8
Eighteenth	63	25.3
Nineteenth (1800–1849)	88	35.3
Nineteenth (1850–99)	91	36.5
Twentieth	3	1.2
Total known	249	99.9
Unknown	4	
Total	253	

b. Authors in American Guides (86)

Century	Authors	Percent of known
Fifteenth		
Sixteenth	2	2.3
Seventeenth	1	1.2
Eighteenth	16	18.6
Nineteenth (1800–1849)	32	37.2
Nineteenth (1850–99)	34	39.5
Twentieth	1	1.2
Total known	86	100.0
Unknown		
Total		86

c. Authors not in American Guides (167)

Century	Authors	Percent of known
Fifteenth		
Sixteenth		
Seventeenth	1	0.6
Eighteenth	47	28.8
Nineteenth (1800–1849)	56	34.4
Nineteenth (1850–99)	57	35.0
Twentieth	2	1.2
Total known	163	100.0
Unknown	4	
Total	167	

Table 9.6 Parrington authors by year born (20 percent sample of 1004)

a. Individual authors (201)

Century	Authors	Percent of known (198)
Fifteenth or earlier	10	5.1
Sixteenth	9	4.5
Seventeenth	17	8.6
Eighteenth	66	33.3
Ninteenth (1800–1849)	71	35.6
Nineteenth (1850–99)	25	12.6
Twentieth	0	
Total known	198	99.7
Unknown	3	
Total	201	

b. Authors in American Guides (45)

Century	Authors	Percent of known
Fifteenth or earlier	0	
Sixteenth	0	
Seventeenth	2	4.4
Eighteenth	14	31.1
Nineteenth (1800–1849)	18	40.0
Nineteenth (1850–99)	11	24.4
Twentieth	0	
Total known	45	99.9
Unknown	0	
Total		45

c. Authors not in American Guides (156)

Century	Authors	Percent of known (153)
Fifteenth or earlier	10	6.5
Sixteenth	9	5.9
Seventeenth	15	9.8
Eighteenth	52	34.0
Nineteenth (1800–1849)	53	34.6
Nineteenth (1850–99)	14	9.2
Twentieth	0	
Total known	153	100.0
Unknown	3	
Total	156	

Table 9.7 Spiller authors by year born (20 percent sample of 1,462 total)

a. Individual authors (292)

Century	Authors	Percent of known (286)
Fifteenth	3	1.0
Sixteenth	10	3.5
Seventeenth	13	4.5
Eighteenth	55	19.2
Nineteenth (1800–1849)	79	27.6
Nineteenth (1850–99)	84	29.4
Twentieth	42	14.7
Total known	286	99.9
Unknown	6	
Total	292	

b. Authors in American Guides (109)

Century	Authors	Percent of known (109)
Fifteenth	0	
Sixteenth	2	1.9
Seventeenth	3	2.8
Eighteenth	19	17.6
Nineteenth (1800–1849)	30	27.8
Nineteenth (1850–99)	49	45.4
Twentieth	5	4.6
Total known	108	100.1
Unknown	1	
Total	109	

c. Authors not in American Guides (183)

Century	Authors	Percent of known (178)
Fifteenth	3	1.7
Sixteenth	8	4.5
Seventeenth	10	5.6
Eighteenth	36	20.2
Nineteenth (1800–1849)	49	27.5
Nineteenth (1850–99)	35	19.7
Twentieth	37	20.8
Total known	178	100.0
Unknown	5	
Total	183	

Table 9.8 Baym (Norton) authors by year born

a. Individual authors (154)

Century	Authors	Percent of known
Fifteenth	2	1.3
Sixteenth	6	3.9
Seventeenth	6	3.9
Eighteenth	18	11.7
Nineteenth (1800–1849)	25	16.2
Nineteenth (1850–99)	37	24.0
Twentieth	60	39.0
Total known	154	100.0
Unknown	0*	
Total	154	100.0

b. Authors in American Guides (66)

Century	Authors	Percent of known
Fifteenth	1	1.5
Sixteenth	2	3.0
Seventeenth	4	6.1
Eighteenth	9	13.6
Nineteenth (1800–1849)	19	28.8
Nineteenth (1850–99)	28	42.4
Twentieth	3	4.5
Total known	66	99.9
Unknown	0	
Total	66	99.9

c. Authors not in American Guides (88)

Century	Authors	Percent of known
Fifteenth	1	1.1
Sixteenth	4	4.5
Seventeenth	2	2.3
Eighteenth	9	10.2
Nineteenth (1800–1849)	6	6.8
Nineteenth (1850–99)	9	10.2
Twentieth	57	64.8
Total known	88	99.9
Unknown	0	
Total	88	99.9

*The birth year of Anne Bradstreet (about 1612) and Olaudah Equiano (about 1745) are unknown but the century for each is clear.

Table 9.9 Pattee authors by ethnicity (20 percent sample of 1,265 total)

a. Individual authors (253)

Ethnicity	Authors	Percent of total	Female	Percent female
African American	0	0.0	0	0.0
Native American	0	0.0	0	0.0
Hispanic	1*	0.4	0	0.0
Total minority				
White, non-Hispanic	252	99.6	0	0.0
Total	253	100.0	0	0.0

b. Authors in American Guides (86)

Ethnicity	Authors	Percent of total	Female	Percent female
African American	0	0.0	0	0.0
Native American	0	0.0	0	0.0
Hispanic	0	0.0	0	0.0
Total minority	0	0.0	0	0.0
White, non-Hispanic	86	100.0	0	0.0
Total	86	100.0	0	0.0

c. Authors not in American Guides (167)

Ethnicity	Authors	Percent of total	Female	Percent female
African American	0	0.0	0	0.0
Native American	0	0.0	0	0.0
Hispanic	1*	0.6	0	0.0
Total minority	1	0.6	0	0.0
White, non-Hispanic	166	99.4	0	0.0
Total	167	100.0	0	0.0

*Vicente Blasco Ibáñez was a popular Spanish novelist and screenwriter whose novel about the First World War, *The Four Horsemen of the Apocalypse* (1919), was a bestseller in the United States.

Table 9.10 Parrington authors by ethnicity (20 percent sample of 1004)

a. Individual authors (201)

Ethnicity	Authors	Percent of total	Female	Percent female
African American	1	0.5	0	0.0
Native American	0	0.0	0	0.0
Hispanic	0	0.0	0	0.0
Total minority	1	0.5	0	0.0
White, non-Hispanic	200	99.5	15	7.5
Total	201	100.0	15	7.5

b. Authors in American Guides (45)

Ethnicity	Authors	Percent of total	Female	Percent female
African American	0	0.0	0	0.0
Native American	0	0.0	0	0.0
Hispanic	0	0.0	0	0.0
Total minority	0	0.0	0	0.0
White, non-Hispanic	45	100.0	5	11.1
Total	45		5	11.1

c. Authors not in American Guides (156)

Ethnicity	Authors	Percent of total	Female	Percent female
African American	1	0.6	0	0.0
Native American	0	0.0	0	0.0
Hispanic	0	0.0	0	0.0
Total minority	1	0.6	0	0.0
White, non-Hispanic	155	99.4	10	6.5
Total	156	100.0	10	6.5

Table 9.11 Spiller authors by ethnicity (20 percent sample of 1,462 total)

a. Individual authors (292)

Ethnicity	Authors	Percent of total	Female	Percent female
African American	5	1.7	0	0.0
Native American	0	0.0	0	0.0
Hispanic	1	0.3	0	0.0
Total minority	6	2.1	0	0.0
White, non-Hispanic	286	97.9	0	0.0
Total	292	100.0	0	0.0

b. Authors in American Guides (109)

Ethnicity	Authors	Percent of total	Female	Percent female
African American	3	2.8	0	0.0
Native American	0	0.0	0	0.0
Hispanic	1	0.9	0	0.0
Total minority	4	3.7	0	0.0
White, non-Hispanic	105	96.3	0	0.0
Total	109	100.0	0	0.0

c. Authors not in American Guides (183)

Ethnicity	Authors	Percent of total	Female	Percent female
African American	2	1.1	0	0.0
Native American	0	0.0	0	0.0
Hispanic	0	0.0	0	0.0
Total minority	2	1.1	0	0.0
White, non-Hispanic	181	98.9	0	0.0
Total	183	100.0	0	0.0

Table 9.12 Baym (Norton) authors by ethnicity

*a. Individual authors (157)**

Ethnicity	Authors	Percent of total	Female	Percent female
Asian	4	2.5	3	75.0
African American	23	14.6	8	34.8
Native American	14	8.9	5	45.5
Hispanic	3	1.9	2	66.7
Total minority	44	28.0	18	40.9
White, non-Hispanic	113	72.0	36	31.9
Total	157	99.9	54	35.1

b. Authors in American Guides (66)

Ethnicity	Authors	Percent of total	Female	Percent female
Asian	0	0.0	0	0.0
African American	9	13.6	0	0.0
Native American	0	0.0	0	0.0
Hispanic	1	1.5	0	0.0
Total minority	10	15.2	0	0.0
White, non-Hispanic	56	84.8	0	0.0
Total	66	100.0	0	0.0

c. Authors not in American Guides (91)

Ethnicity	Authors	Percent of total	Female	Percent female*
Asian	4	4.4	3	75.0
African American	14	15.4	8	57.1
Native American	14	15.4	5	38.5
Hispanic	2	2.2	2	100.0
Total minority	34	37.4	18	52.9
White, non-Hispanic	57	62.6	21	36.8
Total	91	100.0	39	43.3

*The Native American category includes three entries, Stories of the Beginning of the World, Native American Chants and Songs, and Native American Trickster Tales, which bring the Native American total to 13 and the overall total to 157. Since these two categories do not indicate one sex, I have calculated the percentage of females without including these three (so in a. and c. the Native American denominators for calculating percent female are both 11, not 14).

Table 9.13 Pattee authors by place born (20 percent sample of 1,265 total)

a. Individual authors (253)

	Authors	Percent of known (250)
Total born in US	197	78.8
British Isles	36	14.4
Continental Europe	14	5.6
Mexico, New Spain		
Canada	2	0.8
Other	1	0.4
Total non-US	53	21.2
Total known	250	100.0
Unknown	3	
Total	253	

b. Authors in American Guides (86)

	Authors	Percent of known (86)
Total born in US	77	89.5
British Isles	6	7.0
Continental Europe	2	2.3
Mexico, New Spain		
Canada		
Other	1	1.2
Total non-US	9	10.5
Total known	86	100.0
Unknown		
Total	86	

c. Authors not in American Guides (167)

	Authors	Percent of known (164)
Total born in US	120	73.2
British Isles	30	18.3
Continental Europe	12	7.3
Mexico, New Spain		
Canada	2	1.2
Other		
Total non-US	44	26.8
Total known	164	100.0
Unknown	3	
Total	167	

Table 9.14 Parrington authors by place born (20 percent sample of 2004)

a. Individual authors (201)

	Authors	Percent of known (198)
Total born in US	114	57.6
British Isles	49	24.7
Continental Europe	31	15.7
Mexico, New Spain	0	
Canada	1	0.5
Other	3	1.5
Total non-US	84	42.4
Total known	198	100.0
Unknown	3	
Total	201	

b. Authors in American Guides (45)

	Authors	Percent of known (45)
Total born in US	41	91.1
British Isles	2	4.4
Continental Europe	1	2.2
Mexico, New Spain		
Canada		
Other	1	2.2
Total non-US	4	8.8
Total known	45	99.9
Unknown	0	
Total	45	

c. Authors not in American Guides (156)

	Authors	Percent of known (153)
Total born in US	73	47.7
British Isles	47	30.7
Continental Europe[a]	30	19.6
Mexico, New Spain	0	
Canada	1	0.7
Other	2	1.3
Total non-US	80	52.3
Total known	153	100.0
Unknown	3	
Total	156	

[a]Of the 139 authors from the Continent, 46 were from France, 32 from Germany, 22 from Spain, 7 from Italy, 6 from Norway, 5 from Austria, 4 from Switzerland, 4 from the Netherlands, 3 from Denmark, 2 from Belgium, 2 from Sweden, and 1 apiece from Estonia, Greece, Hungary, Lithuania, Portugal, Romania, and Transylvania.

Table 9.15 Spiller authors by place born (20 percent sample of 1,462 total)

a. Individual authors (292)

	Authors	Percent of known (288)
Total born in US	202	70.1
British Isles	42	14.6
Continental Europe	37	12.8
Mexico, New Spain	0	0.0
Canada	1	0.3
Other	6	2.1
Total non-US	86	29.8
Total known	288	
Unknown	4	
Total	292	

b. Authors in American Guides (109)

	Authors	Percent of known (109)
Total born in US	93	85.3
British Isles	9	8.3
Continental Europe	7	6.4
Mexico, New Spain		
Canada		
Other		
Total non-US	16	14.7
Total known	109	
Unknown		
Total	109	

c. Authors not in American Guides (183)

	Authors	Percent of known (179)
Total born in US	109	60.9
British Isles	32	17.9
Continental Europe	31	17.3
Mexico, New Spain	0	
Canada	1	0.6
Other	6	3.4
Total non-US	70	29.2
Total known	179	
Unknown	4	
Total	183	

Table 9.16 Baym (Norton) authors by place born

a. Individual authors (154)

	Authors	Percent of known (154)
Total born in US	132	85.7
British Isles	12	7.8
Continental Europe	5	3.2
Mexico, New Spain	0	
Canada	1	0.6
Other	4	2.6
Total non-US	22	14.3
Total known	154	
Unknown	0	
Total	154	

b. Authors in American Guides (66)

	Authors	Percent of known (66)
Total born in US	58	87.9
British Isles	6	9.1
Continental Europe	1	1.5
Mexico, New Spain	0	
Canada	0	
Other	1	1.5
Total non-US	8	12.1
Total known	66	
Unknown	0	
Total	66	

c. Authors not in American Guides (88)

	Authors	Percent of known (88)
Total born in US	74	84.1
British Isles	6	6.9
Continental Europe	4	4.5
Mexico, New Spain	0	
Canada	1	1.1
Other	3	3.4
Total non-US	14	15.9
Total known	88	
Unknown	0	
Total	88	

Table 9.17 Pattee authors by division (20 percent sample of 1,265 total)

a. Individual authors (253)

	Authors	Percent of known US born (197)
Divisions without major publishing centers		
Division of birth		
ESC	9	4.6
MTN	0	0.0
PAC	2	1.0
SAT	11	5.6
WNC	9	4.6
WSC	3	1.5
Total for six divisions	34	17.2
Divisions with major publishing centers		
Division of birth		
ENC	29	14.7
MAT	62	31.5
NEN	72	36.5
Total for three divisions	163	82.7
Total of nine divisions	197	
Born outside of US	51	
Unknown	5	
Total	253	

b. Authors in American Guides (86)

	Authors	Percent of known US born (77)
Divisions without major publishing centers		
Division of birth		
ESC	5	6.5
MTN	0	0.0
PAC	1	1.3
SAT	5	6.5
WNC	7	9.1
WSC	1	1.3
Total for six divisions	19	24.6
Divisions with major publishing centers		
Division of birth		
ENC	11	14.3
MAT	21	27.3
NEN	26	33.8
Total for three divisions	58	75.3
Total of nine divisions	77	
Born outside of US	9	
Unknown	0	
Total	86	

(continued)

c. Authors not in American Guides (167)

	Authors	Percent of known US born (120)
Divisions without major publishing centers		
Division of birth		
ESC	4	3.3
MTN	0	0.0
PAC	1	0.8
SAT	6	5.0
WNC	2	1.7
WSC	2	1.7
Total for six divisions	15	12.5
Divisions with major publishing centers		
Division of birth		
ENC	18	15.0
MAT	41	34.2
NEN	46	38.3
Total for three divisions	105	87.5
Total of nine divisions	120	
Born outside of US	42	
Unknown	5	
Total	167	

Table 9.18 Parrington authors by division (20 percent sample of 1004)

a. Individual authors (201)

	Authors	Percent of known US born (114)
Divisions without major publishing centers		
ESC	2	1.8
MTN	0	
PAC	1	0.9
SAT	17	14.9
WNC	2	1.8
WSC	2	1.8
Total for six divisions	24	21.1
Divisions with major publishing centers		
ENC	12	10.5
MAT	31	27.2
NEN	47	41.2
Total for three divisions	90	78.9
Total of nine divisions	114	100.0
Born outside of US	84	
Unknown	3	
Total	201	

b. Authors in American Guides (45)

	Authors	Percent of known US born (41)
Divisions without major publishing centers		
ESC	1	2.4
MTN	0	0.0
PAC	1	2.4
SAT	8	19.5
WNC	1	2.4
WSC	2	4.9
Total for six divisions	13	31.6
Divisions with major publishing centers		
ENC	4	10.0
MAT	8	19.5
NEN	16	39.0
Total for three divisions	28	68.5
Total of nine divisions	41	100.1
Born outside of US	4	
Unknown		
Total	45	

(continued)

c. Authors not in American Guides (156)

	Authors	Percent of known US born (73)
Divisions without major publishing centers		
ESC	1	1.4
MTN	0	0.0
PAC	0	0.0
SAT	9	12.3
WNC	1	1.4
WSC	0	0.0
Total for six divisions	11	15.1
Divisions with major publishing centers		
ENC	8	11.0
MAT	23	31.5
NEN	31	42.5
Total for three divisions	62	85.0
Total of nine divisions	73	100.1
Born outside of US	80	
Unknown	3	
Total	156	

Table 9.19 Spiller authors by division (20 percent sample of 1,462 total)

a. Individual authors (292)

	Authors	Percent of known US born (202)
	Divisions without major publishing centers	
ESC	12	5.9
MTN	0	
PAC	4	2.0
SAT	23	11.4
WNC	7	3.5
WSC	4	2.0
Total for six divisions	50	24.8
	Divisions with major publishing centers	
Division of birth		
ENC	32	15.8
MAT	61	30.2
NEN	59	29.2
Total for three divisions	152	75.2
Total of nine divisions	202	
Born outside of US	86	
Unknown	4	
Total	292	

b. Authors in American Guides (109)

	Authors	Percent of known US born (93)
	Divisions without major publishing centers	
ESC	6	6.5
MTN	0	0.0
PAC	3	3.2
SAT	13	14.0
WNC	5	5.4
WSC	0	0.0
Total for six divisions	27	29.1
	Divisions with major publishing centers	
Division of birth		
ENC	18	19.4
MAT	22	23.7
NEN	26	28.0
Total for three divisions	66	71.1
Total of nine divisions	93	
Born outside of US	16	
Unknown	0	
Total	109	

(*continued*)

c. Authors not in American Guides (183)

	Authors	Percent of known US born (109)
Divisions without major publishing centers		
ESC	6	5.5
MTN	0	0.0
PAC	1	0.9
SAT	10	9.2
WNC	2	1.8
WSC	4	3.7
Total for six divisions	23	21.1
Divisions with major publishing centers		
Division of birth		
ENC	14	12.8
MAT	39	35.8
NEN	33	30.3
Total for three divisions	86	78.9
Total of nine divisions	109	
Born outside of US	70	
Unknown	4	
Total	183	

Table 9.20 Baym (Norton) authors by division (154)

a. Individual authors (154)

	Authors	Percent of US born (132)
Divisions without major publishing centers		
Division of birth		
ESC	7	5.3
MTN	4	3.0
PAC	9	6.8
SAT	14	10.6
WNC	10	7.6
WSC	5	3.8
Total for six divisions	49	37.1
Divisions with major publishing centers		
Division of birth		
ENC	18	13.6
MAT	23	17.4
NEN	42	31.8
Total for three divisions	83	62.9
Total of nine divisions	132	85.7 (of 154)
Born outside of US	22	14.3 (of 154)
Unknown	0	
Total	154	

b. Authors in American Guides (66)

	Authors	Percent of US born (58)
Divisions without major publishing centers		
Division of birth		
ESC	3	5.2
MTN	0	0.0
PAC	2	3.4
SAT	7	12.1
WNC	6	10.3
WSC	1	1.7
Total for six divisions	19	32.8
Divisions with major publishing centers		
Division of birth		
ENC	9	15.5
MAT	8	13.8
NEN	22	37.9
Total for three divisions	39	67.2
Total of nine divisions	58	87.9 (of 66)
Born outside of US	8	12.1 (of 66)
Unknown	0	
Total	66	

(*continued*)

c. Authors not in American Guides (88)

	Authors	Percent of US born (88)
Divisions without major publishing centers		
Division of birth		
ESC	4	4.5
MTN	4	4.5
PAC	7	8.0
SAT	7	8.0
WNC	4	4.5
WSC	4	4.5
Total for six divisions	30	34.1
Divisions with major publishing centers		
Division of birth		
ENC	9	10.2
MAT	15	17.0
NEN	20	22.7
Total for three divisions	44	50.0
Total of nine divisions	74	84.1
Born outside of US	14	15.9
Unknown	0	
Total	88	

Table 9.21 Pattee authors by genre

a. Individual authors (253)

Genre	Male	Female	Percent male	Percent female	Total	Percent of 253 total	Percent of 189 genres
Fiction	30	16	65.2	34.8	46	18.2	24.3
Poetry	25	9	73.5	26.5	34	13.4	18.0
Drama	3	1	75.0	25.0	4	1.6	2.1
Subtotal	58	26	69.0	31.0	84	33.2	44.4
Historical	17	2	89.5	10.5	19	7.5	10.1
Folklore	0	0	0	0.0	0	0.0	0.0
Travel	7	0	100.0	0.0	7	2.8	3.7
Archeology, natural history	2	0	100.0	0.0	2	0.8	1.1
Journalism, editorial	23	0	100.0	0.0	23	9.1	12.2
Children's books	2	2	50.0	50.0	4	1.6	2.1
Music, songs	0	0	0	0.0	0	0.0	0.0
Theology, philosophy	11	0	100.0	0.0	11	4.3	5.8
Publishing	9	0	100.0	0.0	9	3.6	4.8
Political	14	0	100.0	0.0	14	5.5	7.4
Literary criticism	15	1	93.8	6.3	16	6.3	8.5
Humor							
Subtotal	100	5	95.2	4.8	105	41.5	55.7
Other, mixtures	55	6	90.2	9.8	61	24.1	
Unspecified	3	0	100.0	0.0	3	1.2	
Total	216	37	85.8	14.6	253	100.0	

b. Authors in American Guides (86)

Genre	Male	Female	Percent male	Percent female	Total	Percent of 86 total	Percent of 68 genres
Fiction	11	8	57.9	42.1	19	22.1	27.9
Poetry	16	3	84.2	15.8	19	22.1	27.9
Drama	0	0	0.0	0.0	0	0.0	0.0
Subtotal	27	11	71.1	28.9	38	44.2	55.8
Historical	9	2	81.8	18.2	11	12.8	16.2
Folklore	0	0	0.0	0.0	0	0.0	0.0
Travel	6	0	100.0	0.0	6	7.0	8.8
Archeology, natural history	1	0	100.0	0.0	1	1.2	1.5
Journalism, editorial	7	0	100.0	0.0	7	8.1	10.3
Children's books	2	1	66.7	33.3	3	3.5	4.4
Music, songs	0	0	0.0	0.0	0	0.0	0.0
Theology, philosophy	2	0	100.0	0.0	2	2.3	2.9
Publishing	0	0	0.0	0.0	0	0.0	0.0
Political	0	0	0.0	0.0	0	0.0	0.0
Literary criticism	0	0	0.0	0.0	0	0.0	0.0
Humor	0	0	0.0	0.0	0	0.0	0.0
Subtotal	27	3	90.0	10.0	30	34.9	44.1
Other, mixtures	14	1	93.3	6.7	15	17.4	
Unspecified	3		75.0	25.0	3	3.5	
Total	71	15	82.6	17.4	86	100.0	

(*continued*)

Table 9.21 (continued)

c. Authors not in American Guides (167)

Genre	Male	Female	Percent male	Percent female	Total	Percent of 167 total	Percent of 121 genres
Fiction	19	8	70.4	29.6	27	16.2	22.3
Poetry	9	6	60.0	40.0	15	9.0	12.4
Drama	3	1	75.0	25.0	4	2.4	3.3
Subtotal	31	15	67.4	32.6	46	27.6	38.0
Historical	8	0	100.0	0.0	8	4.8	6.6
Folklore	0	0	0.0	0.0	0	0.0	0.0
Travel	1	0	100.0	0.0	1	0.6	0.8
Archeology, natural history	1	0	100.0	0.0	1	0.6	0.8
Journalism, editorial	16	0	100.0	0.0	16	9.6	13.2
Children's books	0	1	0.0	100.0	1	0.6	0.8
Music, songs	0	0	0.0	0.0	0	0.0	0.0
Theology, philosophy	9	0	100.0	0.0	9	5.4	7.4
Publishing	9	0	100.0	0.0	9	5.4	7.4
Political	14	0	100.0	0.0	14	8.4	11.6
Literary criticism	15	1	93.8	6.3	16	9.6	13.2
Humor	0	0	0.0	0.0	0	0.0	0.0
Subtotal	73	2	97.3	2.7	75	45.0	61.8
Other, mixtures	41	5	89.1	10.9	46	27.5	
Unspecified							
Total	145	22	86.8	13.2	167	100.1	

Note: a, Ratio of traditional to nontraditional genre mentions: 84/105 = 0.8. *b*, Ratio of traditional to nontraditional genre mentions: 38/30 = 1.27.*c*, Ratio of traditional to nontraditional genre mentions: 46/75 = 0.61

Table 9.22 Parrington authors by genre

a. Individual authors (201)

Genre	Male	Female	Percent male	Percent female	Total	Percent of 201 total	Percent of 144 genres
Fiction	17	4	81.0	19.0	21	10.4	14.6
Poetry	18	0	100.0	0.0	18	9.0	12.5
Drama	3	0	100.0	0.0	3	1.5	2.1
Subtotal	38	4	90.5	9.5	42	20.9	29.2
Historical	16	1	94.1	5.9	17	8.5	11.8
Folklore	0	0	0.0	0.0	0	0.0	0.0
Travel	0	1	0.0	100.0	1	0.5	0.7
Archeology, natural history	0	0	0.0	0.0	0	0.0	0.0
Journalism, editorial	7	0	100.0	0.0	7	3.5	4.9
Children's books	0	0	0.0	0.0	0	0.0	0.0
Music, songs	0	0	0.0	0.0	0	0.0	0.0
Theology, philosophy	18	2	90.0	10.0	20	10.0	13.9
Publishing	5	0	100.0	0.0	5	2.5	3.5
Political	47	1	97.9	2.1	48	23.9	33.3
Literary criticism	4	0	100.0	0.0	4	2.0	2.8
Humor	0	0	0.0	0.0	0	0.0	0.0
Subtotal	97	5	95.1	4.9	102	50.9	70.9
Other, mixture[a]	51	6	89.5	10.5	57	28.4	
Unspecified							
Total	186	15	92.5	7.5	201	100.2	

(continued)

Table 9.22 (continued)

b. Authors in American Guides (45)

Genre	Male	Female	Percent male	Percent female	Total	Percent of 45 total	Percent of 33 genres
Fiction	11	3	78.6	21.4	14	31.1	42.4
Poetry	6	0	100.0	0.0	6	13.3	18.2
Drama	0	0	0.0	0.0	0	0.0	0.0
Subtotal	17	3	85.0	15.0	20	44.4	60.6
Historical	3	1	75.0	25.0	4	8.9	12.1
Folklore	0	0	0.0	0.0	0	0.0	0.0
Travel	0	0	0.0	0.0	0	0.0	0.0
Archeology, natural history	0	0	0.0	0.0	0	0.0	0.0
Journalism, editorial	4	0	100.0	0.0	4	8.9	12.1
Children's books	0	0	0.0	0.0	0	0.0	0.0
Music, songs	0	0	0.0	0.0	0	0.0	0.0
Theology, philosophy	1	0	100.0	0.0	1	2.2	3.0
Publishing	1	0	100.0	0.0	1	2.2	3.0
Political	3	0	100.0	0.0	3	6.7	9.1
Literary criticism	0	0	0.0	0.0	0	0.0	0.0
Humor	0	0	0.0	0.0	0	0.0	0.0
Subtotal	12	1	92.3	7.7	13	28.9	39.3
Other, mixtures Unspecified	11	1	91.7	8.3	12	26.7	
Total	40	5	88.9	11.1	45	100.0	

c. Authors not in American Guides (156)

Genre	Male	Female	Percent male	Percent female	Total	Percent of 156 total	Percent of 111 genres
Fiction	6	1	85.7	14.3	7	4.5	6.3
Poetry	12	0	100.0	0.0	12	7.7	10.8
Drama	3	0	100.0	0.0	3	1.9	2.7
Subtotal	21	1	95.5	4.5	22	14.1	19.8
Historical	13	0	100.0	0.0	13	8.3	11.7
Folklore	0	0	0.0	0.0	0	0.0	0.0
Travel	0	1	0.0	100.0	1	0.6	0.9
Archeology, natural history	0	0	0.0	0.0	0	0.0	0.0
Journalism, editorial	3	0	100.0	0.0	3	1.9	2.7
Children's books	0	0	0.0	0.0	0	0.0	0.0
Music, songs	0	0	0.0	0.0	0	0.0	0.0
Theology, philosophy	17	2	89.5	10.5	19	12.2	17.1
Publishing	4	0	100.0	0.0	4	2.6	3.6
Political	44	1	97.8	2.2	45	28.8	40.5
Literary criticism	4	0	100.0	0.0	4	2.6	3.6
Humor	0	0	0.0	0.0	0	0.0	0.0
Subtotal	85	4	95.5	4.5	89	57.0	80.1
Other, mixtures	40	5	88.9	11.1	45	28.9	
Unspecified							
Total	146	10	93.6	6.4	156	100.0	

Note: a, Ratio of traditional to nontraditional genre mentions: 42/102 = 0.4. *b*, Ratio of traditional to nontraditional genre mentions: 20/13 = 1.5. *c*, Ratio of traditional to nontraditional genre mentions: 22/89 = 0.2.

[a]The category of "Other" is unusually high in the case of Parrington for two reasons. First, he included a number of intellectuals who were not writers or did not fit into my categories, and second, he gave unusually full treatment to writers, often mentioning multiple genres.

Table 9.23 Spiller authors by genre

a. Individual authors (292)

Genre	Male	Female	Percent male	Percent female	Total	Percent of 292 total	Percent of 231 genres
Fiction	38	9	80.9	19.1	47	16.1	20.3
Poetry	39	3	92.9	7.1	42	14.4	18.2
Drama	13	0	100.0	0.0	13	4.5	5.6
Subtotal	90	12	88.2	11.8	102	35.0	44.1
Historical	16	4	0.8	0.2	20	6.8	8.7
Folklore	0	0	0.0	0.0	0	0.0	0.0
Travel	13	0	100.0	0.0	13	4.5	5.6
Archeology, natural history	2	0	100.0	0.0	2	0.7	0.9
Journalism, editorial	18	1	94.7	5.3	19	6.5	8.2
Children's books	1	0	100.0	0.0	1	0.3	0.4
Music, songs	0	0	0.0	0.0	0	0.0	0.0
Theology, philosophy	23	1	95.8	4.2	24	8.2	10.4
Publishing	5	0	100.0	0.0	5	1.7	2.2
Political	26	3	89.7	10.3	29	9.9	12.6
Literary criticism	13	0	100.0	0.0	13	4.5	5.6
Humor	2	1	66.7	33.3	3	1.0	1.3
Subtotal	119	10	92.2	7.8	129	44.1	55.9
Other, mixtures	53	6	89.8	10.2	59	20.2	
Unspecified	2	0	100.0	0.0	2	0.7	
Total	264	28	90.4	9.6	292	100.0	

b. Authors in American Guides (109)

Genre	Male	Female	Percent male	Percent female	Total	Percent of 109 total	Percent of 91 genres
Fiction	21	6	77.8	22.2	27	24.8	29.7
Poetry	18	1	94.7	5.3	19	17.4	20.9
Drama	3	0	100.0	0.0	3	2.8	3.3
Subtotal	42	7	85.7	14.3	49	45.0	53.9
Historical	10	3	76.9	23.1	13	11.9	14.3
Folklore	0	0	0.0	0.0	0	0.0	0.0
Travel	7	0	100.0	0.0	7	6.4	7.7
Archeology, natural history	1	0	100.0	0.0	1	0.9	1.1
Journalism, editorial	12	0	100.0	0.0	12	11.0	13.2
Children's books	1	0	100.0	0.0	1	0.9	1.1
Music, songs	0	0	0.0	0.0	0	0.0	0.0
Theology, philosophy	0	0	0.0	0.0	0	0.0	0.0
Publishing	1	0	100.0	0.0	1	0.9	1.1
Political	4	0	100.0	0.0	4	3.7	4.4
Literary criticism	1	0	100.0	0.0	1	0.9	1.1
Humor	2	0	100.0	0.0	2	1.8	2.2
Subtotal	39	3	92.9	7.1	42	38.4	46.2
Other, mixtures	15	1	93.8	6.3	16	14.7	
Unspecified	2	0	100.0	0.0	2	1.8	
Total	98	11	89.9	10.1	109	99.9	

(*continued*)

Table 9.22 (continued)

c. Authors not in American Guides (183)

Genre	Male	Female	Percent male	Percent female	Total	Percent of 183 total	Percent of 140 genres
Fiction	17	3	85.0	15.0	20	10.9	14.3
Poetry	21	2	91.3	8.7	23	12.6	16.4
Drama	10	0	100.0	0.0	10	5.5	7.1
Subtotal	48	5	90.6	9.4	53	29.0	37.8
Historical	6	1	85.7	14.3	7	3.8	5.0
Folklore	0	0	0.0	0.0	0	0.0	0.0
Travel	6	0	100.0	0.0	6	3.3	4.3
Archeology, natural history	1	0	100.0	0.0	1	0.5	0.7
Journalism, editorial	6	1	85.7	14.3	7	3.8	5.0
Children's books	0	0	0.0	0.0	0	0.0	0.0
Music, songs	0	0	0.0	0.0	0	0.0	0.0
Theology, philosophy	23	1	95.8	4.1	24	13.1	17.1
Publishing	4	0	100.0	0.0	4	2.2	2.9
Political	22	3	88.0	12.0	25	13.7	17.9
Literary criticism	12	0	100.0	0.0	12	6.6	8.6
Humor	0	1	0.0	100.0	1	0.5	0.7
Subtotal	80	7	92.0	8.0	87	47.5	62.2
Other, mixtures	38	5	88.4	11.6	43	23.5	
Unspecified	0	0	0.0	0.0	0	0.0	
Total	166	17	90.7	9.3	183	100.0	

Note: a, Ratio of traditional to nontraditional genre mentions: 102/129 = 0.79. *b*, Ratio of traditional to nontraditional genre mentions: 49/42 = 1.17. *c*, Ratio of traditional to nontraditional genre mentions: 53/87 = 0.6.

Table 9.24 Baym (Norton) authors by genre

a. Individual authors (156)

Genre	Male	Female	Percent male	Percent female	Total	Percent of 156 total	Percent of 139 genres
Fiction	30	21	58.9	41.8	51	32.7	36.7
Poetry	33	16	67.3	32.7	49	31.4	35.3
Drama	5	1	83.3	16.7	6	3.8	4.3
Subtotal	68	38	64.2	35.8	106	67.9	76.3
Historical	6	5	54.5	45.5	11	7.1	7.9
Folklore	*	*	0	0	1	0.6	0.7
Travel	9	1	90.0	10.0	10	6.4	7.2
Archeology, natural history	0	0	0	0	0	0.0	0.0
Journalism, editorial	2	0	100.0	0	2	1.3	1.4
Children's books	0	1	0	100.0	1	0.6	0.7
Music, songs	*	*			1	0.6	0.7
Theology, philosophy	2	0	100.0	0	2	1.3	1.4
Publishing	0	0	0	0	0	0.0	0.0
Political	2	1	66.7	33.3	3	1.9	2.2
Literary criticism	1	1	50.0	50.0	2	1.3	1.4
Humor	0	0	0	0	0	0.0	0.0
Subtotal	22	9	71.0	29.0	33	21.1	23.6
Other, mixtures	10	7	58.8	41.2	17	10.9	
Unspecified							
Total	100	54	64.9	35.1	156	99.9	

(continued)

Table 9.24 (continued)

b. Authors in American Guides (66)

Genre	Male	Female	Percent male	Percent female	Total	Percent of 66 total	Percent of 54 genres
Fiction	16	5	76.2	23.8	21	31.8	38.9
Poetry	14	5	73.7	26.3	19	28.8	35.2
Drama	2	1	66.7	33.3	3	4.5	5.6
Subtotal	32	11	74.4	25.6	43	65.1	79.7
Historical	3	1	75.0	25.0	4	6.1	7.4
Folklore	0	0	0.0	0.0	0	0.0	0.0
Travel	4	0	100.0	0.0	4	6.1	7.4
Archeology, natural history	0	0	0.0	0.0	0	0.0	0.0
Journalism, editorial	2	0	100.0	0.0	2	3.0	3.7
Children's books	0	0	0.0	0.0	0	0.0	0.0
Music, songs	0	0	0.0	0.0	0	0.0	0.0
Theology, philosophy	0	0	0.0	0.0	0	0.0	0.0
Publishing	0	0	0.0	0.0	0	0.0	0.0
Political	1	0	100.0	0	1	1.5	1.9
Literary criticism	0	0	0.0	0.0	0	0.0	0.0
Humor	0	0	0.0	0.0	0	0.0	0.0
Subtotal	10	1	90.9	9.1	11	16.7	20.4
Other, mixtures	9	3	75.0	25.0	12	18.2	
Unspecified	0	0	0.0	0.0	0	0.0	0.0
Total	51	15	77.3	22.7	66	100.0	

c. Authors not in American Guides (90)

Genre	Male	Female	Percent male	Percent female	Total	Percent of 90 total	Percent of 85 genres
Fiction	14	16	46.7	53.3	30	33.3	35.3
Poetry	19	11	63.3	36.7	30	33.3	35.3
Drama	3	0	100.0	0	3	3.3	3.5
Subtotal	36	27	57.1	42.9	63	69.9	74.1
Historical	3	4	42.9	57.1	7	7.8	8.2
Folklore	*	*	0.0	0.0	1	1.1	1.2
Travel	5	1	83.3	16.7	6	6.7	7.1
Archeology, natural history	0	0	0	0	0	0.0	0.0
Journalism, editorial	0	0	0	0	0	0.0	0.0
Children's books	0	1	0	100.0	1	1.1	1.2
Music, songs	*	*	0.0	0.0	1	1.1	1.2
Theology, philosophy	2	0	100.0	0	2	2.2	2.4
Publishing	0	0	0	0	0	0.0	0.0
Political	1	1	50.0	50.0	2	2.2	2.4
Literary criticism	1	1	50.0	50.0	2	2.2	2.4
Humor	0	0	0	0	0	0.0	0.0
Subtotal	12	8	60.0	40.0	22	24.4	26.1
Other, mixtures	4	1	80.0	20.0	5	5.6	
Unspecified							
Total	52	36	59.1	40.1	90	99.9	

Note: a, Ratio of traditional to nontraditional genre mentions: 106/33 = 3.2. *b*, Ratio of traditional to nontraditional genre mentions: 43/11 = 3.9. *c*, Ratio of traditional to nontraditional genre mentions: 63/22 = 2.9.

*The two categories of Native American Trickster Tales and Native American Songs and Chants are included in their respective genres, but are not included in calculating the percentages male and female authors.

Appendix G: US Census Regions and Divisions

The United State Census divides the country into nine divisions, clustered into four large regions. The census adopted the nine divisions in 1910, and the only change since then has been the addition of two new states, Alaska and Hawaii to the Pacific Division in 1960. The nine divisions are the basis for the analysis of the geographical characteristics of the Guides.

Northeast

New England Division (NEN)

Maine, New Hampshire, Vermont, Massachusetts, Rhode Island, Connecticut

Middle Atlantic Division (MAT)

New York, New Jersey, Pennsylvania

Midwest

East North Central Division (ENC)

Ohio, Indiana, Illinois, Michigan, Wisconsin

West North Central Division (WNC)

Minnesota, Iowa, Missouri, North Dakota, South Dakota, Nebraska, Kansas

South

South Atlantic Division (SAT)

Delaware, Maryland, District of Columbia, Virginia, West Virginia, North Carolina, South Carolina, Georgia, Florida

East South Central Division (ESC)
  Kentucky, Tennessee, Alabama, Mississippi
West South Central Division (WSC)
  Arkansas, Louisiana, Oklahoma, Texas

West

Mountain Division (MTN)
  Montana, Idaho, Wyoming, Colorado, New Mexico, Arizona, Utah, Nevada
Pacific Division (PAC)
  Washington, Oregon, California, Alaska, Hawaii

References

Primary

STATE GUIDES

Alabama: A Guide to the Deep South. 1941. "Compiled by Workers of the Writers' Program of the Work Projects Administration in the State of Alabama."[1] Sponsored by the Alabama State Planning Commission. New York: Richard R. Smith.

Arizona: A Guide to the Youngest State. 1940. "Compiled by Workers of the Writers' Program of the Work Projects Administration in the State of Arizona." Sponsored by the Arizona State Teachers College at Flagstaff. New York: Hastings House.

Arkansas: A Guide to the State. 1941. "Compiled by Workers of the Writers' Program of the Work Projects Administration in the State of Arkansas." Sponsored by C. G. Hall, Secretary of State, Arkansas. New York: Hastings House.

California: A Guide to the Golden State. 1939. "Compiled and Written by the Federal Writers' Project of the Works Progress Administration for the State of California." Sponsored by Mabel R. Gillis, California State Librarian. New York: Hastings House.

Colorado: A Guide to the Highest State. 1941. "Compiled by Workers of the Writers' Program of the Work Projects Administration in the State of Colorado." Sponsored by the Colorado State Planning Commission. New York: Hastings House.

1. On April 3, 1939, the president sent to Congress a reorganization plan that relieved the Works Progress Administration of its independent status and changed its name to the Work Projects Administration. Guides published before this date say that they are compiled and written by the Federal Writers' Project (under the Works Progress Administration, although this is not stated); Guides published after say that they were compiled and written by the Writers' Program of the Works Projects Administration for a particular state.

Connecticut: A Guide to Its Roads, Lore, and People. 1938. "Written by Workers of the Federal Writers' Project of the Works Progress Administration for the State of Connecticut." Sponsored by Wilbur L. Cross, Governor of Connecticut. Boston: Houghton Mifflin.

Delaware: A Guide to the First State. 1938. "Compiled and Written by the Federal Writers' Project of the Works Progress Administration for the State of Delaware." Sponsored by Edward W. Cooch, Lieutenant Governor. New York: Viking Press.

Florida: A Guide to the Southernmost State. 1939. "Compiled and Written by the Federal Writers' Project Program of the Work Projects Administration for the State of Florida." Sponsored by the State of Florida Department of Public Instruction. New York: Oxford University Press.

Georgia: A Guide to Its Towns and Countryside. 1940. "Compiled and Written by Workers of the Writers' Program of the Work Projects Administration in the State of Georgia." Sponsored by the Georgia Board of Education. Athens: University of Georgia Press.

Idaho: A Guide in Word and Picture. 1937. "Prepared by the Federal Writers' Projects of the Works Projects Administration." Caldwell, ID: Caxton Printers.

Illinois: A Descriptive and Historical Guide. 1939. "Compiled and Written by the Federal Writers' Project of the Work Projects Administration for the State of Illinois." Sponsored by Henry Horner, Governor. Chicago: A. C. McClurg.

Indiana: A Guide to the Hoosier State. 1941. "Compiled by Workers of the Writers' Program of the Work Projects Administration in the State of Indiana." Sponsored by the Department of Public Relations of Indiana State Teachers College. New York: Oxford University Press.

Iowa: A Guide to the Hawkeye State. 1938. "Compiled and Written by the Federal Writers' Project of the Works Progress Administration for the State of Iowa." Sponsored by the State Historical Society of Iowa to Commemorate the Centenary of the Organization of Iowa Territory. New York: Viking Press.

Kansas: A Guide to the Sunflower State. 1939. "Compiled and Written by the Federal Writers' Project of the Work Projects Administration for the State of Kansas." Sponsored by the State Department of Education. New York: Viking Press.

Kentucky: A Guide to the Bluegrass State. 1939. "Compiled and Written by the Federal Writers' Project of the Work Projects Administration for the State of Kentucky." Sponsored by the University of Kentucky. New York: Harcourt, Brace.

Louisiana: A Guide to the State. 1941. "Compiled by Workers of the Writers' Program of the Work Projects Administration in the State of Louisiana." Sponsored by the Louisiana Library Commission at Baton Rouge. New York: Hastings House.

Maine: A Guide "Down East." 1937. "Written by Workers of the Federal Writers' Project of the Works Progress Administration for the State of Maine." Sponsored by the Maine Development Commission. Boston: Houghton Mifflin.

Maryland: A Guide to the Old Line State. 1940. "Compiled by Workers of the Writers' Program of the Work Projects Administration in the State of Maryland."

Sponsored by Herbert R. O'Conor, Governor of Maryland. New York: Oxford University Press.

Massachusetts: A Guide to Its Places and People. 1937. "Written and Compiled by the Federal Writers' Project of the Works Progress Administration for the State of Massachusetts." Frederic W. Cook, Secretary of the Commonwealth, Cooperating Sponsor. Boston: Houghton Mifflin.

Michigan: A Guide to the Wolverine State. 1941. "Compiled by Workers of the Writers' Program of the Work Projects Administration in the State of Michigan." Sponsored by the Michigan State Administrative Board. New York: Oxford University Press.

Minnesota: A State Guide. 1938. "Compiled and Written by the Federal Writers' Project of the Works Progress Administration." Sponsored by the Executive Council, State of Minnesota. New York: Viking Press.

Mississippi: A Guide to the Magnolia State. 1938. "Compiled and Written by the Federal Writers' Project of the Works Progress Administration." Sponsored by the Mississippi Advertising Commission. New York: Viking Press.

Missouri: A Guide to the "Show Me" State. 1941. "Compiled by Workers of the Writers' Program of the Work Projects Administration in the State of Missouri." Sponsored by the Missouri State Highway Department. New York: Duell, Sloan, and Pearce.

Montana: A State Guide Book. 1939. "Compiled and Written by the Federal Writers' Project of the Work Projects Administration for the State of Montana." Sponsored by Department of Agriculture, Labor and Industry, State of Montana. New York: Viking.

Nebraska: A Guide to the Cornhusker State. 1939. "Compiled and Written by the Federal Writers' Project of the Works Progress Administration for the State of Nebraska." Sponsored by the Nebraska State Historical Society. New York: Viking Press.

Nevada: A Guide to the Silver State. 1940. "Compiled by Workers of the Writers' Program of the Work Projects Administration in the State of Nevada." Sponsored by Dr. Jeanne Elizabeth Wier, Nevada State Historical Society, Inc. Portland, OR: Binfords and Mort.

New Hampshire: A Guide to the Granite State. 1938. "Written by Workers of the Federal Writers' Project of the Works Progress Administration for the State of New Hampshire." Francis P. Murphy, Governor of New Hampshire, Cooperating Sponsor. Boston: Houghton Mifflin.

New Jersey: A Guide to Its Present and Past. 1939. "Compiled and Written by the Federal Writers' Project of the Works Progress Administration for the State of New Jersey." Sponsored by the Public Library of Newark and the New Jersey Guild Associates. New York: Viking Press.

New Mexico: A Guide to the Colorful State. 1940. "Compiled by Workers of the Writers' Program of the Work Projects Administration in the State of New Mexico." Sponsored by the Coronado Cuarto Centennial Commission and the University of New Mexico. New York: Hastings House.

New York: A Guide to the Empire State. 1940. "Compiled by Workers of the Writers' Program of the Work Projects Administration in the State of New York." Sponsored by New York State Historical Association. New York: Oxford University Press.

North Carolina: A Guide to the Old North State. 1939. "Compiled and Written by the Federal Writers' Project of the Federal Works Agency Work Projects Administration for the State of North Carolina." Sponsored by North Carolina Department of Conservation and Development. Chapel Hill: University of North Carolina Press.

North Dakota: A Guide to the Northern Prairie State. 1938. "Written by Workers of the Federal Writers' Project of the Works Progress Administration for the State of North Dakota." Sponsored by the State Historical Society of North Dakota. Fargo, ND: Knight Printing Company.

The Ohio Guide. 1940. "Compiled by Workers of the Writers' Program of the Work Projects Administration in the State of Ohio." Sponsored by the Ohio State Archaeological and Historical Society. New York: Oxford University Press.

Oklahoma: A Guide to the Sooner State. 1941. "Compiled by Workers of the Writers' Program of the Work Projects Administration in the State of Oklahoma." Sponsored by the University of Oklahoma. Norman: University of Oklahoma Press.

Oregon: End of the Trail. 1940. "Compiled by Workers of the Writers' Program of the Work Projects Administration in the State of Oregon." Sponsored by the Oregon Board of Control. Portland, OR: Binfords and Mort.

Pennsylvania: A Guide to the Keystone State. 1940. "Compiled by Workers of the Writers' Program of the Work Projects Administration in the State of Pennsylvania." Cosponsored by the Pennsylvania Historical Commission and the University of Pennsylvania. New York: Oxford University Press.

Rhode Island A Guide to the Smallest State. 1937. "Written by Workers of the Federal Writers' Project of the Works Progress Administration for the State of Rhode Island." Sponsored by Louis W. Cappelli, Secretary of State, Chairman of the Sponsoring Committee. Boston: Houghton Mifflin.

South Carolina: A Guide to the Palmetto State. 1941. "Compiled by Workers of the Writers' Program of the Work Projects Administration in the State of South Carolina." Sponsored by Burnet R. Maybank, Governor of South Carolina. New York: Oxford University Press.

A South Dakota Guide. 1938. "Compiled by the Federal Writers' Project of the Works Progress Administration State of South Dakota." Sponsored by the State of South Dakota. Pierre, SD: State Publishing Company.

Tennessee: A Guide to the State. 1939. "Compiled and Written by the Federal Writers' Project of the Work Projects Administration for the State of Tennessee." Sponsored by the Department of Conservation, Division of Information. New York: Viking Press.

Texas: A Guide to the Lone Star State. 1940. "Compiled by Workers of the Writers' Program of the Work Projects Administration in the State of Texas." Sponsored by the Texas State Highway Commission. New York: Hastings House.

Utah: A Guide to the State. 1941. "Compiled by Workers of the Writers' Program of the Work Projects Administration for the State of Utah." Sponsored by the Utah State Institute of Fine Arts. Cosponsored by the Salt Lake County Commission. New York: Hastings House.

Vermont: A Guide to the Green Mountain State. 1937. "Written by Workers of the Federal Writers' Project of the Works Progress Administration for the State of Vermont." Sponsored by the Vermont State Planning Board. Boston: Houghton Mifflin.

Virginia: A Guide to the Old Dominion. 1940. "Compiled by Workers of the Writers' Program of the Work Projects Administration in the State of Virginia." Sponsored by James H. Price, Governor of Virginia. New York: Oxford University Press.

Washington: A Guide to the Evergreen State. 1941. "Compiled by Workers of the Writers' Program of the Work Projects Administration in the State of Washington." Sponsored by the Washington State Historical Society. Portland, OR: Binfords and Mort.

West Virginia: A Guide to the Mountain State. 1941. "Compiled by Workers of the Writers' Program of the Works Progress Administration in the State of West Virginia." Sponsored by the Conservation Commission of West Virginia. New York: Oxford University Press.

Wisconsin: A Guide to the Badger State." 1941. "Compiled by Workers of the Writers' Program of the Work Projects Administration in the State of Wisconsin." Sponsored by the Wisconsin Library Association. New York: Duell, Sloan, and Pearce.

Wyoming: A Guide to Its History, Highways, and People. 1941 "Compiled by Workers of the Writers' Program of the Work Projects Administration in the State of Wyoming." Sponsored by Dr. Lester C. Hunt, Secretary of State. New York: Oxford University Press.

OTHER AMERICAN GUIDE SERIES BOOKS

A Guide to Alaska: Last American Frontier. 1939. By Merle Colby. Federal Writers' Project. John W. Troy, Governor of Alaska, Sponsor. New York: Macmillan.

New York City Guide. 1939. "A Comprehensive Guide to the Five Boroughs of the Metropolis—Manhattan, Brooklyn, the Bronx, Queens, and Richmond—Prepared by the Federal Writers' Project of the Works Progress Administration in New York City." New York: Random House.

New York Panorama. 1938. "A Comprehensive View of the Metropolis, Presented in a Series of Articles Prepared by the Federal Writers' Project of the Works Progress Administration in New York City." New York: Random House.

Washington: City and Capital. 1937. Federal Writers' Project, Works Progress Administration, American Guide Series. Washington, DC: United States Government Printing Office.

OTHER PRIMARY SOURCES

Automobile Blue Books Inc. (1924). *Official Automobile Blue Book 1924: Standard Touring Guide of America*. Vol. 1. New York and New England [covers New York, New England, southern Ontario, Nova Scotia, New Brunswick]. Chicago: Automobile Blue Books.

Baym, Nina, ed. 2007. *The Norton Anthology of American Literature*. 7th ed. Nina Baym, general editor. New York: W. W. Norton. http://www.wwnorton.com/college/english/naal7/welcome.asp.

Bureau of the Census. 1930. *Statistical Abstract of the United States 1930*. Washington: US Department of Commerce.

Crofutt, George A. 1879. *Crofutt's New Overland Tourist and Pacific Coast Guide*. Vol. 2 1879–80. Chicago: Overland Publishing Company.

Katharine Amend Kellock Papers. 1924–69. Library of Congress, Manuscripts Division, ID MSS55301.

National Archives and Records Administration (NARA), Record Group: 69, Stack area: 530, Row: 69, Compartment 20, Compartment: 20, Entry: 13. This is the WPA, Federal Writers' Project, Editorial Correspondence. I refer to this as NARA 69 in notes.

Parrington, Vernon Lewis. 1927–30. *Main Currents in American Thought: An Interpretation of American Literature from the Beginnings to 1920*. 3 vols. New York: Harcourt, Brace.

Pattee, Fred Lewis. 1915. *A History of American Literature since 1870*. New York: Century.

Pattee, Fred Lewis. 1930. *The New American Literature, 1890–1930*. New York: Century.

Pattee, Fred Lewis. 1935. *The First Century of American Literature, 1770–1870*. New York: Appleton-Century.

Selvaggio, Marc S. 1990. *The American Guide Series: Works by the Federal Writers' Project*. Pittsburgh, PA: Arthur Scharf, Bookseller and Schoyer's Books.

Spiller, Robert E., ed. 1963. *Literary History of the United States*. 3rd ed., revised. Editors: Robert E. Spiller, Willard Thorp, Thomas H. Johnson, Henry Seidel Canby, and Richard M. Ludwig. New York: Macmillan and London: Collier-Macmillan.

Secondary

Aaron, Daniel. 1961. *Writers on the Left: Episodes in American Literary Communism*. New York: Harcourt, Brace and World.

Adamic, Louis. 1934. "What the Proletariat Reads: Conclusions Based on a Year's

Study among Hundreds of Workers throughout the United States." *Saturday Review of Literature* 11 (December 1, 1934).

Arnesen, Eric, ed. 2007. *Encyclopedia of U.S. Labor and Working-Class History*. Vol. 1. New York: Routledge.

Aron, Cindy S. 1999. *Working at Play: A History of Vacations in the United States*. New York: Oxford University Press.

Baxandall, Michael. 1985. *Patterns of Intention: On the Historical Explanation of Pictures*. New Haven, Ct: Yale University Press.

Baym, Nina. 1981. "Melodramas of Beset Manhood: How Theories of American Fiction Exclude Women Authors." *American Quarterly* 33: 123–39.

Beck, P. G., and M. C. Forster. 1935. *Six Rural Problem Areas: Relief, Resources, Rehabilitation; An Analysis of the Human and Material Resources in Six Rural Areas with High Relief Rates*. Washington, DC: Federal Emergency Relief Administration, Division of Relief, Statistics, and Finance.

Beckham, Sue Bridwell. 1989. *Depression Post Office Murals and Southern Culture: A Gentle Reconstruction*. Baton Rouge: Louisiana State University Press.

Berkowitz, Michael. 2001. "A 'New Deal' for Leisure: Making Mass Tourism during the Great Depression." In *Being Elsewhere: Tourism, Consumer Culture, and Identity in Modern Europe and North America*, edited by Shelley Baranowski and Ellen Furlough, 185–212. Ann Arbor: University of Michigan Press.

Billington, Ray Allen. 1961. "Government and the Arts: The W. P. A. Experience." *American Quarterly* 13: 466–79.

Bliss, Carey S. 1972. *Autos across America: A Bibliography of Transcontinental Automobile Travel: 1903–1940*. Los Angeles: Dawson's Book Shop.

Bold, Christine. 1999. *The WPA Guides: Mapping America*. Jackson: University Press of Mississippi.

Bold, Christine. 2006. *Writers, Plumbers, and Anarchists: The WPA Writers' Project in Massachusetts*. Amherst: University of Massachusetts Press.

Boyd, Donald C. 2007. "The Book Women of Kentucky: The WPA Pack Horse Library Project, 1936–1943." *Libraries and the Cultural Record* 42: 111–28.

Brinkley, Alan. 1982. *Voices of Protest: Huey Long, Father Coughlin, and the Great Depression*. New York: Knopf.

Chapman, Edward A. 1938. "WPA and Rural Libraries." *Bulletin of the American Library Association* 32 (10; October 1, 1938): 703. Online at New Deal Network: http://newdeal.feri.org/texts/216.htm.

Cocks, Catherine. 2001. *Doing the Town: The Rise of Urban Tourism in the United States, 1850–1915*. Berkeley: University of California Press.

Cohen, Adam. 2009. *Nothing to Fear: FDR's Inner Circle and the Hundred Days That Created Modern America*. New York: Penguin Press.

Darnton, Robert. 2009. *The Case for Books: Past, Present, and Future*. New York: Public Affairs.

Denning, Michael. 1997. *The Cultural Front: The Laboring of American Culture in the Twentieth Century*. London: Verso.

Downey, Kristin. 2010. *The Woman behind the New Deal: The Life of Frances Perkins,*

FDR's Secretary of Labor and His Moral Conscience. New York: Nan A. Talese/ Doubleday.

Eppard, Philip B. 1986. "The Rental Library in Twentieth-Century America." *Journal of Library History, Philosophy, and Comparative Librarianship* 21: 240–52.

Faust, Drew Gilpin. 2008. *This Republic of Suffering: Death and the American Civil War*. New York: Knopf.

Folsom, Franklin. 1994. *Days of Anger, Days of Hope: A Memoir of the League of American Writers 1937–1942*. Niwot: University of Colorado Press.

Ford, Henry, with Samuel Crowther. 1922. *My Life and Work*. Garden City, NY: Garden City Publishing.

Galbi, Douglas A. 2007. "Book Circulation per U.S. Public Library User since 1856." http://galbithink.org/libraries/circulation.htm.

Gassan, Richard. 2005. "The First American Tourist Guidebooks: Authorship and Print Culture of the 1820s." *Book History* 8: 51–74.

Gilpin, William. 1794. *Three Essays: On Picturesque Beauty; on Picturesque Travel: and on Sketching Landscape; to Which Is Added a Poem on Landscape Painting*. 2nd ed. Ecco Print Editions.

Graff, Harvey J. 1987. *The Legacies of Literacy: Continuities and Contradictions in Western Culture and Society*. Bloomington: Indiana University Press.

Griswold, Wendy. 1987. "A Methodological Framework for the Sociology of Culture." *Sociological Methodology* 17: 1–35.

Griswold, Wendy. 2008. *Regionalism and the Reading Class*. Chicago: University of Chicago Press.

Griswold, Wendy, and Hannah Wohl. 2015. "Evangelists of Culture: One Book Programs and the Agents Who Define Taste, Shape Culture, and Reproduce Regionalism." *Poetics: Journal of Empirical Research on Culture, Media, and the Arts* 50: 96–109.

Griswold, Wendy, and Nathan Wright. 2004. "Cowbirds, Locals, and the Dynamic Endurance of Regionalism." *American Journal of Sociology* 109: 1411–51.

Hall, H. Lark. 1994. *V. L. Parrington: Through the Avenue of Art*. Kent, OH: Kent State University Press.

Haygood, William Converse. 1938. *Who Uses the Public Library: A Survey of the Patrons of the Circulation and Reference Departments of the New York Public Library*. Chicago: University of Chicago Press.

Hibbert, Christopher. 1987. *The Grand Tour*. Thames, UK: Methuen.

Hirsch, Jerrold. 2003. *Portrait of America: A Cultural History of the Federal Writers' Project*. Chapel Hill: University of North Carolina Press.

Hodgson, James Goodwin. 1944. *Rural Reading*. Chicago: n.p.

Homberger, Eric. 1979. "Proletarian Literature and the John Reed Clubs 1929–1935." *Journal of American Studies* 13: 221–44.

Hunter, J. Paul. 1966. *The Reluctant Pilgrim: Defoe's Emblematic Method and Quest for Form in "Robinson Crusoe."* Baltimore: Johns Hopkins University Press.

Hutner, Gordon. 2009. *What America Read: Taste, Class, and the Novel, 1920–1960*. Chapel Hill: University of North Carolina Press.

Jakle, John A., and Keith A. Sculle. 2009. *America's Main Street Hotels: Transiency and Community in the Early Auto Age*. Knoxville: University of Tennessee Press.

Jepperson, Ronald L., and Ann Swidler. 1994. "What Properties of Culture Should We Measure?" *Poetics* 22: 359–71.

Johnson, Samuel, and James Boswell. [1775] 1984. *A Journey to the Western Islands of Scotland and The Journal of a Tour to the Hebrides*. London: Penguin Classics.

Kammen, Michael G. 1991. *Mystic Chords of Memory: The Transformation of Tradition in American Culture*. New York: Knopf.

Korda, Michael. 2001. *Making the List: A Cultural History of the American Bestseller 1900–1999*. New York: Barnes and Noble Books.

Levy, David W. 1995. "'I Become More Radical with Every Year': The Intellectual Odyssey of Vernon Louis Parrington." *American History* 23: 663–68.

Löfgren, Orvar. 1999. *On Holiday: A History of Vacationing*. Berkeley: University of California Press.

Lynd, Robert S., and Helen Merrill Lynd. 1937. *Middletown in Transition: A Study in Cultural Conflicts*. New York: Harcourt, Brace.

Mangione, Jerre. 1972. *The Dream and the Deal: The Federal Writers' Project, 1935–43*. Boston: Little, Brown.

Marling, Karal Ann. 1982. *Wall-to-Wall America: A Cultural History of Post-office Murals in the Great Depression*. Minneapolis: University of Minnesota Press.

Martin, Robert Sidney. 1986. "Louis Round Wilson's *Geography of Reading*: An Inquiry into Its Origins, Development, and Impact." *Journal of Library History (1974–1987)* 21: 425–44.

McDonald, William F. 1969. *Federal Relief Administration and the Arts: The Origins and Administrative History of the Arts Projects of the Works Progress Administration*. Columbus: Ohio State University Press.

McKinsey, Elizabeth. 1985. *Niagara Falls: Icon of the American Sublime*. Cambridge: Cambridge University Press.

Meinig, D. W. 1986. *The Shaping of America: A Geographical Perspective on 500 Years of History*. Vol. 1, *Atlantic America, 1492–1800*. New Haven: Yale University Press.

Miller, Laura J. 2006. *Reluctant Capitalists: Bookselling and the Culture of Consumption*. Chicago: University of Chicago Press.

Miller, R. A. 1936. "The Relation of Reading Characteristics to Social Indexes." *American Journal of Sociology* 41: 738–56.

National Center for Education Statistics. 1993. *120 Years of American Education: A Statistical Portrait*. Edited by Thomas D. Snyder. Washington, DC: US Department of Education.

National Endowment for the Arts. 2004. *Reading at Risk: A Survey of Literary Reading in America*. Research Division Report #46. Washington, DC: National Endowment for the Arts.

National Endowment for the Arts. 2009. *Reading on the Rise: A New Chapter in American Literacy*. Washington, DC: National Endowment for the Arts, Office of Research and Analysis.

Newman, Katherine S., and Elisabeth S. Jacobs. 2010. *Who Cares? Public Ambivalence and Government Activism from the New Deal to the Second Gilded Age.* Princeton, NJ: Princeton University Press.

Norton, Peter D. 2008. *Fighting Traffic: The Dawn of the Motor Age in the American City*. Cambridge, MA: MIT Press.

Odum, Howard W., and Harry Estill Moore. 1938. *American Regionalism: A Cultural-Historical Approach to National Integration*. New York: Holt.

O'Reilly, Kenneth. 2000. "Dies, Martin." *American National Biography Online*. February 2000. http://www.anb.org.turing.library.northwestern.edu/articles/07/07-00076.html. Accessed December 5, 2012.

Park, Marlene, and Gerald E. Markowitz. 1984. *Democratic Vistas: Post Offices and Public Art in the New Deal*. Philadelphia: Temple University Press.

Parks, George B. 1947. "John Evelyn and the Art of Travel." *Huntington Library Quarterly* 10 (3; May 1947): 251–76.

Parsons, Nicholas T. 2007. *Worth the Detour: A History of the Guidebook*. Stroud, UK: Sutton.

Pattee, Fred Lewis. 1896. "Is There an American Literature?" *Dial 21* (November): 243–45.

Pattee, Fred Lewis. 1937. "Gentian, Not Rose: The Real Emily Dickinson." *Sewanee Review* 45: 180–97.

Pawley, Christine. 2001. *Reading on the Middle Border: The Culture of Print in Late Nineteenth-Century Osage, Iowa*. Amherst: University of Massachusetts Press.

Penkower, Monty Noam. 1977. *The Federal Writers' Project: A Study in Government Patronage of the Arts*. Urbana: University of Illinois Press.

Phillips, Harlan. 1963a. *Oral History Interview with Jacob Baker, 1963 Sept. 25*. Archives of American Art. Smithsonian Institution.

Phillips, Harlan. 1963b. *Oral History Interview with Florence Kerr, 1963 Oct. 18–Oct. 31*. Archives of American Art. Smithsonian Institution.

Purchase, Eric. 1999. *Out of Nowhere: Disaster and Tourism in the White Mountains*. Baltimore: Johns Hopkins University Press.

Rassuli, Kathleen M., and Stanley C. Hollander. 2001. "Revolving, Not Revolutionary Books: The History of Rental Libraries until 1960." *Journal of Macromarketing* 21: 123–34.

Reising, Russell J. 1989. "Reconstructing Parrington." *American Quarterly* 41: 155–64.

Sandburg, Carl. 1936. *The People, Yes*. New York: Harcourt, Brace.

Sandoval-Strausz, A. K. 2007. *Hotel: An American History*. New Haven: Yale University Press.

Schindler-Carter, Petra. 1999. *Vintage Snapshots: The Fabrication of a Nation in the W.P.A. American Guide Series*. Frankfurt am Main: Peter Lang.

Schlesinger, Arthur M. Jr. 1958. *The Age of Roosevelt: The Coming of the New Deal 1933–1935*. Boston: Houghton Mifflin.

Sears, John F. 1989. *Sacred Places: American Tourist Attractions in the Nineteenth Century*. New York: Oxford University Press.

Seiler, Cotton. 2008. *Republic of Drivers: A Cultural History of Automobility in America*. Chicago: University of Chicago Press.

Shaffer, Marguerite S. 2001. *See America First: Tourism and National Identity, 1880–1940*. Washington, DC: Smithsonian Institution Press.

Sherwood, Robert E. 1948. *Roosevelt and Hopkins: An Intimate History*. New York: Harper and Brothers.

Shlaes, Amity. 2007. *The Forgotten Man: A New History of the Great Depression*. New York: HarperCollins.

Skard, Sigmund. 1967. "Robert E. Spiller: Bridge Builder and Image Maker." *American Quarterly* 19: 293–96.

Smith, Jason Scott. 2006. *Building New Deal Liberalism: The Political Economy of Public Works, 1933–1956*. New York: Cambridge University Press.

Sporn, Paul. 1995. *Against Itself: The Federal Theatre and Writers' Projects in the Midwest*. Detroit: Wayne State University Press.

Stott, William. (1973) 1986. *Documentary Expression and Thirties America*. Chicago: University of Chicago Press.

Swan, D. W., J. Grimes, T. Owens, K. Miller, J. Arroyo, T. Craig, S. Dorinski, M. Freeman, N. Isaac, P. O'Shea, R. Padgett, P. Schilling, and J. Scotto. 2014. *Public Libraries in the United States Survey: Fiscal Year 2011* (IMLS-2014-PLS-01). Washington, DC: Institute of Museum and Library Services.

Taylor, David. A. 2009. *Soul of a People: The WPA Writers' Program Uncovers Depression America*. Hoboken, NJ: John Wiley and Sons.

Taylor, Nick. 2008. *American-Made: The Enduring Legacy of the WPA: When FDR Put the Nation to Work*. New York: Bantam.

Tebbel, John William, and Mary Ellen Zuckerman. 1991. *The Magazine in America, 1741–1990*. New York: Oxford University Press.

Trease, Geoffrey. 1967. *The Grand Tour*. New York: Holt, Rinehart, and Winston.

Ulrich, Mabel. 1939. "Salvaging Culture for the WPA." *Harper's* 178 (May 1939): 653–64.

VanGiezen, Robert, and Albert E. Schwenk. 2003. "Compensation from before World War I through the Great Depression." US Bureau of Labor Statistics: Compensation and Working Conditions Online. http://www.bls.gov/opub/cwc/cm20030124ar03p1.htm. Accessed December 14, 2010. Originally published in the fall 2001 issue of *Compensation and Working Conditions*.

Verheul, Jaap. 1999. "The Ideological Origins of American Studies." In *Through the Cultural Looking Glass: American Studies in Transcultural Perspective*, edited by Hans Krabbendam and Jaap Verheul, 93–103. Amsterdam: VU University Press.

Waples, Douglas. 1938. *People and Print: Social Aspects of Reading in the Depression*. Chicago: University of Chicago Press.

Weinberger, Michelle F. and Melanie Wallendorf. 2008. "Having vs. Doing: Materialism, Experientialism, and the Experience of Materiality." In *Advances in*

Consumer Research, vol. 35: 257–61, edited by Angela Y. Lee and Dilip Soman. N.p.: Association of Consumer Research.

Wharton, Edith. 1908. *A Motor-Flight through France*. New York: Charles Scribner's Sons.

Wilson, Louis R. 1938. *The Geography of Reading: A Study of the Distribution and Status of Libraries in the United States*. Chicago: American Library Association and University of Chicago Press.

Wind, Herbert Warren. 1975. "The House of Baedeker." *New Yorker*, September 22, 42–93.

Withey, Lynne. 1997. *Grand Tours and Cook's Tours: A History of Leisure Travel 1750–1915*. New York: William Morrow.

Yorke, Douglas A. Jr., and John Margolies. 1996. *Hitting the Road: The Art of the American Road Map*. San Francisco: Chronicle Books.

Author Index

This is an index of authors named in Literature essays and referred to in the text.

State Index

Subject Index

I am including the individual state writers' projects and the individual state guides under the name of the state. Thus, for example, material pertaining to the Louisiana Writers' Project and to *Louisiana: A Guide to the State* will be included under Louisiana in the state index.